Social Studies for Children

A Guide to Basic Instruction

TWELFTH EDITION

Jesus Garcia
University of Kentucky

John U. Michaelis
Late of University of California, Berkeley

Allyn and Bacon

Boston   London   Toronto   Sydney   Tokyo   Singapore

To
Victoria Diane Garcia, Francisco Luis Garcia,
Elizabeth Ann Michaelis, John Barry Michaelis, Susan Ann Michaelis

Series Editor: *Traci Mueller*
Developmental Editor: *Susanna Brougham*
Series Editorial Assistant: *Bridget Keane*
Marketing Manager: *Kathleen Morgan*
Composition and Prepress Buyer: *Linda Cox*
Manufacturing Buyer: *Megan Cochran*
Cover Administrator: *Linda Knowles*
Photo Researcher: *Kate Cook*
Production Administrator: *Deborah Brown*
Editorial-Production Service: *Susan McNally*
Text Design and Electronic Composition: *Denise Hoffman*

Copyright © 2001, 1996, 1992 by Allyn & Bacon
A Pearson Education Company
160 Gould Street
Needham Heights, MA 02494
Internet: www.abacon.com

Between the time website information is gathered and then published, it is not unusual for some sites to have closed. Also, the transcription of URLs can result in unintended typographical errors. The publisher would appreciate being notified of any problems with URLs so that they may be corrected in subsequent editions.

Library of Congress Cataloging-in-Publication Data

Garcia, Jesus
    Social studies for children : a guide to basic instruction / Jesus Garcia — 12th ed.
        p. cm.
    Previous edition entered under John Udell Michaelis.
    Includes bibliographical references and index.
    ISBN 0-205-28316-0
        1. Social sciences—Study and teaching (Elementary)—United States.   I. Michaelis, John Udell, 1912- Social studies for children.   II. Title.

    LB1584.G33 2000
    372.83'044—dc21   00-060901

Printed in the United States of America

10 9 8 7 6 5 4 3 2 1   RRDV   05 04 03 02 01 00

Photo credits: Robert Fox, Impact Visuals, **p. x**; AP/World Wide Photos, **pp. 8, 56**; Carl Dekyzer, **p. 14**; Ariel Skelley, **p. 18**; Library of Congress, **pp. 24, 31**; Prentice Hall, Inc. **pp. 52, 364**; Brian Smith, **pp. 74, 83, 93, 330, 465**; Will Faller, **pp. 89, 145, 167, 182, 272, 336, 342, 345, 352; 376, 386**; Will Hart, **pp. 98, 108, 138, 174, 214, 234, 242, 250, 254, 296, 303, 420, 426, 435**; Michael Newman, **p. 111**; Stephen McBrady **p. 119**; Allan E. Goody, **pp. 186, 217, 225, 277, 286, 367; 415, 454, 461**; Tony Stone Images, **p. 203**; Robert Harbison, **p. 210**; PhotoDisc, Inc, **pp. 264, 312**; Associated Press/AP, **p. 392**; Michael Evans, **p. 406**; Grace Davies, **p. 413**; and Tony Freeman, **p. 444**.

Contents

iii

Preface

This volume is a guide for preparing preservice teachers to offer effective social studies instruction in grades K–8. It aims to promote social studies as education for citizenship in a democracy by (1) presenting and describing principles and classroom practices that lead to effective social studies instruction and (2) encouraging preservice teachers to reflect on and employ these principles and practices as they develop their own perspective on social studies and its role in grades K–8. The twelfth edition of *Social Studies for Children: A Guide for Basic Instruction* draws on the experiences of John Michaelis and myself in K–12 classrooms and teacher education. I hope this new volume will help preservice teachers gain a well-rounded understanding of social studies in the K-8 curriculum.

In addition to editing and rearranging the chapters of the previous editions, I've included two new ones in the twelfth edition: Chapter 3, "Teaching Social Studies in a Culturally Diverse and Global Society," and Chapter 15, "Teaching Social Studies in Today's Classrooms: Am I Prepared?" Chapter 3 describes the students in today's classrooms and provides a sketch of teaching, learning, and living at the beginning of the twenty-first century. Chapter 15 reviews the text, course outcomes, and general learning about teaching social studies; it also asks the preservice teacher to reflect on how well he or she is prepared to support children and adolescents as they learn about active citizenship in a democratic society and a culturally diverse global community.

The major themes of the book—social studies, students, community—are described in Part I, Defining and Teaching Social Studies in Elementary and Middle School Classrooms. I have held as did John Michaelis that this triad of themes is the bedrock of effective social studies teaching. This part of the book builds a case for teaching social studies, introduces the social sciences and other disciplines, and concludes with a description of the children and adolescents who will fill tomorrow's classrooms. It also gives a thumbnail sketch of the world of the twenty-first century. These topics and themes are integrated into later chapters as well.

Part II, Incorporating Contemporary Perspectives into Social Studies Instruction, provides ways to engage children and adolescents in social studies learning. It offers creative approaches to the subject, including ways to incorporate special topics, challenging issues, current events, and contemporary concerns into the curriculum. These topics may touch on students' backgrounds or issues, problems, and challenges related to life in a given neighborhood, the community, the nation, or the international arena. Practical suggestions for projects and learning activities for the whole class, small groups, and individuals will help students appreciate the value of social studies learning in everyday life.

Part III, Planning for Social Studies Instruction, discusses effective planning in social studies, including lesson and unit building, meeting individual needs, fostering reading and communication skills, integrating civic values and creative thinking, incorporating group learning, and evaluating and assessing students' learning, including use of portfolios. These chapters address the "mechanics" of social studies instruction.

We conclude with an epilogue, Chapter 15, "Teaching Social Studies in Tomorrow's Classrooms: Am I Prepared?" This chapter reviews important questions posed throughout the book: Who are the students in my classroom? How do I prepare to teach in culturally diverse classrooms? How do I reach all students? What is my vision of society? of the world? What is social studies? What is its purpose? What is its role in the twenty-first century? How can I become an effective social studies teacher?

With the twelfth edition we say goodbye to John U. Michaelis, who was the author of ten editions of *Social Studies for Children: A Guide for Basic Instruction*. John passed away in February 1996. He will be missed by his many friends and colleagues, by the broader social studies community, by the many teachers whom his book has influenced, and by me. As with the eleventh edition, I have continued to update this text, gradually remolding it to reflect my ideas on how best to prepare elementary and middle school social studies teachers. The book will continue to carry John's name because many of the ideas expressed here are his.

As with past editions, I wish to thank the many people who helped make *Social Studies for Children: A Guide for Basic Instruction* a mainstay in the preparation of elementary and middle school teachers including reviewers of this edition Mohammed Farouk, Florida International University; F. Gene Miller, Western Illinois University; Heidi Schweizer, Marquette University; and Nelly Ukpokudu, Northwest Missouri State. Special thanks go to Traci Mueller, Susanna Brougham, Deborah Brown, Bridget Keane, Denise Hoffman, Susan McNally, and other staff members of Allyn and Bacon. A debt of gratitude is owed to Mary Vass, the education librarian at the University of Kentucky, and her very cooperative staff, especially Amanda Barnes and Bindy Fleischman.

Chapter 1

Historical Highlights and Curriculum Overview

Chapter Objective

To provide a brief historical sketch of social studies in American schools and to outline the main features of curriculum for social studies education

Focusing Questions

- What major development shaped the history of social studies education?
- What issues, problems, and trends are influencing social studies teaching today?
- How has social studies education been defined at different times and places?
- What rationales have been provided for social studies education?
- What major goals and related objectives undergird the curriculum?
- What is the conceptual structure of the curriculum?
- What three types of studies are included in the curriculum?
- How can conceptual, inquiry, and topical approaches be unified?
- What is included in the scope and sequence of the curriculum?

Historical Highlights of Social Studies Education

Any study of the evolution of social studies in American schools will reveal a variety of "ups and downs" in the development of this part of the educational curriculum. Over the course of your career as a teacher, the focus and goals of social studies education will no doubt continue to change. Part of the excitement of teaching social studies is its close connection to the world we live in—the events that occur and the conditions that prevail in the realms of economics, politics, society, culture, law, and so on. These developments in turn influence social studies teaching.

We begin this book with an overview of the history of social studies education so that you can understand the forces that have shaped this area of study and will in turn influence your teaching—both *what* you teach (the content) and *how* you teach (the methodology).

The Eighteenth and Nineteenth Centuries

During the colonial period of American history, schools focused on teaching reading, writing, and arithmetic (the three R's) as well as religion and morality. Toward the end of this period, older students took courses in geography and history as well. The

Revolutionary War brought an emphasis on geography and the study of civil government (later called civics), preparing students for citizenship in the new democracy. Common textbooks of the time included *Geography Made Easy* (1784) by the clergyman Jedidiah Morse, a U.S. history text by John McCulloch (1787), and Noah Webster's *Grammatical Institute of the English Language* (1779–1783) with volumes on reading, spelling, and grammar.

During the nineteenth century, the teaching of geography and history continued to develop. Especially in the upper grades, the curriculum emphasized U.S. history and the documents, institutions, and processes that characterize U.S. government. These focuses were chosen in part to help immigrants develop a sense of patriotism and loyalty to their new country. In the classrooms, students often demonstrated their learning through tests and recitation, and memorization was an important learning technique. Though no national or state curriculum standards existed in this period, some cities, such as Philadelphia in 1888, developed their own curriculum. By the end of the nineteenth century, many states had passed laws requiring instruction in civil government in the public schools.

The Emergence of National Organizations

■ Schools have not and never will be neutral in regard to social, political, economic, and cultural values.

—**William B. Stanley and Jack L. Nelson**

Beginning in the late nineteenth century, national educational organizations emerged to evaluate curriculum and recommend standards. Through published reports, such organizations influenced classrooms across the country. For example, in 1893, the Committee of Ten of the National Education Association suggested that biography and myths be studied in grades 5 and 6, American history in grades 7 and 11, and Greek and Roman history in grade 8. They also recommended that all elementary schools provide instruction in both the local and national levels of government and that teachers incorporate appropriate literature in these studies.

In 1895, the Committee of Fifteen of the National Education Association drew even more specific guidelines: oral lessons in history and biography for sixty minutes a week in grades 1–8; readings in U.S. history in grade 7 and the first half of grade 8; and lessons on the Constitution in the last half of grade 8. By 1908, the American Political Science Association reported that instruction on civics was appropriate in the middle grades and a course in government should be provided in high school. In 1909, the Committee of Eight of the American Historical Association recommended that the following topics be studied at particular grade levels.

Grade 1: American Indian life, Thanksgiving, and George Washington

Grade 2: same as grade 1, with the addition of Memorial Day

Grade 3: heroes, Independence Day, and American Indians

Grade 4: events and people of the colonial period

Grade 5: U.S. history and major industries

Grade 6: Europe

Grade 7: U.S. history through the Revolution and more about Europe

Grade 8: U.S. history since the Revolution and events in European history

As national educational organizations grappled with the best ways to separately teach history, government, and geography, they laid the groundwork for what would become social studies.

The Social Studies Movement

In 1916 the Committee on Social Studies of the National Education Association's Commission on Reorganization of Secondary Education made a report of historic significance. For the first time, the label "social studies" was used to designate an area of the curriculum defined as "studies whose subject matter relates directly to organization and development of human society, and to man as a member of social groups." Social efficiency and good citizenship, beginning in the neighborhood and extending to world society, were cited as key purposes. Local development of the curriculum was recommended. Many educators adopted the key goals outlined in *Cardinal Principles of Secondary Education* (Commission on Reorganization of Secondary Education, 1918), such as citizenship, worthy home membership, and ethical character. Recommendations from these organizations and others led to a formal K–12 social studies curriculum.

A key development in the social studies movement was the founding of the National Council for the Social Studies. Its 1921 charter stated: "Social studies is used to include history and the social science disciplines and those areas of inquiry which relate to the role of the individual in a democratic society, designed to protect his and her integrity and dignity and which are concerned with the understanding and solution of problems dealing with social issues and human relationships." The Council has been a significant force in U.S. education.[1]

Other organizations contributed to the growth of social studies curriculum in the first half of the twentieth century. In the early 1900s the National Society for the Study of Education published influential yearbooks on geography and history. These were followed by others on social studies, curriculum development, the activity movement, child development, audiovisual instruction, international understanding, measurement of understanding, and other topics. The American Historical Association's Commission on the Social Studies supported the publication of the following significant volumes: *A Charter for the Social Sciences in the Schools* (1932); *Tests and Measurements in the Social Sciences* (1934); and *Methods of Instruction in the Social Studies* (1937).

Developments in educational philosophy and psychology also influenced the social studies movement. The scientific movement in education, stressing the attainment of specific objectives, the empirical analysis of human activity, and objective measures of achievement, affected the curriculum.

Even more pivotal was the progressive movement in education, which exerted a powerful influence that lasted until the 1950s. Progressives in the United States,

---

1. NCSS began publication of *Social Education* in 1937 and has published yearbooks, bulletins, how-to leaflets, position papers, and curriculum packets on a variety of issues and topics. In 1988 NCSS began publishing *Social Studies and the Young Learner,* and in the late 1990s it began including a supplement on middle school social studies in *Social Education.*

such as John Dewey, G. Stanley Hall, Francis Parker, and Edward Thorndike, held that students learn best when involved in activities that relate to their own lives and interests. These educators sought to organize meaningful units of study in the curriculum. They wished to change the authoritarian structure of the classroom and championed student-run activities, such as student government and publications. The progressive movement was influenced by educators of an earlier generation: Jean Jacques Rousseau's ideas about children's innate goodness and need for freedom, Johann Pestalozzi's object lessons and use of observation, Friedrich Froebel's emphasis on creativity and a rich learning environment, and Johann Friedrich Herbart's ideas on moral development and steps of instruction.

Social studies education at all levels was influenced by publications of the Educational Policies Commission: *The Purposes of Education in American Democracy* (National Education Association, 1938); *Learning the Ways of Democracy* (1940); and *Education for All American Children* (1948). At the state level California's *Teachers' Guide to Child Development—Manual for Kindergarten and Primary Teachers* (1930) and *Teachers' Guide to Child Development in the Intermediate Grades* (1936) exemplify teaching guides based on progressive education principles that contained integrated content and comprehensive units of work.

During the early and middle years of the twentieth century, the events of the times shaped social studies curriculum as well. Instruction on patriotism, loyalty, and certain ideals of good citizenship characterized the years of World War I. Later, during World War II, the importance of winning the war was emphasized.

An Evolving Curriculum: The 1940s and 1950s

By the 1940s, the social studies curriculum had evolved to include the following educational goals:

- preparation for living as a citizen in a democracy
- development of positive social attitudes, such as concern for others
- development of thinking and problem-solving skills
- understanding of social studies concepts and generalizations
- insight into democratic economic and political values
- appreciation of contributions of various cultures and individuals
- responsibility for promoting social progress

During this decade many school systems adopted the 1944 recommendations of the Committee on American History in Schools and Colleges, directed by Edgar B. Wesley: colonial and early national history in the intermediate grades; 1776–1876, the westward movement, and simple aspects of the industrial revolution in junior high; and the period following 1865, political and economic development, and foreign relations in senior high.

Content, learning activities, and a variety of materials and community resources were organized in units of work, many of them correlated or integrated with other subjects. Some state and local programs used basic social functions such as transportation and communication to define the scope of the curriculum. The expanding horizons (expanding environment or communities) model—beginning with home, school, neighborhood, and community in early grades and moving to state, region, country, and world in later grades—was widely used to define the sequence of the curriculum. Major core concepts, such as interdependence and adaptation were presented with increasing complexity as children moved from the early grades to the later grades. Current events were included, and students' news weeklies were popular.

During this era, activities, projects, problem solving, and learning by doing took precedence over memorization and recitation. Cooperative group work, individual needs and interests, teacher–pupil planning, thinking skills, creativity, social attitudes, behavioral objectives, and democratic values and behavior were stressed. Evaluation was extended beyond testing to include a variety of informal techniques and pupil self-evaluation.

Following World War II studies and projects were designed to improve citizenship education, applications of democratic values and beliefs to daily living, intergroup and intercultural human relations education, and international understanding. Many states required by law that students study American history, civics, the Constitution, selected holidays, and state history and constitution. The formation of the Joint Council on Economic Education in 1949 was to have an impact on instruction in economics at both elementary and secondary levels in the following decades.

A publication that had great impact on social studies and other subjects in regard to framing objectives, questions, and test items was the *Taxonomy of Educational Objectives, Handbook I: The Cognitive Domain* (1956), edited by Benjamin S. Bloom. A companion volume, *Taxonomy of Educational Objectives: Affective Domain*, by David R. Krathwohl and others, was published in 1964. These publications offered classroom teachers methods of developing instructional objectives leading to examples of levels of student understanding in the cognitive (knowledge) and affective (dispositions) domains.

Reform Projects and Social Concerns

Soviet Union advances in the sciences, launching Sputnik in 1957, led many influential Americans to call for reforms in education. During the 1960s and 1970s educational reformers sought to make social studies broader and more rigorous by including history and social science curriculum projects and instruction on social concerns. The curriculum projects highlighted conceptual structures and inquiry processes drawn from the basic disciplines of social studies. Bruner's *Process of Education*, published in 1960, offered this challenge: "Any subject can be taught effectively in some intellectually honest form to any child at any stage of development." Academicians in a variety of disciplines prepared instructional materials, some of which were called "teacher-proof." Although none of the projects gained a lasting place in the curriculum, they did influence instruction by increasing the inclusion of concepts and inquiry processes from the basic disciplines. Development of thinking ability was spurred by publication of *The Central Purpose of American Education* (Educational Policies Commission, 1961).

In the 1970s a variety of individuals and groups demanded instruction on topics of social concern. As a result, black history, ethnic studies, women's studies, and other topics enhanced the social studies curriculum. The NCSS guidelines of 1971 and 1979 took into account these new efforts in their statements of rationale, goals, and curriculum components. In 1976 the organization published specific guidelines on ethnic pluralism, stressing positive interaction between groups. A number of other changes in educational policy, instructional techniques, and skill development characterized this period: accountability, mainstreaming of exceptional students, simulations and games, learning centers, learning styles, thinking processes, decision making, future studies, educational television, and computer-assisted instruction.

Emphasis on Essentials, Geography, History, and Civics

■ The American Sociological Association **http://www.asanet. org** is the organization to turn to if you would like information on how to integrate sociology into the K–8 social studies curriculum.

In the late 1970s and the 1980s, emphasis shifted to basic knowledge drawn from the disciplines, democratic beliefs and values, and skills in thinking, study, and participation. The National Council for the Social Studies issued a position statement, *Essentials of Social Studies* (1981), which noted the knowledge, democratic beliefs, thinking skills, participation skills, and civic action needed to function effectively in our democratic society and interdependent world.

In the late 1980s several organizations focused on the teaching of geography, history, and civics. The National Geographic Society formed a foundation with alliances in many states. The Geographic Implementation Project proposed ways to implement guidelines for geographic education recommended by a committee of the National Council for Geographic Education and the American Association of Geographers. In 1988 CIVITAS was sponsored by the Council for the Advancement of Citizenship and the Center for Civic Education and proceeded to develop *A Framework for Civic Education* (1990).

More, and earlier, history instruction was recommended in the 1980s. For example, in 1988 California published the *History–Social Science Framework* for grades K–12, which placed history in central focus and urged the integration of other content and related literature into history instruction. Also in 1988 the Bradley Commission on History in the Schools recommended a K–6 history-centered curriculum with more history in early grades; state, national, and world history in 4–6; and infusion of biography, geography, literature, and primary sources at all grade levels. The National Center for History in the Schools was set up the same year as a joint venture of the National Endowment for the Humanities and the University of California at Los Angeles.

In 1989 the National Commission on Social Studies recommended that history and geography serve as a framework for social studies and that concepts and main ideas from political science, economics, and other disciplines be integrated into the K–12 program. Some of the commission's recommendations included more content in the early grades; condensation of expanding environment studies; one year each of U.S. history, world history, and world geography in grades 4–6; courses in history, government, economics, anthropology, sociology, and psychology in secondary schools; and community service participation as an option.

There were several other projects and reports of note during this time (O'Neill, 1989). A report by the Joint Council on Economic Education urged more attention to economic literacy. *Education for Freedom* (American Federation of Teachers and others) set forth principles for including history, government, and geography in a more substantial and demanding curriculum. International education was recommended by a task force of the National Governors' Association, and global studies was recommended by a Study Commission on Global Education.

In another major trend in education, several groups responded to the request for national standards. Of special significance were those for history, geography, civics, and social studies.

What are standards? Similar to goals, they describe the main ideas of a discipline (e.g., history, geography, economics) or area of study (i.e., social studies). In this book we highlight the NCSS standards as well as cite examples from social science organizations, in order to show the variety of standards available to teachers. (See Table 1.1.) The primary reason for favoring the NCSS standards, *Curriculum Standards for Social Studies: Expectations for Excellence* (NCSS, 1994), is because they represent the integration of the social sciences, and by extension, an integration

---

■ TABLE 1.1

Organizations That Have Issued Social Science Standards

Civics and Government

The Center for Civic Education
5146 Douglas Fir Road
Calabasas, CA 91203
818-591-9321
http://www.civiced.org

Economics

The National Council on Economic Education
1140 Avenue of the Americas
New York, NY 10036
212-730-7007
http://www.nationalcouncil.org

Geography

National Council for Geographic Education
Indiana University of PA
16A Leonard Hall
Indiana, PA 15705-1087
724-357-6290
http://www.ncge.org

Social Studies

National Council for the Social Studies
3501 Newark Street, NW
Washington, DC 20016
202-966-7840
http://www.ncss.org

History

National Center for History in the Schools
Department of History
University of California, Los Angeles
6339 Bunche Hall
405 Hilgard Avenue
Los Angeles, CA 90095
310-825-4702
http://www.sscnet.ucla.edu/nchs

of the standards from the social sciences. During planning, K–8 teachers are more likely to turn to the NCSS standards than to those from the social sciences. To introduce you to standards, we have included excerpts from the NCSS standards.

Other concerns during the 1990s included the integration of content from other social sciences and literature; more content in the early grades; attention to impacts of science and technology on ways of living; the influence of religions on human affairs; and global, multicultural, gender equality, environmental, and other social concerns.

The Future

In the early twenty-first century, we believe a number of trends and issues will continue to influence K–8 social studies. Four that clearly stand out are citizenship education, global education, technology in the classroom, and the standards movement. First, because of the large number of immigrants coming to this country, much attention will be given acknowledging cultural diversity while addressing methods of bringing all Americans together in order to promote the civic (political) values that lead to a more cohesive society. Second, technological advancement, global economies, and the search for world peace will lead to greater efforts in global education. Technology in the classroom will no doubt evolve rapidly.

Last, it is the standards movement, more than any other trend or issue, which we believe will most significantly influence the K–12 social studies programs in the first decade of the twenty-first century. Over the past two decades most professional organizations (e.g., mathematics, English, vocational education, science, social studies) have developed and published a set of standards describing their discipline area. It is safe to say that standards of some form will influence the planning and teaching of social studies for many years to come.

How would this veteran define social studies? How might his definition be like or unlike yours?

We believe that the twenty-first century will be an exciting time to teach social studies. Technology will revolutionize teaching and learning. Not only will students learn more social studies in elementary and middle schools, but they will also be better prepared for high school and, as adults, will lead more positive and productive lives.

■ Definitions, Rationales, and Purposes in Social Studies Education

In this section, we explore the many ways in which educators have defined social studies. In the preceding section on historical highlights, you may have noticed that educators have defined social studies in somewhat different ways, given different rationales for teaching it, and have stipulated that it serve a variety of purposes. Perhaps, as you read these pages, you might wonder what definitions and purposes of social studies will dominate in the year 2010? in the year 2025?

■ The purpose of the social studies is to help young people understand themselves and the society and world in which they live, so that they may act intelligently and responsibly.
　　　—Matthew T. Downey

Definitions of Social Studies

Stated as simply and concisely as possible, social studies can be defined as the study of human relationships to develop responsible citizenship in a democracy. To be more precise, the social studies may be defined as the area of the curriculum that

> transmits basic aspects of our cultural heritage (subject matter–centered).
>
> is based on content and methods of study drawn from the social sciences and other disciplines (subject matter–centered).
>
> provides instruction on thinking and decision-making skills applied to social problems (society-centered).
>
> provides instruction to develop the competencies needed for social criticism and action (society-centered).
>
> develops students' potential for self-directed participation in group activities (student-centered).

Notice how these facets of social studies are integrated in the definition adopted in 1992 by the Board of Directors of the National Council for the Social Studies:

> *Social studies is the integrated study of the social sciences and humanities to promote civic competence. Within the school program, social studies provides coordinated, systematic study drawing upon such disciplines as anthropology, archeology, economics, geography, history, law, philosophy, political science, psychology, religion, and sociology, as well as appropriate content from the humanities, mathematics, and natural sciences. The primary purpose of social studies is to help young people develop the ability to make informed and reasoned decisions for the public good as citizens of a culturally diverse, democratic society in an interdependent world.* (NCSS, Curriculum Standards, 1994)

Different definitions of social studies emphasize subject matter, society, and students to varying degrees (Barr et al., 1977; Brubaker et al., 1977). We label these elements the triad—social studies, community, students—for planning and implementing elementary and middle school social studies instruction. They are in fact of equal importance, support one another, and are essential to a social studies program. In this chapter and in Chapter 2, the social sciences and other disciplines are described and explored, and in Chapter 3, we discuss the impact of diversity on education in the twenty-first century. These three chapters of Part I are the foundation for the rest of the textbook. Figure 1.1 shows the scope of social studies to be explored in Part I.

Social studies should not be confused with social competence or social education. *Social competence* is the ability to engage in group activities both in and out of school. *Social education* takes place in the school, family, church, and other institutions. Although social studies education contributes to both of these, it is first and foremost an area of the curriculum, as are the language arts and science education.

Rationales for and Purposes of Social Studies

Rationales

A rationale for the teaching of social studies is a statement of reasons. It typically includes the assumptions, beliefs, philosophy, or special characteristics underlying the curriculum. For example, many guidelines for social studies curriculum include goal-

■ **FIGURE 1.1**

The Scope of Social Studies

SOCIAL STUDIES

Learning about human relationships in order to develop responsible citizenship in a democracy

Focused on . . .
- Cultural heritage and global diversity
- Social, political, economic, temporal, and spatial aspects of human activity
- Human activity in the past, present, and future
- Using skills to solve problems, take action, and think critically

Founded on . . .
- History
- Geography
- Civics
- Economics
- Anthropology
- Sociology

related reasons for the importance of social studies instruction. A primary reason is to develop understanding and appreciation of our democratic heritage. Another is to develop concepts and methods of study needed to understand human relationships and to handle social issues and problems. A third reason is to develop thinking skills and competence in social criticism and action, so that students can engage in decision making and participate in activities that improve human welfare.

Some rationales can be inferred from mandated requirements. Although they vary from state to state, those listed here are examples of widely accepted program requirements.

- observance of designated holidays such as Washington's birthday, state admission day, and first settlers in our community
- history and geography of the home state, our country, the Constitution, our legal system and government
- understanding of international relations, global initiatives, and the goal of achieving world peace
- fair and accurate portrayal of the roles and contributions of women and men, ethnic and minority groups, and business and labor
- wise use of resources, conservation of energy, and protection of the environment
- values and principles of morality, justice, patriotism, and responsibilities of American citizenship
- American economic system and principles of free enterprise

A rationale isn't always conveniently labeled as such. Sometimes rationales are embedded in statements of philosophy, point of view, values, the characteristics of a program, or the nature of knowledge. You may also infer rationales from statements of goals.

Goals and Objectives

The purposes of social studies are typically stated as goals and objectives. Goals are long-range desired outcomes of instruction that give teachers a sense of direction. Objectives are related specific and measurable outcomes sought by teachers at each grade level. The goals and objectives of social studies are related directly to our democratic heritage, views of citizenship, societal expectations, legislative mandates, and accountability programs.

Goals   Broad social studies goals are often expressed as strands that are woven throughout the curriculum at all or at certain grade levels. For example, California's *History–Social Science Framework* includes these strands in the K–12 curriculum:

- knowledge and cultural understanding of historical, ethical, cultural, geographic, economic, and sociopolitical elements

- democratic understanding and civic values with emphasis on our national identity, constitutional heritage, civic values, and rights and responsibilities
- skills attainment and social participation with emphasis on study, thinking, and participation skills

Specific areas of knowledge, skills, attitudes, values, appreciations, and social participation are typically stated in program goals. Examples of specific goals related to each of the three strands cited are given in Table 1.2.

■ TABLE 1.2
Social Studies Strands and Specific Goals

Knowledge and Cultural Understanding	Democratic Understanding and Civic Values	Skills Attainment and Social Participation
Historical, ethical, cultural, geographic, economic, and sociopolitical literacy	National identity as a democracy rich in diversity	Critical and creative thinking, problem solving, decision making, metacognition
Relationships between people and their social and physical environments	The Constitution and its amendments	Analysis of bias, stereotype, prejudice, propaganda, assumptions, and opinions
Impact of science and technology on human relationships and conditions	Knowledge of the Bill of Rights	Skills in reading, writing, listening, speaking, and study
Social institutions such as government, education, and religion	The branches of government	Work with maps, globes, graphs, charts, diagrams, cartoons, and other visuals
World regions, cultures, history, geography, civilizations, and political systems	Government institutions such as the U.S. Postal Service and the armed forces	Use and understanding of available technology
Relationships between groups, locally, nationally, and globally	Local, state, and national government	Positive attitudes toward others and appreciation of diversity
Diverse ethical and religious beliefs and their effects on ways of living	The election process	Commitment to values such as justice, equality, patriotism, freedom, and human rights
Universal concern for ethics and human rights	Civic values such as the importance of voting	Ability to judge conflicts in terms of justice, equality, and other democratic values
Art, literature, values, and ideas as reflecting people's thoughts and feelings	Rights and responsibilities	Constructive group interaction skills such as using persuasion and negotiation
	The criminal justice system	Competence in social and political action such as accepting consequences for action

Social studies also contributes to the broad goals of education in many ways.

Self-realization: Social studies fosters each individual's growth in knowledge, skills, and values.

Human relationships: Students gain knowledge of the cultural diversity of our nation and the world, develop interpersonal skills, and analyze intergroup problems.

Civic responsibility: Social studies emphasizes the importance of civic activities in and out of school, the legal rights of individuals, and competent decision making.

Economic competence: Students explore concepts, attitudes, and skills related to high-quality work, career awareness, contributions of different workers, and use of resources.

Thinking ability: Learning activities involve students in critical thinking, creative thinking, problem solving, and decision making.

Learning how to learn: Students engage in independent study activities, apply reading and writing skills, and learn how to direct and evaluate their own work.

> ■ Social studies is concerned with developing reflective, democratic citizenship within a global context.
> —**H. Michael Hartoonian and Margaret A. Laughlin**

Objectives   Instructional objectives are a key element in social studies programs. They indicate what students will learn and how they will reveal what they have learned. Objectives state the precise behavior expected from students—what they will make, do, demonstrate, say, or write as evidence of their learning.

The following examples of student instructional objectives are derived from goals for social studies and illustrate the level of specificity that teachers can reach when planning for instruction. Each one describes the expected behavior and performance level as well as the conditions in which the behavior will take place.

Knowledge objective: Students will write [behavior] a definition of stereotype similar to the one in the textbook [performance level], without referring to the textbook or a dictionary [conditions].

Thinking skill objective: Using classroom sources other than the textbook [condition], students will generalize by writing [behavior] one [performance level] main idea about the role of government in a community.

Study skill objective: Students will make [behavior] a map of trails westward, using crayons and an outline map of the United States [conditions] to show three trails in different colors [performance level].

Value objective: Students will state [behavior] the extent to which justice was upheld in a story read by the teacher [conditions], giving one [performance level] reason for the judgment.

Participation objective: Students will show sensitivity to feelings of others by always [performance level] making constructive comments [behavior] in group discussion [conditions].

In Chapter 5, we describe instructional objectives in detail, noting reasons for their use, how to write them, and examples of cognitive (knowledge), skills, and values objectives. In addition, we provide sample units and lesson plans that incorporate objectives. Further examples can be found in other chapters too.

■ The Curriculum

The curriculum is the heart of social studies instruction. It can be defined as the organization and delivery of instruction. Curriculum also includes materials used, assessment, and evaluation. In this section we focus on the organization of content.

Patterns of unit and course organization range from the widely used interdisciplinary approaches, in which disciplines are melded together, to separate subject approaches, in which geography, history, and other disciplines are focused on separately. Interdisciplinary patterns are used, for example, in units on family life, communities around the world, improving the environment, and cultural diversity; in middle and high schools this pattern is also found in courses such as career exploration, youth and the law, current problems, and international relations.

The separate subject approach is used in units on such topics as history of our community, geography of our state, and local government. Separate subject instruc-

How is learning about the United Nations a part of social studies? What are the connections among global, national, and local issues?

tion is predominant in secondary school courses such as U.S. history, American government, and economics.

In between the interdisciplinary and separate subject approaches are multidisciplinary studies that bring the perspectives of different disciplines to bear on certain topics and problems. This approach is often used in units on our state, the New England states, Canada, Latin America, and the Middle East. In multidisciplinary approaches the geographic, historical, economic, political, and sociocultural features of the area under study are considered and relationships among them highlighted. Each discipline is clearly visible, and the content is not brought together into an amalgam that renders the separate disciplines indistinguishable.

Conceptual Structure

The content of social studies can be broken into different interrelated categories, and understanding them can help you structure social studies instruction. These categories include facts, vocabulary, concepts and concept clusters, themes, and generalizations. They are defined as follows.

Facts, such as "The capital of New York is Albany," are statements of information that include concepts, but they apply only to a specific situation. A set of related facts can form a generalization, such as "All states have a capital." Facts can also be used to support generalizations.

Vocabulary, or words such as *capital, Civil War,* and *urbanization,* encompasses the terms, names, or labels given to objects, events, qualities, or processes. Vocabulary can be used meaningfully by students only if they understand the concepts that the words represent.

Concepts, represented by terms such as *cooperation, equality,* and *ethnic group,* are abstractions that apply to a class or category of objects or activities that have certain characteristics in common.

Concept clusters, such as *natural resources* (water, soil, plants, animals, minerals), are sets of concepts subsumed under a major concept. All concepts within a cluster must be developed in a way that enables students to associate them with the major concept.

Themes, such as *growth of the community, the westward movement,* and *industrial growth in the South,* combine concepts in a phrase that indicates a topic, issue, or trend. Themes highlight the emphasis of a unit or part of a unit. Broad themes, such as *school and family, living in communities,* and *world cultures,* indicate the focus of instruction in various grades.

Generalizations, such as "People use resources to meet basic needs," are broadly applicable statements that contain two or more concepts and show the relationship between them. Generalizations are stated as main ideas, basic understandings, principles, laws, rules, and conclusions. *Descriptive* generalizations are based on what currently exists, for example, "Members of minority groups have not experienced equality of opportunity." *Prescriptive* generalizations are based on what ought to be, for example, "Steps must be taken to extend equality of opportunity to minority groups." Additional examples are provided in other chapters.

Studies in Generalizing, Particularizing, and Decision Making

A strong social studies curriculum will give students opportunities to make generalizations, delve into the particulars of many topics, and gain skills in decision making. K–8 teachers target three areas when developing instructions.

Generalizing Studies

Learning to make generalizations and to recognize sound and unsound generalizations should be prominent in the social studies classroom. As a foundational concept, students should learn that a generalization needs to be based on an adequate number of cases or situations. For example, if a lesson objective is to develop a generalization about the public services that cities provide, students should identify the public services in several cities before making a general statement about them.

Several other concepts should be taught concerning generalizations. Students need to learn that a good generalization should not consist of a circular statement, such as "The primary role of the mayor of our city is to be the mayor of our city." Generalizations need to contain more information than that. Also, some generalizations need to be revised from time to time to account for additional information, insight, or experience. A generalization about how technology affects standards of living may need to be refined as a student gains more understanding about technology. Also, teachers should provide learning experiences to show that a generalization that holds up in one context may not be applicable in a different context.

Learning what can be generalized from a reading, a set of data, or an argument calls upon skills in analysis, logic, recognizing bias and stereotyping, and observation. The ability to analyze and make generalizations is one aspect of sound judgment. Students can apply this ability both at school—in taking tests, writing papers, participating in debates, and other activities—and beyond.

Particularizing Studies

An important concept for students to learn is that every person, city, region, country, culture, and historical event has distinctive characteristics that set it apart from others. There is only one Abraham Lincoln, one Alabama, one New England, and one Japan; no other person, state, region, or country is quite like another. Particularizing studies focus on the distinctive characteristics of a person, place, or event, asking questions such as these:

- What is special about the families of members of our class?
- What were the main periods in the development of our state?
- What events took place in the Boston Tea Party?
- What were the special contributions of Susan B. Anthony?

In particularizing studies, students make a thorough investigation of the topic at hand. They learn the vocabulary unique to that topic, such as the Loop in Chicago, the French Quarter in New Orleans, and the caste system in India. They also discover that a broadly applicable concept, such as democracy, has different shades of meaning in different contexts—the democratic process as employed in the United States and in China differs a good deal.

Whenever possible, particularizing studies should include contributions from the humanities. Art, music, and literature can enrich students' understanding of the people, places, events, and cultures they study. For example, a unit on the Civil War could include cartoons caricaturing Abraham Lincoln, an excerpt from the poetry of Walt Whitman, letters written by soldiers, Matthew Brady's photography, and recordings of ballads sung about the war.

Decision-Making Studies

Because it is essential to personal and community life, decision making should also be a focus in the social studies classroom. It involves students in many types of higher-order thinking: clearly defining a problem, generating and evaluating alternatives, weighing pros and cons, predicting outcomes, and so on. Decision making also engages students in considering values: will a given decision be fair to everyone? Here are sample questions that might be used to spark decision-making activities:

- How should we set up the books in the reading center? How can we take better care of them?
- How can we increase student participation in student government? What plans can we think of? Which plan is best?
- How would you propose improving safety on school buses? Which proposal would be most effective?

As students progress through the grades, they can be given more challenging decision-making tasks that require analysis of complex situations.

More information on decision making is given in Chapters 9 and 11.

The Inquiry, Conceptual, and Topical Approaches: How to Unify Them

Three general approaches to the social studies curriculum are the inquiry, conceptual, and topical approaches. The *inquiry approach* stresses the inquiry process: generating questions, making hypotheses to answer the questions, and then testing the hypotheses. The *conceptual approach* emphasizes mastery of social studies concepts, and the *topical approach* focuses on topics, such as the civil rights movement or the major cultures of Southeast Asia. We recommend an approach that blends all of these together: an inquiry–conceptual model used to guide the study of topics.

There are a number of advantages to this approach. The inquiry component challenges students to be active participants in the learning process, drawing on their previous learning as they ask questions and make hypotheses. As students gather information to test their ideas, they gain new knowledge and develop cognitive skills such as observing, classifying, and synthesizing. The conceptual element of the approach lets students work with previously mastered concepts, learn new ones, and

■ Social Studies School Service **http:// socialstudies.com** offers teachers an array of materials in most social studies areas.

build richer concept clusters as they study a variety of topics in social studies. This approach gives students the confidence to become independent learners.

Asking questions and finding answers are at the heart of the inquiry–conceptual approach. Teachers can bring up questions that focus on a concept and involve students in a particular thinking skill. The sample questions that follow are drawn from a unit on Canada. Each question focuses on the concept of natural resources; question 3 also includes the concept of economy.

1. What natural resources are shown in this video? (thinking skill: observing)
2. Into what main groups can we place Canada's natural resources? (thinking skill: classifying)
3. Which natural resources do you think are most important in Canada's economy? (thinking skill: hypothesizing)
4. How should we organize and present our findings on Canada's use of natural resources? (thinking skill: synthesizing)

Other examples of ways to link concepts and thinking skills are presented in other chapters, particularly Chapter 9.

Scope and Sequence of the Curriculum

The scope of the curriculum indicates its breadth—which areas of knowledge, skills, values, and experiences are needed to achieve the goals of the program. The scope is usually expressed as a particular theme for each grade level.

What is the significance of July fourth to all Americans? What civic values do these Americans share? How important will patriotic holidays be in your curriculum?

The sequence of the curriculum indicates the order in which each theme, and the topics within each theme, will be studied. A typical social studies sequence is based on the concept of the expanding environment: the curriculum usually begins by exploring the immediate environment (family, home, school, neighborhood, and community) and moves outward to state, regional, national, and international environments. Because this sequence has been criticized for limiting students' understanding of the wider world in the early grades, comparative studies of families, schools, communities, and regions have been added to help students develop a global perspective.

Several states issue frameworks to guide the scope and sequence of the social studies curriculum, as shown in Table 1.3. Textbook publishers also provide a scope and sequence to show the arrangement of themes and topics in a social studies program. You can evaluate any scope and sequence by using the checklist shown in Table 1.4.

■ TABLE 1.3

Themes and Topics in Three K–8 Frameworks

Grade	California	Texas	New York
K	Learning and Working, Now and Long Ago	Needs for Food, Shelter, and Clothing	Self, Family, Community
1	A Child's Place in Time and Space	Family, School, Community	pre-K
2	People Who Make a Difference (supply needs, many cultures)	How People Depend on Others	through grade 2
3	Continuity and Change (local history, literature, holidays)	Community Comparisons Around the World	Communities Around the World
4	California: A Changing State (early times to modern times)	Texas, Selected World Regions Western Hemisphere	Local Community and U.S. History
5	U.S. History and Geography: Making a New Nation (to 1850)	U.S. History, Geography, Government	Contemporary U.S., Canada, Latin America
6	World History and Geography: Ancient Civilizations (to 500)	Ancient Egypt, China, and India	Contemporary Europe, Mediterranean Region, Africa, Asia
7	World History and Geography: Medieval and Early Modern Times (500–1789)	Texas History and Geography	U.S. and New York State History, Pre-Columbian Times to 1876
8	U.S. History and Geography: Growth and Conflict (1783–1914)	Texas and U.S. History	U.S. and New York State History, 1876 to Present

Sources: History–Social Science Framework. Sacramento, CA: State Department of Education, 1988, 1994; *Social Sciences Essential Elements for K–6, 7–8, 9–12.* Austin, TX: Texas Education Agency, 1994: Selected from several elements for each grade; *Curriculum Frameworks,* Social Sciences. New York, 1994.

■ **TABLE 1.4**

Criteria for a K–8 Scope and Sequence

_____ Clear goals and rationale
_____ Balanced local, state, national, and global content
_____ Balanced past, present, and future content
_____ Significant content from history and social sciences
_____ Integration of skills, methods, and materials
_____ Inclusion on content providing multiple perspectives
_____ Emphasis on a variety of teaching strategies
_____ Provisions for active learning and social interaction
_____ Commitment to democratic beliefs and values
_____ Appreciation of our cultural heritage and that of others
_____ Emphasis on self-esteem and individual and group responsibility
_____ Progressive development of thinking, study, and participation skills
_____ Application of learning to life situations

The following list gives sample names of units and topics at each grade level.

Units of Instruction in the K–8 Curriculum

Kindergarten: Working, Learning, and Playing Together; Myself and Others; My Family: Other Families; Why Rules Are Needed; Using My Senses to Learn

Grade 1: How Families Meet Needs; Roles of Family Members; Our School; Roles of School Workers; Living in Neighborhoods; How We Depend on Others

Grade 2: How We Get Food, Shelter, and Clothing; Urban and Rural Communities; Groups That People Form; Roles in Groups; Changes in Neighborhoods

Grade 3: Our Community; Other Communities; Local History; Community Groups; Cities and Towns; How Our Community Is Governed; How Communities Change; Future Communities

Grade 4: History and Geography of Our State; How Our State Is Governed; Links to Other States; Resources and Industries; Regions of the United States (or in grade 5); World Regions—Desert, Mediterranean, Mountain, Tropical, Grassland

Grade 5: History—Before Columbus; Exploration, Colonial Life, and Pioneer Life; Beginning a Nation; Westward Expansion: Our Country in a Global Setting; Contributions of Individuals and Ethnic and Minority Groups; Our Neighbors—Canada and Mexico; Geography—North America; Regions of the United States—Northeast, Middle Atlantic, Southeast, North and South Central, Mountain, Pacific

Grade 6: The Earth's Geographic Features; Where People Live; Uses of Natural Resources; The Western Hemisphere; The Eastern Hemisphere; Early Civilizations, Greece, Rome, the Middle Ages, the Renaissance, and Other Topics in World History

Grade 7: Prehistoric People; Beginning of Civilization; Ancient Egypt, Greece, and Rome; The Middle Ages; The Renaissance; Global Exploration; Industrialization; Western Europe; Eastern Europe and the former USSR; The Middle East; Africa; Third World Countries; South Asia; East Asia; Oceania; State History and Government

Grade 8: Coming of Europeans; Winning Independence; Founding a New Nation; The Constitution; Building a Strong Nation; the Civil War; Reconstruction; Industrial America; Contributions of Men, Women, and Ethnic and Minority Groups; Relations with Other Countries; Current Problems

Not shown above are the many topics and units of study offered at many high schools, such as peace studies, environmental studies, career education, and law-related education. Examples of how these topics might be treated in the K–8 curriculum are shown in Chapter 4.

■ Conclusion

In this chapter we provided historical highlights to chronicle the evolution of social studies and to illustrate societal influences on the K–8 curriculum. We also reviewed definitions, rationales, purposes, and goals and objectives to explore the foundations of social studies and to validate its place in the K–8 curriculum as a core subject area.

 Questions, Activities, and Evaluation

1. Indicate your position on the following by writing *A* if you agree, *D* if you disagree, and *?* if you are uncertain. Discuss your views with a colleague, and explore reasons for any differences.

    _____ **a.** However social studies is defined, primary emphasis should be given to transmission of the best of our cultural heritage.

    _____ **b.** Teachers in all grades should use the same rationale for teaching social studies.

    _____ **c.** In most situations, knowledge and skill goals should have priority over value and participation goals.

    _____ **d.** Teachers should feel free to substitute topics they believe students need to study to replace those specified in the curriculum.

    _____ **e.** Geography, history, and civics should have a central place in the K–8 curriculum.

2. Examine a local curriculum guide or teacher's editions of adopted textbooks and note the following:

   a. How is social studies defined? How does the definition resemble or differ from the definitions presented in this chapter?

   b. What rationale is given for social studies education? What changes, if any, do you think should be made in the rationale?

   c. What goals and objectives are identified? How do they resemble or differ from those presented in this chapter? What legal requirements are stated?

   d. What recommendations are there for including multicultural and multiethnic studies, instruction on gender equity, law-related education, global studies, environmental education, and futures studies?

   e. What themes and topics are recommended for each grade? How do they differ from the examples presented in this chapter?

   f. What historical movement or trends in social studies are included?

3. Identify a set of articles that argue for or against the use of standards in the K–8 classroom. Report what you find, and conclude by providing the class with your position on standards.

4. Using information from the chapter, develop an argument for a definition and purpose for social studies in the K–8 curriculum. Hypothesize what social studies would be like without a definition and purpose.

5. Review recent issues of the following journals and note any articles that contain ideas you might use: *Social Education, Journal of Geography, The Social Studies, Early Years, Instructor, Learning, Teacher Magazine, Teaching and Change,* and *Social Studies and the Young Learner.*

General References

Bradley Commission on History in the Schools. (1988). *Building a history curriculum.* Washington, D.C.: Educational Excellence Network.

Brubaker, D. L., Simon, L. H. & Williams, J. W. (1977). A conceptual framework for social studies curriculum and instruction. *Social Education, 41,* 201–5. Five definitions of the social studies.

Butts, R. F. (1988). *The goals of democratic citizenship: Goals for civic education in the republic's third century.* Calabasas, CA: Center for Civic Education.

Citizens for the 21st century. (1988). *Social Education, 52,* 414–21. Series of articles in this and following issues on role of social studies.

National Commission on Social Studies in the Schools. (1989). *Charting a course: Social studies for the 21st century.* Washington, DC: National Commission. Available from National Council for the Social Studies.

National Commission on Social Studies in the Schools. (1991). *Voices of teachers.* Dubuque, IA: Kendall Hunt. Current status of social studies.

National Council for the Social Studies, Position Statements in *Social Education:* Revision of NCSS curriculum guidelines, *43* (April 1979), 261–73; Essentials of social studies, *45* (March 1981), 162–64; Including study about religions, *49* (May 1985), 413–14; Social studies for early childhood and elementary school children preparing for the 21st century, *53* (January

1989), 14–23; In search of a scope and sequence for the social studies, *Social Education, 53* (October 1989), 376–87; Citizenship needs of new Americans, *54* (January 1990), 16; Teaching about science, technology and society in social studies: Education for citizenships in the 21st century, *54* (April/May 1990), 189–93; The freedom to teach and the freedom to learn, *54* (October 1990), 343; Revised code of ethics for the social studies profession, *54* (October 1990), 344–45; Testing and evaluation of social studies students, *55* (September 1991), 284–86; Social studies in the middle school, *55* (September 1991), 287–93; The Columbian quincentenary, *55* (October 1991), 346–48; Standards for the preparation of social studies teachers, *56* (September 1992), 271–73; Ability grouping in social studies, *56* (September 1992), 268–70; Curriculum guidelines for multicultural education [revised], *56* (September 1992), 274–94; A vision of powerful teaching and learning in the social studies: Building social understanding and civic efficacy, *57* (September 1993), 213–3; Ten thematic strands in social studies, *58* (October 1994), 365–68.

National Council for the Social Studies. (1994). *Curriculum standards for social studies: Expectations for excellence* (Bulletin 89). Washington, DC: National Council for the Social Studies.

O'Neill, J. (1989). Social studies: Charting a course for a field adrift. *ASCD Curriculum Update.*

Parker, W. C. (1997). Navigating the unity/diversity tension in education for democracy. *The Social Studies, 88,* 12–17.

Shaver, J. P. (Ed.). (1990). *Handbook of research on social studies teaching and learning.* New York: Macmillan.

The social studies professional. Newsletter of the National Council for the Social Studies, 3501 Newark St., N.W., Washington, DC 20016.

Sources of Objectives

Anderson, L. W., & Sosniak, L. A. (Eds.). (1994). *Bloom's taxonomy of educational objectives.* NSSE Yearbook 1993. Chicago: University of Chicago Press. A forty-year retrospective.

Bloom, B. S. (Ed.). (1956). *Taxonomy of educational objectives, handbook I: The cognitive domain.* New York: David McKay Co.

Krathwohl, D. R., Bloom, B. S., & Masia, B. B. (1964). *Taxonomy of educational objectives: Affective domain.* New York: David McKay Co.

References on History of Social Studies

Cremin, L. A. (1962). *The transformation of the school: Progressivism in American education, 1876–1957.* New York: Alfred A. Knopf.

Grossman, R. H. (1964). *Development of the elementary social studies curricula in the public schools of New York City and San Francisco, 1850–1952.* Dissertation. Berkeley: University of California.

Hertzberg, H. W. (1981). *Social studies reform 1880–1980.* Boulder, CO: Social Science Education Consortium.

Jenness, D. (1990). *Making sense of social studies.* New York: Macmillan.

Michaelis, J. U. (1966). New directions in social sciences education. *Influences in Curriculum Change.* Washington DC: Association for Supervision and Curriculum Development. Review of project impacts.

Tanner, D. & Tanner, L. (1990). *History of the school curriculum.* New York: Macmillan.

Tyron, R. M. (1935). *The social sciences as school subjects.* New York: Charles Scribner's Sons.

Wesley, E. B. (1944). *American history in schools and colleges.* New York: Macmillan.

Wronski, S. P., & Bragaw, D. H. (Eds.). (1986). *Social studies and social sciences: A fifty-year perspective.* Bulletin 78. Washington, DC: National Council for the Social Studies.

Chapter 2

Incorporating Content from Basic Disciplines

Chapter Objective

To identify substantive and process knowledge of enduring value and to give examples of discipline-based questions, study guides, and learning activities for social studies

Focusing Questions

- What are primary sources of content for social studies?
- What content is recommended in recent reports on geography, history, and civic education?
- What substantive knowledge—concepts, concept clusters, themes, and generalizations—are drawn from core disciplines?
- How can concepts and themes be used to generate questions and improve thinking and learning?
- What are examples of discipline-based study guides and learning activities?
- What process knowledge—values, attitudes, models, and methods of inquiry—may be used to improve learning?
- How does children's and adolescent literature support social studies instruction?
- How can content from the disciplines, process knowledge, and literature be incorporated into social studies instruction?

■ The Core Disciplines

History and geography are primary sources of content for social studies. Content is also drawn from political science, economics, anthropology, sociology, and psychology. These disciplines are interrelated by concepts and methods of investigation as well as by their focus on human relationships. Geography and history draw freely from a variety of disciplines but do so with reference to the space and time dimensions of human relationships. All the disciplines have their own historical dimensions, and all are concerned with the study of various aspects of human behavior.

Each discipline has its own unique characteristics. Regional geography, social history, and cultural anthropology are highly integrative disciplines. Regional geography provides a well-rounded view of cultural and physical elements in areas under study. History provides an integrated view of significant past events in a time framework. Cultural anthropology provides a holistic view of ways of living in selected cultures. These three fields of study are used extensively to synthesize content: geography in a spatial context, history in a temporal context, and anthropology in a cultural context.

Political science and economics are policy sciences that study processes and decision making in two realms of human activity. Material from these two disciplines may be included in units based primarily on geography or history, or in separate units on local, state, and national government or economic activities. Political science is a key source of content for civic education, as shown later in this chapter.

Three behavioral sciences—anthropology, sociology, and psychology—are sources for the study of concepts such as roles, groups, institutions, and processes of social interaction. These fields contribute to the study of social problems, social change, and human interaction in a variety of cultures and societies.

Not listed here, but discussed later in this chapter, is philosophy. Philosophy is useful in social studies because it provides definitions, critiques of the methods of study and conclusions of other disciplines, and methods of reasoning and analysis. Inferring, critical thinking, valuing, using criteria to make judgments, finding fallacies in statements, and examining the grounds for claims and beliefs all call for reasoning and logical analysis. Teachers also employ literature and other areas of the humanities to enrich the social studies curriculum. And, as you have already gathered, K-8 teachers make effective use of the humanities in social studies instruction.

This breadth of content is widely accepted as central to the goals of social studies education. Recommendations in recent frameworks and reports illustrate the central place of history and geography as a matrix of time and place for the study of human relationships (Bradley Commission, 1988; California, 1988; National Commission on Social Studies, 1989). They also urge the integration of content from other social sciences and the humanities. This multidisciplinary approach is highlighted in the six types of literacy put forth in the goals of the California framework (California, 1988):

> *Historical literacy:* sense of historical empathy; meaning of time and chronology; cause and effect; continuity and change; history as memory with political implications; importance of religion, philosophy, and other major belief systems in history
>
> *Ethical literacy:* of life and dignity of the individual; how societies have tried to resolve ethical issues; how ideas affect behavior; universal concern for ethics and human rights as aspirations in every time and place
>
> *Cultural literacy:* complex nature of culture—history, geography, politics, literature, art, drama, music, dance, law, religion, philosophy, architecture, technology, science, education, sports, social structure, economy; relationships among parts of a culture—mythology, legends, values, and beliefs; literature and art as reflection of inner life of people; multicultural perspective that respects dignity and worth of people

Geographic literacy: awareness of place; locational skills and understandings; human and environmental interaction; human movement; world regions and their historical, cultural, economic, and political characteristics

Economic literacy: economic problems confronting all societies: comparative economic systems; economic goals; performance and problems of our society; international economic system

Sociopolitical literacy: relationships between social and political systems; relationships between society and law; comparative political systems

History

To quote two history educators, "Knowledge of history is the precondition of political intelligence" (Nash & Crabtree, 1996, p. 1). Effective history instruction invites students to appreciate their common heritage and core civic values and allows them to learn about self, others, and communities near and far.

Historical content is incorporated in social studies education at all grade levels, including family life from colonial times to the present, community and state history, background on current and special events, and American and world history.

Oral history projects have become a popular means for students to do their own historical research. Students interview key individuals, tape-record their accounts, and replay and interpret them. Also, taped accounts such as *Geronimo: His Own Story, Hard Times,* and *The Immigrant* help bring history to life. Local history can be studied in sourcebooks and at active local historical associations. For example, *The Worcester Sourcebook, The Small Town Sourcebooks I* and *II,* and the *Guide to Small Town Sourcebooks* are replete with teaching suggestions, photos, drawings, and other source materials.[1] The sourcebooks are useful in comparative studies of the growth of communities and as models for developing materials on any community.

A variety of computer programs simulate trekking westward, exploring, trading, ruling ancient kingdoms, and other events. Examples are *Oregon, The Oregon Trail, Trailwest, Westward—1847, Lincoln's Decisions, Fur Trading, Voyageur, Hammurabi, Kingdom,* and *Sumer.* Folksongs from different historical periods can enrich learning.[2] A variety of books and historical literature may be used at all levels to nurture empathy and convey nuances of different time periods.[3]

1. Available from New England Bookstore, Old Sturbridge Village, Sturbridge, MA 01566.

2. For example, see music textbooks and recently published books such as the following: Memphis Orff Teachers. (1981). *Hearing America.* Memphis Musicraft Publishers: Memphis, TN; W. K. McNeil. (1993). *Southern Mountain Folksongs: Traditional Folksongs from the Appalachians and the Ozarks* (The American Folklore). August House Publishers: Little Rock, Arkansas; A. Paredes, & M. Pena. (1995). *A Texas-Mexican Cancionero: Folksongs of the Lower Border.* University of Texas Press: Austin, Texas.

3. There are a number of sources to turn to when looking for social studies trade books. For example, each year the April/May issue of *Social Education,* the official journal of the National Council for the Social Studies (NCSS), publishes the "Notable Children's Trade Books in the Field of Social Studies." This committee, a collaborative effort between NCSS and the Children's Book Council, highlights outstanding trade books in the areas of human relations, creativity in the area of cultural diversity, scholarship, and high literary quality.

Habits of Mind

As they learn about history, students should be encouraged to cultivate certain habits of mind. These habits help students open up to the study of history in ways that develop empathy, sound judgment, and understanding of content on a number of levels. You can use the evaluation checklist provided in Table 2.1 to help discern your own habits of mind, and you might develop a similar checklist for students, appropriate to their grade level.

History Concepts, Themes, and Generalizations

Many concepts used to interpret and synthesize historical information are drawn from other disciplines. For example, the economic concept of division of labor is useful in learning about the history of family or community life in different time periods, as is the anthropological concept of cultural borrowing.

■ TABLE 2.1

Habits of Mind for Historical Studies

_____ Do I know how the past is significant to me? to my society? to other societies?

_____ Can I separate important information from unimportant information?

_____ Do I have historical empathy? Can I view past events the way they might have been viewed when they were happening?

_____ Do I understand the diversity of world cultures? Do I avoid prejudice in favor of my own cultural heritage?

_____ Do I understand that, despite cultural diversity, all peoples of the world share a common humanity?

_____ Do I try to understand the forces that cause historical change? Do I look for causes and effects? people who are the agents of change? new ideas that precipitate change?

_____ Can I grasp the interplay of change and continuity in a given period of history?

_____ Am I careful in making judgments about the past? Do I avoid simplistic "lessons from history"?

_____ Do I recognize the importance of individuals in the shaping of history? the effect of personal character on the common good?

_____ Do I understand history and geography as a matrix of time and place? as a context for events?

_____ Do I read widely and critically? Can I frame useful questions as I study?

_____ Can I distinguish fact from opinion? real evidence from faulty evidence?

Time, processing, and organizing concepts are also fundamental to the study of history. It would be hard to think of teaching history without using these concepts. Here are examples of each.

Time Concepts

time	decade	era
day	generation	prehistory
week	millennium	medieval
season	period	modern
year	epoch	

Process Concepts

criticism	synthesis	interpretation
analysis	periodization	reconstruction of events

Organizing Concepts

event	place	trend
theme	movement	chronology
period		

Themes

Themes drawn from history are also a hallmark of social studies instruction. Within the context of each theme, particular historical events and developments can be studied. Here are some examples.

Theme: The History of Our Town

- the arrival of the first settlers
- the establishment of homes, schools, and houses of worship
- the development of business
- contributions of individuals and groups

Theme: Early American History

- discoverers and explorers
- contacts with native peoples
- establishment of settlements
- development of economy
- relationship between colonies and European powers

To employ the inquiry–conceptual model described in Chapter 1, teachers can develop questions to engage students in the content of each theme. The following summary of themes (from the Bradley Commission, 1988) includes sample questions that combine social studies concepts with thinking tasks. The questions guide the students' exploration of content. (Notice that the themes in this list are not historical periods or movements; they are instead broad conceptual themes.)

Theme

Civilization, cultural diffusion, innovation: evolution of human skills and means of exerting power over nature and people; centers of power; flowering of civilizations; social, religious, and political patronage of the arts; importance of the city

Questions (for analyzing, synthesizing)

- How did early civilizations emerge in river valleys?
- How did ideas spread among societies?
- What are significant contributions of ancient Greece and Rome?

Theme

Human interaction with the environment: geography/technology/culture relationships and their effects on economic, social, and political developments; choices made possible because of climate, resources, and location and the effect of culture and beliefs on choices; gains and losses of technological change; role of agriculture; effects of disease and disease-fighting on people, plants, and animals.

Questions (for interpreting)

- What adaptations have been made to climate in our community?
- How did early settlers adapt to the environment?

Theme

Values, beliefs, political ideas, institutions: religions and ideologies; political and social institutions at various stages of industrial and commercial development; interplay among ideas, material conditions, moral values, and leadership, especially in democratic societies; tensions between aspirations for freedom and security, liberty and equality, distinction and commonality.

Questions (for analyzing, synthesizing)

- What has been the impact of religions and ideologies in China? in Japan? in Middle Eastern countries?
- What has been the impact of European ideologies such as Marxism? nationalism? others?

Theme

Conflict and cooperation: causes of war and approaches to prevention and peace making; relations between domestic affairs and ways of dealing with the outside world; contrasts between international conflict and cooperation and between isolation and interdependence; consequences of war and peace for societies and their cultures.

Questions (for interpreting)

- What were the causes of the American Revolution? the French Revolution?
- What were the immediate consequences? the long-range consequences?

How would you help students become aware of social injustices? Would you use a historical approach? Would a multidisciplinary approach be more effective?

Theme

Comparative history of major developments: revolutionary, reactionary, and reform periods across time and place; imperialism; comparative instances of slavery and emancipation; feudalism and centralization; human successes and failures, wisdom and folly; comparative elites and aristocracies; role of the family; wealth and merit.

Questions (for analyzing, synthesizing)

- What foundations of western ideas can be traced to the ancient Hebrews and Greeks? to the ancient Romans? to the Renaissance?

Theme

Patterns of social and political interaction: changing patterns of class, ethnic, racial, and gender structures and relations; immigration, migration, and social mobility; effects of schooling; new prominence of women and minorities in the study of history and their relation to political power and influential elites; characteristics of multicultural societies; forces for unity and disunity.

Questions (for analyzing, recalling)

- How has the status of minority groups changed since the Civil War?
- What has been the impact on politics? on business? on freedom and justice?
- What have been the contributions of immigrants to our multicultural society?

In the following section we illustrate how to use standards as another basis for developing history instruction for K–8 learners.

History Standards

The History Standards, developed by the National Center for History in the Schools, is a product of the 1990s reform movement and represents an attempt to provide better focus to the teaching of history in K–12 schools, particularly in the early grades.

These standards are based on five fields of historical thinking: (1) chronology, (2) comprehension, (3) analysis, interpretation, (4) issue analysis and decision making, and (5) research (Nash & Crabtree, 1996).

Historical chronology includes the ability to distinguish between past, present, and future; identify the temporal structure of a historical narrative; establish temporal order when constructing historical narratives; measure calendar time by days, weeks, months, years, decades, centuries, and millennia; calculate calendar time B.C. and A.D.; compare our system of measuring time with other systems; interpret the data in time lines; create time lines; reconstruct patterns of historical succession and use them to explain continuity and change; and compare models for periodization.

Historical comprehension includes the ability to reconstruct the literal meaning of a passage; identify the central question; read narratives imaginatively; evidence historical empathy; use data in historical maps; use data in charts, tables, graphs, Venn diagrams, and other graphic organizers; use visual data in photographs, cartoons, paintings, and architectural drawings to elaborate data in a historical narrative.

Historical analysis and interpretation include application of critical thinking to identify authors and sources of documents; compare and contrast ideas, values, personalities, behaviors, and institutions; differentiate between historical facts and interpretations; consider multiple perspectives; incorporate multiple causes in analyses and explanations of historical action; challenge arguments of inevitability; compare competing narratives; hold interpretations as tentative; evaluate historians' debates; and hypothesize the influence of the past on the present.

Historical issue analysis and decision making include identifying past issues and problems and analyzing interests and views of those involved in a situation; gathering evidence on past and present factors that contribute to a problem and alternative courses of action; identifying relevant antecedents and historical analogies, differentiating them from inappropriate and irrelevant ones; evaluating alternative courses of action; formulating a position or course of action; evaluating implementation of the decision by analyzing the interests served, actions of each player, ethical dimensions, and costs and benefits from various perspectives.

Historical research includes creative thinking in developing narratives and arguments; formulating historical questions; obtaining needed data; analyzing the data in terms of its social/political/economic context, credibility, consistency, and completeness; evaluating bias, distortion, and propaganda by omission, suppression, or invention of facts; detecting gaps in available records and marshaling contextual knowledge of the time and place in order to elaborate upon the evidence, fill gaps, and construct a sound narrative.

All of these fields of thinking are applied in various grades. For example, students in grades 5–6, as they study historical documents, should be able to pose questions such as:

- Who produced this document?
- When, how, and why?
- What does the document tell about the person(s) who created it?
- What information is needed to tell a story about the document and the people and events connected to it?

Students in grades 7–8 should be able to pose questions to guide research; use primary and secondary sources such as diaries, letters, periodicals, literature, oral histories, artifacts, art, photographs, and films; prepare a meaningful report; identify omissions; and challenge interpretations and generalizations.

The following activity ideas can engage students in the study of history in a variety of ways.

ACTIVITY IDEAS　*Learning about History*

➤ Get students involved in an oral history project. They might find out about their town in the 1950s, about changes in an industry or business that is based locally, or about an important event or development in their city's history that is still within living memory. Help students set goals for the project and plan how to implement it. To support them as they plan interviews, you might give them a checklist like this one.

Before the Interview

_____ Brainstorm a list of questions to ask the person you will interview. Include questions that ask *who, what, when, where, why,* and *how.*

_____ Choose the most interesting questions. Put them in an order that makes sense. Avoid questions that can simply be answered with "yes" or "no."

_____ Arrange a time and a place to meet the person. Make plans to arrive promptly.

During the Interview

_____ Introduce yourself in a friendly way.

_____ Start the tape recorder, or begin taking notes. Ask your questions one by one.

_____ Give the interviewee time to elaborate. Don't rush.

_____ Listen carefully. The person may mention some things that are so interesting, you'll want to ask more about them. Do so, even if the questions aren't on your list.

_____ Ask questions to clarify anything that seems unclear.

_____ Express your thanks sincerely.

After the Interview

_____ If you took notes, review them while the interview is still fresh in your mind. Fill out details that you might have missed.

_____ Write a note of thanks to the person you interviewed.

➤ As a writing assignment, have students use their knowledge of a historical event to write a diary entry as if they were someone who experienced the event. Encourage them not only to include historical detail but also to use imagination as they report the person's thoughts and feelings and describe what was seen and heard.

➤ Spend time focusing on definitions of important terms in the study of history. For example, have students use the index of the textbook to find discussions of scalawags, muckrakers, and carpetbaggers and then write a definition for each of these three terms. As a class, compare and refine the definitions.

➤ In small groups, have students investigate state history. Assign each group a number of questions from a list like the following one. Or create a list suited to your grade level and learners. Students might report their findings to the whole class or create a bulletin board display about state history.

> Which native peoples have lived in the territory that is now our state?
>
> Who were the early explorers of this area? Why did they explore it?
>
> What were some of the early settlements? Who settled them?
>
> What was the first main highway? the first railroad?
>
> On what date did this area become a state?
>
> What is the state capital? Why is it located where it is?
>
> Who was the first governor? Who are other important political leaders?
>
> What was the first university or college?
>
> What are the state's important natural resources? important products?
>
> What are the significant industries in our state? How have they changed over time?
>
> Find four or five examples of accomplished artists, writers, actors, athletes, or inventors from your state. Tell a little about each one.

➤ In a lesson on primary and secondary sources, you might include a worksheet like this one.

> The main features of primary sources are _____.
>
> The main features of secondary sources are _____.
>
> Write **P** for primary source and **S** for secondary source.
>
> | _____ novel | _____ diary entry |
> | --- | --- |
> | _____ biography | _____ letter |
> | _____ textbook | _____ newspaper editorial |
> | _____ news article | _____ autobiography |
> | _____ minutes of a meeting | _____ recording of a speech |

➤ To add depth to a study of the history of space exploration, have each student research biographical information about an astronaut or scientist. They might choose Neil A. Armstrong, Edwin "Buzz" Aldrin, Guion Bluford, Yuri A. Gagarin, John H. Glenn Jr., Virgil "Gus" Grissom, Mae Carol Jemison, Christa McAuliffe, Ellen Ochoa, or Sally K. Ride. They might present the reports orally or in writing, including pictures or drawings with their reports.

➤ Ask students to compare the characteristics of modern communities and one or more earlier ones. Students might use a chart like this one as they gather information. Later, ask them what generalizations can be made about community life in each time period.

Characteristics	Eighteenth-Century Americans	Twentieth-Century Americans
Food, shelter, and clothing		
Schools, houses of worship, and other public buildings		
Transportation		
Communication		
Health and medical services		
Recreation and sports		
Work done by men, women, and children		
Use of natural resources		

➤ To learn about long-term historical trends, students might study a table of population growth in the American colonies or a similar chart or graph. Questions like these may guide such a study.

What years are shown in the first column? _____

What colonies are shown across the top? _____

Which colony had the least growth in 1680 and the greatest growth eighty years later? _____

Which colony had the smallest population in 1760? Which had the second largest in 1760? _____

In general, what can be said about population growth in this period?

_____

_____

➤ Studying a map that shows historical developments adds a visual element to learning about history. Here is a sample worksheet to support this type of study.

> **Territorial Expansion of the United States**
>
> Read the text, and study the map in today's assignment. Write the name of the area acquired by the United States in these years:
>
> 1803 _____   1867 _____
>
> 1818 _____   1846 _____
>
> 1848 _____   1853 _____

➤ Ask students to take notes as they read a history assignment. Build on any instruction in note taking that they have experienced so far. For example, you might ask them to read a passage about how the southern states were readmitted to the Union after the Civil War. They might list the requirements and the years in which each southern state was readmitted. Then have the students use the notes as they participate in a class discussion.

➤ As a handy reference, you might have the class keep a chart on information about U.S. presidents to use as they study American history. The chart could be kept on a bulletin board or easel. Ask different students to add information about different presidents. The chart could look something like this.

Name	Term	Party	Major Contributions
George Washington			
John Adams			
Thomas Jefferson			
James Madison			
James Monroe			
John Quincy Adams			
Andrew Jackson			

Geography

Geography bridges the social and natural sciences. It provides information on the spatial variation of the cultural and physical elements that make each place on earth unique. The study of geography enriches understanding and appreciation of the earth as the home of people, of variations in human habitats and cultures, and of human interaction with the natural and cultural environments. Students explore people–land relationships, paying attention to the past, present, and future uses of resources, population growth, the impact of technology, adaptation to the environment, and global interdependence.

The social studies program draws from the two main branches of geography—physical and human. *Physical geography* provides information on landforms, water bodies, climate and weather, and plant and animal life that is relevant to the study of human activities. *Human geography* provides information on the interaction between people and their physical and cultural environments, ranging from ways of living in particular cultures to historical, demographic, urban, economic, political, and other aspects of human settlement of the earth.

Regional and topical studies along with spatial analysis are included in social studies. *Regional studies* reveal the unique features of a particular region, such as mediterranean, tropical, and desert areas. *Topical studies* provide data on a single element, such as climate, population, resources, and land use. *Spatial analysis* identifies patterns of surface features, elements that tend to be in close proximity, and interaction between elements and areas.

Special fields of study within geography, such as urban, economic, political, and historical geography, are also drawn upon to enrich learning. Concepts from urban geography—city zones, specialized cities, and central places—are used to study communities; to classify manufacturing, commercial, and other specialized cities; and to identify settlement patterns that range from village and town to metropolis and megalopolis (for example, the area stretching from north of Boston through New York to south of Washington, DC is a megalopolis). Major cities such as New York, Chicago, Los Angeles, London, and Tokyo are studied as central cores that serve large areas. Students learn about patterns of urban sprawl by studying cities that have mushroomed outward in concentric circles or strips. The internal structure of a city may be analyzed, beginning with streets in the neighborhood and extending to land use in inner, middle, and outer zones for business, industrial, residential, recreational, and other uses.

Geography Concepts, Themes, and Generalizations

Concepts from economic and political geography are used to study relationships between communities, states, and nations; changing boundaries; use of resources; and trade. Wise use and conservation of resources are stressed in units on energy and resource use, beginning with the local community and extending to countries and regions around the world. Resources, capital, labor, and know-how (a central concept cluster in economics and economic geography) are studied as learners analyze economic activities. The concept of interdependence is emphasized on local, regional, national, and global levels.

Historical geography considers spatial changes over time in units on growth of the community, rural to urban population shifts, early settlements, growth of cities, and territorial changes. Studies of exploration and colonization, westward expansion, the growth and decline of the Roman Empire and other great domains, and the emergence of early civilizations in different parts of the world may be found in upper elementary grades and middle school.

A major contribution of geography is instruction on globes and maps, as shown in Chapter 10. The following conceptual components show how geography makes a substantive contribution to the social studies curriculum.

Examples of Geography Concepts

adaptation	equator	poles
capital	interdependence	resources
community	latitude	state
conservation	longitude	spatial distribution and differentiation
continent	maritime	temperate
country	metropolis	tropical

Concept Clusters

The environment: natural, cultural, spheres (hydrosphere, lithosphere, atmosphere, biosphere, or life layer); human elements (people and their cultures); physical elements (land, water, climate); biotic elements (plants, animals)

Earth-sun relationships: source of energy; rotation, revolution, inclination and parallelism of axis; circulation of atmosphere; seasons, night and day

Environmental concerns: acid rain, pollution, ozone layer, wetlands, rain forests

Major landforms: plains, hills, plateaus, mountains

Water bodies: rivers, lakes, bays, straits, seas, oceans

Natural resources: water, soil, animal life, plant life, minerals, climate

Population: size, distribution, centers, density, composition, growth rate, movement, prediction, control, problems, productive potential

Settlement patterns: isolated, village, town, suburb, city, metropolis, megalopolis

Urbanization: growth of urban centers, central cities, location; functions; internal structure (residence, business, industry); interaction with other places, accessibility; migration, invasion, segregation, desegregation, redevelopment

Specialized cities: manufacturing, commercial, transport, port, government, other

City structure: inner, middle, outer zones; central business district; residential, industrial, suburban

As students study concepts in geography, they will soon gain enough knowledge to make helpful generalizations.

Generalizations

People use resources to meet their needs in ways that are shaped by their culture and influenced by their environment.

Each region of our country interacts with other regions and makes unique economic contributions.

Human activities and natural forces cause changes on the earth's surface.

Themes

A variety of themes characterize education in geography. The following are adapted from a national report.[4] Teachers can employ the inquiry–conceptual model in geography studies, raising questions that employ geography concepts and focus on particular thinking skills in the context of a given theme.

Theme

Location: position on the earth's surface; absolute and relative location to indicate positions of physical and cultural features

Questions (for interpreting, observing)

■ What is this feature's location in relation to our community? our state? our country?

■ What is its latitude? its longitude?

Theme

Place: physical and human characteristics; description of characteristics that distinguish a place from other places

Questions (for interpreting, observing)

■ What are distinctive human features of this place, such as settlement patterns and population density?

■ What are its geographical features?

Theme

Human-environment interactions: relationships within places; how people modify and adapt to the environment; consequences of changes in the environment

Questions (for analyzing, synthesizing)

■ How have people changed their environment?

■ What are the consequences of changes?

Theme

Movement: movement of people, goods, services, and ideas; local to global interdependence; interaction by means of communication and transportation

Questions (for analyzing, synthesizing)

■ How do networks of transportation speed the movement of people and goods?

■ How do networks of communication affect the spread of ideas?

---

4. Adapted from reports of Geographic Education National Implementation Project, 1987, 1989. Compare these themes with the Geography Standards in the next section. For information on related materials from Geography Alliances set up in states around the country, write to Geographic Education Program, National Geographic Society, 1145 17th Street, Washington, DC 20036-4688.

Theme

Regions: how they are defined by unifying features of the physical or human environment; how they are formed and changed for geographic study; types of physical and cultural regions

Questions (for analyzing, synthesizing)

- What are unifying features of the Corn Belt? the Middle East? other regions?
- How would you describe a mountain region? a desert region?

Geography Standards

The standards movement has also affected the study of geography. Six essential elements are included in the National Geography Standards, *Geography for Life:* spatial elements, places and regions, physical systems, human systems, environment and society, and applying geography (Bettis, 1994).

Spatial elements: These include working with maps and globes, other representational models, and tools and technology to process information from a spatial perspective; use of "mental maps" to put items in a spatial context; and the ability to analyze spatial organization.

Places and regions: This component includes knowledge of physical and human characteristics of places, how regions are defined to assist in interpreting the complex surface of the earth, and how culture influences human perceptions of places and regions.

Physical systems: This involves knowledge of the processes that shape the physical patterns on the earth and knowledge of ecosystems.

Human systems: This area of study includes the distributions and migration of peoples, the nature of cultural mosaics, the nature of economic interdependence, the characteristics of human settlement, and the forces of cooperation and conflict.

Environment and society: Studies in this area examine the impact of human actions on physical systems, the effect of physical systems on human systems, and knowledge of changes in the meaning, distribution, and importance of resources.

Applying geography: This features the interpretation of the past in terms of geography and using geography to interpret the present and plan for the future.

You can approach geography in many ways in the classroom. The following ideas will help get you started.

 *Learning about Geography*

➤ Give students practice in identifying U.S. time zones. Using a map, have them first identify the different time zones. Then ask them to work out the answer to a problem like this one: What time is it in Central, Mountain, and Pacific time when it is 1:00 P.M. in New York City? What time would it be in Alaska? in Hawaii?

➤ Urge students to use computer programs to develop proficiency in the concepts and content of geography. To find information on places being studied, they might use *World GeoGraph, Africa Trail, The Silk Road, Crosscountry USA, 3D Atlas 98, Carmen Sandiego Social Studies Library,* or *Star Sites.* To build a database on the places they study, students might use *AppleWorks, Bank Street Filer, pfs: File, Easy Working,* or *Data Manager.*

➤ Encourage students to develop greater accuracy in describing a given place or region. You might use a checklist like this one.

_____ Describe the location of the place. Tell where it is in relation to other places.

_____ State the place's main physical and cultural features.

_____ Describe the relation between people and the environment.

_____ Note urban, suburban, or exurban features of the place. Tell whether the population is growing, shrinking, or moving within the area.

_____ List other distinctive features of the place.

➤ As they study regions of the United States, challenge your class to fill out a chart like this one, noting the key features of each region. Students could keep their own individual charts, or they could work on one as a class.

Regions of the United States				
Region	*States*	*Major Cities*	*Economy*	*Special Features*
New England				
Middle Atlantic				
Southeastern				
North Central				
South Central				
Southwestern				
Midwest				
Pacific				

➤ Students can examine where people live and why they live there by focusing on population. Choose a country, region, or place for study. Then let students explore number of inhabitants, population density and growth rate, patterns of settlement and areas of concentration, and shifts in population over time. You may include a forecasting activity in which students predict what population patterns will prevail in the future.

➤ To orient students to the study of regions that are unfamiliar to them, you could begin by examining a map with the whole class. Use a questioning strategy to help them grasp key features of these regions. Here is a list of questions that could be used to introduce a study of North Africa and the Middle East.

> What countries are shown on this map of North Africa and the Middle East?
>
> Which country is largest?
>
> Which one is smallest?
>
> Which country is farthest east? farthest west? farthest north? farthest south?
>
> How far is it across the area shown from west to east? from north to south?

➤ To learn more about geographical concepts, have students compare two or more regions, countries, or states. They might compare geographic features of Canada, the United States, and Mexico or the geographic similarities and differences among the states of the Deep South. One approach might be to divide the class into small groups, giving each group a particular topic to research. Encourage students to use reference works in the classroom reference center or the library. Each group might use a worksheet like this one as a research guide.

The Physical Features of _____

Describe the space (area, relative size, shape, natural and political boundaries, neighbors, and so on).

_____

Describe the landforms (plains, hills, plateaus, mountains, valleys, and so on).

_____

Describe bodies of water (rivers, lakes, bays, straits, ocean coasts, underground water systems, and so on).

_____

Describe the climate (average temperatures and precipitation per season, effects of latitude, elevation, ocean currents, land and water distribution, mountain barriers).

_____

Describe the resources (soil, water, vegetation, animal life, minerals, and so on).

_____

Describe the population (number, density, growth rate, settlement patterns, and so on).

_____

Pitfalls to Avoid in Teaching Geography

Because so much information is available on various regions and cultures, it is easy to overemphasize facts at the expense of higher-level learning. However, educators generally conclude that a more valuable learning experience is gained from studying a selected area in depth and from using facts to develop concepts, answer questions, test hypotheses, and develop understanding and appreciation of human uses of the environment. Facts take on more meaning when structured around concepts and main ideas; students should use facts to explain adaptations to the environment, why cities have developed in some places and not in others, the impact of technology, and so on.

A related pitfall is to overemphasize the bizarre and exotic features of various lands and peoples. This approach inevitably produces stereotypes and misconceptions.

It also helps to develop clear distinctions between easy-to-confuse concepts such as weather and climate. *Weather* refers to the atmospheric conditions—temperature, precipitation, air pressure, and wind—that prevail at a given time in a given place. *Climate* refers to temperature and other conditions over a period of years. Other concepts that are easy to confuse include country and continent, and physical region and cultural region.

In the upper elementary and middle grades, weigh the value of an in-depth study of selected cultures in an area against that of an overall study of cultures in the area. This issue has been resolved in some schools by following an overview of an area with an intensive study of one or more representative cultures or countries within the area. Be sure that students do not generalize about all countries on the basis of the single country studied in depth. Although certain common geographic, economic, political, and cultural characteristics are to be found among countries in the Middle East, in Africa, or in Latin America, their specific differences can be grasped only by studying each country in detail. For example, many countries in Africa aspire to improved standards of living, better educational and health services, increased industrial output, and stable government, but the specific ways and means employed to attain these goals vary greatly from country to country.

The outmoded concept of environmental determinism has been rooted out of most current teaching materials and should be avoided. Geographers take the position that although environmental conditions are important to consider when studying ways of living, they do not *cause* those ways of living. If this were so, all people in desert areas, for example, would live the same way. Students can quickly discover differences in ways of living in similar environments and interpret them in terms of differences in culture. And they can discover how interaction with the environment is transformed as cultural changes occur by studying their own community, state, and nation as well as the Inuit, Nigerians, and people in other lands.

When referring to places relative to the equator, the terms *middle latitudes, high latitudes,* and *low latitudes* should be used. The terms *temperate, frigid,* and *torrid zones* are climatic rather than locational terms, and they are not accurate descriptions of climatic conditions. Since some writers still use the terms, however, children should become acquainted with them and understand the inaccuracies and limitations that characterize them.

The following activities are designed to help students avoid confusion as they learn such concepts.

 **ACTIVITY IDEAS** *Clarifying Geographic Concepts*

➤ To aid in learning about latitudes, you might provide a study guide like this one.

What Are the Different Latitudes?

1. Low latitudes are between 23 1/2 degrees north and south of the equator. This area is sometimes called the torrid zone.

2. Middle latitudes are between 23 1/2 and 66 1/2 degrees north and between the same degrees south of the equator. These areas are sometimes called temperate zones.

3. High latitudes are between 66 1/2 degrees north of the equator and the North Pole and 66 1/2 degrees south of the equator and the South Pole. These areas are sometimes called the frigid zones.

➤ While studying concepts such as different climates, you might give students practice in remembering the names of continents. Try using a worksheet like this one.

For each climate listed below, name the continents on which such a climate can be found.

1. tundra: _____

2. continental: _____

3. marine: _____

4. steppe: _____

5. desert: _____

6. Mediterranean: _____

7. rain forest: _____

8. savanna: _____

Hint: When you are finished, check your work. Make sure you have used the names of continents, not of countries.

Civics: Political Science and Law

Most K–8 programs focus on traditional civics content and move beyond this area to include concepts such as power and authority in the family, the school, and the community. Recent events (such as legislative debates about gun control, violence in the schools, and peer mediation programs in middle schools) may influence civics instruction in the K–8 curriculum. As a result of pressure from parents and other groups, schools might increase the attention given to safety issues, rights of individuals, and programs that offer students nonviolent ways of resolving disputes.

Civics Concepts, Themes, and Generalizations

Most elementary schools provide instruction in making rules, carrying out rules, and the settling of disputes in situations familiar to children, during the early grades. Later these concepts are extended to legislative (rule-making), executive (rule-applying), and judicial (rule-adjudicating) processes of local, state, and national government. In community studies students learn about the roles of the mayor, the city council, teachers, police, and other public employees; public services such as education, protection, and recreation; city planning and redevelopment; and metropolitan planning to solve transportation and other cross-community problems.

State and national studies include concepts such as authority, separation of powers, due process and equal protection of law, and processes of government. Historical studies include the contributions of the Greeks and the Romans to government, the Magna Carta, changes in laws in England, law and government in early America, case studies of struggles for justice, and great documents such as the Declaration of Independence and the Constitution. Examples of key conceptual components follow.

> ■ The citizens of the United States enjoy rights and freedoms found in very few other places in the world.
> —*Creating America*

Examples of Civics Concepts

the Bill of Rights	equal protection	political systems
civil rights	justice	separation of powers
the Constitution	laws	responsibilities
due process	legal systems	

Concept Clusters

Tasks of government: external security, internal order, justice; public services; freedom (under democracy)

Processes: rule making (legislative branch), rule applying (executive branch), rule adjudicating (judicial branch)

Public services: police, postal service, education, health, conservation, labor, business

Due process of law: protection against arrest without probable cause, unreasonable search and seizure, forced confession, self-incrimination, and double jeopardy; right to public trial, counsel, fair judge and jury, habeas corpus, knowledge of accusation; right to confront and cross-examine witnesses, to have witnesses for one's defense, to the assumption of innocence until proven guilty

Sources of law: the Constitution, statutes, common law, decrees

As students learn about concepts and concept clusters, they will soon be able to make meaningful generalizations about civics, such as these.

Generalizations

Rules are needed to guide individual and group activities.

Due process of law is needed to provide equal opportunity, protection, and justice for all individuals and groups.

Conflicts arise when individuals and groups have competing goals, apply different standards of conduct, and interpret laws differently.

Themes

The following themes are drawn from a project based primarily on political science and law (CIVITAS, 1991). The questions under each topic illustrate how civics concepts and a variety of thinking skills can be employed in each theme.

Theme

The nature of politics and government: political power and authority; sources of authority; purposes and types of government; ethics and politics; religion and public life; economics; race/class/ethnicity; gender issues; human rights; purposes of law; legal systems

Questions (for interpreting, analyzing)

- What are the purposes of government?
- What is constitutional government?
- What are problems of morality in politics and government?
- How has religion impacted government?

Theme

Politics and government in the United States: fundamental values—common good, individual rights, justice, equality, diversity, truth, patriotism; fundamental principles—popular sovereignty, constitutional government, rule of law, separation of powers, checks and balances, minority rights, civilian control of the military, separation of church and state, power of the purse; conflicts over rights, between individuals and groups, between liberty and equality, between diversity and unity, and between liberty and authority

Questions (for interpreting, analyzing, comparing)

- What is meant by "the common good"?
- What are the rights of the individual?
- What is justice?
- Why is truth essential to decent and effective government?
- What is patriotism, and why is it important?
- What is the place of dissent?
- How does separation of powers work?
- How does the principle of checks and balances work?
- What are the functions of Congress? the executive branch? the judicial system?
- How are public services similar to and different from private services?

Theme

The role of the citizen: responsibilities of citizens, rights of citizens, formation of policy, civic and community action, civil disobedience

Questions (for interpreting, evaluating, analyzing)
- What are citizens' rights?
- How can citizens help to form public policy?
- How effective have various forms of civil disobedience been?

Theme

Civic virtue: Dispositions—civility, self-discipline, civic-mindedness, compromise, respect for diversity, patience and persistence, compassion, generosity; commitments, values—right to life and liberty, personal, political, and economic freedom, right to pursuit of happiness, the common good, justice, equality, diversity, truth, patriotism; commitments, principles—popular sovereignty; constitutional government—rule of law, separation of powers, checks and balances, minority rights, civilian control of the military, separation of church and state

Questions (for analyzing, interpreting, evaluating)
- What civic dispositions are of key importance in American democracy? How can they be put to productive use?
- To what fundamental values should citizens be committed?
- How can differences in views regarding individual rights and the common good be resolved?
- To what principles of constitutional government should citizens be committed?
- Which ideas are best for ensuring the equality of all groups in our community?

Civics Standards

Similar to the other social sciences, political science (civics/government) also has developed a set of standards. Among the standards proposed by the Center for Civic Education (1994) are the following questions that U.S. students should focus on as they learn about civics.

- What is government, and what should it do?
- What are basic values, principles, and ideals of American democracy?
- How does the government set up by the Constitution embody the purposes and principles of American democracy?
- What is the relationship of the United States to other nations and to world affairs?
- What are the roles of the citizen in American democracy?

Each of these questions is elaborated with subquestions. For example, the fourth question in the previous list is extended in this set of questions:

■ From the day they declared themselves citizens of a new nation, Americans have built their society around the principles of a democracy.
—Creating America

A. How is the world divided into nations?

B. How do nations interact with one another?

C. How have Americans and peoples of other nations influenced each other?

D. How do world affairs affect Americans?

The following activities can help you teach students about civics.

 **ACTIVITY IDEAS** ➤ *Learning about Civics*

➤ To help students understand the differences that characterize rules, rights, and responsibilities, you might provide a worksheet like this one. After students complete their worksheet, the class can discuss the results.

Rules

What rules are required at our school for these purposes?

to maintain safety _____

to participate in a discussion _____

to take care of personal property _____

to use computer equipment _____

Rights

What rights does each of us have in these categories?

speech _____

education _____

religion _____

owning property _____

Responsibilities

What responsibilities does each citizen have in each of these areas?

following the law _____

treatment of people in other groups _____

➤ To reinforce important civics concepts, give students a list of terms. Then have them find and write the meaning of each one. They may use the index or glossary in their textbooks or look up terms in classroom reference works. The list may include terms like these.

democracy	rights	representative government
republic	freedoms	legislative branch
due process	responsibilities	executive branch
equal protection	power	judicial branch
majority rule		

➤ Encourage students to explore civics concepts and content by using computer programs. They may want to try *Lincoln's Decisions, Jury Trial, Bill of Rights, the Constitution*, or *Congress*.

➤ To explore the early foundations of U.S. government, have students focus on particular questions as they study. You might provide a list of questions like this one.

> How were early colonies governed?
>
> What ideas about government emerged?
>
> What branches of government were set up in the Constitution?
>
> What rights were guaranteed by the Bill of Rights?

➤ To prevent confusion about the roles and responsibilities of workers in different levels of government, you might provide students with a worksheet like this one. Students could complete the worksheet individually, in small groups, or as a class.

> **Community Government**
>
> 1. How is our community governed?
> 2. What is the role of the mayor? the city council? *or* What is the role of the town manager? the selectmen?
> 3. What public services (health, education, fire and police protection, and so on) are provided in our community?
>
> **County Government**
>
> 1. What are the main services provided by our county?
> 2. What is the role of the county commissioner?
> 3. What court is in our county? What is its role?
>
> **State Government**
>
> 1. What is the role of the governor?
> 2. What is the role of the treasurer?
> 3. Describe the legislative branch of our state government. What elected officials work in it?
> 4. What is the highest court in the state? Who are the members of the judiciary branch?
> 5. How are state and local services related?

The following lesson plan shows how a civics topic relevant to students can be played out in the classroom.

 **LESSON PLAN   *Rules***

Objectives   To name rules students must follow at home and in school

To state why rules are needed and must be followed

Materials   Textbook, pages 72–73

Video on rules

Introduction   Ask, Who can give an example of a rule that must be followed at home? Who can give an example of a rule that must be followed at school?

Development   1. Ask students to find as many rules as they can as they watch the video on rules. List their responses on the chalkboard under these two headings:

Rules at Home   Rules at School

2. Tell students to look at pages 72–73 in their textbooks. Ask them to tell what rule is being followed in each picture. Add any new ones to the list on the chalkboard.

3. Ask students to think of other rules, for example, for games, for safety, or for watching TV.

4. Discuss why rules are needed at home and in school. Ask what happens when rules are broken.

Conclusion   Have students summarize rules under headings such as family rules, school rules, personal rules, safety rules, play rules, and property rules.

Follow-up   Have students keep a record for a week of rules that are easiest and hardest to follow.

Economics

Similar to political science, economics has gained renewed interest among educators, but for a different reason. A robust economy and the growth of a global economy have resulted in a K–8 curriculum that introduces students, at an earlier age, to basic economic principles and in elementary and middle school grades to the interrelationship of national economies and the formation of global economy. As a result, curriculum and materials are available to provide students with local and global perspectives on economic ideas.

Concepts such as division of labor are introduced in the beginning grades as children compare the production of favors or other items on an "assembly line" with individual production. The differences between producers and consumers and between goods and services are discovered as children study roles of family members, community workers, and people in other places. Price, cost, supply, market, production, and other concepts are presented in computer programs such as *Sell Apples, Lemonade, Markets, Factory,* and *Market Place.* The opportunity–cost principle is used as students consider questions such as "What does Joan give up if she spends her allowance for candy?" "What does a family give up when they take a trip instead of spending the money for other things?" The world of work, roles of various workers, and careers in different fields of work are included in some units.

In the area of global economy, students examine products and identify how they are put together, find out how to buy and sell stock in worldwide markets, discover how businesses appeal to a culturally diverse clientele, and discuss the social issues that emerge when countries experience economic setbacks.

The following are important concepts, concept clusters, and generalizations in the study of economics.

> ■ An important economic issue is to find ways of ensuring that the people have opportunities to share fully in the nation's wealth.
>
> —*Creating America*

Examples of Economics Concepts

benefits	division of labor	money	saving
capital	economic system	needs	scarcity
consumer	goods	price	services
costs	investment	production	spending
credit	labor	resources	supply and demand
distribution	market		

Concept Clusters

Basic economic problem: conflict between wants and resources, need to make choices, need for an economic system to allocate resources to alternative uses

Specialization: division of labor by occupations, technological applications, and geographic situation; resulting interdependence

Productive resources: human (workers, managers, know-how), capital (tools, machines, factories), natural (soil, water, climate, minerals, forests)

The market: means of allocating resources; interaction of supply and demand; use of money, transportation, and communication; modification by policies related to economic goals; global economy

Economic goals: equity, growth, stability, security, freedom, employment, efficiency

Career clusters: agriculture, communication, education, health, recreation, transportation, and so on

Generalizations

Members of families, people in communities, and societies meet the basic economic problem by finding answers to these questions: What shall we produce? How shall we produce? How much shall we produce? How shall we distribute what we produce?

Division of labor increases production and leads to interdependence among individuals, communities, states, and nations.

What economic concepts should be introduced to children and adolescents? How would you integrate economics into the social studies curriculum?

You may use the following activity ideas as you plan for economics instruction.

 **ACTIVITY IDEAS** ▶ *Learning about Economics*

➤ To help students learn what sorts of products and services different people offer, assign each student a particular type of worker to research. Encourage them to gather detailed information. Have each student report his or her findings to the class. You might choose assignments from this list.

accountant	dentist	nurse
author	doctor	pilot
bus driver	farmer	plumber
carpenter	florist	software engineer
cartographer	librarian	teacher

➤ Challenge students to evaluate their decision-making skills as consumers. Have them fill out an inventory like this one as they consider making a particular purchase.

Am I a Wise Consumer?

Why should I buy this? _____

Do I need this item, or do I want it? _____

What is my reason for needing this item? _____

What might be reasons for not buying it? _____

How reasonable is the price? _____

Do I need to give up buying something else to buy this item? How will that affect my decision? _____

How good is the quality? _____

What criteria did I use to evaluate the quality? _____

Should I wait for a sale or buy now? Why? _____

Am I just following a habit by buying this? _____

How have advertisements or sales pitches affected me? _____

What have consumer reports said about this item? _____

What have people who own this item said about it? _____

➤ Have a "definition bee," on the same principle as a spelling bee, in which students define terms from economics. You might use the list of economics concepts listed earlier in this section, or create your own. Students who do not give a correct definition of the term have to sit down. The team with the most students left standing wins the bee.

➤ In small groups, ask students to work on cost–benefit analyses for different projects that could be undertaken at school. Students might answer questions such as these as they work.

What would be the benefits?
Who would get the benefits?
What would be the costs?
Who would pay the costs?
What would be gained by whom?
What would be given up?

➤ Have students explore the division of labor in different settings, such as a housing construction company, a supermarket, or an airport. Students might list the different workers, what they do, and how they contribute to the overall goals of the organization.

■ For more information on the National Council on Economic Education visit their website **http://www. nationalcouncil.org**

The following lesson plan shows how a lesson on economic concepts can be played out in the classroom.

LESSON PLAN *Goods and Services*

Objective   To identify goods and services

Materials   Textbook pages 101–103, worksheet

Introduction   Let's review yesterday's lesson. Who remembers the meaning of *goods?* What are some examples? Who remembers the meaning of *services?* What are some examples?

Development   Study the pictures and the text on pages 101–103 of your textbook. How many goods and how many services can you find? Mark an X on this worksheet by each one you find.

Goods and Services

Goods

____ Baseballs	____ Bread	____ Maps
____ Beds	____ Chairs	____ Toys
____ Books	____ Clothes	____ Wagons

Services

____ Bookkeeping	____ Garbage pickup	____ Selling cars
____ Cleaning	____ Library work	____ Transportation
____ Education	____ Police work	____ TV repair
____ Fire fighting	____ Shoe repair	___ Watering lawns

Conclusion and Evaluation   Which goods in the first column did you find? in the second column? in the third column? Which services did you find?

Follow-up   Look out for other examples of goods and services, and be ready to share them on Friday. Remember that goods are things people make. Services are what people do to serve others.

Sociology

Concepts and key ideas from sociology are included in many units of studies in the social studies curriculum. The family and school, two basic social institutions, are usually studied early in the program. Values and expectations of children, adolescents, parents, teachers, and others are considered in the context of children's relationships to one another and to adults. Norms and sanctions and their relation to social control are discovered through the students' own experiences and in units that include material on customs, regulations, rewards, punishment, and laws in communities and other places near at hand and far away. Understanding of social interactions, such as cooperation, competition, and conflict are also developed. Historical and geographic studies centered on the community, state, nation, and other places typically include sociological concepts such as role, groups, institutions, values, and social change.

Structural elements drawn from sociology are closely related to those drawn from anthropology and psychology, as shown in the following examples of sociology concepts, concept clusters, and generalizations that are typically part of the K–8 social studies curriculum.

■ U.S. History is not learning about Buffalo Bill's wild west shows.
—*Creating America*

Examples of Sociology Concepts

expectations	social problems	norms
socialization	social process	roles
group behavior	minority groups	status
group interaction	majority groups	social class

Concept Clusters

Values: personal, social, economic, political, religious, aesthetic

Social institutions: family, economy, politics, educational system, scientific organizations, religious organizations, recreational organizations, welfare, arts organizations

Processes of social interaction: cooperation, competition, conflict, assimilation, accommodation, acculturation

Types of groups: primary, secondary, ethnic, minority, reference

Social control: dependency, rewards, sanctions, norms, laws

Generalizations

The family is a basic social institution in all societies.

The work of society is done by organized groups.

Societies need a system of social control in order to survive.

Social institutions are shaped by societal values and norms.

The following activity ideas may be useful as you plan for sociology instruction.

ACTIVITY IDEAS *Learning about Sociology*

➤ In a class discussion have the children talk about what they do at home to help their families. Have the students focus on their individual and group responsibilities (e.g., keeping their rooms clean, cleaning up the table after dinner). Next, have the students discuss what their family does for them to make them feel loved, secure, wanted, and appreciated (e.g., providing shelter, food, entertainment). Have the students draw two generalizations that describe their role as a family member and the role of the family in meeting their individual needs.

What sociological concepts would you introduce to children and adolescents in a unit on the 1960s Civil Rights movement?

➤ Working in small groups, have the students review the definition of social institutions provided in their textbook. Next, have them list the many social institutions in their neighborhood. As they identify each institution, they should describe the societal groups it serves and the services it provides. As a class, have the students develop an informational flyer for their parents listing these institutions, their addresses and telephone numbers, hours open, and the services they provide.

➤ In the middle grades, have the students do a content analysis of their U.S. history textbook. One approach might be to focus on the illustrations depicting humans and identifying the individuals as male or female, whether they are in the background or foreground, and their level of activity. You might assign pairs of students one or more chapters and ask them to report their content analysis. Then, as a class, develop a generalization that describes how the textbook depicts males and females in the context of U.S. history.

➤ Have the students review the following handout and define the terms. Then have the students use the terms to describe an aspect of the community.

Introduction to Sociology

Define each term on this list. Be prepared to use these terms in a class discussion.

role	norms	institution	customs
cooperation	ethnic	traditions	competition
innovation	minority	values	
leadership	status	socialization	

➤ Have the children think of someone other than a family member who has helped them in their immediate neighborhood—for example, someone who has helped them purchase an item or fix a bike. Have the students draw a picture of this individual and, in a sentence or two, describe why this person should be considered a "neighborhood helper."

Cultural Anthropology

Knowledge of both universal and particular traits of the diverse peoples of the world is provided by cultural anthropologists, who study the wholeness or totality of human cultures. From this rich storehouse of knowledge is drawn content on topics including beliefs, values, traditions, customs, technology, tools, institutions, social organization, and aesthetic and religious expression. The all-inclusive "culture" concept brings together these diverse elements to present a unified view of a way of living.

Examples of social studies units rooted in cultural anthropology are comparative studies of families, villages, communities, early civilizations, and prehistoric peoples. Specific units on American Indians, peoples of Africa, indigenous peoples of South America and Central America, and other groups include anthropological material on food, shelter, clothing, tools, arts, crafts, rituals, ceremonies, folklore, and other aspects of culture. This material depicts the main characteristics of a culture. The following concepts, concept clusters, and generalizations about cultural anthropology may inform your instruction.

Examples of Cultural Anthropology Concepts

adaptation	culture	society
beliefs	cultural change	technology
civilization	customs	traditions
community	social organization	values

Concept Clusters

Culture: learned patterns of behavior; ways of living; arts, crafts, technology, religion, economic activities, language, other learned behaviors

Processes of cultural change: invention, discovery, diffusion, adaptation

Food-getting activities: gathering, hunting, fishing, herding, gardening, agriculture

Societies: folk or preliterate, preindustrial, transitional, industrial

Characteristics of civilization: writing, accumulation of food and other goods for managed use, division of labor, government, arts, sciences, urbanization, trade

Generalizations

Culture is socially transmitted in all societies, differs from society to society, and is a prime determiner of behavior.

Families around the world have common needs, but they meet those needs in different ways.

Major differences among people are cultural, not biological.

The culture of modern societies has evolved from the culture of earlier societies.

The following activities can support learning about cultural anthropology in your classroom.

ACTIVITY IDEAS ➤ *Learning about Cultural Anthropology*

➤ Divide the class into four groups. Assign each group the job of cutting out or drawing pictures that illustrate one of the following aspects of culture: language, tools, institutions, and beliefs. Have each group design a display of the pictures, perhaps on a poster, in a booklet, or on the bulletin board.

➤ To further their understanding of artifacts, have students complete a worksheet like this one.

What Is an Artifact?

What is an artifact? _____

What can we learn about a culture by examining its artifacts? _____

_____

Mark an X by the items that are artifacts.

____ acorns	____ blankets	____ fish	____ trees
____ aprons	____ canoes	____ pots	____ wagons
____ baskets	____ clothing	____ sandals	____ women
____ berries	____ corn	____ spoons	

➤ Have students choose two different contemporary cultures. Have them compare their similarities and differences in these areas.

family life	literature
community life	customs
economic and political systems	values
responses to the environment	borrowings from other cultures
arts and crafts	contributions to other cultures

➤ As a class, have students hypothesize answers to a question about early cultures, such as "What might have been the main causes of the shift from hunting to herding?" Then have students do research to find out whether their hypotheses are supported by evidence.

➤ Have students compare family life in two or more cultures of the present. They might look for similarities and differences in food, cooking, clothing, the setup of homes and individual rooms, furnishings, health care, roles of children and adults, rules for children, recreational activities, holidays, and other distinctive features.

➤ As students become familiar with the basic concepts of cultural anthropology, you might challenge them with more difficult concepts. In small groups, have them look up definitions of these terms and provide examples of each.

accommodation	competition	innovation
assimilation	conflict	norms
cooperation	ethnicity	socialization

➤ To evaluate students' understanding of anthropological concepts, you might give them a simple matching worksheet to complete.

Directions: For each activity, write the letter of the aspect of culture that it belongs with.

Aspects of Culture	Activities
A. beliefs	____ talking on the telephone
B. institutions	____ making a bird house
C. language	____ taking part in a family celebration
D. tools	____ placing a high value on honesty
	____ repairing a bicycle
	____ working in a store

Psychology

Concepts and ideas from psychology are embedded in all levels of social studies instruction. For example, the concept of individual differences is important in studies of families, schools, community workers, and people in other places. How the senses—seeing, hearing, touching, and so on—help one to observe and to learn may be included early in the program. The importance of attitudes, motives, and interests in human behavior is brought home in both contemporary and historical studies of people near and far away. How to deal with feelings is considered in the context of children's own experiences and in studies of others. Students are taught how to remember and use what is learned and how to improve critical thinking and problem solving.

Examples of Psychology Concepts

attitudes	intergroup relations	personal–social needs
feelings	learning	self-concept
individual differences	memory	senses

Concept Clusters

Using our senses to learn: seeing, hearing, smelling, touching, tasting, balancing

Learning and remembering: clear purposes, meaning, practice, use, review, application, grouping around main ideas, contrast, comparison, concentration, knowledge of results, ideas in own words

Personal–social needs: acceptance, belonging, security, achievement, self-expression, interaction with others, learning, self-actualization

Individual differences: appearance, personality, role, attitudes, beliefs, family, customs, learning, abilities, habits

Social roles: leadership, followership, aggression, submission

Generalizations

Individual differences exist among family members, children, and people in communities.

Perceptions of others vary from individual to individual and are conditioned by motives, attitudes, and other factors.

An individual takes different roles in different groups and situations.

The following activities show how psychology can be integrated into social studies.

ACTIVITY IDEAS ➤ *Learning about Psychology*

➤ In pairs, have students analyze the individual differences that make each of them unique. They might use a chart like this one to guide their discussion and record the outcomes.

How Are We Alike? How Are We Different?		
	Person A	*Person B*
Things I like		
Things I don't like		
My hobbies		
My strongest skills		
My interests		
My personality		
My favorite school subjects		
My height		
My values		

➤ Dealing with feelings is a challenge for people at any age! To help students analyze their feelings and learn constructive ways of handling them, you might focus a class discussion on pairs of questions like the following ones.

What makes you afraid? How do you deal with feelings of fear?

What makes you sad? How do you deal with feelings of sadness?

What makes you excited? How do you deal with feelings of excitement?

What makes you angry? How do you deal with feelings of anger?

Which feelings are most difficult to handle? How might we learn to handle them better?

➤ To develop their abilities in metacognition, give students opportunities to focus on "learning about learning." A class discussion based on questions like the following ones will allow students to share their ideas on this topic.

What are the five senses? How do they help us learn?

What study habits help us learn?

How do we learn attitudes? How do they affect our learning?

How do we learn values? How do they affect our learning?

Philosophy

Philosophy is included in this chapter because values, inquiry, and reasoning are part of social studies. Students need to learn about values such as freedom, equality, responsibility, loyalty, and patriotism, along with the positive attitudes and feelings needed to reinforce such values. Students should also understand the nature of logical fallacies, the meaning of the spirit of philosophical inquiry, and the processes involved in making judgments. The following value-related elements are found in most social studies materials.

Examples of Philosophy Concepts

the common good	ethical behavior	moral conduct
cooperation	freedom	open-mindedness
creativity	justice	responsibility
duties	loyalty	rights
equality		

Concept Clusters

The spirit of inquiry: longing to know and understand, questioning of all things; search for data and their meaning; demand for verification; respect for logic; consideration of premises, causes, and consequences

Logical fallacies: appeal to force, argument from ignorance, appeal to pity, emphasis on false cause, snob appeal, neglect of all causes, false premises

Making judgments: clarifying what is to be judged, defining related criteria, analyzing in terms of criteria, making the judgment, checking the judgment with others

Generalizations

The basic value of human dignity underlies our way of life.

Criteria should be defined in terms of values and used to decide what is good or ought to be.

Ideas and proposals must be subjected to critical examination if their value is to be determined.

The following activities offer ideas for using concepts from philosophy in the social studies classroom.

ACTIVITY IDEAS ➤ *Learning about Philosophy*

➤ In the middle school, students can gain sophistication in recognizing forms of logical fallacy that crop up in political argument, advertising, and other persuasive forms of expression. As a class or in small groups, ask students to find the definition of each of these logical fallacies and then give examples of each.

appeal to force	generalization based on inadequate evidence
false cause	mass appeal
false conclusion	snob appeal
false premise	

➤ As an exercise in making good judgments, choose a topic such as a political issue of the day or a school policy that is currently being debated. To help students judge the soundness of an argument or a proposed course of action related to the issue, give them a step-by-step guide to making judgments, such as this one.

Making Sound Judgments

1. Clarify what is to be judged.

2. Define the criteria you will use in judging it.

3. Apply all of the criteria.

4. Make a judgment that is fair.

5. Test the judgment. Ask these questions:

   ■ Is it consistent with similar judgments I have made?

   ■ What will be the consequences if it is applied? Will it cause new problems?

   ■ Is it fair?

➤ Challenge students to examine the truth of a set of statements by analyzing the criteria they are using to judge the truth. This set of questions may help them articulate these criteria.

Is it true by definition?	Is it true based on values?
Is it true based on observation?	Is it true according to experts?
Is it true based on a certain set of criteria?	

■ Process Knowledge

In the preceding section we identified areas of knowledge associated with each of the social sciences. In this section we describe process knowledge, the form of inquiry that social scientists assume when examining a particular problem, issue, or personality. For example, if you wanted to study community with a group of middle school learners, how would you proceed? A historian would suggest one approach (e.g., a look at the settlers who migrated to the area), whereas a sociologist might offer another (e.g., a look at social interactions in the building of community). How might other social scientists, such as geographers or anthropologists view community? As you may have gathered, how we look at phenomena depends on our experiences and formal preparation. Here we examine two important aspects of process knowledge: the values and attitudes that shape inquiry and the models, methods, and materials used to study human relationships.

Incorporating process knowledge in instruction provides greater depth and breadth of study in social studies. An understanding of process knowledge offers teachers the freedom to choose the best approach to examine a particular topic with a particular group of learners—certain discipline may give students the best "way in" to an area of knowledge. Students also benefit because process knowledge helps them "learn how to learn." They discover that different social scientists take different approaches to certain issues, problems, and historical figures, and the whole spectrum of interpretations resulting from their approaches offers legitimate information and insights into the topic at hand. As students learn to think and act as historians, geographers, and other social scientists, they gain a variety of perspectives. Integrating process knowledge into the curriculum offers a genuine alternative to "learning as the accumulation of knowledge."

■ Constructivism refers to a theory that learners construct their own knowledge and their version of reality from their own unique experiences.
—**Arthur K. Ellis and Jeffrey T. Fouts**

Values and Attitudes

The following values and attitudes are fostered by teaching about process knowledge:

- high regard for clear thinking, respect for differing views, and clear definition of problems and terms
- objectivity in gathering and reporting information, demand for evidence to support conclusions, awareness of how feelings can affect thinking
- corroboration of findings by double-checking them; by analyzing assumptions, biases, and possible errors; and by evaluating study procedures to find ways to improve

You can help students attain these values by posing questions that stimulate analysis and evaluation, such as these:

What is good about the idea? How can we use it? How can we improve it?

How can we restate the problem to make it clearer? What terms need to be clarified?

Will we get the same result a second time? Why do we need to check that information? What other source can we use?

What is unfair in this statement? How is it biased? What changes are needed?

What evidence supports that idea? What evidence does not support it?

What additional information do we need? Where can we get it?

How do feelings affect thinking about this issue? How can we deal with these feelings?

Models of Study

Scholars in all the fields encompassed by social studies follow this general model as they carry out their studies:

1. Define the problem and clarify the objectives for the study.
2. State questions or hypotheses to guide the study.
3. Make and use a plan to gather data.
4. Appraise, organize, and interpret the data.
5. Make conclusions, and check them for soundness.
6. Consider needs for further study.

The models presented in Table 2.2 (page 66) are adapted from reports and recent social studies materials. The table shows more specific models of study or inquiry used in various disciplines. More information on how geographers, historians, archaeologists, and other scholars conduct their studies may be found in social studies textbooks. The model given for anthropology may be useful when planning field trips and field studies. Social studies decision-making models are closely related to those presented for political science and economics.

You can introduce middle school students to discipline-specific modes of inquiry. The lesson plan on page 65 offers an example of this type of instruction.

Source Materials

A wide variety of source materials are available in media centers, community resource centers, textbooks, and related curriculum. Many such resources include methods of study and suggestions for using them. Students should take an active role in finding sources for many topics of study in social studies.

It may be helpful to guide students in a planning discussion focused on the following questions:

- How shall we gather information?
- What sources shall we use?
- How shall we present information?

Almost any social studies unit can present opportunities for students to do research. This section presents sources of information and ideas for studying a topic and reporting and evaluating the findings.

LESSON PLAN *How Historians Work*

Objectives	To define history and describe the work of historians
	To identify sources of information used by historians
Learning Resources	Textbook, pages 26–28
	Historian as resource visitor
Introduction	List these questions on the chalkboard, and ask students to give preliminary answers to them:
	What is history? What do historians do? What sources do they use?
Development	Ask students to read pages 26–28 in their textbooks to find out if their answers agree with those in their books.
	Discuss each question, and note students' responses under each question.
	Ask students to indicate ideas that are new to them.
	Ask students to explain in their own words the difference between primary and secondary sources and to give examples of each.
	Invite a high school history teacher or a historian from a nearby college to speak to the class and give answers to the three questions.
	Discuss new ideas that students obtained from the resource visitor.
Conclusion	Ask students to summarize answers to the three questions, combining ideas obtained from their textbook and the resource visitor.
	Ask students to suggest how they can apply what they have learned to the study of historical events.

Gathering Information

An obvious place for students to begin their studies is the printed word. They can delve into different kinds of written materials available through libraries, historical societies, families in the neighborhood, and school. Here is just a sampling of what they might access:

textbooks
reference books
letters, published or unpublished
diaries and journals
current newspapers
old newspapers

government documents
biographies
case studies
nonfiction children's books
magazines

■ **TABLE 2.2**

Models of Study in the Social Studies

Geography

1. Identify and define the topic or the problem to be studied.
2. Consider all factors that may be related.
3. State questions or hypotheses related to each factor.
4. Gather data related to each hypothesis or question.
5. Evaluate and organize data to test hypotheses or answer questions.
6. Interpret findings and draw conclusions.
7. Suggest other needed studies.

History

1. Define the question or problem to be studied.
2. State hypotheses or questions to guide study.
3. Collect and evaluate sources of information.
4. Analyze and synthesize data in the sources.
5. Organize findings to answer questions and test hypotheses.
6. Interpret findings in relation to social, economic, and political developments.

Political Analysis

1. Define the problem and clarify related values.
2. Consider different choices or solutions.
3. Evaluate each choice or solution in terms of values, facts, and historical background.
4. Identify possible consequences of each choice or solution.
5. Evaluate the consequences in light of values.
6. Make judgments as to which choice or solution is best in terms of values.

Anthropology

1. Define objectives or questions for the field study.
2. Make a plan for gathering and recording data for each objective or question.
3. Make necessary arrangements.
4. Gather data by direct observation, interview, and participation (if feasible).
5. Organize and interpret data in light of objectives.
6. Summarize findings and draw conclusions.
7. Compare findings and conclusions with those of others.

Sociology

1. Define the problem and relate it to existing knowledge.
2. State hypotheses to guide study.
3. Select an adequate sample.
4. Use appropriate techniques to gather data.
5. Organize and analyze the data to test each hypothesis.
6. Interpret findings and draw conclusions.
7. Suggest other studies.

Economic Analysis

1. Define the problem. Where are we and where do we want to go?
2. Identify goals, and rank them in order of priority.
3. Consider alternative ways to attain goals with usable resources.
4. Use concepts to explore the problem and the effects of alternative proposals.
5. Complete an analysis of each alternative in terms of goals.
6. Choose the best alternative to achieve goals.

Also, forms of early writing, such as inscriptions on clay tablets, hieroglyphics, and Norse runes, can enrich certain social studies units. Examples can be found in books and in museums.

Students can explore databases to find information. The Internet has revolutionized access to information, and databases are readily available for students to use. Other sources include libraries and school and classroom databases.

Sources from the fine arts can enhance many areas of study. Students can find such images in library books, on the Internet, or at a museum. Think of ways for students to research and gain appreciation of art objects such as the following:

murals	medals
tapestries	paintings
vases	sculpture
jewelry	pottery
plaques	wood carvings

Architecture, in the form of buildings from different time periods and historic monuments, can be viewed in books and on field trips to enhance the study of communities or certain time periods. Studying artifacts of material culture can also bring to life different eras and different communities. Such artifacts might include the following:

coins	musical instruments
textiles	tools and utensils
furniture	articles of clothing
weapons	grave markers
baskets	

Other visual materials that can contribute to social studies learning include slide presentations, photographs, objects brought from home that illustrate a cultural or ethnic heritage, maps and globes, and information given in graphic form such as charts, tables, flow charts, and graphs.

Students may find orally transmitted information on videotape or tape recordings; it's even more interesting to invite a community member to class who can tell about a local legend, give an eyewitness account of an event, or speak about an area of expertise. Ballads, speeches, the national anthems of different countries, or the popular music of a certain era can provide interesting information and a chance to develop listening skills in the social studies classroom.

Processing Information

As students gather and synthesize information, they make take a variety of approaches to gain knowledge and deepen their understanding. Their choice will depend on the topic at hand and the available resources.

Students may focus on *analyzing content* as they study printed materials, videos, and other instructional media. They may gather information about areas such as the following:

- the meaning of key terms
- changes and trends that have occurred over time
- how words are used to stir the emotions
- how gender bias may be inferred from the use of language
- what assumptions underlie the text

Many learning activities take students away from books and study tables. In the following activities, students gather data in a variety of ways.

 *Gathering Information*

➤ Together with students, plan a field trip that will enrich their study of a unit or specific topic. Rather than letting them watch passively, make sure they have an active role to take in gathering information on the trip. They might collect data on farming, business activities, conservation, modes of transportation or communication, exhibits of artifacts, or the construction of a bridge.

➤ Give students practice in taking careful notes as they observe certain activities and phenomena. These observations might occur at a single setting or over time. Here are some ideas:

noting recreational activities of family members

noting how family members share chores

observation of workers such as graphic designers, farmers, or chefs

taking notes at a town meeting or at meetings of the city council or the school board

➤ Help students set up activities in interviewing and taking polls and surveys. Support them as they plan, implement, and assess their work. They might use these tools to gather information from fellow students, teachers, business people, health workers, experts on conservation, members of certain political parties, or other groups.

➤ Students may learn from role-playing activities. They might play out scenarios in which families make decisions, markets are evaluated by economists, or policies are developed by local officials. Role playing can help students better understand the dynamics that operate in certain situations, sparking new insights and better synthesis of knowledge.

➤ Students may conduct experiments to test their hypotheses. They may test fellow students' visual perceptions under different conditions of lighting or distance, or they may test a prediction about the proportion of their neighbors who favor a particular referendum.

After gathering information, students may organize and present their findings in different ways. They may share their conclusions through written or oral reports. They may plot data on graphs or charts, make diagrams, or use flow charts to show processes. Maps can be constructed to present a variety of information: the distribution of homes and businesses in a given area, transportation networks, or the flow of people, goods, and services. Drawings and exhibits are also effective ways to share information.

Though the presentation of information may seem to be the final step in a study, there is in fact one more. Students should evaluate their own work, perhaps writing journal entries on what went well and what could be improved in the next study they undertake. They can review their records, drafts, and finished product as they evaluate the stages of their work. Such evaluations can take place in discussions or by filling out rating scales or charts customized to evaluate the project. To make sure that students get the maximum learning experience from their work, it is important to evaluate many projects, both group and individual work, in this way.

■ Literature in Social Studies

In the preceding two sections we described the core disciplines and the dynamics of process knowledge, both of which are central to identifying, acquiring, using, and evaluating knowledge in social studies. In this section we briefly describe how children's literature can add depth and breadth to a social studies program.

Children's literature is an integral part of most social studies programs in grades K–6 and in the middle grades, particularly those programs stressing integrated learning. In some programs, literature is used to supplement textbook instruction, whereas in others, it is the mainstay of the curriculum, and teachers provide background information. Walk into any K–8 classroom, and you will find children's and adolescent literature in use in social studies programs.

Why do so many teachers use literature in teaching social studies? To answer this question, we need only turn to you for a response. What do you remember most about your social studies experiences in elementary and middle school? Probably some experiences that come to mind involve a teacher reading to the class or a friend describing an exciting book. Did your teacher read to you about Paul Revere's ride as you explored the Revolutionary War? Did you learn about the game of lacrosse as you read about the Iroquois? Did your teacher read stories of young children who lived through the Holocaust as you examined World War II? Did you have a favorite fable, myth, or tall tale? Perhaps you can recite a poem that enriched your social studies education.

Why is it that when we think of social studies the pleasurable memories relate to literature (trade books) rather than to textbooks? The answer is quite simple. Textbook writers strive for objectivity as they present information. Literature, on the other hand, includes feelings, emotions, and biases. It imaginatively expresses the experiences of historical characters. Authors focus on individuals, the famous and the not-so-famous, to describe historical events and eras. They write about Martin Luther

King Jr., for example, to provide insights into Dr. King's character as he helped shape an important period of American history. Authors and illustrators of children's and adolescent literature are adept at depicting human relationships. Their works can add dimension to the content of social studies.

Forms of this literature include historical fiction, which provides realistic depictions of past events, issues, and individuals. Biographies accurately portray the flavor of an era as they narrate the experiences of a particular individual. Folk literature (myths, tall tales, folktales, and legends) chronicle the oral traditions of past cultures. Teachers use all of these genres in the classroom.

Children's literature is popular in K–8 classrooms because it can be used in so many ways. For example, a biography of Martin Luther King Jr. can provide a description of the civil rights movement, a look at black leadership and black–white relations, and a link to studying human rights movements across the globe. But by far, teachers employ literature in social studies classroom because it provides a human dimension to learning about the past. Literature transports students to another time and connects them to themes, issues, and people of that period. Students can step into the shoes of an individual and relive the past. They can experience Amelia Earhart's adventures in flying, the fears of slaves as they traveled the Underground Railroad with Harriet Tubman, and the satisfaction Gandhi felt as Indians accepted nonviolence as a method of bringing about change. Textbooks cannot do this.

When you include works of historical fiction in instruction, it's important to consider just one limitation. Although such stories can deepen students' empathy and understanding, these works may not in all details be historically accurate; the writer may have taken minor or major liberties with the facts to heighten the drama or make a character more compelling. Such practices are the stock and trade of fiction; simply being aware of them and helping students recognize such techniques, when appropriate, is enough. Thus, trade books can be viewed as providing another interpretation of the past. It may be a highly personal interpretation or one that is rigorous in its recounting of historical detail. With this in mind, do use literature to support social studies education.

The lesson plan on page 71 shows how literature can be the focus of a history lesson.

■ Conclusion: Constructing Knowledge in Social Studies

Now that you have reviewed the core disciplines, process knowledge, and the use of literature in social studies, it must be obvious that construction of knowledge is inherent in social studies. Even if you have a defined curriculum and scope and sequence from which to work, the way you plan many elements of instruction is up to you. And there are many variables to consider.

Authors of social studies textbooks, for example, construct knowledge. They present specific information, develop questions to motivate learning, and construct

LESSON PLAN *Using Literature to Study the Harlem Renaissance*

Objectives	To describe the Harlem Renaissance and the contributions of African Americans to the arts
	To identify many of the African American musicians who flourished during this time period
	To gain an appreciation of the contributions of African Americans to music
Learning Resources	Textbook, pages 686–688
	Chamber, Veronica, *The Harlem Renaissance*
	Igus, Toyomi, *I See the Rhythm*
Introduction	Ask the students to recall background information from the textbook on the Black Renaissance by answering the following questions:
	When did the Harlem Renaissance occur? Where?
	How would you characterize this time period?
	Identify one or more black artists who you feel exemplify the time period.
Development	Ask students to read pages 686–688 in their textbook.
	Discuss each question, and place some of the responses on the chalkboard.
	Read excerpts of *The Harlem Renaissance* to the class that support the textbook, and ask the students to use this new information to augment their textbook responses to the questions on the chalkboard. Have students review the books in the Reading Corner on the Harlem Renaissance.
	Next, read and share *I See the Rhythm* with the class to highlight the many ways music has been a part of the life of African Americans. Discuss new ideas that students obtained from this trade book.
Conclusion	Ask students to review their responses to the questions on the board and to add further information learned from the trade books.
	As a culminating activity, have the students, working in groups or individually, illustrate examples of black contributions to American music.

chapters with themes such as family, community, and the world community. You too will construct knowledge as you prepare a unit of instruction. You will integrate knowledge and methods from some of the core disciplines into the unit, choose resources and learning experiences for students, develop questions to guide study, and set goals for the knowledge students are to attain.

Students will be following the planning that you have laid down. As they work through the unit, they will reconstruct the knowledge that you present, interpret it in their own way, synthesize it as they participate in various learning experiences and activities, and then demonstrate to you, in a way that suits their age and skill level, what they have learned and how they interpret it.

Therefore, you should consider carefully the questions you ask and the materials you use while planning instruction. You should also be prepared for unique, unpredictable, and valuable contributions from students. Their life experiences and the context of the world around them will influence and enrich the social studies class.

 Questions, Activities, and Evaluation

1. Examine a social studies textbook and note examples of the following:
   a. Concepts, concept clusters, themes, generalizations, and questions that include social science concepts
   b. Values and attitudes, models, materials, and methods of study
   c. Relative attention to material from core disciplines.

2. Examine a course of study and do the same.

3. Examine a unit of instruction and do the same.

4. Which of the study guides, sample learning activities, and models presented in this chapter do you prefer? Discuss your choices with others, and tell how you may use them.

5. Note how you might use several of the methods and materials in a unit.

6. Prepare five or six illustrative questions or study guides, using concepts, concept clusters, or themes.

7. Complete the following, and discuss your responses with a colleague, exploring reasons for differences:
   a. A primary reason for basing the social studies program on content from the social sciences is _____
   b. The concepts from the following social sciences that I believe will be most useful in units I plan to teach are:
      (1) Geography: _____
      (2) History: _____
      (3) Economics: _____
      (4) Political Science: _____
      (5) Anthropology: _____
      (6) Sociology: _____
      (7) Psychology: _____
   c. Models, methods, and materials most useful in elementary social studies are
      _____

References

Avonna, S. (1994). What does a historian do?—Middle school students present their views, *The Social Studies, 85*, 114–16.

Banks, D. (1998). From Hiroshima to Homer Simpson: Using literature to confront the impact of nuclear energy. *Social Education, 62*, 196–200.

Barton, K. C. (1997). History—it can be elementary: An overview of elementary students' understanding of history. *Social Education, 61*, 13–16.

Berson, M. J., Ouzts, D. T., & Walsh, L. S. (1999). Connecting literature with K–8 national geography standards. *The Social Studies, 90*, 85–92.

Bettis, N. C. (1994, April). National geography standards. *Perspective*, National Council for Geographic Education.

Beyer, B. K. (1990). What philosophy offers to the teaching of thinking. *Educational Leadership, 47*, 55–60.

Bradley Commission on History in the Schools. (1988). *Building a history curriculum*. Washington, DC: Educational Excellence Network.

Center for Civic Education. (1994). *National standards for civics and government*. Calabasas, CA: Author.

Epstein, T. L. (1997). Sociocultural approaches to young peoples' historical understanding. *Social Education, 61*, 28–31.

Gardner, C. C. (1997). Treasures from the past: Using archaeology in upper-elementary social studies. *The Social Studies, 88*, 83–86.

Geography Education Standards Project. (1994). *Geography for life: National geography standards*. Washington, DC: National Geographic Research and Exploration.

History—social science framework. (1988). Sacramento, CA: State Department of Education.

Kent, S. I. (1999). Saints or sinners?—The case for an honest portrayal of historical figures. *Social Education, 62*, 8–13.

Manzo, K. K. (1997). Advocates battle to find home for state history curriculum. *Education Week, 16*, 26–27.

Maxim, G. (1998). Writing poetry in the elementary social studies classroom. *Social Education, 62*, 207–210.

Palmer, J., et al. (1996). Button up your social studies classroom. *The Social Studies, 87*, 52–55.

Plavin, A. K. (1993). A simple economics project that students enjoy. *Social Education, 57*, 137–38.

Schlene, V. J. (1993). Teaching economics in the elementary school: An Eric/ChESS sample. *Social Studies and the Young Learner, 5*, 13–14.

Singleton, L. R. (1995). *H is for history: Using children's literature to develop historical understandings*. Boulder, CO: Social Science Education Consortium.

Soldier, L. L. (1990). Making anthropology a part of the elementary social studies curriculum. *Social Education, 54*, 18–19.

Sunal, C. S., & Sunal D. W. (1996). Interdisciplinary social studies and science lessons with a Native American theme. *The Social Studies, 87*, 72–77.

Thornton, S. (1997). First-hand study: Teaching history for understanding. *Social Education, 62*, 11–13.

Valentine, G. P. (1994). Economics for grades K–9. *Social Studies, 85*, 218–21.

Whelan, M. (1996). Right for the wrong reason. *Social Education, 60*, 55–57.

Yell, M. M. (1998). The time before history: Thinking like an archaeologist. *Social Education, 62*, 27–31.

Chapter 3

Teaching Social Studies in a Culturally Diverse and Global Society

Chapter Objective

To describe the diversity that characterizes K–8 students and the world beyond the classroom in the twenty-first century

Focusing Questions

- How does K–8 social studies instruction connect with students, the world beyond the classroom, and the purpose of social studies?
- What factors have influenced the growing diversity found in America's schools?
- How might teachers gain a basic understanding of K–8 students?
- How might teachers gain a deeper understanding of K–8 students?
- Why is getting to know your students a prerequisite to planning for social studies instruction?
- What are some general descriptors of the world at the beginning of the twenty-first century?

■ Making Connections

A favorite topic of conversation among student teachers is the difficulty they experience in making meaningful connections between social studies instruction and students and their experience in the world beyond the classroom. Student teachers describe students who say, "This is so boring, I hate social studies"; others who are daydreaming, asleep, or exhibiting off-task behavior; and still others who display disruptive behavior or show little interest in learning social studies. They have also observed teachers who are having difficulties with instruction. In these classrooms students sit at their desks and passively read their social studies textbook; students are involved in a daily curriculum that includes little social studies learning. These scenarios represent exceptions to most K-8 classrooms. Generally, teachers develop and deliver instructional programs that are valuable, interesting, and fun, which connect with students and the goals of social studies education.

How do teachers make these meaningful connections? This challenge is present in all areas of teaching. Whether the scene is a one-room classroom in the 1800s, a recently integrated urban classroom of the 1960s, or a rural classroom at the turn of the twenty-first century, connecting social studies learning with students has always been a challenge. Since it is not unusual for 25–30 students to be assigned to K–6 teachers and 75–100 students to be assigned to middle school teachers, these educators don't expect connections to occur naturally—they learn *how* to make them!

In this chapter we describe student diversity and offer beginning teachers a method of gaining more than a superficial understanding of students. We also suggest integrating information about students into the planning process to create social stud-

■ Perhaps our most important contribution to the twenty-first century will be to demonstrate that people from different races, cultures, and ethnic backgrounds can live side by side … and over time form a common culture.

—**Robert J. Cottrol**

ies programs that are truly engaging. In the second part of the chapter we encourage beginning teachers to gain an understanding of many aspects of the twenty-first century world and to use this information to prepare students for the multiple roles of "citizens of a culturally diverse, democratic society in an interdependent world" (NCSS, 1994, p. 3).

■ Diversity in the Classroom and in Our World

Social studies programs do not exist in a vacuum; they exist for a purpose. Its very name suggests what this area of study is about—learning to live together in a community, state, nation, and global village. The NCSS definition of social studies seems to suggest that social studies education is about living together: "to help young people develop the ability to make informed and reasoned decisions for the public good as citizens of a culturally diverse, democratic society in an interdependent world" (NCSS, 1994, p. 3). Walter C. Parker, a leading social studies educator, elaborates on this theme.

> *Being American, after all, is to live with others who are culturally different while committing to an overarching political community that strives to be neutral. Being American means being politically one (this is our citizenship identity) while culturally many (these are our other identifications). Being American, then, means having multiple identities.* (Parker, 1997, p. 14).

K–8 teachers who subscribe to a similar definition of social studies accept this premise: knowing students well is a prerequisite to developing instructional programs that prepare them to assume multiple responsibilities as political citizens in a culturally diverse country and world. This means recognizing and valuing student diversity and acknowledging its existence beyond the classroom. Such teachers help students understand themselves, one another, and people outside the classroom. These teachers appreciate cultural commonalities, differences, and conflicts among students, and they find ways of addressing challenges that may surface when groups of students come together in classrooms.

Teachers sensitive to diversity also are aware of its role in the American experience. They focus on moments in U.S. history in which issues of diversity played a formative role. Whether they study race relations, exceptionalities, or religious or socioeconomic differences, students learn many ways in which Americans have resolved and acclimated to differences. In short, good social studies programs connect with students and help them in turn connect with peers, neighborhood, community, country, and the global community.

Diversity in U.S. History

The late president John F. Kennedy described the United States as "a nation of immigrants." Any basic course in U.S. history would reveal this statement to be true. The original inhabitants, the Native Americans, were as diverse as the early European settlers: Germans, Jews, English, Spanish, and Scots-Irish. In the eighteenth and nineteenth centuries more immigrants arrived from the continents of Europe, Africa, Asia, and other parts of the Americas. They arrived on the east coast and the west coast, emigrated from Mexico and Canada, and scattered about or settled in ethnic enclaves in the large and small cities dotting the United States. Most Africans came in chains and were enslaved; for generations they were not permitted to participate in the American dream.

In the late nineteenth and early twentieth centuries, countless immigrants came to the United States to work in cities, to find that "mountain of gold," and to claim land in sparsely populated areas, such as the Southwest and the Midwest. The majority of the people came from Europe (e.g., the Irish, the German and Russian Jews, and the Italians), but significant numbers came from China and Mexico. Similar to past immigrants, they too formed ethnic enclaves or scattered about the country. Some groups, because of their physical characteristics, experienced difficulties in realizing the American dream; they were referred to as minorities (e.g., Mexican, African, Native, Chinese, and Japanese Americans). The Civil War brought an end to slavery, and African Americans began migrating to the Northeast, the Midwest, and other areas of the country where land and jobs were available.

In the latter half of the twentieth century, immigrants from around the globe continued to come to the United States; however, a shift in numbers occurred as the stream of immigrants coming from Mexico, Central America, the Caribbean, Puerto Rico, Cuba, and Asia grew significantly. Across America, but particularly on the coasts, the new arrivals included Mexicans, Colombians, Vietnamese, Cambodians, Chinese, and Filipinos. In the late twentieth century international incidents—wars in Yugoslavia and Africa; economic mishaps in Asia and South America, the collapse of the Soviet Union, and a change of government in Hong Kong—brought a new variety of immigrants and political refugees seeking to make the United States their new home. In the twenty-first century the flow of immigrants and political refugees will continue to be influenced by international events (e.g., economic catastrophes, political upheavals, wars, famines) and the belief expressed by immigrants—the United States is a "mountain of gold" where political freedom is cherished, economic opportunities abound, and dreams can become realities.

Yet many immigrants found great challenges in their new country. Racism and discrimination have been part of the experiences of immigrants and political refugees. Some have faced formidable obstacles—job and housing discrimination, segregated schooling—while seeking the American dream. Today, these forces continue to restrict the opportunities of some Americans and new immigrants.

Diversity in America's Classrooms

What is meant by the concept of diversity used in phrases such as "diversity in the classroom," "culturally diverse students," "a culturally diverse America," and "a culturally diverse global village"? In all of these phrases, *diversity* refers to the many ways in which students, Americans, and our global neighbors are different from each other. Diversity refers to what makes each of us unique; it's not a liability but an asset.

■ For more information
on multicultural
education, visit the
National Association
for Multicultural
Education's website at
**http://www.inform.
umd.edu/NAME**

Ethnicity and race represent two forms of diversity. But in the context of the American classroom, it means much more. Diversity also refers to gender differences, socioeconomic differences, student exceptionalities, differences in learning styles, and the individual differences that make each person unique.

Does focusing on differences ignore the commonalities students share and that teachers should use to build group cohesiveness in the classroom? Absolutely not. At a most basic level, we highlight differences to help identify qualities students share in common. Group cohesiveness is important. And, regardless of different backgrounds, there is much that binds students together, which social studies teachers can use to highlight the experiences all Americans share.

At the same time, diversity can help students connect with teachers, peers, and instruction. By knowing about gender issues in education, services provided by schools to help children with exceptionalities, and the school experiences of children of recent immigrants, teachers can overcome challenges, modify instruction, and help students learn. On another level, differences among students (e.g., ethnicity, languages, family experience) can enrich social studies units of study. Diversity in the classroom helps students understand the role of diversity in a democratic society, acknowledge diversity as part of the American identity, appreciate the value of diversity, and learn to address and resolve conflicts that arise in a diverse society. And from a global perspective, students can gain a greater appreciation of diversity by examining differences and similarities between Americans and their neighbors and efforts by Americans to work with their neighbors for the betterment of humanity.

Some Pitfalls to Avoid

Critics of diversity believe it is overemphasized in the educational process and minimizes the common history Americans share. Some see it as a technique used by overzealous politicians to promote particular ideologies in the educational process. In fact, care must be taken to avoid a narrow ideological stance on this issue in the classroom and to bear in mind the broader goals that diversity awareness serves. The following ideas may help you avoid potential problems.

1. Diversity is a concept used in education to refer to the differences among students in the classroom. Teachers who appreciate diversity work to identify the unique qualities of individuals. This information is used to enhance connections between students and the goals of social studies.

2. Exploring student diversity allows teachers to focus on experiences and needs—those that enhance social studies learning and enable all students to fully participate in social studies learning.

3. Exploring diversity does not involve extolling or ignoring the contributions and experiences of particular groups to the American experience.

4. Exploring diversity does not involve promoting a particular brand of social studies instruction.

5. Exploring diversity allows teachers to connect students' common and unique experiences with those that Americans share in common.

■ Gaining a Baseline Understanding of Students

Have you wondered why educators stress individual differences over the characteristics shared among students? First, individual differences are readily apparent. Walk into a classroom, and what do you see? Individuals of all shapes and colors. When you speak to classroom teachers, they may comment on the general characteristics of students, but their conversations usually focus on describing individual students. Second, differences are not only obvious but also valued. Individualism and developing the individual are viewed as very important in our society. Much of education is geared toward helping individual students develop to their fullest potential and addressing challenges that may hinder them from doing so. In many classrooms we seek to know the individual and to develop an environment where individualism can prosper and grow.

In some classrooms, the amount and variety of differences among students may seem overwhelming. How can teachers make sense of it and use differences to enhance instruction? We recommend developing two main areas of knowledge about students: baseline knowledge and then more elaborate knowledge of diversity. These areas of knowledge and the categories within each are illustrated in Figure 3.1.

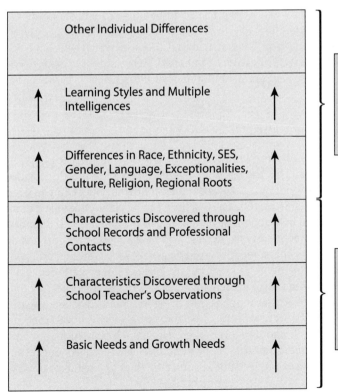

■ **FIGURE 3.1**

Levels of Knowledge about Students

To acquire baseline knowledge, teachers reflect on the needs and wants of children and adolescents, use observation, and employ the knowledge available at the school. This pool of information offers teachers both general information and insights into particular students who are experiencing difficulties in social studies. Knowing how teachers in earlier grades helped a student with difficulties and identifying strategies that did not work gives the teacher a helpful context in which to plan instruction. However, in assessing needs in their classroom, teachers do well to begin with the basic needs that all students share.

Basic Needs and Growth Needs

If a group of first-, fifth-, and eighth-grade teachers were asked to identify the qualities K–8 students share in common, what do you think they would say? What would their list of common qualities look like? We suspect it would touch on the basic needs and growth needs cited in the hierarchy of needs developed by the psychologist Abraham Maslow (see Figure 3.2).

Maslow's hierarchy of needs is an excellent tool for gaining an appreciation of the basic needs of children and adolescents and identifying the many ways in which teachers can help students satisfy them. At a most basic level, students need an environment where they feel safe and secure and their basic needs can be met (e.g., for water and food). They need to interact with adults who value them, who care, and who offer a sense of belonging. They also need instruction that offers opportunities to build self-esteem—to be acknowledged and respected by others. As basic needs are met, students and teachers can attend to growth needs such as justice and beauty.

Reflect on the classrooms you have visited and those in which you have observed. How safe and secure were these environments? Were student growth needs being met? Not enough can be said on the importance of these needs in the development of instruction.

The Teacher's Observations

Observing your students carefully can improve your knowledge of and sensitivity to their basic and growth needs. This excellent technique, when formalized, provides teachers with a wealth of information. (Many examples of how to collect and analyze information are provided in this textbook.) Teachers can observe students before school begins, at play, during instruction, at the library, in the cafeteria, and among friends. The information gathered early in the year will be elaborated and refined as the year goes on. The obvious characteristics—physical size, racial, ethnic, and gender differences—are the starting point; later, more subtle clues can be gathered, such as hints to the socioeconomic status of students gained by looking at clothes, grooming habits, and the quantity of school supplies they bring to school. Teachers can observe whether students are extroverts or introverts, and verbal or physical in their interactions with peers. At still another level, they can gain information on how students learn by observing their physical actions and intellectual efforts during social studies instruction. These examples should suffice to show the value of observing students while developing social studies programs.

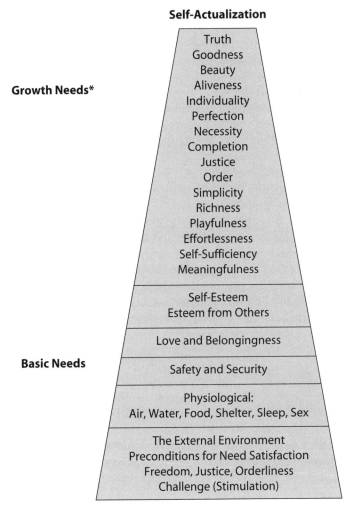

Self-Actualization

Growth Needs*

Truth
Goodness
Beauty
Aliveness
Individuality
Perfection
Necessity
Completion
Justice
Order
Simplicity
Richness
Playfulness
Effortlessness
Self-Sufficiency
Meaningfulness

Self-Esteem
Esteem from Others

Love and Belongingness

Basic Needs

Safety and Security

Physiological:
Air, Water, Food, Shelter, Sleep, Sex

The External Environment
Preconditions for Need Satisfaction
Freedom, Justice, Orderliness
Challenge (Stimulation)

■ **FIGURE 3.2**

Maslow's Hierarchy of Needs

Source: From *The Third Force: The Psychology of Abraham Maslow* by Frank Goble. Copyright © 1970 by Thomas Jefferson Research Center. All rights reserved. Reprinted by permission of Grossman Publishers.

*Growth needs are all of equal importance (not hierarchial).

Consistent practice of observation can over time reveal to teachers which teaching approaches prove most successful with particular students. Teachers might recruit colleagues or support staff to help in further developing these approaches. Gathering observations might extend to noting developments in students' written work and speaking with parents and support staff. Can you think of other ways in which teachers could collect valuable information about students?

School Information

The school itself is another rich source of information. Student files, for example, provide notes on the academic achievement of students, family background, medical history, interactions with support staff, referrals to specialists, any challenges students have experienced in school, and evaluations from school personnel, including teachers. Most schools employ specialists, such as a psychologist, counselor, nurse, reading specialist, and community liaison person, who can offer valuable insights about particular students. Casual and formal conversations with a cross-section of teachers, administrators, and support staff can inform teachers about the general characteristics of the students, the school, and the community. Teachers at other grade levels who have taught students in your classroom can provide especially valuable information on the strengths and weaknesses of students, family background, and the successes and failures they experienced while teaching these students.

Another rich source of information are the individualized educational plans (IEPs) of students with exceptionalities. Each IEP states which special education teachers are involved with a particular student, a plan for addressing the needs of the student, and information on the past experiences of teachers who have interacted with the student.

Basic and growth needs, teacher observations, and school information form the baseline information that teachers need to develop effective social studies programs. They provide sufficient information to begin planning for instruction. Teachers know that their understanding of students can never be completely objective; they acknowledge the subjectivity in this process. More important, they recognize bias that may be present in the information they receive about students and minimize its impact planning. Part of being a teaching professional is to recognize bias (one's own or others') and prevent it from coloring one's treatment of any student.

■ Understanding Differences among Students

The rich diversity found in America's classrooms may sound abstract and general when discussed in textbooks and reference books. It is, however, a powerful source of learning, at many levels, when it is explored and appreciated in a classroom of students.

Cultural Differences

Culture is a broad concept that has been defined in many ways. One useful definition is Nieto's (1996, p. 390): "the ever-changing values, traditions, social and political relationships, and worldview created and shared by a group of people bound together by a combination of factors (which can include a common history, geographic location, language, social class, and/or religion) and how these are transformed by those who share them." This definition is broad, and rightly so. It is difficult to target a particular belief, behavior, or area of knowledge that is not influenced by culture. In the United States, our taken-for-granted way of viewing ourselves and others has been called "the Anglo–Western European macroculture" (Bennett, 1998, p. 47). As you recall from your educational foundations course, a major purpose of education is the transmission of culture, and not surprisingly, schools in the United States transmit and reflect the Anglo–Western European macroculture.

Why are basic and growth needs a part of social studies? How would you address the basic needs of students? growth needs?

Beginning teachers must ask, "How do groups of culturally diverse students coexist in my classroom?" Do all the students claim an Anglo–Western European culture? Do all the students seem to fit into the culture of the classroom? If not, what other cultures are represented? How would you characterize the students who seem to do well in school? those who become lost in the day-to-day experiences of school? those who do not do well in school? Does culture affect these students' school performance?

In our society and our schools, a variety of cultures coexist with the macroculture. Conflicts can arise when the culture in the home differs from the culture of the school. These conflicts may spring from differences in the value placed on verbal ability, in communication styles, in the organization of time and space, and in numerous other areas. Notice the children who receive praise in a given classroom. Are they those students who raise their hands, answer questions correctly, and interact with their peers in what is considered an appropriate manner? Children who don't exhibit this behavior may do so for cultural reasons. For example, generally speaking, in Hispanic cultures children learn that greater value is placed on nonverbal than verbal behavior. They are taught to learn by listening and watching parents and other responsible adults and to demonstrate learning by imitating their actions. What might happen to some Hispanic children who enter our schools? They might appear less interested or responsive than their peers from the macroculture, yet they are behaving in accordance with the standards of the culture in the home. When cultural conflicts are not addressed in the classroom, they can cause much distress both to the teacher and students.

Ethnic Differences

According to Banks (1994), an ethnic group "shares a common ancestry, culture, history, tradition, and a sense of peoplehood" (p. 91). We have noted a few of the many ethnic groups who have settled in America (e.g., the Irish, the German and Russian

Jews, Italians, Mexicans, Salvadorians, the Chinese). Some members of these groups have assimilated into American culture, but others have maintained their own culture and sense of peoplehood over the years. Today, some members of recent immigrant groups have continued this tradition and established ethnic enclaves in small and large communities across the United States. Some rural communities in central Illinois, for example, continue to exhibit a strong German influence, and in cities such as San Francisco, in numerous neighborhoods groups of people (e.g., Latinos, Chinese Americans, African Americans, Japanese Americans) continue to observe cultural patterns that differ from those of mainstream Americans and other ethnic groups.

Members of ethnic groups, for example, may adhere to particular family roles and patterns for carrying on daily activities. They also may value their group's own historical experiences (outside and inside the United States), celebrate particular holidays, and prefer certain foods. Children and adolescents from these groups may be influenced by these ethnic differences and may express particular inclinations toward school, adults, and modes of learning.

These differences in ethnic background may create challenging dynamics in the classroom, but they can also enhance social studies learning. A student who is continually talking about the ways in which he and his family celebrate their Irish heritage might have a lot to contribute to studies of immigration, culture, holidays, or community. A creative teacher will find ways to tap into this student's knowledge and experience to benefit the whole class.

Racial Differences

According to Campbell (1995, p. 49), race is a "term used to describe a large group of people with a somewhat similar genetic history. Many observers believe that they can describe a racial group based on hair color and texture, skin color, eye color, and body type." Today, many biologists and physical anthropologists contend that there are no pure races and therefore no basis for this form of scientific classification of peoples. Race, they state, is a social category adopted by some to categorize particular people.

In this study of diversity, racial diversity refers to "people of color" such as African Americans, Latinos, Native Americans, and Asian Americans—people who are physically different from white Americans. And as previously mentioned, these groups also are referred to as minorities, a term that denotes their numerical proportion to white Americans and connotes the inordinate amount of prejudice and discrimination these groups have encountered. African Americans, for example, were brought to the United States enslaved in chains, and although they gained their freedom at the end of the Civil War, they continue to encounter obstacles that other Americans and recent immigrant groups do not experience. The term *Latino* refers to the many peoples of Latin American origin and descent (e.g., Mexican Americans, Colombians, Cubans, Puerto Ricans) who, like African Americans, as a group also experience the forces of racism—prejudice and discrimination. For example, for many years Mexican Americans attended "Mexican schools" in the Southwest, and during the Great Depression some were illegally deported to Mexico. Reflect on what you learned in U.S. history courses with respect to Asian Americans and Native Americans. How are their experiences similar to those of African Americans and Latinos? How are those experiences similar to and different from those of white ethnic groups and Americans who express no ethnic affiliations?

Children and adolescents who belong to these groups, just like those from various ethnic groups, may bring to the classroom a wealth of information about the history and culture of other countries and their group's historical experiences in this country. They may share their own experiences as they moved from one culture to another—home, neighborhood, school, and the mainstream. They may tell stories of relatives and friends who have come to this country recently and how they maintain contact over distances with relatives and friends. Because some members of these groups have experienced prejudice and forms of discrimination, they can provide detailed firsthand information about America's contemporary challenges in this area. These children and adolescents come from a variety of backgrounds, and some may experience academic challenges that need attention as you attempt to connect them with social studies learning.

Differences in Socioeconomic Status (SES)

Socioeconomic status (SES) refers to one's material wealth. Generally, social scientists classify individuals according to the following categories: (1) the underclass, (2) the working class, (3) the middle class, and (4) the upper class. Members in each class tend to share similar levels of career status, education, and power (money and influence). It is generally agreed that U.S. schools reflect the Anglo–Western European macroculture and a middle-class outlook on life. This means that a member of the middle class has a better chance of succeeding in school than a member of the lower or working class does. Members of the working class who are striving to join the middle class also have a better chance of succeeding in school since they, too, accept middle-class values.

■ Poverty must not be a bar to learning, and learning must offer an escape from poverty.
—**Lyndon B. Johnson**

Think of your K–8 school experiences. Would you characterize them as positive? Did you like your teachers? Did you enjoy learning in the classroom? Perhaps one of the reasons you succeeded in school was because your education reflected the cultural values instilled in you as you grew up. How did your family's SES influence your preschool experiences? Were your experiences more or less limited than those of your classmates? Did your pool of friends expand beyond your neighborhood? Did you learn in classrooms that were culturally diverse? Did success in school help you fit in with your peers, or did it lead to isolation? Your own school experiences will likely affect the way you perceive students when you begin teaching. Being aware of your own cultural and socioeconomic background and how it has influenced your education will help you understand how powerful culture and social class are in shaping the lives of children.

A major challenge for beginning teachers is learning to communicate with children and adolescents of all socioeconomic classes and to involve all these students in learning social studies. Although teachers easily interact with most children of their own socioeconomic class, other children can be a challenge. Why? Generally, most beginning teachers have had limited experiences with children and adults from different parts of society. Although teacher preparation programs emphasize America's diverse society, new teachers have studied this information in an academic setting. They often have few real-life experiences with connecting a cross-section of U.S. students with school culture.

In your field experiences, student teaching, and the first years of your professional career, you will learn about class differences and gain experience in drawing all students into social studies learning. You will find ways for students from all social classes to enrich your social studies program and ways to foster understanding and respect among all students.

Exceptionalities

Effective social studies teachers make it their business to appreciate their students as individuals; to discover the unique needs, talents, and interests of each; and to plan social studies instruction accordingly. The logical conclusion of such a viewpoint is that *all* students have special needs that make them "exceptional": however, in common educational parlance, the term *exceptionality* refers to the growing array of student characteristics that qualifies individual students to receive special services. Currently, these exceptionalities include (1) mental retardation, (2) learning disabilities, (3) emotional and behavioral disorders, (4) communication disorders, (5) physical and health impairments, (6) hearing impairments, (7) visual impairments, (8) severe or multiple disabilities, and (9) giftedness (Culatta & Tompkins, 1999).

Traditionally, students with these characteristics have received special services in programs that removed them from the general education classroom. More recently, a trend toward inclusive schools has integrated many students with exceptionalities into regular education programs. This means that you, as a prospective K–8 teacher, will probably have exceptional students in your classroom. How will you respond?

Full inclusion allows teachers to take advantage of the rich experiences that students with exceptionalities bring to social studies, while also addressing their unique needs. Their presence makes the classroom more accurately reflect the diversity of society in general—a big advantage, from a social studies perspective. In your field experiences, notice how teachers make use of individualized education programs. How does this affect social studies instruction? How does the teacher highlight the abilities and contributions of exceptional students in order to enrich learning for all students? Think of ways in which you too could enhance social studies instruction by drawing on the skills and experiences of these students.

Linguistic Differences

Though most students arrive at school speaking Standard English, sizable numbers do not. In the early twentieth century, the children of immigrants spoke a language other than English when they entered school. Many quickly learned the dominant language, but others struggled and left school. The programs available to students who did not speak English required full immersion—the learning of English as quickly as possible. Later, as the public and some educators became concerned about the number of students who dropped out before graduating, some efforts were made to address linguistic diversity in the classroom. However, not until the 1960s civil rights movement did significant changes occur. Latinos, for example, fought for bilingual programs. Across the country, particularly on the west coast and in the Southwest, schools instituted programs providing Latinos the opportunity to maintain Spanish while learning Standard English.

Today, some schools continue to offer these programs for Spanish-speaking students as well as others. However, for a variety of reasons, schools have been unable to develop and maintain bilingual programs for all students who speak a language other than English. Although immersion programs are usually available, more needs to be done to help these students connect with school and social studies learning. What can you do? First, you can welcome the students to your classroom, establish a buddy system, and contact the district's foreign language or ESL teacher to find options to support the education of these students. You should also integrate the students into the culture of the classroom, paying particular attention to their basic and growth needs. Learn a few phrases in the students' languages. Speak with the students' parents. If the parents do not speak English, communicate through an interpreter. Think of ways for these students' experiences to be incorporated into your social studies program, and modify your instruction to address their language needs.

Gender Differences

Although discrimination against girls and women is against the law, subtle (and blatant) forms of sexism remain present in society and can surface in the classroom. Think back to your K–8 experiences. Can you think of instances in which teachers or other students limited your opportunities to pursue areas of interest because they weren't considered appropriate for your gender? Did you feel you needed to act in a certain way because that is the way that boys or girls are supposed to act? Did your teachers pay equal attention to boys and girls? Were the experiences of women integrated across the curriculum? How much do you know about the contributions of women to the American experience?

As you prepare to teach, keep in mind the overall goal of education and one purpose of social studies—to provide *all* students with the opportunity to meet their potential and to learn about the many people who have contributed to the American experience. To meet these goals, you will need to become familiar with students' perception of gender issues. If you detect biases, stereotypes, and the like among the students, you should address those issues. This can be challenging.

To eliminate sexism from the classroom, teachers should serve as role models, offer praise to both boys and girls in a variety of activities, and provide instruction in which girls and boys assume several different roles, including taking responsibility for their learning. Teachers should also give high priority to intergroup relations, understanding the dynamics between girls and boys as they interact at different grade levels. With respect to social studies, teachers should provide opportunities for students to learn about the role of women in the history of the United States and other countries. And, in those instances where teachers detect weakness among the students (e.g., biases, stereotypes), they should modify their instruction.

Religious Differences

What does it mean to be Muslim in a predominantly Christian country? to be Jewish in a predominantly Protestant community? to be a person with no religious affiliation in a classroom where everyone else is deeply religious? Diversity in religion is foundational to U.S. society, and from the beginning, religious freedom has been held as an ideal in our country. In classrooms, religion should be recognized and respected; that is, teachers should acknowledge a student's religious beliefs and, where appropriate, incorporate diversity in religion into social studies. (Social studies teachers teach *about* religion; they do not promote religious beliefs in the classroom.)

■ The Center for Multi-lingual Multicultural Research **http:// www.usc.edu/dept/ education/CMMR** offers teachers information on multilingual education, English-as-a-second-language, and related areas.

To accomplish this, teachers can learn about diversity in religion and, with the help of parents and community members, identify the religious beliefs of individual students. Teachers should be alert for potential conflicts as students with particular religious affiliations interact with others in the classroom. Diversity in religion offers teachers a wealth of opportunities to enrich social studies learning. Religious beliefs, practices, and holidays can be integrated into instructional programs to illustrate similarities and differences among the world's religions. At another level, teachers can examine diversity in religion among immigrant groups; the role of Protestantism in the formation of this country, and the ways in which groups have maintained their religious identities. On a global level, teachers could survey the role of religion in the formation of civilizations and historical movements and its influence on historical figures.

Regional Differences

If you have lived in different parts of the country, you have probably noticed that, although we are all Americans, regional differences exist. That is, Americans differ in dialect, the foods they eat, communication patterns, religious affiliations, and cultural traditions, based on where they live. Historically, these differences can be seen among different Native American peoples and among various early immigrant groups as they settled in places. As the country grew, these regional differences flourished and changed as new groups arrived. Today, new immigrants add to this diversity.

Differences also exist among Americans living in rural, suburban, and urban settings. Were you born and raised in a large metropolitan area? Did you grow up in a small town in Nebraska? Did you grow up in a suburban community outside of Atlanta? Most likely, where you were born and raised had an impact on your K–8 education. If you move to a different part of the country to teach, regional differences might require that you adapt your communication style or other aspects of instruction in order to succeed in your new position.

Teachers are also sensitive to the changes students must make when they move from one region of the country to another or from a rural to an urban environment. Students may feel embarrassed about a different accent in their speech, misinterpretation of slang words common in their new environment but unfamiliar to them, or other differences. To welcome students who are new to the school, teachers can focus on the basic and growth needs, establish a buddy system, and use observation techniques to gauge how well a new student is getting along with others and adjusting to

What differences and similarities do you see among these students? Why are student differences and similarities powerful information to a teacher?

a new school culture. Teachers are mindful of name calling and other negative behavior directed at new students. Some teachers address this potential problem by integrating the new student's experiences into the curriculum. Think of the possibilities if a new student in your classroom had lived close to the Golden Gate Bridge, near a cotton field in Mississippi, near a catfish farm near Sioux Falls, in a mining community in Utah, or near the coast in Florida. Students can easily fit in when they are accepted as individuals, their past experiences are valued, and they see themselves as classroom contributors.

Learning Styles and Multiple Intelligences

Another level of diversity lies in the learning styles and multiple intelligences students bring to the classroom. Observe K–8 students to discover the ways in which they like to learn best (e.g., by way of a lecture, group work, project, class discussion) and ways in which they like to demonstrate learning (e.g., through linguistic, spatial, or musical expression). The research on these two areas (see Dunn, Beaudry, & Klavas, 1989; Gardner, 1983, 1995) has given educators a constructive way to view differences among students and how they learn. If you have observed in several classrooms, you have seen teachers using a variety of teaching strategies and students demonstrating learning in a variety of ways.

Learning Styles

Learning styles may be defined as "the unique ways whereby an individual gathers and processes information and are the means by which an individual prefers to learn" (Davidson, 1990, p. 36). Proponents of learning theory attempt to make teachers aware that (1) students have different styles of learning, (2) teachers tend to teach according to their own preferred learning style, (3) school success often hinges upon being able to learn in a single style, and (4) teachers need to vary their instructional styles to address the varied learning styles of their students.

In general, current U.S. schools seem to work best for learners who can deal in the abstract, who tend to think logically and sequentially, who learn from listening and the written word, and who are autonomous or easily motivated by authority figures. However, many students exhibit a propensity to learn differently: some learners prefer the concrete and immediate to the abstract; others think intuitively, imaginatively, or globally; some learn best when they receive a lot of feedback from adults or can talk to their peers. When schools and teachers are inflexible about learning styles, these variations can sometimes land students in academic or disciplinary difficulty.

How do teachers address this level of diversity in social studies? First, they begin with self-awareness and identify their own learning preferences. They note the style they prefer, the times they used it in the classroom, instances when other styles were used, and missed opportunities for varying the teaching style. They also note the teaching strategies they used that successfully engaged the students in learning. This reflective activity acquaints teachers with the many ways in which students learn and encourages teachers to use a variety of teaching strategies (lecture, group work, independent study, projects, and so on). Teachers also find that varying teaching style is helpful in addressing difficulties that individual students may have in learning.

Multiple Intelligences

Do you recall taking an IQ (intelligence quotient) test? Do you know what numbers designate the high range of intelligence? the low range? Have you thought about what it means to represent a person's intelligence by a single number, say, 120? Who is most intelligent—Al Gore, Michael Jordan, Toni Morrison, or Bill Gates?

When we recognize that individuals are gifted in very different ways, it becomes impossible to talk about a single narrow concept of intelligence. Al Gore may not become president of Microsoft, and Toni Morrison is not likely to be recruited by a women's professional basketball team, but each has a unique genius and has made a lasting contribution to our society and culture.

Howard Gardner's theory of multiple intelligences (e.g., Gardner, 1983, 1995) gives educators a soundly researched and scrupulously documented means to identify and describe the many ways in which people are intelligent. Prior to Gardner's work, it was widely assumed that intelligence could be determined through a paper-and-pencil test, which focused on students' verbal, mathematical, and logical skills. Thanks to Gardner and others, educational psychologists have identified other intelligences.

According to Gardner, there are at least seven intelligences: (1) logical/mathematical, (2) linguistic, (3) musical, (4) spatial, (5) bodily–kinesthetic, (6) intrapersonal, and (7) interpersonal. Generally, schools emphasize the first two types and provide few opportunities for students to demonstrate learning in other ways. In the elementary grades, however, teachers do encourage children to use their special talents to demonstrate learning. Today, in the middle grades, as a result of a greater emphasis on understanding children and adolescents and the advent of block scheduling and portfolios, teachers are employing teaching strategies that encourage students to demonstrate learning in creative ways.

In most teacher preparation programs, prospective social studies teachers are being introduced to topics like multiple intelligences, learning styles, portfolios, and integrated learning. They are learning the many ways in which students can express learning and the strategies that will encourage even greater creative expression.

Individuality

In addition to differences related to culture, ethnicity, race, socioeconomic status, exceptionalities, language, gender, religion, geographic region, and learning style, one more area of diversity remains: that of the distinct individual.

The essence of a given student cannot be grasped only by labeling him or her as a member of the particular groups described in this section. A person cannot be categorized so easily; a unique spark of personality, ability, and experience gives each student in your classroom an absolutely unique contribution to make and a set of individual learning needs as well.

Observant teachers consider each student as an individual and are wary of simplistic labels. They look for areas of growth still needed for "model students." They search for the hidden strengths in students who don't easily adapt to the classroom or have struggles with social studies learning. They don't lose sight of the individual as they plan instruction.

It takes judgment to create a student profile that accounts for all the important features discussed in this section. However, it is the best way to ensure that your instruction will engage your students, relate to their lives, interest them, and make classroom learning a model for lifelong learning. Understanding the diversity in your classroom is a key to reaching your students.

■ Diversity beyond the Classroom

In this section, we embark on an odyssey to explore diversity beyond the classroom, to make you aware of the world around you, beyond your immediate surroundings, and interactions among people and nations locally, regionally, nationally, and internationally.

I've got a great idea! It's early afternoon—forget about the university and go shopping! Drive to the nearest large indoor shopping mall in your community, and spend the afternoon people-watching. Buy a cup of coffee, locate a busy traffic area, and find a comfortable seat. Bring a notebook, and jot down notes based on your observations. You might answer questions like these:

- How are people dressed? What might this tell you about their socioeconomic status?
- Do individuals shop alone? What groups do you observe?
- What languages are being spoken?
- How do the various people differ from you?
- What forms of interaction do people use to communicate?
- How do parents and other adults discipline children and adolescents?
- How do adolescents without adult supervision behave? Do boys and girls behave differently?

■ Education must
teach us that all our
actions on this planet,
physical and social, are
irrevocably interlocked.
—**Ernest Boyer**

Are you tired of observing people? It's time to shop! Look at items in different shops to see where they were manufactured and assembled. Start by visiting your favorite department store and its clothing and shoe departments. Look at the labels. Where were these items manufactured? Stop by the entertainment area, and look at television sets, cellular phones, audio systems, and camcorders. Where were these items assembled? How many were manufactured and assembled in the United States? Stop at a toy store, a music store, and a craft shop. Does it seem that businesses in countries around the world, including the United States, interact as they develop, manufacture, and assemble goods and to distribute them internationally? Can you offer a hypothesis on global interdependence?

If you are hungry, stop at the food court. You might order Cajun, Chinese, Mexican, or Japanese food—another example of diversity in your community.

Visit the dealership selling your favorite American car. Ask a sales associate to describe where the automobile's parts were manufactured and where the automobiles were assembled. How "American" are American cars?

Now it's time to go home. You need to send an e-mail to your parents who are in Australia for a month-long vacation, and then you'll do some shopping on the Internet. Later, your social studies chat group is meeting to talk about diversity in the classroom. And, if time permits, you are going to take a hot shower, crawl into bed, turn on the television, and review the news of the day.

This make-believe odyssey illustrates the diversity in the United States and the interdependence that exists among the countries of the world. During the twenty-first century these trends will continue. Immigrants will continue arriving, minority populations within the United States will increase significantly, and technological advancements and business ventures are expected to bring countries around the world closer and closer together. Diversity is a part of the fabric of American and international life.

◼ Diversity and Social Studies

How should K–8 social studies teachers address diversity? To respond to this question, we turn to the purpose of social studies as described by NCSS, "to help young children develop the ability to make informed and reasoned decisions for the public good as citizens of a culturally diverse, democratic society in an interdependent world." According to Walter Parker, the purpose of social studies is to help students sharpen their cultural identities (e.g., gender, ethnicity, race) while learning to become citizens of the United States and of an interdependent world.

Teachers bear these purposes in mind as they identify and nurture students' cultural identifies. First, they survey the classroom and reflect on its particular areas of diversity and how these dynamics might be used to reinforce and enrich social studies learning. They address questions such as the following: How will I address the basic and growth needs of students? How will I gather student information? What ethnic groups are represented in my classroom? What religions? Is anyone a recent immigrant? Teachers use this information as they develop a social studies program.

Describe the student diversity you have observed in K–8 classrooms. How do teachers incorporate diversity in social studies instruction?

Second, teachers identify students' special strengths and needs. A teacher may identify an African American student who just returned from visiting Africa with her parents to trace their historical roots; a gifted girl who is an expert on developing webpages; a boy who is interested in examining human rights abuses against children in the twenty-first century. Teachers also identify special needs, such as a student who is not reading at grade level, another who lacks social skills, and another with a behavior disorder.

Third, teachers reflect on the knowledge, skills, and core values important in living in the world today, and ask themselves the following questions: How might I prepare my students to become U.S. citizens in an interdependent world? What knowledge do children and adolescents need? What skills and values? What can I do to help students know themselves and their peers?

ACTIVITY IDEAS ➤ *Celebrating Diversity*

➤ Ask students to carry out a language survey of their community or region. Have some students focus on languages that influenced the area in the past; other students can find out about languages spoken there presently. They might use these resources:

- The library or historical society can provide information about language groups of the past.
- Hints can be found in street names or names of geographic features. Do Native American terms (such as Massachusetts) show the influence of a particular native people? Does the town name show Norwegian or Hispanic presence?
- The Internet can yield a great deal of information. Look for sites on local and state history.

- School administrators, social agencies, and government offices can provide current language information.
- Students can canvass different neighborhoods to find out about languages spoken there. They may find some surprises!

Each group can present their findings to the class. Wrap up the activity by discussing how, overall, different language groups have influenced your community or region.

➤ In the primary grades, ask students to draw pictures of themselves, adding any words or symbols that show what makes them unique. Then ask each student to share his or her picture with the class, describing what makes him or her special. List these characteristics on the board. After each student has had a turn, discuss the list with students. Guide them in noting what they have in common and what makes each person different.

➤ For a week or two, ask students to find items in local and national news about current immigration patterns and problems in the United States. As they gather information, they might focus on these questions:

- From what parts of the world are people now emigrating to our country?
- What motivates them to do so?
- What do they have in common with immigrants of the past?
- What challenges do they face?

Children in elementary school might make a bulletin board display focusing on today's immigrants. At the middle school level, you might challenge teams of students to debate a particular policy or problem in immigration today.

➤ Have students make a comparison between their community today and in the 1970s (or some other decade, but preferably one within living memory). They should focus on the cultural and ethnic makeup of the community. Divide students into groups who undertake library and Internet research, carry out interviews, and write for information from social or government agencies. You might provide them with focusing questions such as the following:

1. What were the major racial and ethnic groups in our community in the 1970s?
2. What are the major racial and ethnic groups here today?
3. Describe each group. What part of the world did they come from? What language do they speak? When did they arrive in this area?
4. Since the 1970s, which groups of people have settled in the area? left the area? Why?
5. What have different groups contributed to our community?

Focusing on specifics—the particular Caribbean island a group emigrated from, the exact events that caused them to leave, both the language and the dialect spoken by a group—can help students avoid making bland stereotypical statements about ethnic and racial groups.

When the research is done, each class group can report on its findings. Encourage the groups to include maps, charts and graphs, pictures, or other resources to capture the changing or stable cultural mosaic of the community.

➤ In the upper elementary grades, have students target their community, state, or metropolitan area and identify the number and kinds of ethnic restaurants found there. Students can do research using telephone directories, the Internet, tourist information, restaurant guides, and their own knowledge. Then have students focus on a few ethnic foods that interest them. Taking account of the preferences of fellow classmates, guide students in planning and preparing a lunch including some of these ethnic dishes. Emphasize special ingredients, preparation methods, and how the food should be eaten (for example, with chopsticks, with the fingers, and so on). Make the meal as authentic as possible. Then have students discuss what they have learned about culture and food from this activity.

Diversity and Citizenship Identity

According to NCSS, a purpose of social studies is "to help young people develop the ability to make informed and reasoned decisions for the public good." To promote "the public good," young people need to learn what that phrase means. Most educators would agree that it refers to a cluster of democratic beliefs and ideas: (1) rights of individuals, (2) freedoms of the individual, (3) responsibilities of the individual, and (4) beliefs concerning societal conditions and governmental responsibilities. Social studies teachers develop and implement programs that include year-long goals focusing on the foundational ideas of U.S. government, which distinguish this country from others.

Whether you teach social studies in the early grades or in middle school, the heart of your program should be core civic values. You can celebrate diversity in the classroom and make use of it in teaching, but you should also promote those civic values we all cherish as Americans. These values can foster group cohesiveness.

■ Conclusion

In this chapter we examined the issue of diversity as it affects making connections between students and social studies. First, teachers must get to know their students. At a basic level, teachers observe students and examine school information. Then they explore the spectrum of diversity among their students—gender, ethnicity, race, exceptionalities, and so on—to enrich social studies, identify students' strengths and challenges, and develop programs that reflect life in the twenty-first century.

Teachers can use diversity to promote the goals of social studies education. An appreciation of diversity helps students form individual identities and prepares them to live in culturally diverse environments. In addition, diversity promotes political identity. Students learn to appreciate the rights and responsibilities of citizens in a democracy that values cultural identities.

Questions, Activities, and Evaluation

1. Examine a textbook or other curricular material, and identify information describing different aspects of diversity in U.S. history. How might this information be used in the development of a social studies unit of study?

2. You are being interviewed by a site-based council for a social studies position. How would you respond to a question about the purpose of social studies education in the K–8 curriculum? How might you make use of the NCSS definition and purpose statement and Parker's interpretation of the purpose of social studies education?

3. Test this hypothesis: we live in a world that is culturally diverse and interdependent. Form a small group. For a week-long period, collect and review newspaper and magazines stories on related topics. Watch news programs of TV. Can you use the information you have gathered to support this hypothesis? Report to the class on your findings.

4. Develop a unit of study that includes the experiences of one or more groups described in this chapter. Describe how this unit addresses the purpose of social studies.

5. Form discussion groups, and debate the accuracy of the following statement by Parker: "Being American means being politically one (this is our citizenship identity) while culturally many. . . . Being American, then, means having multiple identities."

6. While observing, focus on diversity as you survey a number of classrooms. Are the classrooms you visited diverse? Describe the forms of diversity you observed.

7. As you reflect on a classroom you have observed, write about how you would make use of diversity to develop and enrich social studies instruction in that setting?

8. In social studies, the topic of diversity in our country is often set in the present. Ask a teacher how he or she incorporates diversity issues into units on earlier periods of history, such as lessons on the Civil War or the Roaring Twenties. How does the teacher give students a grasp of the changing makeup of the people of the United States? Brainstorm with the teacher to come up with more ideas.

9. Ask your educational psychology instructor for examples of learning styles inventories. Then, in your classroom observations, ask a teacher how he or she incorporates knowledge of students' learning styles into classroom instruction. If possible, arrange to complete learning styles inventories as you observe a few students for two to three days. Discuss your findings with the cooperating teacher. How should they affect instructional planning?

References

American Association of University Women & the National Education Association. (1992). *How schools short-change girls.* Commissioned by AAUW Educational Foundation and researched by Wellesley College Center for Research on Women. Washington, DC: Author.

Armstrong, T. (1996). *Multiple intelligences in the classroom.* Alexandria, VA: Association for Supervision and Curriculum Development.

Banks, J. A. (1994). *An introduction to multicultural education.* Boston: Allyn & Bacon.

Baruth, L. G., & Manning, L. M. (1999). *Multicultural education of children and adolescents.* (2nd ed.). Boston: Allyn & Bacon.

Bennett, C. I. (1998). *Comprehensive multicultural education: Theory and practice.* (4th ed.). Boston: Allyn & Bacon.

Caldwell, G. P., & Dean, W. (1996). Differences in learning styles of low socioeconomic status for low and high achievers. *Education, 117,* 141–147.

Culatta, R. A., & Tompkins, J. R. (1999). *Fundamentals of special education: What every teacher needs to know.* Upper Saddle River, NJ: Merrill.

Campbell, D. E. (1996). *Choosing democracy: A practical guide to multicultural education.* Englewood Cliffs, NJ: Prentice Hall.

Dilg, M. (1999). *Race and culture in the classroom: Teaching and learning through multicultural education.* New York: Teachers College Press.

Dunn, R., Beaudry, J. S., & Klavas, A. (1989). Survey of research on learning styles. *Educational Leadership, 46,* 50–58.

Farlow, L. (1996). A quartet of success stories: How to make inclusion work. *Educational Leadership, 53,* 51–55.

Gardner, H. (1995). Reflections on multiple intelligences: Myths and messages. *Phi Delta Kappan, 77,* 200–203, 206–209.

Gardner, H. (1983). *Frames of mind.* New York: Basic Books.

Hardin, D. E., & McNelis, S. J. (1996). The resource center: Hub of inclusive activities. *Educational Leadership, 53,* 41–43.

Heward, W. L. (1996). *Exceptional children.* (5th ed.). Upper Saddle River, NJ: Prentice Hall.

Kaltsounis, T. (1997). Multicultural education and citizenship education at a crossroads: Searching for common ground. *The Social Studies, 86,* 18–22.

Knapp, M. S., & Woolverton, S. (1995). Social class and schooling. In J. A. Banks (Ed.), *Handbook of research in multicultural education,* (pp. 548–569). New York: Macmillan.

National Council for the Social Studies. (1994). *Curriculum standards for social studies: Expectations of excellence.* Washington, DC: Author.

Nieto, S. (1996). *Affirming diversity: The sociopolitical context of multicultural education.* (2nd ed.). New York: Longman.

Parker, W. C. (1997). Navigating the unity/diversity tension in education for democracy. *Social Studies, 88,* 12–17.

Reid, J. M. (1987). The learning style preferences of ESL students. *TESOL Quarterly, 21,* 87–111.

Roach, V. (1995). Supporting inclusion. *Phi Delta Kappan, 77,* 295–299.

Sadker, M. P., & Sadker, D. M. (1993). *Failing at fairness: How America's schools cheat girls.* New York: Charles Scribner's Sons.

Sapon-Shevin, M. (1995). Why gifted students belong in inclusive schools. *Educational Leadership, 52,* 64–71.

Van Til, W. (1974). *Education: A beginning.* (2nd ed.). Boston: Houghton Mifflin.

Chapter 4

Topics of Public Concern, Current Affairs, Controversial Issues, and Special Events

Chapter Objective

To present guidelines and strategies for including topics of public concern, current affairs, controversial issues, and special events to engage students in social studies

Focusing Questions

- How do various programs contribute to social studies objectives?
- What guidelines are helpful in incorporating instruction on multicultural issues, gender issues, law, global studies, and the environment?
- How are goals and objectives of various topical programs different from and similar to the goals and objectives of social studies?
- How can teachers generate focusing questions that guide study and encourage higher-order thinking?
- What criteria are used to select events and issues that are meaningful to students?
- What are commonly used approaches to the teaching of current affairs?
- What guiding principles are helpful in dealing with controversial issues?
- What principles and strategies are helpful in providing instruction on holidays and other special events?

■ How These Topics Contribute to Social Studies

Every day, events in the news cast light on a variety of social studies topics: political developments in different parts of the world, conflicts and conflict resolutions at both local and national levels, rallies or speeches expressing ideas on controversial social issues, festivals celebrating a particular cultural heritage, environmental problems or breakthroughs, and so on. Showing how current happenings and controversies relate to students' studies in history, geography, civics, and other social studies disciplines keeps social studies instruction on the cutting edge of new ideas and events. It also piques students' interest and more deeply involves them in this important part of their education.

Here are specific ways in which study of topics of public concern can benefit students:

- Issues related to a given student's ethnic or cultural heritage, country of origin, or religious background help the student make a personal connection to social studies.
- Such studies reinforce concepts and concept clusters (such as economic concepts, due process of law, and particular social institutions) introduced in other contexts.
- Meaningful bridges can be built between life in the classroom and life outside it.
- Thinking and study skills can be engaged to analyze issues of real urgency.
- Attitudes and values develop as students appraise the actions and decisions of policy makers and political leaders.
- Appreciation of other places, peoples, and ways of life can grow as students become engaged in a broad range of issues and events.
- Students can interrelate the past, present, and future by linking current events to past developments and by making projections about the future.

Topics of public concern focus on two kinds of relationships: those between humans (such as gender studies and multicultural education) and those between humans and the environment (such as energy and conservation studies). These topics can be interwoven with all social studies programs, both those that are interdisciplinary (drawing on the social sciences) and multidisciplinary (combining the social studies and the humanities). Building on the discussion of global change and classroom diversity in Chapter 3, this chapter will give you many ideas for incorporating current affairs, controversial issues, and special events into your social studies curriculum. The end result of these studies could be deeply significant: a healthier planet, a more peaceful global society, equality among peoples and between genders, and respect for and interest in the law. If students make these concerns their own, social studies education will have succeeded admirably.

Guidelines and Goals

To incorporate issues of public concern into your social studies curriculum, you should first consider the goals of your curriculum as well as the overall goals of social studies education. How can public concerns enhance and enliven instruction? Although you may wish to devote a whole unit to such issues, they are more typically dovetailed into other units and become the focus of certain lessons. For example, multicultural issues can be integrated into units on community, state, or nation. Peace education could be taken up in units on communities around the world, our country, or other lands.

Base your instruction on solid conceptual foundations. Identify key concepts, concept clusters, themes, and generalizations to serve as tools of study, as a structure for organizing information, and as a way to generate focusing questions. A foundation of concepts will also help you determine which vocabulary words to discuss, which main ideas to teach, and which resources (books, videos, and so on) to employ.

As we cover several topics of public concern in this chapter, we will give you sample goals and objectives, focusing questions, and activity ideas to help you create instruction that shows how relevant social studies is to the challenges of contemporary life.

Pitfalls to Avoid

Remember that current affairs, controversial issues, and special events can be integrated into other parts of the school curriculum. For example, a newsworthy development concerning the environment may be incorporated into a science lesson rather than a social studies lesson. A celebration of the Chinese New Year might be featured in an art lesson. You don't need to "do it all" in social studies.

Avoid slanting historical data to favor a particular group, exaggerating to point up the problems that a group has faced or the progress that has been achieved in a given area, or using scare tactics or preachy exhortation to influence students' thinking. Instead, make critical thinking the touchstone of such studies. Make sure to reflect on different viewpoints in controversial issues; do not extol one viewpoint as the only right one. It requires a good deal of balance to help students delve into the dynamics that make people come to different conclusions and support different decisions while also encouraging students to develop their own well-thought-out convictions and opinions.

Also, keep focusing on concepts, concept clusters, and generalizations as a way to organize information. Without such a framework, these studies can devolve into a loose gathering of facts or truisms about a particular issue, event, or group of people. For example, studying the Chinese presence in San Francisco is contextualized and enriched by including the concepts of culture and immigration, the concept cluster of social interaction (including the concepts of cooperation, conflict, and accommodation), and the generalization "San Francisco's culture has been enriched by the achievements of the Chinese and other groups of immigrants." A list of stray facts contributes less to the student's progress in social studies understanding.

Over the course of a year, make sure to take a broad-based approach to addressing issues of public concern. Dip into a variety of such topics: the environment, cultural groups in the United States and in other countries, the political issues of the day, and questions of social justice. And within each broad area, vary your focus. For example, in environmental issues, don't focus only on conservation and neglect other issues such as pollution. Aim for a rich cross-section of topics and the issues within each one.

Finally, avoid the temptation to present issues that are too complex to approach in the elementary and middle school grades. The technical aspects of nuclear waste disposal and details of the diplomatic relationship between North Korea and China can wait for high school or college! Consider your students' ages, backgrounds, and maturity as you select topics of public concern to introduce in class.

■ Multicultural Education

In the broadest sense, the aim of multicultural education is to include multiethnic and ethnic heritage studies in a comparative culture context. Such studies highlight differences while accentuating similarities among individuals and groups. In a classroom, the goal of multicultural education is to recognize differences while building cohesiveness among students. At local, national, and global levels it is aimed at studying cultural groups within the totality of the human experience. In all such studies, high priority is given to developing an appreciation of one's own and other cultures and to eradicating racism, classism, sexism, ethnocentrism, prejudice, and discrimination. Value systems, lifestyles, cultural heritages, and current conditions are examined. Students develop answers to these questions: *Who am I? Who are they? What is special about each individual? Who are we?* As they discover answers, they learn about their root culture, the cultures of others, and the common culture all of us share.

■ Education is a kind of continuing dialogue, and a dialogue that assumes different points of view.
—Robert M. Hutchins

Over the years, multicultural education has been integrated into the K–12 curriculum. Banks and McGee (1995) and others have observed the implementation of multicultural principles in K–12 social studies instruction and have categorized efforts as follows: (1) the contributions approach—discrete pieces of information are added to existing curriculum (e.g., ethnic holidays, heroes/heroines), (2) the additive approach—concepts, concept clusters, and generalizations chronicling the experiences of minority and racial groups are integrated into the existing curriculum, (3) the transformation approach—the structure of the curriculum is modified to include racial and minority perspectives on issues, problems, and challenges, and (4) the social action approach—the curriculum includes examining the social, moral, and ethical issues and problems important to students as well as taking action on them. According to many multiculturalists, most K–12 program initiatives in multicultural education are at levels 1 and 2. Ideally, in the K–8 curriculum, students should be offered a form of multicultural education that allows them to move from level 1 to level 3.

Sample Goals, Objectives, and Focuses

The following goals show the breadth of multicultural studies. Each goal is followed by an example of a related instructional objective that illustrates a desired student attainment.

Goal: To develop understanding of cultural diversity in our society, of diversity within and among societal groups, of ethnic heritage as a factor in lifestyle, and of the history, culture, and achievements of ethnic groups

Objective: Describe gaps between the professed ideals of our society and current realities for Hispanics; list three ways the gaps can be closed.

Goal: To apply thinking and decision-making processes to societal issues through such activities as interpreting events from various perspectives and evaluating proposals and actions

Objective: Evaluate proposals for eliminating racism, prejudice, and discrimination by ranking them in order according to your judgment of their effectiveness.

Goal: To develop skills needed for communicating with both majority and minority groups, for resolving conflicts, and for taking action to improve current conditions

Objective: Describe the steps of a procedure that may be used to clarify a problem in our school and make a plan to resolve it.

The following is a sampling of concepts, concept clusters, themes, and generalizations that can be highlighted in lessons focused on multicultural issues.

Concepts

culture	ethnicity	discrimination	stereotype
prejudice	pluralism	assimilation	social protest

Concept Clusters

Social interaction: cooperation, competition, conflict, assimilation, accommodation

Democratic values: justice, equality, liberty, concern for others, use of intelligence to solve problems, respect for human dignity

Americans: African, Cuban, Chinese, Japanese, Jewish, Puerto Rican, and so on

Themes

cultural and ethnic pluralism	unity and diversity in our society
social protest and action	discrimination against societal groups

Generalizations

American culture has been enriched by the achievements of members of many different cultures.

Civil rights guaranteed by the Constitution must be extended to all groups in our society.

To guide the study of multicultural issues, develop focusing questions that use the inquiry–conceptual model discussed in Part I. Tie social studies concepts to particular thinking skills to help students focus on the issue at hand. Here are sample questions.

Focusing Questions

- Why might certain ethnic groups resist assimilation? (thinking skill: inferring)
- Why might some groups form ethnic enclaves in cities? (thinking skill: hypothesizing)
- How can we organize and present our findings on the achievements of the ethnic, racial, and cultural groups that we have studied? (thinking skill: synthesizing)

Here are several activities that you may use to involve and challenge students.

 *Learning about Multicultural Issues*

➤ As a class, have students organize and present a multiethnic fair. Encourage groups of students to make scrapbooks, drawings, murals, or multimedia reports related to their study of ethnic heritage. They also might find audio recordings of music to play at the fair and ethnic foods to share. Schedule a date for the fair, and invite parents and other classes in the school to attend.

➤ To gather specific information about each ethnic or cultural group that your class will study, ask students to create a database. Working individually or in groups, they can fill out fact sheets like this one. As a class activity, ask students to point out the differences and similarities that characterize selected groups.

Fact Sheet on Jewish Americans

Countries they left: _____

When they left: _____

Why they left: _____

Problems on arrival: _____

Ways of adapting: _____

Work they did at first: _____

How they helped each other: _____

Their status in society today: _____

Examples of achievements: _____

_____

➤ View a video about a particular ethnic, racial, or cultural group (for example, a selection from Hispanics of Achievement Video Collection). Follow the video with a discussion, focusing on questions such as these:

What dreams did these people have?
What problems did they encounter?
How did they solve the problems?
To what extent did their dreams come true?
What still needs to be done to make their dreams come true?
What is life like for these people right now?

➤ To encourage students to think about their own values, attitudes, and actions, have them complete statements such as these:

When I hear name calling, I_____.

When I have been caught name calling, I _____.

When someone prejudges other people, I _____.

When I am told that I have prejudged others, I_____.

➤ You can involve students in a creative writing activity that draws on their knowledge of a particular multicultural issue. Here are some topic ideas.

Write a diary entry as if you were someone who has just become an American citizen. Give details about what you think and feel about this experience.

Write a letter to a friend, telling about the discrimination you have faced in getting a job. Give details about what happened to you.

Write a diary entry as if you were someone who has just fled to the United States to gain political or religious freedom. Tell about your thoughts and feelings about your new country and the one you left behind.

➤ Encourage students to find and write to a pen pal from a different culture. You might use one of the resources given in Table 4.1 to find suitable contacts. Students might like to write by "snail mail" or by e-mail.

■ **TABLE 4.1**

Pen Pal Organizations

International Friendship League
P.O. Box n.111
Catania, Italy

Student Letter Exchange
211 Broadway, Suite 201
Lynbrook, NY 11563

World Pen Pals
P.O. Box 337
Saugerties, NY 12477

Pen pal organizations have decreased in the past decade. One reason is the popularity of e-mail and the Internet. E-mail allows teachers and students to establish instant communication with social studies classrooms near and far. On the Internet, you will find organizations and individual teachers from around the globe seeking specialized pen pals (e.g., students with exceptionalities, those wishing to learn a foreign language) and requests for pen pals that are not related to education. One source we recommend is World Wise Schools sponsored by the Peace Corps, http://www.peacecorps.gov. While we encourage you to surf the Internet, use your professional judgment when helping students seek pen pals.

Resources in
Multicultural Education

Americans All, a national nonprofit education program, offers *The peopling of America: A timeline of events that helped shape our nation,* two volumes of facts on the contributions of various societal groups to the American experience. Write to Americans All, 5760 Sunnyside Avenue, Beltsville, MD 20705 for further information.

Bainbridge, J. M., Pantaleo, S., & Ellis, M. (1999). Multicultural picture books: Perspectives from Canada. *The Social Studies, 90,* 183–189.

Banks, J. A., and Banks, C. A. M. (Eds.). (1995). *Handbook of research on multicultural education.* New York: Macmillan.

Boyle-Baise, M. (1996). Multicultural social studies: Ideology and practice. *The Social Studies, 87,* 81–87.

Denton, K. L., & Muir, S. P. (1994). Making every picture count: Ethnicity in primary grade textbook photographs. *Social Education, 58,* 156–58.

Dublin, T. (1997). Drawing on the personal: "Roots" papers in the teaching of American History. *The Social Studies, 88,* 61–64.

Earthmaker's lodge, a resource book of Native America histories, folklore, activities, and food, is available through Cobblestone Publishing, Inc., 7 School Street, Peterborough, NH 03458.

Fuller, C., & Stone, M. E. (1998). Teaching social studies to diverse learners. *The Social Studies, 89,* 154–157.

GPN, a service agency of the University of Nebraska–Lincoln, offers a catalog of educational media on issues including cultural awareness, African American studies, Asian American studies, and ESL. To inquire about a catalog write to GPN, P.O. Box 80999, Lincoln, NE 68501-0669.

Heath, I. A. (1996). The social studies video project: A holistic approach for teaching linguistically and culturally diverse students. *The Social Studies, 87,* 106–113.

Lacks, C. (1992). Sharing a world of difference. *Social Studies and the Young Learner, 4,* 6–8.

McCallum, A. L. (1996). Making a difference: Integrating social problems and social action in the social studies curriculum. *The Social Studies, 87,* 203–209.

Pang, V. O., & Evans, R. W. (1995). Caring for Asian Pacific American students in the social studies classroom. *Social Studies and The Young Learner, 7,* 11–14.

Sesow, F. W., Van Cleaf, D., & Chadwick, B. (1992). Investigating classroom cultures. *Social Studies and the Young Learner, 4,* 3–5.

Simon, K., Clarke-Ekong, S., & Ashmore, P. (1999). Effects of a hands-on multicultural education program: A model for student learning. *The Social Studies, 90,* 225–229.

The Stanford Program for International and Cross-Cultural Education offers *SPICE,* a catalog filled with information for multicultural and global education. Write to the Institute for International Studies, Littlefield Center, Room 14C, Stanford University, Stanford, CA 94305-5013.

White, J. J. (1998). Helping students deal with cultural differences. *The Social Studies, 89,* 107–111.

Wraga, W. G. (1999). Organizing and developing issue-centered social studies curricula: Profiting from our predecessors. *The Social Studies, 90,* 209–217.

Zephyr Press offers elementary and middle school teachers a catalog filled with curricular materials on multicultural education. Write to Zephyr Press, 3316 N. Chapel Ave., Tucson, AZ 85716-1416.

■ Gender Equality

The long and continuing struggle for social, economic, and political equality for women merits attention in all areas of the curriculum. Although significant progress has been made in this area, at the start of the twenty-first century, sexism and gender-role stereotyping remain in all realms of human activity, including the arts, law, education, medicine, industry, government, sports, family life, and politics. The advance toward gender equality needs to be accelerated so that the democratic ideals of equality, justice, and freedom will become a reality for everyone.

Studies concerning gender equality fit well within the social studies curriculum. To provide different lenses through which students may view this issue, you might discuss long-held traditions and perceptions regarding gender in the United States, roles that men and women tend to play in different cultures, and the history of social movements aimed at gaining suffrage and equal rights for women. Introduce students to some of the women and men who have combated sexism, as well as the women who blazed a trail in professions and organizations that had barred their participation; such biographical studies could include people from a variety of backgrounds—ethnic, racial, religious, and so on. As you design instruction involving gender issues, strive for balance—neither overstating nor understating the challenges that still exist or the progress that has been made.

Sample Goals, Objectives, and Focuses

These goals and objectives will give you an idea of how instruction in gender issues might be planned.

Goal: To develop an understanding of how tradition influences views of the roles of males and females and the differences between views based on biological characteristics and views based on cultural beliefs

Objective: Describe how traditions have limited the participation of women in the world of work, and give two examples of recent changes.

Goal: To develop skills in detecting gender stereotypes, bias, and inequalities in daily activities, current affairs, and various media

Objective: List three biased statements (or stereotypes) found in reading materials or observed on TV, and rewrite them to eliminate the bias.

■ Look to the National Organization for Women **http://now. org** to identify current issues.

Goal: To develop positive attitudes and an appreciation of freedom of choice as a basic right of both sexes

Objective: Describe two examples of how freedom to choose has opened new fields of work for both men and women.

You may use the following concepts, concept clusters, themes, and generalizations as you plan instruction—or you may wish to use others.

Concepts

discrimination   sexist language   equality of opportunity
gender roles   reform movements   nontraditional roles

Concept Clusters

Gender bias: males in active roles, women in passive roles; high status ascribed to males, low status ascribed to females; narrower interests assigned to females; less attention paid to females; use of masculine pronoun (*he, him, his*) to refer to people in general

Freedom to choose: lifestyle, career, hobby, recreation, other activities

Themes

women's suffrage movement
struggle for equal rights

Generalizations

Women of all walks of life have contributed to the growth and development of the United States.

Men and women should work together to ensure gender equality.

Instruction about gender issues can be provided at all grade levels. In the early grades, students may focus on the roles of girls and boys, women and men, in the family, neighborhood, and community. In later grades, the emphasis could shift to these issues as played out on the level of a state, a geographic region, our country, or other countries. Consider biographical, historical, analytical, and descriptive ap-

What gender concepts should be incorporated in K–3 social studies instruction? 4–6? 7–8? What themes and generalizations should be incorporated at all levels?

proaches as you prepare instruction. You might prepare focusing questions such as the following to guide study.

Focusing Questions

- In general, what goals have been basic in reform movements led by women? (thinking skill: generalizing)
- What stereotypes and sexist language can you find in this reading assignment? (thinking skill: analyzing)
- What changes in the roles of boys and girls in the home are likely to occur in the future? (thinking skill: predicting)
- Which of the books we have read is most objective in its treatment of girls and boys? Why do you think so? (thinking skill: evaluating)

You may wish to use some of the following activities as you discuss gender issues in the social studies classroom.

ACTIVITY IDEAS ▶ *Learning about Gender Equality*

➤ Have students find and share news reports on advances and setbacks in gender equality in the United States. They may gather newspaper and magazine clippings, download news items from the Internet, or watch and take notes from videos or TV news programs. They may want to look for news items on these topics:

court decisions
state and federal laws
appointment of women to leadership positions
important awards won by women
political demonstrations or speeches on gender issues
activities of the National Organization of Women (NOW)

➤ Individually or in small groups, have students find the dates on which each U.S. state granted women the right to vote. You might provide a map worksheet on which they can write the dates.

➤ Challenge students to gather examples of gender bias, gender stereotyping, and sexist language. They may review textbooks, television advertisements, storybooks, photographs and other visual art, news reports, and so on. Then, as a class, discuss how selected examples might be changed to reflect a viewpoint of gender equality.

➤ Create a learning center that focuses on the achievements of women. You might include materials such as *The Encyclopedia of Women's History in America, American Women Activities, Speeches of Famous Women* (video), *Women's Activities Poster Set, Equality: A History of the Women's Movement in America* (video), *American Women of Achievement Video Library,* and other resources for reading, listening, and viewing.

➤ As a class, create a database on women who have made significant contributions to the United States. Include a wide variety of women: leaders of political and social movements, leaders or groundbreakers in various professions, writers, artists, and so on. Students may place information on cards like this one.

> **Harriet Tubman, 1821–1913**
>
> Harriet Tubman escaped from slavery in 1849. She became known as "the Moses of her people." She risked her life as a conductor on the Underground Railroad, a network of people who took slaves to freedom. There was a reward of $40,000 for her capture, but she was never caught. She worked for the Union Army during the Civil War. She later started a school for old and needy blacks. The city of Auburn, New York, put up a bronze tablet to honor her.

➤ Suggest a research project in which students find out how World War II affected the roles of women in the United States. Individual students might research topics such as the roles of women in various occupations (not just limited to Rosie the Riveter), how women participated in the armed forces (for example, as aviators), how advertising portrayed women during this period, and the long-term effects of this social transformation.

➤ Focus on nontraditional roles for women. Invite women from the community to class to discuss work in fields formerly dominated by men; you might find a radio disc jockey, a trial lawyer, an electrician, a surgeon, or a police officer. In advance, students might prepare questions to ask the speakers about the special challenges of being a woman in their field, how they navigated their career paths, who inspired them, and so on.

➤ As they study American history, have students create a time line showing important achievements of American women. They can add to the time line as they learn about more women. Make sure to include women from various groups: Native Americans, African Americans, Japanese Americans, and so on.

Resources in the Study of Gender Equality

Biklen, S. K. (1995). *School work: Gender and the cultural construction of teaching.* New York: Teachers College Press.

Hauser, M. E., & Hauser, J. C. (1994). Women and empowerment: Part I. (pull-out section). *Social Studies and the Young Learner, 7,* 1–4.

Janeway, E. (1973). *Women: Their changing roles.* Salem, NH: Ayer Publishing, 1989. Reprints of *New York Times* items, 1880s–1970s.

Opdycke, S. (2000). The Routledge historical atlas of women in America. New York: Routledge Press.

Schur, J. B. (1995). Students as social science researchers: Gender issues in the classroom. *Social Education, 59,* 144–48.

Seager, J. (1197). *The state of women in the World Atlas.* New York: Penguin Press.

Shelly, A. C., & Wilen, W. W. (1988). Sex Equity and Critical Thinking. *Social Education, 52,* 168–72.

Sommers, M. (1994). Women and empowerment: Part II. (pull-out section). *Social Studies and the Young Learner, 7,* 5–7.

Stilt, B. A., et al. (1988). *Building gender fairness in schools.* Carbondale, IL: Southern Illinois University Press.

Styer, S. (1988). Sex equity: A moral development approach. *Social Education, 52,* 173–74.

Theme: Women's Studies. (1988). *The History and Social Science Teacher, 25,* 5–28. Special section.

Wilkins, M. E., & Freeman, M. E. (1997). *The shoulders of Atlas: Rediscovered fiction by American women.* Salem, NH: Ayer Co. Publishers.

Women's history curriculum guide. National Women's History Project, P.O. Box 3716, Santa Rosa, CA 95402. Revised annually; activities, materials for students, references.

■ Law-Related Education

Educators have recognized that a basic understanding of law is essential to civic competence and personal welfare, and this recognition has led to a rapid growth in law-related studies in the school curriculum. Other factors have influenced this development. Ongoing concern about juvenile delinquency, justice for all people, the rights of the individual, improvement in the operation of the legal system, and the obligation of all citizens to obey the law is reflected in this emphasis in education.

Law-related studies focus on knowledge needed for effective citizenship, an understanding of Constitutional guarantees as well as rights and responsibilities, procedures to follow when legal help is needed, and holding authorities accountable. In the early grades, students learn about the rules and procedures that help people work,

What are the rights and responsibilities of a citizen of the Unites States? How does law-related education promote citizen rights and responsibilities?

play, and live together at home, in school, and in the community. In later grades, the focus can be broadened to include contemporary and historical events as they relate to concepts such as justice, due process, and civil rights. It is natural to emphasize issues that are especially relevant to students as they enter adolescence, such as rules and regulations related to health, safety, recreation, and property.

This part of the curriculum will continue to evolve to address issues of concern as they arise in society. No doubt the isolated but highly publicized incidents of school violence in the late 1900s will influence law-related studies in the years to come.

Sample Goals, Objectives, and Focuses

Goal: To develop understanding of concepts such as justice, equal protection, authority, responsibility, due process, property, civil liberties, and privacy

Objective: State the meaning of property rights, and describe ways to protect property rights in school.

Goal: To develop understanding and appreciation of the Constitution as the basis of our legal system and the roles and responsibilities of representatives within our legal system

Objective: List civil liberties guaranteed by the Constitution, and give an example of how each one is important in our daily lives.

Goal: To develop thinking processes and decision-making ability through activities that call for analyzing and evaluating legal issues and procedures

Objective: Evaluate procedures for settling a dispute by stating whether all parties had a fair hearing, whether wrongs or injuries were corrected, and whether a fair decision was made.

Goal: To increase students' sense of the law's efficacy and reduce feelings of indifference and alienation related to laws and legal processes

Objective: Describe at least three procedures that an individual or a group can use to challenge the misuse of authority.

The following are examples of concepts, concept clusters, themes, and generalizations drawn from political science and jurisprudence; you might focus on these or others in social studies instruction.

Concepts

authority	responsibility	laws	privacy
due process	rights	property	legal system

Concept Clusters

Rights: of minors, citizens; to public trial, bail, privacy, property, vote; due process, equal protection, protection from unreasonable search and seizure

Freedoms: religion, speech, press, assembly, petition

Themes

the need for rules and laws

the resolution of conflicts

individual rights and responsibilities

extension of civil liberties

Generalizations

The Constitution serves as the basis of our legal system.

Individuals must exercise their rights and assume responsibilities to make our legal system work.

You might use questions like these to begin studies of law-related issues.

Focusing Questions

- How is the concept of fairness defined in this case study? (thinking skill: interpreting)
- How can we show on a chart the freedoms guaranteed by the Bill of Rights? (thinking skill: synthesizing)
- Which of the housing regulations suggested in this reading will best serve members of minority groups? Why? (thinking skill: evaluating)

You might use or adapt some of the following activities as you develop instruction about law.

ACTIVITY IDEAS ➤ *Learning about the Law*

➤ To involve students in a discussion about authority, show the class pictures of people who have certain types of authority, such as parents, teachers, police officers, and judges. Raise these questions about each picture.

What authority does this person have? Why is it needed?

What do we expect this person to do? Why is that important?

What might happen to a person who does not respect this person's authority? Is that consequence fair? Why or why not?

➤ Have students make a study of rules. You might begin by having the school principal visit class to discuss current rules at school, how rules have changed over time, and what happens when rules are violated. Then, as a class, have students fill out a chart about rules on certain topics. As they learn more rules, they can add them.

Topic	Rules	Penalties
Riding the bus		
Dogs		
Trespassing		

➤ To help students understand the various functions of the law, you might have them gather law-related news reports from print media and the Internet. Then discuss how these reports illustrate the functions. You might provide a list like this one to use during the discussion.

Some Functions of the Law
1. To reflect what people value
2. To set standards of behavior and penalties for infractions
3. To define procedures for settling disputes
4. To define and set limits on authority
5. To provide a means of achieving justice
6. To evolve in response to new conditions

➤ Give students the opportunity to learn about part of the court system by inviting a speaker to class to talk about juvenile court. You might choose a judge, an attorney, or a police officer. Students might prepare a list of questions to ask your guest, such as the following:

What is juvenile court? What is its purpose?
Who is in charge of juvenile court?
How does it operate?
What rights do minors have?
What legal assistance is available to minors?
What current issues are being debated about minors and the law?

Resources for Law-Related Studies

American Bar Association, Division for Public Education, 514 N Fairbanks Court, Chicago, IL 60611.

Bennett, L. (1996). The universal rights of the child. (pull-out section). *Social Studies and the Young Learner, 8,* 1–4.

Bryant, C. J. (1999). Build a sense of community among young students with student-centered activities. *The Social Studies, 90,* 110–113.

Center for Civic Education, 5146 Douglas Fir Road, Calabasas, CA 91302. Units on Authority, Justice, Privacy, Responsibility; booklet *We the People* on the Constitution.

Center for Human Rights and Constitutional Law, 256 S. Occidental Blvd., Los Angeles, CA 90057.

Constitutional Rights Foundation, 601 South Kingsley Drive, Los Angeles, CA 90005.

Harvey, K. D. (1996). Teaching about human rights and American Indians. *Social Studies and the Young Learner, 8,* 6–9.

Jennings, T. E., Crowell, S. M., & Ferlund, P. F. (1994). Social justice in the elementary classroom. *Social Studies and the Young Learner, 7,* 4–6.

Lapid, L. (1995). From the Hobbesian floor to the Kantian ceiling: UN intervention as a practical–idealist challenge. *The Social Studies, 86,* 101–104.

Lewis, C. (1998). The need for a center for public integrity. *The Social Studies, 89,* 196–198.

Peters, M. M., & Bjorklun, E. C. (1996). Torts and tales. (pull-out section). *Social Studies and the Young Learner, 8,* 5–8.

Solovitch-Haynes, S. (1996). Street smart second-graders navigate the political process. *Social Studies and the Young Learner, 8,* 4–5.

Wade, R. C. (1995). Developing active citizens: Community service learning in social studies teacher education. *The Social Studies, 86,* 122–128.

■ Global Studies

In Chapter 3 we provided a rationale for infusing a global perspective into social studies programs. This section presents practical guidelines for doing so.

A perfect time to introduce global studies is in the early grades, when students learn about families, schools, and communities. Studies of families, schools, and communities in other lands is a natural fit and a fascinating topic for students. In the later grades, discussion of relationships between the United States and other countries easily emerges in the study of history. Concepts such as cultural borrowing, interdependence among countries and regions, and the evolving global system of human interaction can surface in studies of the environment, geography, economics, lifestyles, and history.

As students explore diversity on a global scale, they can employ analytical thinking skills to ask *what, where, when, among whom, how,* and *why* differences exist. They can explore cause-and-effect relationships to discover how the actions of one group or nation can affect others. They can celebrate the richness of diversity while at the same time learning about ways in which problems can be resolved when differences lead to conflict.

Sample Goals, Objectives, and Focuses

Goal: To develop understanding of human interconnections in a global system marked by cultural diversity, change, conflict, search for peace, and networks of communication and transportation

Objective: Describe common human needs and concerns in one's own culture and in others and explain why ways of meeting needs differ.

Goal: To apply thinking and decision-making skills by exploring the impact on other people of personal decisions regarding the use of resources, lifestyle, and other matters

Objective: Describe how decisions about lifestyle, use of resources, or ways to resolve conflicts may affect others here and in other places.

Goal: To develop attitudes and behavior that reflect respect for cultural diversity, appreciation of differences, understanding of why differences exist, and interest in exerting influence through appropriate activities

Objective: Make a list of things one might do to help curb pollution and to influence others to do the same.

You might use the following concepts, concept clusters, themes, and generalizations as you design instruction in global studies.

Concepts

peace	global village	urbanization
communication	global system	interdependence

Concept Clusters

Interdependence: among families, communities, states, nations; improving the environment; transportation and communication; maintaining peace

Change: scientific, technological, social, economic, political, environmental

Themes

cultural similarities and differences	resolution of conflicts
increasing interdependence of people	movement of peoples

Generalizations

International networks of transportation and communication link communities and countries around the world.

All countries have a responsibility to cooperate in solving environmental, energy, economic, political, and other problems.

You might use these questions to focus on social studies concepts and to spark critical thinking.

■ Global Youth Network **http://youthwhocare. com** is an organization run by young people who strive to increase awareness of global challenges.

Focusing Questions

■ How are families in Japan like ours? How are they different? (thinking skill: comparing)

■ How can we bring together our findings on communication systems that link communities around the world? (thinking skill: synthesizing)

■ What hypothesis can we make about relationships between developing and industrial countries based on data in the computer programs about *India* and *Latin America?* (thinking skill: hypothesizing)

The following activity ideas can be used to incorporate global studies into your social studies curriculum.

 *Learning about Global Connections*

➤ Use visuals to engage students in the study of various peoples around the world. Divide students into small groups, and assign to each a particular societal group in a particular country (not including the United States). Have students gather pictures that show how the assigned group meets the needs for food, shelter, clothing, and security that exist among all peoples. Let them display their pictures on charts, with captions.

➤ In pairs, have children make "we books." In the booklet each pair should describe in pictures and in words what makes the two of them alike and different. Humor and creativity are welcome!

➤ Students might research the place of origin of many foods that we now take for granted; they might show their findings on a world map. Similarly, you might ask students to find the country of origin of various inventions, games, and furnishings that are common today.

➤ In small groups, have students research the origins, purposes, and ongoing work of several international agencies. You might include the United Nations, UNESCO, UNICEF, the World Health Organization, CARE, the YWCA, the YMCA, and the Red Cross.

➤ As part of their global studies, have students reflect on efforts toward world peace. You might have each student complete a worksheet like this one.

What is the meaning of the word *peace?* _____

_____

What makes world peace so difficult to achieve? _____

_____

What are sound bases on which peace can be built? _____

_____

What has the United States done to promote peace? _____

_____

What have other nations done to promote peace? _____

_____

➤ As a creative activity, have the class plan and make a mural or collage to highlight the ways in which immigrants have contributed to American life. They might depict immigrants from a variety of backgrounds and their inventions and achievements in art, music, medicine, sports, and politics.

Resources for Global Studies

Ad Hoc Committee on Global Education. (1987). Global education: In bounds or out? *Social Education, 51,* 24–49.

Bagley, D. (1993). Using vacations to increase the global awareness of students. *Social Studies and the Young Learner, 5,* 18–20 + .

Branson, M. S., & Torney-Purta, J. (Eds.). (1982). *International human rights and the schools* (Bulletin 68). Washington, DC: National Council for the Social Studies.

Dufour, J., & Sears, J. F. (Eds.). (1994). *Social Education, 58,* special issue on the fiftieth anniversary of the United Nations.

Fleming, D. B. (1991). Social studies and global education. *The Social Studies, 82,* 11–15.

Lickteig, M. J., & Danielson, K. E. (1995). Use children's books to link the cultures of the world. *The Social Studies, 86,* 69–73.

Nickell, P., & Kennedy, M. (1987). *Global perspectives through children's games.* How to Do It, Series 5, No. 3. Washington, DC: National Council for the Social Studies.

Pesce, L., Faughnan, K., & Kurtzberg, R. L. (1996). Addressing society's problems in a global studies class. *The Social Studies, 87,* 60–63.

Reardon, B. A. (Ed.). (1998). *Educating for global responsibility.* New York: Teachers College Press.

Reardon, B. A. (1988). *Comprehensive peace education.* New York: Teachers College Press.

Schlene, V. J. (1992). Teaching global studies in elementary school: An ERIC/ChESS sample. *Social Studies and the Young Learner, 4,* 19–20.

Sherman, H. (1993). An international store to integrate global awareness, math, and social studies. *Social Studies and the Young Learner, 6,* 17–18.

Titus, C. (1994). Civic education for global understanding. *ERIC Digest,* Bloomington, IN: Clearinghouse for Social Studies/Social Science Education.

Tye, K. E. (Ed.). (1990). *Global education.* Alexandria, VA: Association for Supervision and Curriculum Development. Guidelines and illustrative practices.

Wade, R. C. (1994). Conceptual change in elementary social studies: A case study of fourth graders understanding human rights. *Theory and Research in Social Education, 22,* 74–95.

■ Environmental and Energy Studies

Concern for the conservation and improvement of the environment is an important value to foster among students, and there are ample opportunities to do this in the social studies classroom. You might focus attention on the history of conservation and environmental movements in our country over the past century: early efforts by Theodore Roosevelt and Gifford Pinchot to expand public lands; developments in conservation and management of natural resources in the 1930s; and the ongoing effort, which began in the 1970s, to reduce air and water pollution, conserve energy, and restore damaged areas in the environment. You can also highlight developments in the news, on the regional, national, or international levels, to engage students in up-to-the-minute reporting of environmental issues.

The following topics might play a part in your instruction on environmental and energy issues

public lands	global warming
wilderness preservation	the ozone layer
endangered species	fuel consumption
protection of rain forests	nuclear and toxic wastes
protection of wetlands	energy conservation
oil spills	offshore oil drilling
acid rain	alternative sources of energy

In the early grades, you might introduce children to conservation by discussing conserving resources and energy at home, at school, and in the community. They might also learn basic information about pollution problems, endangered species,

How important are environmental and energy studies in social studies? What contemporary themes would you include in your social studies program?

and human practices that threaten the environment. These issues may be examined in greater detail in the upper grades. To make environmental and energy studies come alive, you might get students involved in a community project to better the local environment.

Sample Goals, Objectives, and Focuses

These goals and objectives illustrate those you might develop as you plan instruction.

Goal: To develop awareness of environmental problems and conditions, causes and consequences of deterioration, corrective measures currently under way and needed in the future, and action that should be taken

Objective: Describe three environmental problems in our community and the steps that are being taken to solve them.

Goal: To take part in decision-making processes by analyzing problems, taking and defending a position on issues, and evaluating proposals

Objective: Evaluate energy-saving projects developed by two or more nations working together; describe their effectiveness and the reasons why these nations joined forces.

Goal: To promote attitudes, values, and appreciations related to quality of life and a commitment to improve the human and physical environment

Objective: Demonstrate a commitment to conservation by carrying out a plan to reduce waste pollution at home and in school.

Think about incorporating the following concepts, concept clusters, themes, and generalizations into environmental and energy studies. You may also use others.

Concepts

environment	pollution	ecosystem
resources	greenhouse effect	biodegradable

Concept Clusters

Conservation: human, water, soil, crop and grazing lands, wetlands, rain forests, public lands, recreational areas; wise use, restricted use, substitution, recycling

Quality of life: personal, social; physical, mental, emotional; rural, suburban, urban, inner city, state, regional, national, global

■ A problem is a chance for you to do your best.
—**Duke Ellington**

Themes

interaction and interdependence	variety and pattern
adaptation and survival	continuity and change

Generalizations

Critical current problems are overpopulation, food supply, energy use, pollution, and preservation of endangered species, rain forests, and wetlands.

Industrialized nations, in cooperation with others, must devise programs that will restore and maintain the environment.

The following questions can help you guide study of these issues.

Focusing Questions

■ In general, what does the evidence show about progress in forest conservation in our country? (thinking skill: generalizing)

■ What are the main causes and effects of acid rain? (thinking skill: analyzing)

■ What do you think will be the main environmental or energy problem in the year 2050? (thinking skill: predicting)

The following activities will engage students in issues related to the environment and energy conservation.

 ACTIVITY IDEAS ▶ *Learning about Environmental and Energy Issues*

➤ To learn about the variety of natural resources, have small groups of students list examples of natural resources available in our country and those we get from other countries. After generating these lists, the students can identify which resources are renewable, nonrenewable, and inexhaustible.

➤ Assign students to research conservationists who made a significant contribution to preserving the environment; they might choose Rachel Carson, John Muir, Theodore Roosevelt, or others. They might create oral, written, or multimedia reports to share with their classmates.

➤ Using physical and land-use maps of a given region, have students locate concentrations of various natural resources, such as forests, mineral deposits, and bodies of water. Then have them research how these resources are being used and conserved, noting any potential problems for the environment.

➤ Take a field trip to introduce students to efforts in your area to preserve and improve the environment. You might visit a water treatment plant, a soil conservation project, or a farm that avoids use of pesticides. Schedule time for a professional to explain to students the processes used at that site to improve quality of life and protect the environment.

➤ In small groups, have students investigate different types of pollution. After each group has gathered information, they can report to the class on the sources of a given type of pollution, its effects on the environment, and how to prevent it. Then the class might work together to complete a chart like this one.

Types	Pollutants	Effects	Prevention
Air			
Water			
Soil			
Food			
Solid wastes			
Toxic wastes			
Aesthetic			
Noise			
Acid rain			

➤ Focusing on what is available in your area, make a study of national or state parks. Students can research when and why these areas were set aside as public lands, what they contribute to quality of life, and how they help preserve wildlife, watersheds, ecosystems, soil, coastline, wilderness, and timber supply. You might write to the National Forest Service to obtain maps and other materials. If possible, plan a class visit to one of the parks.

▶ For practice in interpreting graphs, provide a worksheet with a graph and series of questions. You might use the one presented here, or develop your own on other topics in environmental and energy studies. After students complete the worksheet, they can discuss their results as a class.

Major Sources of Pollution

What is the main source of air pollution?

What is the second main source?

What percentage do other sources contribute?

What main idea can be stated about sources?

What sources are not shown?

How can we find out about them?

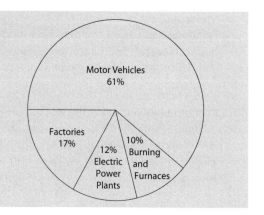

Motor Vehicles 61%

Factories 17%

12% Electric Power Plants

10% Burning and Furnaces

Resources for Environmental and Energy Studies

Allen, M. G., & Stevens, R. L. (1996). People and their environment: Searching for the historical record. *Social Studies, 87,* 156–160.

Brown, R. G. (1998). Outdoor learning centers: realistic social studies experiences for K–6 students. *Social Studies, 89,* 199–204.

Center for Renewable Energy and Sustainable Technology (CREST), 1612 K. St. NW, Suite 202, Washington, DC 20006.

Conservation Directory. National Wildlife Federation, 9825 Leesburg Pike, Vienna, VA 22184-0002.

Environmental Defense Fund, 257 Park Avenue South, New York, NY 10010.

Environmental Support Center, 4420 Connecticut Ave. NW, Suite 2, Washington, DC 20008-2301.

EnviroWatch, Inc., P.O. Box 89-3062, Mililani, HI 96789.

ERIC Clearinghouse for Science, Mathematics, and Environmental Education, Ohio State University, 1929 Kenny Road, Columbus, OH 43210-1080.

International Wildlife Coalition, 70 Falmouth Highway, East Falmouth, MA 02536.

International Wildlife Education & Conservation, 237 Hill St., Santa Monica, CA 90405.

Love Canal: A chronology of events that shaped a movement. Center for Health, Environment and Justice, P.O. Box 6806, Falls Church, VA 22040-6806.

National Audubon Society, 700 Broadway, New York, NY 10003.

North American Association for Environmental Education, 1825 Connecticut Ave. NW, Suite 800, Washington, DC 20009-5708.

Renew America, 1200 18th St., NW, Suite 1100, Washington, DC 20036.

Resources for the Future, 1616 P. St. NW, Washington, DC 20036.

Sunal, C. S., & Sunal, D. W. (1999). Nuclear reactions: Studying peaceful applications in middle and secondary schools. *Social Studies, 90,* 164–170.

U.S. Environmental Protection Agency, Ariel Rios Building, 1200 Pennsylvania Ave., Washington, DC 20460.

World Resources Institute, 10 G. St. NE, Suite 800, Washington, DC 20002.

Worldwatch Institute, 1776 Massachusetts Ave. NW, Washington, DC 20036-1904.

World Wildlife Fund, 1250 24th St. NW, P.O. Box 97180, Washington, DC 20037.

■ Current Affairs and Controversial Issues

Guidelines and Goals

Just like the issues of public concern already discussed in this chapter, the study of current affairs and controversial issues should be tied into social studies in a way that reflects the definition, purposes, and stated goals of the program in your school. Social studies concepts, themes, and generalizations should inform the study of these issues as well. This will keep a particular current event or controversial issue from commandeering the curriculum—conflict in Kosovo, peace talks in the Middle East, drought in the local community, or a hot political debate should be dealt with in the context of broader goals and purposes in social studies.

That said, it is also important to treat these topics with some seriousness, not glossing over them superficially. The timeliness of these events and issues gives students a chance to "think on their feet"—to use a variety of thinking skills to analyze, interpret, and suggest solutions or predict outcomes. You might follow these steps as you prepare instruction about a current event or controversial issue:

1. Think of an engaging way to introduce the topic.
2. Find out enough about the topic to give students a historical perspective.
3. Identify concepts and concept clusters in the social sciences that relate to the topic.
4. Consider students' interests, strengths, and weaknesses.
5. Consider how the topic fits into your school's goals in social studies instruction.
6. Decide whether to examine the topic separately or to integrate it into other parts of the program.
7. Develop specific goals, objectives, and lesson plans.

Current Affairs

The scope of current affairs encompasses events of local, state, national, and international importance. Examples include the construction of a new road between towns, the election of a state official, a disastrous storm in a different part of the country, the appointment of a new justice of the Supreme Court, the end of a civil war on a different continent, and the development of new technology to speed global communication. Studying current affairs lets students listen in as history is being made—and sometimes to participate in it as well. Learning about an earthquake may motivate students to organize a shipment of care packages to agencies helping the survivors. Finding out about a bill before the state assembly may motivate students to write letters encouraging elected officials to vote for or against the measure.

The great wealth of material on current affairs makes it no simple task to choose what to include in instruction. Though you may sometimes plan to focus on what is offered in students' weekly newspapers, you should largely base your choices on criteria such as the following:

> *Educational value:* How will a given event or issue contribute to the overall social studies program and the goals of social studies education? Will students gain knowledge of significant value? What will studying the topic contribute to them in terms of mastery of social studies concepts, skill development, and values education?
>
> *Appropriateness:* Do students have the level of maturity to deal with this topic? Do feelings and conditions in the wider community make this an appropriate topic to study?
>
> *Relevance:* Does the topic connect to students' prior knowledge? to topics that they will study in the future? Does the topic fit in with basic units of study? Will students be able to relate to it?
>
> *Available information:* Can I find helpful background information to introduce the topic? Are suitable teaching materials available?
>
> *Available time:* Is there enough time for students to develop a meaningful depth of understanding about this topic?
>
> *Reliability:* Can I be sure that the information I have is accurate? Can facts be differentiated from opinion? If the information contains bias, can it be readily be detected and analyzed by students?
>
> *Timeliness:* Is the information up-to-date? Does it reflect current trends?

Approaches to the Study of Current Affairs

Each approach to the study of current affairs described here has certain strengths and weaknesses. Many teachers use a combination of approaches, depending on the objectives to be achieved, the significance of the events involved, time available, the units under study, and the materials available.

Relating Current Affairs to Basic Units

In general, the teacher should relate current affairs to basic units of instruction; then the problem of obtaining background material and giving perspective becomes less difficult. In regional units, such as our state, midwestern United States, and regions of South America, current events can be selected to highlight recent developments in the places being studied. In historical units, such as early times in our state and colonial life, current events can be selected to contrast then and now.

The greatest problem in relating current affairs to units of instruction concerns timing. As one teacher put it, "Significant events occur either before or after I teach a unit." Many teachers address this problem by using current events to launch units and, when possible, by timing the introduction of certain units to coincide with events such as sessions of the state legislature and of Congress. They relate current events to past units and continue certain strands, such as transportation, communication, and conservation, from unit to unit. They assure their classes of a good supply of current materials by continually asking students about current affairs that interest them and reflecting on ways of incorporating them into social studies instruction.

Weekly Study of Periodicals

Many teachers allot one period each week to the study of students' periodicals. It is convenient and relatively easy to assign readings, carry on discussions, and have students complete activities and tests included in each issue. But there are limitations to this approach. It may lead to routine reading and answering of questions, superficial learning caused by covering too many topics, and failure to relate current events to basic topics and units. The suggestions presented below should help teachers to avoid these limitations.

1. Skim the newspaper first to get a general idea of the contents.
2. Review pictures, maps, charts, tables, and graphs.
3. Read assigned articles.
4. Note articles on which background material is given.
5. Note articles on which background material is needed.
6. Look up the meaning of any words you do not understand.
7. Look for facts, opinions, and differing points of view.
8. Be ready to raise questions and make comments during discussion.
9. Check your understanding by completing the tests.

You may want to assign reading from a variety of student news publications and national newspapers and magazines. Publications such as the following may be available in your library:

Children's Express	*The New York Times*	*U.S. News & World Report*
Current Events	*Scholastic News*	*Vocal Point*
Junior Scholastic	*Time*	*Weekly Reader*
Newsweek		

Student Reports on Current Affairs

It can be fun and educational to give students opportunities to report the news. In the early grades, students may give spoken news reports on topics such as their parents' work, trips they have taken, community activities they have participated in, changes in seasons, responsibilities that they have at home, or creative projects that they have completed. These reports may be given during the daily sharing period. In the middle school, you might organize students into committees who report regularly on news developments in areas such as the environment, technology, and government. Such reporting might be done on a weekly basis or at other assigned times.

Potential weaknesses in this approach include reporting of trivial events, superficial study of current events, isolation from basic units of study or prior knowledge, and a tendency for the discussion to wander. These weaknesses may be overcome by keeping the discussion on track and by clearly stating the criteria for selecting news items to report. The criteria can be simple and straightforward, such as the following:

- Is it important?
- Do I understand it?
- Can I explain the main ideas?
- Is it interesting?
- Is it related to our unit?
- Can I relate it to other topics or events?

Teachers should be prepared to tactfully redirect the discussion when students bring up inappropriate topics. In the early grades, students may report on family matters unsuitable to class discussion; older students may raise issues that are beyond the class's level of maturity to address. These topics should be acknowledged, but the teacher should make an unobtrusive shift to other subjects. Sometimes it is wise to suggest that the student discuss a particular topic later, with the teacher.

Short Current Affairs Units

Current affairs of special significance cannot always be dealt with during daily or weekly reports, nor can they always be incorporated in units of work. An important community or state event or problem, a major election, a nation's significant role in international affairs, individual's internationally prominent achievement—any of these may require an intensive short unit. Sometimes special units featured in students' weekly periodicals need a more extended period of study. By noting related materials and suggestions contained in the teacher's edition of the weekly newspaper and by collecting pamphlets, books, videos, and other resources, a teacher can achieve important objectives by introducing special units.

Whichever approach or combination of approaches is used, every effort should be made to have students attain three levels of thinking and understanding: The *first level* is the routine reporting of events. Each child has seen, read, or heard about an event and shares it with the group with little discussion or analysis. At the *second level* the reporting is followed by discussion of the most interesting points. This level requires more thinking and may stimulate interest. Usually it does not uncover basic concepts, trends, and relationships; it does not encourage any critical analysis. At the *third level* students use problem-solving and critical thinking skills to explore the significance of the event or issue. They review supporting facts, consider differing points of view, and collect additional information. To be sure, this third level cannot and should not be applied to all current affairs. When truly significant events are selected for study, however, students can usually be guided from the first to the third level, thus increasing the value of the experience.

Whatever approaches you use to incorporate the study of current affairs into social studies, you may find the following activities helpful to strengthen learning and increase students' interest.

 *Learning about Current Affairs*

➤ Vary the ways in which students deliver news reports. They might present individual reports, group reports, panel discussions, dramatizations, cartoons, exhibits, webpage news items, or annotated maps.

➤ Have students deepen their knowledge of a current event by interviewing a local expert. Find out whether local colleges or professional associations can provide contacts.

➤ Provide students with a list of questions to help them evaluate the soundness of the information they read in news reports. Here is an example.

> Is the information up-to-date? How do you know? _____
>
> Who reported the information? _____
>
> How can the facts be checked? _____
>
> What opinions are given? How are they supported? _____

➤ Make a "Who's Who in the News" bulletin board. Have groups of students take turns posting news items, photographs, and clippings about current people in the news whose actions or achievements relate to the social studies unit currently being studied.

➤ Conduct mock television or radio newscasts. Students can take roles such as anchorperson, on-the-scene reporter, editorial commentator, weather reporter, and sports reporter. If possible, use audiotape or videotape equipment to record the newscasts. Have students set criteria for the news items they will present.

➤ With students, analyze proof or evidence used to substantiate news reports. You might focus on the use of statistics, eyewitness accounts, personal experience, expert opinion, legal precedent, research findings, appeals to common sense, or references to published works.

➤ Use students' weekly newspapers to provide practice in the skills of skimming, scanning, and using an index to locate information.

Controversial Issues

According to recent surveys, students, particularly those in the middle grades, rank social studies low among their favorite subjects in the curriculum. Many would argue that students find textbook content boring and irrelevant to their lives. Today some social studies educators are advocating the use of controversial issues as a viable approach to social studies instruction. They believe that social studies will gain in appeal if teachers follow a well-known educational principle: make use of student interests.

Some believe, however, that elementary school children lack the background to study controversial issues. They mean that children are unable to study critical issues currently being debated by adults and achieve adult levels of understanding. Certainly, many current issues are beyond a child's understanding; but controversial issues do come up in social studies, and experienced teachers wisely select some of them to study. Some issues must be approached as unanswered questions; the spectrum of possible answers should be studied in a thoughtful manner. Some may be handled briefly, others may simply be introduced as continuing problems that will be reviewed in the future, and still others may be studied in detail.

In the early grades, attention is generally given to issues and problems close to the lives of children—issues and problems that come up in school, in the neighborhood, and in the community. Examples include differences of opinion on ways of carrying out classroom activities, how to conserve resources, ways of using parks and playgrounds, fair play in the treatment of others, the contributions of others, and conflicts between individuals and groups. At times, the teacher may include issues raised by students—perhaps a labor dispute, a demonstration, housing problems, or ways of preventing discrimination. Problems growing out of community living should not be ignored, nor should they be handled in a way that is beyond the ability of students to understand. A simple answer, an explanation of the problem, a clarification of the issue, or a brief discussion may suffice. The important thing is to keep the way open for such questions, to discuss them on an appropriate level, and to begin to lay a foundation for ongoing study of issues.

In the elementary and middle grades, more involved issues and problems are encountered as students undertake units such as our state, the United States, Mexico, Canada, countries of Latin America, the Middle East, Russia, Africa, or growth of democracy. Current events periodicals raise issues that may be related to basic units of study. Students may be exposed to other issues through the Internet, television and radio programs, newspapers, and discussion at home.

The board of education often sets policy governing the study of controversial issues and problems. The following statement is typical of the policies established in many school systems:

1. Only significant issues and problems understandable to children, and on which children should begin to have an opinion, should be selected for study in elementary and middle schools.

2. Instructional materials must present differing points of view, discussion should include all points of view, and respect for the views of others should be shown.

3. Teachers must guide learning so as to promote critical thinking and open-mindedness, and they must refrain from taking sides or propagandizing one point of view.

4. Special attention must be given to background factors, possible consequences of various proposals, the need for additional information, and the detection of fallacies of thinking, logic, and argumentation.

5. The importance of keeping an open mind—that is, the willingness to change one's mind in the light of new information—should be stressed.

When teachers are unsure whether an issue should be examined in the classroom, they can consult with the school principal or department chair. Experienced teachers provide depth and breadth to a controversial issue by integrating it into a unit of study. Many activity ideas in the previous section can be adapted for instruction on controversial issues.

Resources for Studying Current Affairs and Controversial Issues

Brabham, E. G. Holocaust education: Legislation, practices, and literature for middle-school students. *The Social Studies, 88,* 139–142.

Evans, R. W., Avery, P. G., & Pederson, P. V. (1999). Taboo topics: Cultural restraint on teaching social issues. *The Social Studies, 90,* 218–224.

Heitzman, W. R. (1986). *The newspaper in the classroom* (2nd ed.). Washington, DC: National Education Association.

Kirman, J. M. (1993). Using satire to study current events. *Social Education, 57,* 139–41.

Lockwood, A. L. (1996). Controversial issues: The teacher's crucial role. *Social Education, 60,* 28–31.

McBee, R. H. (1996). Can controversial issues be taught in the early grades? The answer is yes. *Social Education, 60,* 38–41.

McGeown, C. (1995). The King Edward Debating Society adds current events to elementary and middle-school social studies. *The Social Studies, 86,* 183–186.

National Council for the Social Studies. Guidelines for teaching science-related social issues. *Social Education, 47* (April 1983), 258–61; Including the study about religions in the social studies curriculum: A position statement and guidelines. *Social Education, 47* (May 1985), 413–14; Science, technology, society and the social studies. *Social Education, 54* (April/May 1990), 189–214. Position statement and strategies.

Onosko, J. J. (1996). Exploring the issues with students despite the barriers. *Social Education, 60,* 22–27.

Passe, J. (1998). Developing current events awareness in children. *Social Education, 52,* 531–33. Approaches and strategies.

Rossi, J. A. (1996). Creating strategies and conditions for civil discourse about controversial issues. *Social Education, 60,* 15–21.

Soley, M. (1996). If it's controversial, why teach it? *Social Education, 60,* 9–14.

■ Special Events

Special events—holidays, special weeks, and commemorations—are a vital part of every cultural heritage. They have been set aside as a time for celebration and the expression of treasured values, ideals, and beliefs. Many call attention to significant events, institutions, documents, men and women, and customs. The study of special legal holidays can contribute to the development of patriotic attitudes and deeper appreciations of citizenship. International understanding is increased as students learn about the significance of Pan-American Day, United Nations Day, and special days in other countries under study.

Although celebrations of religious holidays are a primary responsibility of families and religious institutions, learning about them may extend students' understanding and respect for cultural diversity. Care should be taken to respect differences in beliefs, activities, and modes of celebration. Sensitivity also must be shown to the feelings and views of those who do not participate in religious holidays. The right of all individuals and groups to religious freedom must be respected.

Special events are only as "special" as teachers make them. When teachers develop the year-long social studies program, they should consider the time to be spent on events, depth of coverage, whether to study them in isolation or integrate them into social studies units. Teachers should reflect on their students and consider selecting dates reflecting that diversity. This information can be found by visiting the school or neighborhood library and by inquiring about the local community and diversity in the school. Scouting out important dates for cultural and ethnic groups in your area may give your students a chance to appreciate holidays such as those listed here, which many Americans aren't even familiar with.

Chinese Moon Festival	Madonna Del Lume (Italy)
Finnish Independence Day	Irish Festival Week
Republic Day (India)	Russian Easter (Orthodox Easter)
St. Patrick's Day (Ireland)	Cinco de Mayo
Polish Constitution Day	Norwegian Constitution Day
Saint Lucia's Day (Sweden)	Asian-Pacific Heritage Week
Mexican Independence Day	Oktoberfest (Germany)
Greek Independence Day	

Some schools post a calendar of special days, ethnic holidays, weeks, and months so that teachers can plan ahead and consider ways to celebrate them. You may use the calendar given in Table 4.2. Remember to fit in state and local requirements. Although they are not cited on this calendar, it may be worthwhile to note special days on religious calendars, such as Christmas, Rosh Hashanah, and Ramadan. Some days and weeks are not set; check resources such as *Instructor* magazine, *Social Studies and the Young Learner,* and *Diversity Fair Notebook* (published by the American Library Association) for updates.

Because many special days and weeks are given attention in each grade, make sure that students develop deeper appreciations and understandings as they progress through the grades.

Special Events in the Primary Grades

At this level, you can introduce customs, traditions, ceremonies, rituals, the special meaning of terms, and the significance of selected special days and weeks. Match activities and materials to the children's maturity and background. Begin with storytelling, simple art activities, and participation in classroom and school activities; you may then progress to reading stories, reporting and sharing ideas, and more advanced activities.

■ **TABLE 4.2**

Special Days, Weeks, and Months

September

Labor Day (first Monday)

Grandparents' Day
(second Sunday)

Citizenship Day (Sept. 17)

Native American Day
(fourth Friday)

Constitution Week

Hispanic Heritage Week

October

Fire Prevention Day (Oct. 9)

Columbus Day
(second Monday)

United Nations Day (Oct. 24)

Halloween (Oct. 31)

Social Studies Week

November

Veterans Day (Nov. 11)

Thanksgiving
(fourth Thursday)

American Education Week

Children's Book Week

December

Human Rights Day (Dec. 10)

Bill of Rights Day (Dec. 15)

January

New Year's Day (Jan. 1)

Martin Luther King Jr.'s
Birthday (Jan. 15)

Franklin D. Roosevelt's
Birthday; March of Dimes
(Jan. 30)

February

Abraham Lincoln's Birthday
(Feb. 12)

Valentine's Day (Feb. 14)

Susan B. Anthony's Birthday
(Feb. 15)

George Washington's Birthday
(Feb. 22)

W. E. B. DuBois's Birthday
(Feb. 23)

Black History Month

March

Luther Burbank's Birthday
(Mar. 7)

Arbor Day

Conservation Week

Women's History Month

Red Cross Month

April

Pan-American Day (Apr. 14)

Earth Day

National Youth Week

Library Week

May

May Day (May 1)

International Goodwill Day
(May 18)

Law Day

National Teacher Day

Mother's Day (second Sunday)

Armed Forces Day
(third Saturday)

Memorial Day (last Monday)

Teacher Appreciation Week

June

Flag Day (June 14)

Father's Day (third Sunday)

July

Independence Day (July 4)

August

National Aviation Day (July 19)

Women's Equality Day (July 26)

Nisei Week

Units of instruction in social studies provide many opportunities for deeper study of special days and weeks. The home and family unit gives background to Mother's Day and Father's Day. The contributions of many different workers, a key aspect of Labor Day, takes on greater meaning as school and community workers are studied. Many teachers use Valentine's Day to study the post office. As communities in other lands are studied, their holidays may be celebrated.

Special Events in Later Grades

Instruction in the elementary and middle grades should be planned to increase students' depth and breadth of understanding. Both the teacher and the class should search for new stories, poems, pictures, articles, and activities related to special days and weeks. After discussing what students have learned in earlier grades about a given day or week, some teachers use leading questions to guide the search for new ideas and materials: How did this special day originate? How was it celebrated in early times? What early customs have we kept for our own? How is it celebrated in other lands? What individuals worked to make it a holiday in our country? What are some famous stories and poems about this holiday?

Here are examples of specific questions geared to two holidays:

Veterans Day: When was Armistice Day first proclaimed? Why was Armistice Day changed to Veterans Day? Why is the unknown soldier honored each year at the National Cemetery in Arlington? What is meant by "preservation of fundamental principles of freedom"? What obligations should each individual assume for the peace, welfare, and security of our country?

Washington's Birthday: Where did Washington live as a boy? What was his home like? How was he educated? What are the main periods of his service to our country? What traits of leadership caused his countrymen to call on him to be the first president? Why is he honored as "the father of our country"? What is meant by "First in war and first in peace"?

Certain special days and weeks are explored in detail while the class is studying a particular unit; this may be in addition to a short observance held as a part of classroom or school activities. For example, Constitution Day, Bill of Rights Day, United Nations Day, and the contributions of Franklin, Lincoln, Washington, and other historic leaders are included in units on the United States and the growth of democracy. Pan-American Day and International Goodwill Day take on deeper significance when tied in with units such as South America and other lands. Notable men and women and special days of importance in the student's state should be included in the unit on our state. Table 4.3 shows how Arbor Day and Conservation Day may be observed from kindergarten through eighth grade. Notice which activities may fit in with units on the family, our community, living in our state, and conservation.

Short units may be needed to give background on a certain special day or week. Students need such information to understand fire prevention, American Education Week, United Nations Day, and Red Cross Week. It is certainly worthwhile to devote time to learning about the purposes and activities of organizations and agencies that render services of benefit to both children and adults. Other short units may be developed on men, women, or days of special importance in the community or state. Students can gain much from individual study and preparation of reports on these topics. Figures 4.1 and 4.2 (page 134) show excerpts from such reports written by fifth-grade students.

■ **TABLE 4.3**

Activities for Arbor Day and Conservation Week

Kindergarten–Grade 2

- Take a nature walk in the neighborhood.
- Read and hear stories and poems about trees.
- Write original poems and stories.
- See videos on forest animals.
- Draw pictures of trees, flowers, and animals.
- Take a study trip to see a house under construction.
- Make picture books and scrapbooks.
- Participate in a tree-planting ceremony.

Grades 3–4

- Learn about the commercial, recreational, and decorative values of trees.
- Learn about the importance of trees in the conservation of water, soil, and animal life.
- Learn about our state's watersheds and water supply.
- Learn about new uses of wood in construction, industry, and hobbies.
- Use the Internet to learn more on logging, reforestation, and water resources.
- Make charts or a mural to summarize basic concepts.

Grades 5–8

- Invite conservation experts to discuss questions and problems raised by the class and to report on newer practices.
- Learn about the consequences of poor conservation practices in ancient civilizations in China and the Middle East.
- Read and report on contributions to the conservation movement made by individuals such as Gifford Pinchot and Rachel Carson.
- Study and make maps of forest areas and state and national parks.
- Create poems, pageants, and programs that highlight conservation needs, problems, and forward-looking practices.
- Plan and carry out a tree-planting ceremony.
- Develop a video on Arbor Day and Conservation Week.

Some teachers take time before the school year ends to consider special days that occur during summer vacation. For example, Independence Day and the events leading up to it can be studied as part of units on the United States. Students can be asked to watch for special reports and activities as celebrations take place during the summer. National Aviation Day, August 19, should not be overlooked as an opportunity for students to collect clippings and other materials for use in transportation and aviation units when school starts in the fall. Similarly, Labor Day celebrations and activities in early September are sources of experience and information that can be put to use at the beginning of the school year.

The following activity ideas can add interest to studies of special days, weeks, and months.

■ **FIGURE 4.1**

Student Report

Harvest Festivals before the Pilgrims Had Their First Thanksgiving

The oldest known harvest festival, Succoth, was in Israel. The people gave thanks for finding a place to live and for the harvest.

In ancient Greece there was a celebration that lasted nine days. It was in honor of the goddess of the harvest, called Demeter. Demeter was also the goddess of corn.

The festival of the harvest moon was held in old China long ago. The Chinese would bake moon cakes. They also thought that a rabbit lived in the moon.

Some of our early settlers had learned about harvest festivals in England. The English would have feasts and share what had been raised. People in the villages would get together, and each family would bring something.

The peasants in Old Russia had feasts and dancing. One custom was to place a wreath of grain by the house. A new one was put there each year. They thought it would help make a good harvest.

■ **FIGURE 4.2**

Student Report

What Susan B. Anthony Did

Susan B. Anthony worked hard to get the right for women to vote. She also wanted equal rights for women in other things. She was a teacher once and only got paid $10 a month while men teachers were getting $40 a month. She said that this was not fair. She also said that women should choose their own jobs and take care of their own property. She also said that they should be able to go to college just the same as men.

I didn't know that women never used to have all these rights. It is a good thing that Susan B. Anthony came along. My mother says that some women take these rights for granted. They should remember what Susan B. Anthony did. I am going to remember her birthday on February 15.

 **ACTIVITY IDEAS** ➤ *Celebrating Special Events*

➤ As a class, make an international calendar of patriotic holidays in different countries. Investigate the history behind these holidays and how they are celebrated. Discuss how they are different from and similar to U.S. patriotic holidays.

➤ Involve students in planning ways to observe Women's History Month. Have them brainstorm ideas for studies and activities to do individually and as a class. They might focus on the following topics:

women leaders in our city or state
women who led reform movements
women in politics and government
women in the arts
women of various ethnic groups
important events in U.S. women's history

➤ To celebrate a holiday focused on a historical event or person, ask a local expert to speak to the class on the topic. Have students prepare questions beforehand to ask the expert. If possible, visit a special museum exhibit or historic site related to the topic.

➤ Find ways for students to learn about different festivals and pageants celebrated around the world. You may find videos or websites that give a sense of the color and atmosphere of these events. Even better, research local opportunities to partake in festivities—sponsored by museums, cities, or cultural organizations—that highlight a particular cultural heritage, such as the Mexican Día de los Muertos, the Caribbean Carnival, or the Chinese New Year. Your school might also host such a celebration, bringing together several classes.

➤ Ask individual students to research and report on particular holidays. Encourage them to include poems, folktales, or recorded music related to the holiday. They can share their reports in small groups or with the whole class.

➤ Decorate the classroom to reflect the holiday you are celebrating. Put background information and fun facts about the holiday on the bulletin board. You might have students make hats, masks, or puppets if they are a traditional part of the celebration. Put on a recording of traditional music, and share foods typical of the holiday.

Resources for Special Events

Accent on Current Events, St. Patrick's Press, Box 5189, Columbus, GA 31906.

Berger, M. A. (1994). Social studies now! What makes a community click. *Instructor, 104,* 45–46.

Gitelman, H. F. (1997). Sharing Hanukkah with young students. *The Social Studies, 88,* 39–41.

Harris, J. J. (1988). *Celebrate Thanksgiving.* New York: Media Books.

Kellman, J. L., & Kellman, N. L. (1986). *Birthday bonanza.* Glenview, IL: Scott, Foresman. Seventy birthdays of notable people.

■ Conclusion

This chapter provided you with a pool of ideas and practical suggestions to help you connect with your students and create an exciting K–8 social studies program. Topics of public concern, current affairs, controversial issues, and special events present a wealth of information to enrich a social studies program with local, national, and global perspectives. These topics can make social studies vital and interesting to a diverse student population.

 Questions, Activities, and Evaluation

1. Several of your students are interested in gauging the progress of women in the arts and sciences in the latter half of the twentieth century. Identify the steps you might suggest to the students to help them organize their "mini unit" and the sources of information they might use. Encourage the students to present their findings to the class.

2. Middle school students are concerned about a small river near the school that appears to be strewn with debris. Articles on the problem have appeared in the local newspaper, and citizens living near the river have complained to city officials. How should these students express their concern? How might you connect this problem with social studies instruction?

3. A local African American has been knocked unconscious by a group of ruffians, tied to the back bumper of a automobile, and dragged to his death. Is this event worthy of study? Does it fall within the area of social studies? Would you incorporate the event into your social studies instruction? How would you present the event to the students?

4. Recent national events have led to a proliferation of school rules aimed at protecting students and ensuring that schools remain safe environments. Develop a "mini unit" in which students examine their school rules and offer suggestions to school officials on how to create a safe school environment.

5. Two students, recent arrivals from Kosovo, have joined your classroom. List ways of incorporating events in the former Yugoslavia into your social studies program and helping these two students become a part of your classroom. Share your ideas with the class.

6. Select a current event from a local newspaper, using the criteria suggested in this chapter. Note social studies objectives that might be achieved by focusing on it, and make a plan for using the event, including a selection of learning activities from this chapter.

7. Select a holiday or some other special event and make a plan for teaching it, including objectives and learning activities. Use resources listed in this chapter.

8. Review several periodicals for students and identify articles, maps, charts, test items, and other material that you might use in a unit of instruction. Prepare an assignment for students similar to this example: "Look at the map of the former Soviet Union on page 5 of your weekly news magazine. How many Soviet republics are shown? Which republic is largest in area? In which republic is Moscow? Which republics have voted to withdraw from the Soviet Union, according to the text below the map? Why?"

9. Make a calendar of special days and weeks that are celebrated in your community. Indicate the grades in which certain days and weeks might be emphasized.

10. Complete the following to indicate your point of view. Discuss your views with a colleague and explore reasons for any differences.
    a. The main contribution of current affairs study to achievement of social studies objectives is _____.
    b. The best approach to the study of current affairs is _____.
    c. The main criterion for selecting controversial issues for children should be _____.
    d. A teacher's position on the study of religious holidays should be _____ _____.
    e. The main criterion for choosing from the ever-increasing number of special days and weeks should be _____.
    f. When students ask the teacher to state what side should be taken on an issue, the teacher should _____.

Chapter 5

Preparing Plans for Instruction

Chapter Objective

To describe planning guidelines and present formats and examples of plans for teaching

Focusing Questions

- What approaches to planning may be used?
- Why are instructional (teacher and student) objectives, authentic assessment, and portfolio options major elements of the planning process?
- How does block scheduling influence planning?
- What are the main features of plans for lessons, modules, and units?
- What formats are used for lessons, modules, and units?
- What procedures are helpful in planning units?
- What introductory, developmental, and concluding activities may be included in plans?
- How can teaching and learning activities be sequenced to elevate thinking to higher cognitive levels?
- Where can sample units and other plans be obtained?

Planning Instruction: The Big Picture

In the next few pages we describe different approaches to planning for instruction. You will learn that well-thought-out planning leads to effective teaching (i.e., teacher success in the classroom), and good planning occurs when teachers are in command of the planning process. While student teaching, you will do planning with your co-operating teacher, but when you begin your career you will plan independently. However, as you may have realized during your field experiences, there is a growing trend at the K–6 level for cooperative planning at each grade level and across the grades; and, in the middle grades, this trend is equally pronounced as more and more teachers adopt block scheduling. Teachers also turn to curriculum specialists, principals, department chairs, and state department educators for assistance. The key to planning, whether you plan independently or cooperatively, is remaining at the center of the planning process.

By now, you are familiar with the history of social studies; definitions and purposes for social studies, concept and concept clusters in the social sciences; and local, national, and global perspectives on the twenty-first century. In short, you possess general knowledge of students in K–8 schools and a pool of social studies information and process knowledge to help you engage students in social studies learning. And, as you may have guessed, this is the information teachers reflect on when planning for instruction.

There are a variety of ways of planning. Some teachers begin with evaluation and work their way back; others begin with activities; still others begin by reflecting on standards in social studies or the social sciences or a definition of social studies. All approaches are fine, and teachers adhere to the approach followed by the school in which they teach. For example, if you begin your teaching career in a state like Kentucky, heavily involved in educational reform (which also means teacher education), state agencies will influence what approach you use when planning for instruction.

Many teachers initiate the planning process by establishing an overview of work for the year or term. Long-range planning is followed by unit and lesson planning. Teachers also employ the documents described in Part I of this book: district and school courses of study (brief or somewhat detailed explanations of specific courses) and curriculum guides.

Student records, teacher's edition textbooks, school study guides and units, school catalogs of materials available (e.g., videos, CD-ROMs, posters, textbooks, literature), and commercial catalogs are useful sources of information during planning. Study and unit guides include examples of activities, evaluation techniques, technology, and student projects.

The planning guidelines and formats in this chapter provide a framework for placing strategies described in the following chapters (e.g., providing for individual differences, group learning activities, thinking skills) in useful and practical teaching plans. You may select those that best mirror your approach to social studies as you make planning a major part of your professional life.

■ Approaches to Planning

■ It is a bad plan that admits to no modification.
—**Publilius Syrus**

The *textbook-based* approach includes a review of the adopted textbook and the related teacher's guide to note objectives and introductory, developmental, and evaluation activities. Many guides suggest supplementary materials and activities to enrich and individualize learning.

A *topic, problem,* or *thematic* approach begins with the selection of a unit from the course of study, textbook, or current affair. Objectives, learning activities and materials, and evaluation techniques are noted. Content, thinking, language, and other skills; related art and music, and other elements may be integrated.

Teacher-guided group planning is the least formal approach. Tentative objectives, available materials, possible learning activities, individual and group work, and evaluation techniques are identified. A plan is made to guide students in a series of inquiry or problem-solving activities that will involve them in planning, implementing, and evaluating the unit of study. This approach may be incorporated into others or used with small groups and individuals to involve students more completely in the learning process.

In many middle schools, 40–50 minute periods have given way to block scheduling (70–90 minute periods), giving teachers greater flexibility in planning. With this schedule, teams of teachers plan multiple activities (e.g., large group instruction, small group discussion, library work) that allow students to experience subject areas in an integrated fashion at a realistic pace that reflects their needs.

Planning and teaching in block scheduling will include making plans to cover an extended period of time, working with a team of teachers, and planning interdisciplinary lessons. Adjusting to a 70–90 minute period of time can be challenging. It is best to view that big chunk of time as a series of time increments (see Figure 5.1). Teachers can plan a series of minilessons over the course of that block of time.

■ FIGURE 5.1

Block Scheduling Worksheet

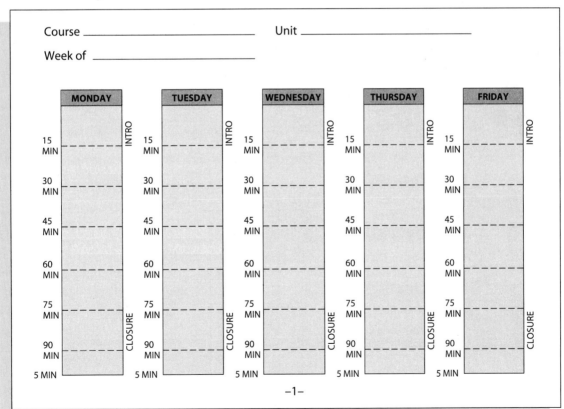

Source: Gary Kunce, Wasson High School, 2115 Afton Way, Colorado Springs, CO.

Figure 5.2 gives an example of such a plan. Mr. Blacknall, the business teacher, developed an interdisciplinary unit (mathematics, social studies, business) based on the following question: What would it take to bring a team from the Women's National Basketball Association to New Orleans and keep it there? In the introductory lesson, one 90-minute block, he emphasized student-directed activities; in the second lesson, he proposed the students find ways of keeping the team in New Orleans.

■ **FIGURE 5.2**

Sample Time-Management Plan for Block Scheduling

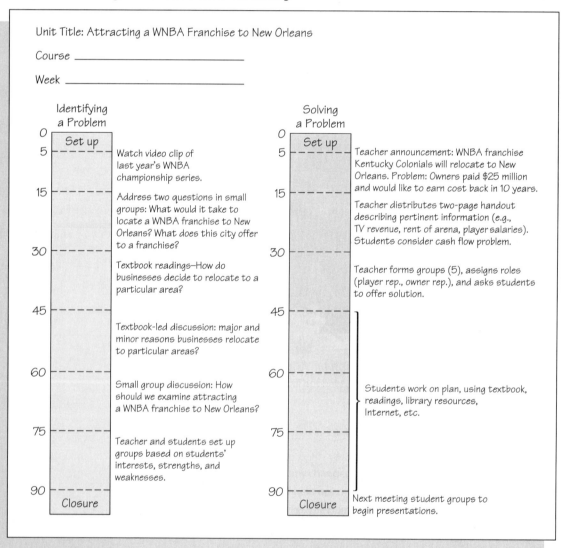

Unit Title: Attracting a WNBA Franchise to New Orleans

Course _____

Week _____

Identifying a Problem

0	Set up
5	Watch video clip of last year's WNBA championship series.
15	Address two questions in small groups: What would it take to locate a WNBA franchise to New Orleans? What does this city offer to a franchise?
30	Textbook readings—How do businesses decide to relocate to a particular area?
45	Textbook-led discussion: major and minor reasons businesses relocate to particular areas?
60	Small group discussion: How should we examine attracting a WNBA franchise to New Orleans?
75	Teacher and students set up groups based on students' interests, strengths, and weaknesses.
90	Closure

Solving a Problem

0	Set up
5	Teacher announcement: WNBA franchise Kentucky Colonials will relocate to New Orleans. Problem: Owners paid $25 million and would like to earn cost back in 10 years.
15	Teacher distributes two-page handout describing pertinent information (e.g., TV revenue, rent of arena, player salaries). Students consider cash flow problem.
30	Teacher forms groups (5), assigns roles (player rep., owner rep.), and asks students to offer solution.
45	
60	Students work on plan, using textbook, readings, library resources, Internet, etc.
75	
90	Closure Next meeting student groups to begin presentations.

You might use these suggestions as you plan lessons based on a block schedule.

1. At the beginning of each semester, use "ice breaker" activities to help students to get to know one another and you.
2. Allow students to be creative. In various settings—alone, in pairs, and in small groups—encourage them to write poems, illustrate a short story, develop a game complete with rules, or set up a science experiment for others to complete.
3. Change the physical layout of the class. Arrange desks differently, hold the class at different locations (e.g., library, gym, outside), and redecorate your classroom on a regular basis.
4. Use cooperative grouping techniques, such as jigsawing, to complete lengthy tasks and place responsibility on the students to get tasks done.
5. Plan and use guest speakers and short field trips to connect students to their community.
6. Plan activities in which students serve as teachers, and in a variety of settings, teach their peers. Probe and make use of student interests.
7. To provide breadth and depth, tie in and reinforce information being taught by other team members and in other disciplines.
8. Role-play situations to enhance understanding and teaching. Have students pick a particular incident and, alone or in a small group, develop a skit. The drama teacher would love to help!
9. Arrange for other teachers to come into your classroom and teach a minilesson. (You teach their class while they teach yours.)
10. Become friends with the school librarian and media specialist. Plan to have your students spend regular amounts of time researching and locating information and finding novel ways of presenting information.

Regardless of the planning approach you use, the following questions will assist you as you begin planning for instruction. Though not exhaustive, the questions focus on key issues that you won't want to ignore.

1. What are the most important concepts or skills to be learned as a result of this lesson?
2. What do your students already know about the concepts or skills you are going to teach?
3. How will you help the students make connections to previous learning?
4. What activities could create interest in the lesson?
5. Are there difficult words or concepts that may need clarification or additional instruction?
6. What procedures will the students need to know and follow to complete the activities?
7. What materials will be needed? Will students need to learn how to use them? How will you distribute them?
8. How will your instruction address different learning styles?

9. If activities require students to work in groups, how will the groups be formed? How will you encourage productive group work?

10. What examples and questioning strategies will you use? Prepare a list of potential examples or questions.

11. How much time will you allocate for different parts of the lesson?

12. What presentation alternatives are there if students have trouble with the skills or concepts (e.g., peer explanation, media, visuals)?

13. Will any students need extra help or more attention? How will you handle this?

14. How will you make sure all students will participate? How will you make sure that all students have an opportunity to answer?

15. What proactive classroom management strategies are needed?

16. How will you adjust the lesson if time is too short or long?

17. What will students do if they finish early?

18. How will you evaluate the students' performance and give feedback?

19. How have you fostered self-evaluation?

20. How will the skills or concepts learned be used in future lessons and learning?[1]

Lesson Plans

Many social studies teachers use search engines such as Yahoo!, Netscape, Webcrawler, and Excite to maneuver the Internet and locate resources to build units of instruction.

Lesson plans are the backbone of the daily instruction you will offer students. Their basic elements are illustrated in the two examples on pages 146 and 147. The first shows the lesson plan format that the Kentucky Department of Education encourages new teachers to follow when completing their first-year internship; it can be adapted to meet your planning needs. In this format, the last step is completed after the lesson. The other example is a sample lesson developed by a fifth-grade teacher in California.

Instructional Objectives

Instructional objectives spell out what the teacher will accomplish in a given class and what the students will learn. Teacher objectives (1) direct the instruction the teacher will deliver, (2) suggest possible student objectives, and (3) offer methods to assess student learning. The following are examples of teacher instructional objectives in the areas of knowledge, skills, and values:

> *Knowledge:* Explain how England and Spain became bitter rivals, and describe the outcome of this rivalry.

> *Knowledge:* Identify groups in the community who are responsible for maintaining a safe environment.

1. Adapted from *Field Guide for Professional Planners,* produced by the College of Education, University of Kentucky, Lexington, KY.

Why is planning an integral part of social studies instruction? What approach to planning do you favor? Is one approach more effective than another?

Skill: Demonstrate how to build a time line.

Skill: Have students practice the use of maps by tracing the routes of major eighteenth-century explorers.

Participation (value): Promote sensitivity to the feelings of others in large and small group discussions.

Appreciation (value): Build appreciation for the contributions of colonists in the building of the thirteen colonies.

Though somewhat broad, teacher objectives are specific enough to impart purpose to lessons. Most teachers combine different types of objectives (such as knowledge, skills, appreciation) as they develop lessons.

Student objectives can be general, similar to teacher objectives, or may focus on very specific behaviors. Objectives should indicate what students will learn and how they will reveal what they learn—how they will perform and what they will be able to do, say, write, make, or demonstrate. Four elements usually included are object, behavior (performance), performance level (criterion), and conditions, as shown in these examples:

Knowledge: To write [behavior] a definition of *stereotype* [object] similar to the one in the textbook [performance level], without referring to the textbook or a dictionary [conditions]

Thinking skill: Using classroom sources other than the textbook [condition], students will generalize [object] by writing [behavior] one [performance level] main idea about the role of government in a community

Study skill: To make [behavior] a map of trails westward [object], using crayons and an outline map of the United States [conditions] to show three trails in different colors [performance level]

SAMPLE LESSON PLAN FORMAT

Name: **School:**

Grade: **Number of Students/Number of Students with IEP:**

Unit/Topic: **Date and Time:**

Objectives	*Guiding Question(s):* What will students be able to answer at the end of the lesson?
	Global: State your overall goals for the lesson, for example, to improve students' ability to follow directions.
	Specific: State exactly what you expect students to accomplish during the lesson, for example, to make puppets, using directions and materials provided.
	Kentucky Learner Goals: List specific goals lesson will meet.
	National Standards: List specific standards lesson will meet.
Materials	List all materials you will use during the lesson.
Procedure	Outline the steps you will take to teach the lesson and the activities for student involvement. Include reasons for choices, directions for activities and assignments, and examples of questions and follow-up questions you will use.
Assessment Method	Describe the process you will use to assess student progress.
Modifications	Outline the steps you will take to modify the procedure and assessment for special needs students.
Follow-up Activity	Describe suggestions for subsequent activities that will extend learning based on the objectives put forth in the lesson. In other words, suggestions should be based on the progress in the activity.
Reflection/ Evaluation	Discuss student progress or achievement in relation to the stated objectives— how students demonstrated success. Include evidence to support how objectives were met with examples as appropriate (i.e., was the lesson aimed at the appropriate level of difficulty for the students; were instructions clear; were students engaged in the lesson—if not, why not; were expectations for management met—why or why not?)

LESSON PLAN   *The Inca Empire*

Major Understanding	The Inca developed a great empire and made unique adaptations to their environment.
Objectives	To describe the extent and achievements of the Inca Empire and to improve map interpretation skills by locating places and determining the distances between them.
	To develop vocabulary by defining *empire, terraces,* and *terraced land.*
	To improve picture interpretation ability by describing what is shown and stating inferences based on the picture.
Materials	Textbook and materials in the learning center.
Introduction	Write the word *Inca* on the chalkboard, and ask if anyone knows what it refers to. Print *empire* on the chalkboard, and ask if anyone knows what it means.
Development	Ask students to read pages 196–197 of their textbook to find out who the Inca were and what an empire is.
	Ask students to compare their earlier responses with what they found by reading.
	Direct students to look at the picture on page 197. Ask what it shows. (Machu Picchu) (thinking skills: interpreting, analyzing)
	Ask students how they think the Inca built a city hidden in mountains. (thinking skill: inferring)
	Ask why the Inca might have built it there and why no one lives there today. Also ask how students think the Inca traveled over such a large empire. (thinking skill: hypothesizing)
	After comments, ask students to read pages 198–199 to find out about the actual means of travel.
	Ask students how they think the Inca sent messages from one part of the empire to another. After comments, ask them to review the textbook and examine the pictures. Ask if they found other means of communication. (thinking skills: hypothesizing, analyzing, recalling)
Conclusion and Evaluation	Ask students to state a main idea that summarizes key learning about the Inca. (thinking skill: generalizing)
	Evaluate learning as students participate in discussion.
Follow-up	Ask students to find related information in the learning center. (thinking skills: interpreting, synthesizing)

Value: To state [behavior] the extent to which justice was upheld [object] in a story read by the teacher [conditions], giving one [performance level] reason for the judgment

Participation: Students will show sensitivity to feelings of others by always [performance level] making constructive comments [behavior] in group discussion [conditions]

Guidelines for Writing Objectives

When writing objectives, include only enough information to make the objective clear. Conditions need not be stated when they are obvious. It is not necessary to state "given an outline map" as part of an objective that includes "to complete an outline map." Who will attain the objective need not be specified when it is obvious that all students should, as in the objective "to show respect for others during discussion."

Keep objectives condensed and concise. For example, one may write "to describe" instead of "to be able to describe." As one teacher put it, "Why write *to be able to* over and over when we know it is implied?" When it comes to objectives, brevity often shows clarity of thinking. Keep it short! And keep in mind the following special points.

Object

State the knowledge, thinking process, skill, or value that is the intended object of instruction. This basic step makes one's intent clear, provides a focus for instruction, and indicates the desired learning outcome. For example, the intent may be able to develop concepts such as stereotype, justice, or public services; the ability to interpret or generalize; skill in reporting; or positive attitudes toward members of various ethnic groups.

Behavior

State what a student will be able to do after the objective is achieved, for example, to *explain* the meaning of stereotype, to *state* a generalization, to *write* a report, to *describe* contributions of ethnic groups. Use active verbs such as these:

point to	explain	mark	pantomime
group	tell	circle	make
sort	present	underline	draw
arrange	report	outline	construct
match	name	demonstrate	prepare
put in order	write	act out	produce
select, choose	list	show	assemble
describe	label	role play	compose
state			

To state objectives on increasing levels of cognitive complexity, use verbs such as these:

Knowledge: define, describe, name, select, state, tell, write

Comprehension: conclude, distinguish, interpret, summarize, state in own words

Application: demonstrate, act out, apply, use, infer, predict

Analysis: break into parts, distinguish features, separate into groups

Synthesis: assemble, draw, create, make, plan, produce, prepare, write

Evaluation: assess, judge, examine, apply criteria, distinguish

To state objectives on increasingly levels of value/complexity, use verbs such as these:

Receiving: answer, follow, select, reply, identify, listen, watch

Responding: answer, comply, describe, help, present, report, select

Valuing: compare, complete, explain, initiate, judge, justify, propose

Organization: adhere, defend, explain, integrate, organize, take a stand

Characterization: act, influence, propose, question, use consistently

Verbs expressing nonobservable behavior are sometimes used in statements of objectives. These verbs include *understand, know, appreciate, believe, develop insight into, enjoy,* and the like. Using such terms can create difficulties, as the following examples illustrate. The comment following each example shows how the objective can be clarified by using terms that express observable behavior.

To *understand* the basic services provided by government [How will the student reveal understanding? It is better to use *describe, state, outline,* or *name.*]

To *appreciate* the achievements of African Americans in literature, art, science, medicine, education, and sports [How will students show appreciation? It is better to use *describe, report,* or *list.*]

You may also clarify the objective by adding a phrase, as shown in these examples:

To develop appreciation of the achievements of American Indians by choosing five examples from materials in the learning center and *presenting* them to the class

To demonstrate understanding of the rights guaranteed in the First Amendment to the Constitution by *explaining* the meaning of each one

Performance Level

When the acceptable standard of performance is not obvious, state a criterion or desired level of achievement. For such an objective as "to describe achievements of Irish Americans," the standard may be "five or more," or another criterion depending on the capabilities of students and the available sources of information. Examples of other phrases include "at least eight out of ten," "according to standards in the textbook," or "similar in quality to [a map, report, or other model used as a standard]."

Conditions

Note any special conditions that should be provided and are not obvious, such as materials, equipment, or restrictions. If special materials are needed or if students may not use references to demonstrate achievement of the objective, state these conditions—for example, "given a dictionary," "using notes," "without the aid of references," or "working in groups of three."

Other Elements

Two elements may be added when detailed statements are needed for accountability programs, specification of details for a performance-based assessment program, or clear communication of details to others. These two elements are *time* of attainment and *who* (which students) will attain the objective, as shown in these examples:

> At the end of the unit [time], students studying independently [who] will state [behavior] from memory [conditions] at least five [performance level] public services provided by cities [object].

> By the end of the year [time], students reading at the fifth-grade level [who] will list [behavior] five or more [performance level] contributions of African Americans to science [object], without referring to reading materials [conditions].

Notice that all of the preceding examples focus on what students will learn, not on what the teacher will do. A mistake to be on guard against is writing statements such as the following:

> The teacher will demonstrate interviewing techniques.
> Contributions of members of minority groups will be presented.

These statements focus on the teacher, not on students. To rewrite them as objectives for students, the teacher must state what students will be able to do after instruction. The following example has been rewritten:

> After a demonstration of interviewing [condition], students will write [behavior] a plan for an interview [object] that includes an introduction and five questions [performance level].

Both open and closed objectives are used in social studies. *Open objectives* are useful to individualize instruction, provide choices, and tap students' creativity. Divergent thinking is emphasized, as shown in this example designed to elicit differing responses from students:

> To develop creative thinking by finding and describing three or more new ways to encourage community support for recycling efforts

Closed objectives are useful in making plans to develop concepts, skills, and values that all students should achieve. Convergent thinking is emphasized, as shown in this example designed to elicit similar responses from students:

> To demonstrate respect for others in group work by helping to set and by adhering to group work standards

Now that you are familiar with lesson plans and methods of writing teacher and student instructional objectives, it's time to turn to other instructional approaches leading to effective instruction. The examples listed here are but a few of the ways K–8 teachers plan for instruction.

▉ Modules

Modules are referred to as individual study guides and individualized learning packages. They are designed to direct students' learning, are complete within themselves, and may be used alone or in conjunction with units, textbooks, and other media. Modules vary in length from those that can be completed in a single class period to those that require several hours. Some are based on a single source, such as a textbook; others are based on technology; and some are designed for use with computers.

> ■ Use **http://www.netscape.com** and the phrase "K–3 (K–6 or K–8) social studies materials" to locate resources to build a unit of instruction on a topic of your choice. Keep track of the number of sites where materials are available.

Some modules are designed to develop and assess performance of a skill such as map reading. A pre-assessment and a post-assessment test may be included. Students who do well on the pre-assessment move to other activities. Other modules are similar to lesson plans in that they include objectives and other components; they are written with precise directions so that students can do them on their own.

The sample module included here is to be used as an individual study guide. Most students would be able to complete it in one or two class periods. Time should be flexible, however, so that time on task can be varied to provide for individual differences and promote mastery learning. The module may be adapted to serve as a guide to making retrieval charts, building a dictionary card file, gathering information on past or current events, compiling information for a report, and organizing data on a variety of topics. An example of how modules may be used to develop geographic skills through individualized instruction is presented in Chapter 6.

SAMPLE MODULE
Making Database Cards on Notable Americans of Diverse Backgrounds

Our multiethnic database includes information on a cross-section of Americans who make up our multiethnic society. We have added data cards as we have studied various periods and movements in the history of our country. The cards include descriptions of notable Native Americans and Irish, Jewish, Italian, German, and African Americans, but we have very few cards on Hispanic Americans. We need to add cards on the roles, achievements, and contributions of these people. Our textbook discusses several notable Hispanic Americans. The librarian has placed additional sources on a special shelf for our use. A list of people who are featured on tapes and videos is posted by the listening and viewing centers.

Objectives   To add to the multiethnic database by making cards on the roles, achievements, and contributions of Hispanic Americans

To increase appreciation for the multiethnic makeup of our society and for the contributions of ethnic groups to American culture by describing activities of notable Hispanics

Procedures   1. Select the person you wish to investigate. You may choose one you have heard about, one you locate in our textbook or in another source, or one of the following:

Rudolfo Anaya	Jaime Escalante	Ricardo Montalban
Herman Badillo	Jose Feliciano	Joseph Montoya
Joan Baez	Ernesto Galarza	Julian Nava
Ruben Blades	Henry B. Gonzalez	Tomas Rivera
Vikki Carr	Ralph Guzman	Edward R. Roybal
Lauro Cavazos	Oscar Hijuelos	Julian Samora
Cesar Chavez	Rolando Hinojosa	George I. Sanchez
Henry Cisneros	Dolores Huerta	Carlos Santana
Sandra Cisneros	Nancy Lopez	Reies L. Tijerina
Roberto Clemente	Vilma Martinez	Lee Trevino

You may look for other prominent Hispanic Americans in these books: Calihan, *Our Mexican Ancestors*; de la Garza, *Chicanos: The Story of Mexican-Americans*; Meier and Rivera, *The Chicanos: A History of Mexican-Americans*; Nesmith, *The Mexican Texans*; Newlon, *Famous Mexican-Americans*; Pinchot, *The Mexicans in America*; Samora and Simon, *A History of Mexican-American People*; Trejo, Ed., *The Chicanos: As We See Ourselves*. Also, find others reported in *Newstime*.

SAMPLE MODULE *Continued*

2. Be sure to follow the model we set up for database cards. The following example shows what to include on the front and back of each card.

(Front)
Romana Acosta Banuelos

Born in 1925 in Arizona, she was appointed treasurer of the United States in 1971. She was the 34th treasurer and the sixth consecutive woman to serve as treasurer. She was the first Mexican American woman appointed to such a high office.

When only 22 years old, she moved to Los Angeles and started a taco stand business with $400. Her business did very well and she later became head of a Mexican food company that earned about $5 million a year.

When she was 39 she started a bank in Los Angeles. This was the only bank that Mexican Americans owned and operated.

(Back)
Who Am I?

1. I was appointed treasurer of the United States in 1971.
2. I founded a bank in 1964.
3. I ran a food business that earned about $5 million a year.
4. I started a taco stand with only $400.
5. I was born in Arizona in 1925.

(Note: Write *Who Am I?* questions that give good clues to use in a guess-who card game.)

---

3. Look up the person you selected in the index of your textbook. If he or she is in it, take notes.
4. Do the same for books in the reading center, using two or more sources.
5. If you cannot find a second source, go to the library. Or see if the person you selected is portrayed on a tape or a filmstrip in the listening and viewing centers.
6. After you have taken enough notes on your subject, write a first draft of your data card. Proofread it for accuracy.
7. Bring your draft to me for approval. Then complete your card.
8. Proofread both sides of the card, and place it in the file on my desk.

■ Activity Cards and Worksheets

Similar in design but shorter in length are individual activity cards and worksheets. As with modules they contain a clear statement of objectives, directions, and materials to use. Here is an example; others are included in later chapters.

■ Units of Study

Units are designed to study a topic, problem, or theme over an extended period of time, ranging from a few days to several weeks. They may focus on a region, a case study, concepts from disciplines, a chronological sequence of events, or a main idea. Teaching units are prepared for a particular class, often as a sequence of lesson plans.

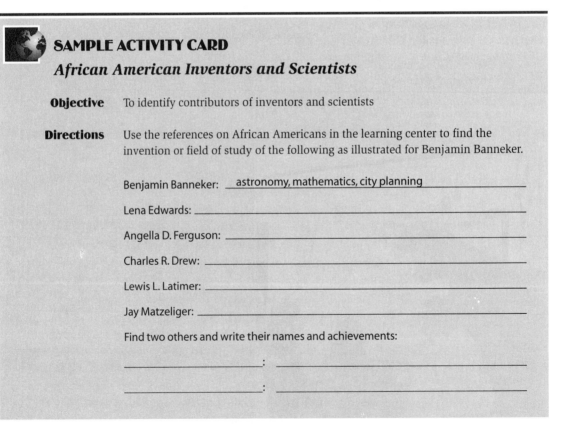

SAMPLE ACTIVITY CARD

African American Inventors and Scientists

Objective   To identify contributors of inventors and scientists

Directions   Use the references on African Americans in the learning center to find the invention or field of study of the following as illustrated for Benjamin Banneker.

Benjamin Banneker: astronomy, mathematics, city planning

Lena Edwards: _____

Angella D. Ferguson: _____

Charles R. Drew: _____

Lewis L. Latimer: _____

Jay Matzeliger: _____

Find two others and write their names and achievements:

_____ : _____

_____ : _____

Resource units contain a variety of suggestions for general use; teachers select and adapt suggestions from them to fit individual classes. Main sections are as follows:

1. *Title:* topic, problem, or theme, such as *The Pacific States, Living in Desert Regions,* or *How Can Acid Rain Be Stopped?*
2. *Background information:* content, main ideas, key concepts
3. *Teacher and students objectives:* knowledge, skills, attitudes/values/appreciations, social participation
4. *Initiation:* suggestions for beginning the unit
5. *Learning activities:*
   a. *Introductory* activities to focus attention on each main idea or problem to be investigated
   b. *Developmental* activities to provide for intake, organization, application, and expression of content
   c. *Concluding* activities to state main ideas, express ideas creatively, and culminate the unit
6. *Evaluation:* suggestions for assessment of learning during and at end of unit
7. *Bibliography:* references for students and teachers

Although different terms may be used, the listed items comprise the major sections of the typical unit (see pages 161–165).

Guidelines for Unit Planning

Although the suggestions in this section focus on unit planning, you may find some useful in planning lessons and modules.

Selecting Units

The most widely used procedure is to refer to the course of study or teacher's guide for the textbook and select units that match the backgrounds and capabilities of students. If an optional unit of special interest to the teacher or students is to be selected, these criteria should be used:

- What contributions will it make to social studies objectives?
- Is it of equal or greater value than the unit it will replace?
- Is it feasible in terms of time, available materials, and the students' abilities?
- What opportunities are available to address the needs of exceptional students?

Building Background

Building background information for a unit requires reviewing textbooks, supplementary books, and other materials available to students. Most teachers review adopted textbooks and related teacher's guides first, noting main ideas, concepts, and background information. They create an outline of content and expand it as other materials are reviewed. The following should be examined carefully:

> *Printed materials:* textbooks, booklets, references, pamphlets, children's literature, library resources
>
> *Nonprint materials:* films, videos, CD-ROMs, maps, transparencies, computer resources, the Internet, and other audiovisual resources
>
> *Community resources:* study trips, resource visitors, interviewees, museums, historical associations, and local publications

Stating Goals and Objectives

The models for lessons and modules presented earlier in this chapter show ways of stating goals and objectives. Teacher's guides for textbooks include statements of goals and objectives for units and lessons, as do local resource units. Instructional objectives should indicate observable and assessable performance, as described in this chapter.

What are some questions you will ask yourself when preparing plans for social studies instruction? Are some questions more important than others? Why?

Main ideas may be identified in various materials or generated when sources for them are not available. Teacher's manuals for textbooks and for other materials include main ideas under headings such as Major Understandings. Main ideas may also be generated by using key concepts and generalizations from the social sciences as shown in Chapter 2.

Selecting and Sequencing Learning Activities

Ideas for learning activities are presented in Table 5.1 (pp. 158–159). They include introductory, developmental, and concluding activities. This sequence parallels the problem-solving and inquiry process in that it provides for defining the problem, collecting and organizing information, and using the information to answer questions, test hypotheses, and draw conclusions. It also provides for the movement of thinking skills from the recalling and interpreting levels to such higher levels as generalizing, analyzing, and synthesizing. Teacher evaluation may be included in all activities to diagnose needs during the introduction of a unit, to assess learning as a unit develops, and to appraise outcomes at the end of a unit.

Introductory Activities

Sometimes referred to as opening or initiating activities, introductory activities begin to initiate units and introduce a main idea or another section of a unit. They build readiness, develop anticipatory set and interest, raise questions, explore what students know about the topic, identify misconceptions, recall relevant information, make plans, and set the stage for the first data-gathering activities. Many initiating activities grow out of the unit that preceded them. Some are based on an arrangement of pictures or other items that stimulate interest and questions. Others may be based on questions posed by the teacher, a stimulating current event, or photo essays or other introductory material in the textbook.

Developmental Activities

Developmental activities should grow out of opening activities to provide a smooth learning sequence. A complete series of developmental activities should flow from data-gathering or intake activities to data-organizing activities, to applicative activities, and on to creative and expressive activities. *Data-gathering* or *intake activities* provide the input needed to handle questions and hypotheses. *Organizing activities* help students structure and summarize information. *Applicative activities* extend learning and develop the ability to use concepts and skills. *Creative and expressive activities* enrich learning and develop the ability to improvise and apply learning in original ways.

Some activities overlap and can be used to organize information, to apply learning, and to express ideas creatively. For example, a student may complete an

CHAPTER 5 *Preparing Plans for Instruction*

outline map to organize information, make a map of an area with a key to apply map concepts and skills, and create a map to portray information gathered on transportation, resources, or other items.

Concluding Activities

Closely related to and flowing from expressive activities are concluding activities of two types. The first type are activities related to each main idea in the unit. The second are those culminating activities that encompass the entire unit and bring together

---

■ TABLE 5.1

Learning Activities for Unit Planning

■ Introductory Activities

Observing, Recalling, Interpreting, Hypothesizing

Arrange a display	Pose questions	Use a current event
Link to past unit	Elicit questions	Use a resource person
Suggest a topic	Elicit hypotheses	Show video without sound
Preassess content	Present an unfinished	Discuss a dilemma
Show new book(s)	sentence, chart, time line,	Plan first activities
Show audiovisual media	map, or story	

■ Developmental Activities

Intake and Data-Gathering Activities: Observing, Recalling, Interpreting

Read	Take a poll	Use graphs
Listen	Keep records	Use indexes, tables of contents,
Observe	Use tables	headings, subheadings
Ask	Take notes	Use library
Use maps	Outline	Use databases
Interview	Make collections	Use learning centers
Do a survey	Take field trips	

Organizing and Summarizing Activities: Comparing, Classifying, Generalizing

Find main ideas	Complete time lines	Summarize
Answer questions	Outline	Complete contracts
Test hypotheses	Diagram	Complete outline maps
Group items	Chart	Make database cards
Tape-record	Graph	Make semantic maps

the different main ideas. Culminating activities usually result in a presentation to parents or to other classes, with emphasis on educational outcomes rather than "putting on a show."

Planning Questions

Productive questions are related to objectives, tap important content, provoke thinking, and invite participation. They may be designed in a sequence to develop concepts, analyze information, and move thinking to higher cognitive levels as shown in

Applicative Activities: Inferring, Analyzing, Synthesizing, Hypothesizing, Predicting

Make maps	Reclassify	Make plans
Make graphs	Judge	Debate
Make charts	Predict	Participate in forums, panels, and action projects
Make checklists	Report	Simulate
Make time lines	Demonstrate	
Conclude	Take roles	

Creative and Expressive Activities: Interpreting, Analyzing, Synthesizing

Dramatize	Write articles	Construct models
Role play	Write playlets	Create maps and charts
Pantomime	Draw	Process materials
Simulate	Make murals	Compose songs
Brainstorm	Make collages	Create rhythms
Write poems and stories	Make dioramas	
Write pen pals	Make exhibits	

■ Concluding Activities

Generalizing, Analyzing, Synthesizing, Evaluating

State main ideas	Put on a program	Discuss ways to improve
Share projects	Take a field trip	Use charts, tests, and checklists
Have a quiz program	Have a panel discussion	Relate to next unit
Review objectives	Complete booklets	

later chapters. For example, these questions may be used in a variety of situations to move thinking from the knowledge level to the evaluation level:

> *Knowledge:* What do you recall about this topic?
>
> *Comprehension:* Can you summarize it in your own words?
>
> *Application:* How can we use this information?
>
> *Analysis:* What are the main parts? How is it organized?
>
> *Synthesis:* How can it be organized in a new way?
>
> *Evaluation:* How should it be rated in terms of the listed criteria?

Sequences also may be used to achieve specific objectives, such as to develop concepts, as shown by this example:

> What did you see? hear? note?
>
> Which items can be grouped together? How are they alike?
>
> What is a good name for this group?

Use a variety of questions. For example, *definitional questions* focus attention on precise meaning—What is meant by gender equity? *Empirical questions* focus attention on what has been read, observed, or reported—What happened? Who did it? When? Where? Why? *Evaluative questions* elicit appraisals or judgments—To what extent was gender equality provided? *Rhetorical questions* emphasize an idea or suggest a response—Why is provision for gender equality fair and just? *Open* or *divergent questions* spark differing responses—How many ways can you think of to solve this problem? *Closed* or *convergent questions* elicit a desired correct response—What is the main idea in this report? *Follow-up questions* clarify ideas—What do you mean by that?

As a general rule, the following types of questions should be avoided or rarely used.

- Questions requiring a yes or no answer—Did John Adams serve as president?
- Questions that are ambiguous—What happened in Vietnam and Cambodia?
- Questions that are slanted or biased—Why should women be satisfied with the gains they have made?
- Questions with obvious answers—Should everyone work for gender equality?

The following excerpts from a unit on Japan should be followed by studies of history, government, the arts, family life, and other topics.

PARTS OF A UNIT PLAN
The Geography of Japan

Background Information

1. Located about 5,000 miles from the United States off the coast of China, in same latitude as eastern United States from Maine to Florida

2. Archipelago of about 3,000 islands more than 1,850 miles long with four main islands: Honshu (over one-half of the area and three-fourths of the population), Shikoku, Kyushu, and Hokkaido

3. Part of the "Rim of Fire" volcanoes located around the Pacific Rim

4. Area of about 145,800 square miles, slightly smaller than Montana or California, one-twentieth the size of the United States, with over 16,500 miles of coastline indented with bays and harbors

5. Forests on mountains that cover about 70 percent of the land, plains, and terraces

6. Variety of climates similar to those from Maine to Georgia; climate influenced by ocean currents and monsoons

7. Lack of resources for industry; forests, water resources, fishing

8. Major cities: Tokyo (capital), Osaka, Nagoya, Yokohama, Kyoto, Kobe

Main Ideas

Japan is a mountainous island nation with a variety of environmental features.

The history of Japan is distinctive, yet it has been influenced by other people.

Japan is a leading industrial nation with a variety of economic activities.

Concepts

climate	landforms	population density
culture	physical features	resources

Objectives

To describe the location of Japan in relation to the United States and other Pacific Rim nations

To describe the main natural features and the climate

To locate the four main islands and major cities

To make comparisons of population and population density between Japan and other areas in Asia

To identify Japan's limited natural resources

Materials

Map of Japan, globe, world map, outline maps of Japan

Students' textbooks with section or chapter on Japan

Film, video, or Internet source on geography of Japan

Photographs, postcards, news stories, clippings on Japan

(continued)

PARTS OF A UNIT PLAN *Continued*

Initiation   Arrange a display that includes pictures, objects, news articles, and other materials around a large map of Japan. Guide discussion of the display, and pose questions such as *What comes to mind when you hear the word Japan? What have you seen on TV or read about Japan? What do you think we will find about the geography of Japan?* (thinking skills: recalling, hypothesizing)

Learning Activities   *The Geography of Japan*

Introductory Activities   Place the following question on the display to begin the unit:

WHAT ARE THE MAIN FEATURES OF JAPAN'S NATURAL ENVIRONMENT?

Ask students to respond to the question. List student's responses on a chart or the chalkboard for future use. (thinking skill: hypothesizing)

Developmental Activities

1. Ask students to locate Japan on the globe and/or on a wall map. Discuss location and distance relative to the United States and other nations around the Pacific Rim. (thinking skill: interpreting)

2. Ask, Why is Japan called an island nation? What are the four main islands? Where is the Sea of Japan? What body of water is east of Japan? (thinking skill: interpreting)

3. Show video on geography of Japan and discuss the features that are shown. Compare them with features stated by students during opening activities. (thinking skills: interpreting, comparing)

4. Have students read pages 422–425 of their textbook and ask, What is an archipelago? About how many islands are included in Japan? Why are there so many earthquakes? Where is the Kanto Plain? Why is it so important? (thinking skill: interpreting)

5. Discuss climate, guided by questions like these: How is the climate of northern Japan similar to that of Maine? How does it differ from the climate of southern Japan? What is the average annual rainfall? What are the effects of ocean currents and the monsoons on the climate? (thinking skills: comparing, analyzing)

6. Compare the population of Japan with the population of the United States, California, and other areas, using the latest *World Almanac* and Blig's *Geography Book* as references. Discuss population density of the same areas, highlighting the high density in Japan. Point out that in relation to arable land, Japan is the most densely populated major country. (thinking skill: comparing)

PARTS OF A UNIT PLAN *Continued*

7. Have students locate and describe major cities, using their textbooks and books in the reading center. Discuss how they are located near harbors and plains. (thinking skills: interpreting, analyzing)

8. Show the video on Japan's human and economic geography. Discuss this statement: Human resources are Japan's greatest resources. Discuss the importance of forests, water resources, and fishing. Discuss the lack of mineral resources and the need to import raw materials. (thinking skill: interpreting)

9. Invite an expert on Japan to show slides, describe natural features, and respond to questions such as these: How are the seasons and the climate similar to and different from ours? How frequent and serious are earthquakes? (thinking skill: interpreting)

10. Arrange for individuals, teams, or small groups to investigate and report on topics such as features of each of the four main islands; uses of water resources; uses of forests; fishing resources; Kanto Plain; Rim of Fire; ocean currents and monsoons. (thinking skill: synthesizing)

11. Have students write haiku and tanka poems that highlight features of the geography of Japan. (thinking skill: synthesizing)

    Haiku with 17 syllables in 3 lines in a 5, 7, 5 pattern:

    Snow on Hokkaido
       Fallen during the cold night
          Greets the morning sun.

    Tanka with 31 syllables in five lines in a 5, 7, 5, 7, 7 pattern:

    Lightning and thunder
    Followed by a drenching rain
    And then a rainbow
    Trees and plants dripping water
    A glistening green landscape.

12. Have students watch the video *Windows to the World—Japan* and share new information learned.

Concluding Activities

1. Make a retrieval chart that includes information on Japan's natural environment: mountain ranges, major plains, natural resources, climate, and other features.

2. Have students complete outline maps on which they show the location of the four main islands, Kanto Plain, major cities, and other features.

3. Guide students in creating a mural that shows main features of the natural environment.

(continued)

PARTS OF A UNIT PLAN   *Continued*

4. Have small groups make and share box movie rolls or paper filmstrips that include photographs and/or drawings of landscape scenes.

5. Have students share the main findings of individual and group reports and their haiku and tanka poems.

6. Discuss students' responses to this statement: The most surprising thing I learned about Japan's geography is _____.

Evaluation

1. Observe students during discussion and other activities to note development and use of concepts, application of thinking and other skills, and expression of attitudes and appreciations.

2. Examine students' completed outline maps, reports, and other written work.

3. Assess knowledge by use of test items such as these: Which of the four main islands is the largest?

   A. Hokkaido   B. Honshu   C. Kyushu   D. Shikoku

   Which of the four main islands has the coldest climate?

   A. Hokkaido   B. Honshu   C. Kyushu   D. Shikoku

4. Examine students' responses to completion statements such as these:

   Japan is called an island nation because _____.

   The largest and most populated island is _____.

   The capital of Japan is _____ . Other main cities are _____.

   Japan is about _____ as large in area as the United States, yet it has around _____ the population of the United States.

Sample Resources

The American Forum for Global Education, 120 Wall Street, Suite 2600, New York, NY 10005, Phone 212-624-1300, E-mail globed120@aol.com, Web http://globaled.org.

Anti-Defamation League of B'nai B'rith, Department JW, 823 United Nations Plaza, New York, NY 10017, Phone 212-490-2525.

Consulate General of Japan in New York, 299 Park Avenue 18th Floor, New York, NY 10171, Phone 212-371-8222, Web http://ny.cgj.org.

The East Asian Studies Center, Indiana University, Memorial West #207, Bloomington, IN 47405-6701, Phone 812-855-3765, E-mail easc@indiana.edu, Web http://easc.indiana.edu.

ERIC Clearinghouse, Social Studies/Social Science Education, 2805 East Tenth Street, Suite 120, Bloomington, IN 47408-2698, Phone 800-266-3815, E-mail ericso@indiana.edu, Web http://indiana.edu/ ~ ssdc/eric_chess.htm.

PARTS OF A UNIT PLAN   *Continued*

East Asian Institute, Columbia University, Mail Code 3333, 420 West 118th St., New York, NY 10027, Phone 212-854-2592, E-mail nre3@columbia.edu.

Japanese American Curriculum Project Inc., P.O. Box 1587, 234 Main Street, San Mateo, CA 94401, Phone 800-874-2242.

Massachusetts Asian American Educators Association, P.O. Box 630, Needham, MA 02192, Phone 617-524-0560.

Social Studies School Service, 10200 Jefferson Boulevard, Room 1811, P.O. Box 802, Culver City, CA 90232-0802, Phone 800-421-4246.

Stanford Program on International and Cross-Cultural Education (SPICE), Institute for International Studies, Littlefield Center, Room 14C, Stanford University, Stanford, CA 94305-5013, Phone 1-800-578-1114, E-mail SPICE.SALES@forsythe.stanford.edu.

The following are examples of publishing houses offering trade books in the area of social studies education: The Children's Book Council Inc., 568 Broadway, Suite 404, New York, NY 10012, Web http://www.CBCbooks.org; Cobblestone Publishing Co., 30 Grove Street, Suite C, Peterborough, NH 03458-1454, Phone 603-924-7209; World Almanac Education, 15355 NEO Parkway, Cleveland, OH 44128, Phone 800-321-1147; Chelsea Curriculum Publications, Dept. MCC, 1974 Sproul Road, Suite 400, Broomall, PA 19008-0914, Phone 800-848-2665.

Ways to Build Units

A popular method of building units is to begin with an idea and use one of the multi-column formats suggested in Figure 5.3 (p. 166) to brainstorm components of the unit. As the brainstorming continues, columns may be added to each sheet.

■ A great teacher makes hard things easy.

—**Ralph Waldo Emerson**

Some new teachers, faced with the multiplicity of problems that typically arise, rely primarily on the adopted textbook for social studies instruction. It is possible to move from textbook to unit teaching in a series of steps as time permits. First, identify other reading materials on various levels of difficulty and other materials that complement textbook units. Note related field trips, resource visitors, and other community resources. In the beginning these materials may be used with chapters in the textbook and learning activities suggested in the accompanying teacher's manual. Next, make plans that are structured around main ideas, key concepts, and guiding questions that are central to the topic of study. Then list learning activities and instructional materials (including the textbook) under the main ideas, concepts, and questions as appropriate. Assessment should also be planned to assess objectives related to all of the instructional materials used.

Another procedure that some teachers use to develop units, particularly in new areas of study, is to begin by making lesson plans related to new videos, reading ma-

■ **FIGURE 5.3**

Formats for Brainstorming Ideas

Objectives	Learning Activities	Materials

Objectives	Content	Teaching Procedures	Materials	Evaluation

Generalizations and Concepts	Learning Activities and Materials	Evaluation

terials, or other resources. For example, a new CD-ROM on energy conservation may be available or a new textbook may be adopted. The accompanying manuals are checked, ideas on needs of students are noted, ideas from past experience are drawn upon, and plans for using the new materials are made. After several plans are made, they are brought together, revised, and combined as a section of a unit clustered around a main idea or generalization. Then plans are made for other parts of the new textbook or other materials, clustering them around another main idea. A practical teaching unit is thus developed inductively by moving from daily planning to an overall plan that is a synthesis of specific plans.

Preplanned units are an excellent resource. They save teachers valuable time by bringing together resources on a particular topic or main idea. However, commercial units, those appearing in teacher's manuals, or those prepared by a fellow teacher need to be modified to match the teacher's objectives and student abilities.

Preplanned units are available from local and county school districts, state departments, curriculum laboratories and media centers, and libraries in colleges and universities. Many have been placed in ERIC (Educational Resources Information Center) and are listed in *Resources in Education.* Some may be found in magazines such as *Instructor, Social Education, Teacher Magazine,* or *Learning.* Teacher's manuals that accompany social studies textbooks contain unit plans directly related to the text and supplemented by a variety of activities and related materials. Other sources are noted in the references at the end of the chapter.

Using Taxonomies

The taxonomies noted as sources of objectives in Chapter 1 may be used to plan objectives, activities, questions, and evaluation on various levels. The following examples from a unit on early civilizations shows the various cognitive levels that students should attain:

Knowledge Level
Objective: To name early civilizations in river valleys

Question: What civilizations arose in river valleys?

Activity: Study pages 80–82 and list the described civilizations.

Evaluation: Civilizations that arose in river valleys were _____.

Comprehension Level
Objective: To describe early civilizations in one's own words

Question: Who can describe the river valley civilizations?

Activity: Guide discussion in which students describe early civilizations.

Evaluation: Write a one-paragraph description of one river valley civilization.

Effective social studies teachers employ a variety of approaches when preparing plans for instruction. What are the strengths of a textbook-based approach? weaknesses?

Application Level

Objective: To use information on early civilizations in studying later ones

Question: How were later civilizations alike and different from early ones?

Activity: Make a retrieval chart to compare early and later civilizations.

Evaluation: Make a summary of similarities and differences.

Analysis Level

Objective: To identify the main elements of early civilizations

Question: What were the main features of early civilizations?

Activity: Make an outline of the main elements of early civilizations.

Evaluation: Ask students to list main elements of early civilizations.

Synthesis Level

Objective: To create a mural that shows main features of early civilizations

Question: What features should we include in a mural on early civilizations?

Activity: Make drawings for a mural on early civilizations.

Evaluation: Guide development and application of evaluative criteria.

Evaluation Level

Objective: To rate quality of life in early civilizations

Question: How do you rate quality of life, using the criteria on page 92?

Activity: Do the rating on a scale from 1 to 10: 1 is very good and 10 is very poor.

Evaluation: List ways the rating system can be improved.

■ Integration of Instruction

■ No one ever became wise by chance.

—**Seneca**

Consider how to integrate material from other subjects into the social studies and vice versa. For example, art and music activities should be a key part of some social studies units to clarify aspects of culture. At other times instruction in art and music can be related to holidays, festivals, and other social studies topics. At times science and social studies can be unified as climate, weather, environmental problems, impact of science and technology, and other topics are studied. Social studies content can be used to teach outlining, writing, and other skills in the language arts program, and communication skills should be applied and improved in social studies. The guiding principle is to identify meaningful relationships and then decide in which subject(s) that instruction should be provided.

Topics such as futures studies, teaching about religion in the social studies, multiethnic and gender equity studies, and law-related instruction also can be integrated into various units. For example, futures studies may be a part of units at all levels to help students identify trends, learn how to influence change, make forecasts, analyze possible, probable, and preferable changes, and weigh possible consequences of alternative actions. To aid planning, future changes may be differentiated as follows:

Value shifts related to work, quality of life, resource use, peace

Social changes in roles, careers, public services, group activities

Cultural diffusion of ideas, values, technology, the arts, leisure activities

Demographic changes in population, family structure, life span, rural-urban balance

Technological innovations, such as computers, robotics, information networks

Ecological changes in the environment, resource base, water and food supply

Systems changes in transportation, communication, economics, government

These and other changes are included in regular units, current affairs studies, and mini units on alternative futures. The three sections of Table 5.2 suggest ideas for futures studies.

■ TABLE 5.2

Ideas for Future Studies

Projecting Basic Trends	The Year 2100		Ways to Influence Change
What are current trends in each of these areas?	What will be the most important values?		Know what we and others value.
■ Freedom and equality for all	■ Community life	■ Jobs for everyone	Consider causes and effects.
■ Changes in the family and other institutions	■ Conservation	■ Justice	Consider alternative proposals.
■ Careers for women and men	■ Education	■ Leisure	Consider consequences of actions.
■ Conservation of resources and energy	■ Environment	■ Recreation	Join with others to take action.
■ Quality of life and lifestyle	■ Family life	■ Wealth	Make plans for the future now.
■ Uses of science and technology	■ Health	■ Peace	Evaluate action and plans.
■ Restoration of rainforests and wetlands	■ Housing	■ Creativity	
■ Growth of democracy in other nations	■ Human rights	■ Gender equality	
	■ Food supply	■ The arts	
	■ Cooperation		

■ Incorporating Teaching Strategies

Table 5.3 shows many teaching strategies that can be incorporated into instruction plans. To give students a broad range of approaches to learning, you'll want to use a variety of these strategies. You'll find that some are especially appropriate to particular instructional focuses. For example, the first—expository instruction—may be used for films, presentations by visitors, and other direct instruction. The problem-solving strategy is helpful when studying environmental, community, state, or other problems. The critical thinking strategy may be used at many points when students are asked to make appraisals or judgments. Refer to this table as you plan instruction.

■ Assessment, Evaluation, and Portfolio Building

Assessment is the process teachers use that leads to evaluation—making judgments about student learning. How to generate opportunities for assessment in planning is always on the minds of teachers. They are keenly aware of the need to develop strategies that lead to nonobtrusive assessment. A variety of devices may be used to appraise achievement of the objectives of the unit. Social studies teachers use traditional forms of assessment (tests and written assignments) and nontraditional forms (play, speech, project). These nontraditional forms are sometimes referred to as authentic, alternative, and performance assessment. Assessment is ongoing (formative) and summative (at the end of the unit). Many teachers include numerous opportunities for formative assessment and use a culminating activity for summative assessment. Some devices are prepared as a part of learning activities, and standards for using materials. Many devices, such as tests and inventories, may be constructed ahead of time. The following list gives examples of devices and procedures. Specific examples and a more detailed discussion appear in Chapter 14.

quizzes	checking of written work
attitude and interest inventories	essay tests
checking by a partner	group discussion
individual self-checking	reviewing files of each student's work
keeping logs or diaries	objective tests
rating scales and checklists	teacher observation

Portfolio building is the collection of student work over a designated period of time—a series of lessons, a unit, a semester, a year—that document student growth in social studies. Portfolios can be put together by teacher, student, or both, and they are used by teachers to demonstrate to interested parties (i.e., students, school officials, parents) student strengths and weaknesses and growth in social studies. It may include written reports, completed quizzes, teacher observations, or any other materials that the teacher or school deems important to demonstrate learning.

■ **TABLE 5.3**

Teaching Strategies

Expository Instruction

Introduction: Clarify objectives, create interest, set the stage.

Procedures: Follow sequence of steps to provide instruction.

Conclusion: Wrap up the lesson to bring closure.

Follow-up: Provide practice or application to clinch and extend learning.

Problem Solving

Identify and define the problem.

Discuss key elements of the problem and propose a solution.

Collect and interpret related evidence.

Use the evidence to decide whether the proposed solution is warranted.

If so, use the solution to solve the problem.

If not, propose another solution and repeat the above steps.

Group Inquiry

Clarify topic or problem to be investigated.

State questions or hypotheses to guide study, using prior knowledge.

Plan and do small group study to gather data to answer questions or test hypotheses.

Share, organize, and evaluate findings, and use them to answer questions or test hypotheses.

State conclusions, note needs for more study, and evaluate procedure.

Inductive-Discovery

Observe and discuss specific examples.

Identify and describe common elements of features.

Discuss other examples and note common elements.

State a main idea based on common elements and check it against additional examples.

Decision Making

Define the issue or topic.

Clarify goals and values and note alternatives for achieving them.

Assess consequences of alternatives and prioritize them in terms of goals.

Choose the best alternative.

Evaluate the decision-making process, the decision, and any action taken.

Individual Inquiry

Choose a topic or problem and define.

Recall prior learning and list questions you have.

Select reliable sources and gather, appraise, and organize needed information.

Use organized information to answer questions; gather more data if needed.

State conclusion, needs for more study, and evaluation.

Deductive-Discovery

Present a main idea that can be checked against evidence.

Have students find supporting evidence or examples.

Have students state why the evidence is supporting.

Have students find other evidence or proof.

Critical Thinking

Define what is to be appraised or judged.

Define standards or values.

Use data to determine how well standards are met.

Consider emotional appeals, inconsistencies, and biases.

Separate facts from opinions and causes from effects.

Make judgment based on facts and sound reasons.

Creative Thinking

Think of a goal, activity, or topic to pursue in new ways.

Imagine new ways to use what you know.

Add new ideas and imagine new ways to express them.

Synthesize thoughts and feelings and express them freely.

Contemplate ways to improve creativity and make desired changes. Imagine modifications, novel applications, and original uses.

Keeping a Log to Evaluate the Unit

Teachers also evaluate their own work and the progress of the class as a whole. Teachers who have kept a log say that it is a great help in evaluating the unit and in gathering ideas to use in revising the unit. A satisfactory log is a brief running account of the unit and includes notes on strengths and weaknesses of instructional materials, changes to be made in learning experiences, and other ways in which the unit should be modified. Items are entered during or at the end of the day and kept in a folder. After the culmination of the unit, notes related to all main ideas or problems should be brought together and used as a basis for revising the unit.

Because tape-recorders are inexpensive, some teachers use this device to log their comments. They might allocate a short period at the end of each day and at the conclusion of the unit to record notes, ideas, and concerns. Some teachers also allocate an extended period of time to reflect on all of ideas and concerns raised before making unit changes.

■ Conclusion

Planning is at the heart of good social studies instruction. Prerequisites to planning are knowledge of the social sciences, integration of the social sciences, and knowledge of students. Some of the elements of effective planning include a definition and purpose for social studies, familiarity with social science or social studies standards, and a grounding in pedagogy. Social studies teachers develop instructional programs that are varied and reflective of the diverse needs of the classroom. They use a variety of ways to develop objectives, modules, lessons, and units of study.

 Questions, Activities, and Evaluation

1. Make a plan for a lesson similar to one presented in this chapter. Base it on a textbook or other resource. Ask a colleague to critique it.

2. Make a plan for a module similar to the one presented in this chapter. Ask a colleague to critique it.

3. Obtain a teacher's edition textbook and do the following:
   a. Note the contents of each major section. Does the unit include the same general sections noted in this chapter?
   b. How are the goals and objectives stated? What changes, if any, might be made to improve them?
   c. Summarize the introductory, developmental, and concluding activities that you believe to be most helpful.
   d. Note suggested techniques for assessment.
   e. Note references that may be useful in your own future planning.

4. Plan a short teaching unit similar to the examples in this chapter. Review as many related instructional resources as time permits. As you obtain ideas from subsequent chapters, add them to the unit.

5. Prepare a kit or box of materials that can be used with the unit you are planning. Include pictures, maps, free or inexpensive materials, songs, directions for arts and crafts, and other resources.

6. Arrange to visit a classroom where a unit of instruction of interest to you is in progress. Try to visit several times so as to observe the initiation, subsequent activities, and the culmination. Have questions ready to ask the teacher in charge.

References

Berg, M. (Ed.). (1989). Making the connections. *Social Studies and the Young Learner, 1,* 3–18. Special section on integrating art and architecture, math and science, and language arts with social studies.

Freeland, K., & Smith, K. (1993). A thematic teaching unit on flight. *Social Studies and the Young Learner, 5,* 15–17.

Harms, J. M., & Lettow, L. J. (1994). Criteria for selecting picture books with historical settings. *Social Education, 58,* 152–154.

Hunkins, F. P. (1989). *Teaching thinking through effective questioning.* Norwood, MA: Christopher-Gordon Publishers. Variety of examples.

Hunter, M. (1982). *Mastery learning.* El Segundo, CA: TIP Publications.

Kon, J. H. (1995). Teachers curricular decision making in response to a new social studies textbook. *Theory and Research in Social Education, 23,* 121–146.

Reissman, R., et al. (1994). Curriculum boosters: Social studies, math, language arts. *Learning, 22,* 56–62.

Rogers, V., Roberts, A. D., & Weinland, T. P. (Eds.). (1988). *Teaching social studies: Portraits from the classroom.* Washington, DC: National Council for the Social Studies. Reports by teachers.

Ruff, T. P. (1994). *Teaching social studies in grades K–8.* Boston: Allyn & Bacon.

Sanchez, T. R. (1997). The social studies teachers lament: How powerful is the textbook in dealing with knowledge of ethnic diversity and attitude change? *Urban Education, 32,* 63–80.

Smith, R, E., & Manley, S. A. (1994). Social studies learning activities packets. *The Social Studies, 85,* 160–64.

Social studies grade 5—The Western Hemisphere. (1985, 1987). New York: City Board of Education. Learning activities for Planet Earth and countries in the Western Hemisphere.

Chapter 6

Planning and Providing for Individual Differences

Chapter Objective

To describe guidelines and strategies for providing individualized instruction that enhances each student's learning

Focusing Questions

- What strategies are useful in identifying individual needs and differences and in making plans to accommodate them?

- How can learning centers, contracts, activity cards, modules, worksheets, reports, and other independent study activities enhance learning?

- How can social studies reading and reporting be individualized?

- What procedures may be used to teach children to individualize work for themselves?

- How can teachers meet the needs of students with exceptionalities?

- How can the needs of students from minority groups and recent immigrant groups be met?

■ Differences: A Challenge and an Opportunity

The 1960s civil rights movement revealed that public education was far from reaching the goal of providing for all students. During the 1960s and 1970s, social activists, students, teachers, and administrators recounted story after story about policies and practices that prevented children and young adults of minority groups from reaching their potential. And, as proponents of this movement studied this problem further, they discovered other groups whose educational needs were not being met. These groups included students living in poor communities and students with exceptionalities. Throughout the second half of the twentieth century, schools reaffirmed their commitment to educational equity by (1) abandoning policies and practices that discriminated against children and young adults based on socioeconomic status, race, and disabilities, and (2) hiring teachers who understood student differences and possessed the expertise to address the educational needs of diverse students. In the twenty-first century the thrust for equity will continue as schools modify twentieth-century ideas about diversity to include the children of new immigrants.

In Chapter 3, we presented two levels of diversity that exist in schools. One level comprises the cultural richness that students bring to school and how their experiences can be integrated into the curriculum to enhance instruction. In social studies this means highlighting the cultural experiences of a student in your class who is from the Middle East or from Kosovo when you discuss current events. It also means including the rich heritage of Latinos to enhance a unit on Latin America as well as the historical experiences of your community's African Americans to add a personal dimension to studies of both of these groups and their roles in the story of America.

The other level of diversity consists of providing for diverse students, including students with exceptionalities (e.g., giftedness, hearing impairments, and emotional disorders), those who speak a language other than English, and those who have difficulties experiencing success because their intellectual, social, or physical needs are not being met. In this chapter we suggest individualized instruction as one method of addressing the needs of students who experience various difficulties. Such instruction is a hallmark of all good teaching.

As they plan individualized activities, teachers focus on student's strengths and weaknesses. During class they carefully note which students seem unchallenged and which ones are falling behind. They also consider individual differences when assessing student learning. In any K–8 social studies classroom, you will observe teachers energetically providing helpful instruction for all learners. Individualizing instruction has always been a goal of education.

In Chapter 3 we discussed the pluralistic society of the United States and the cultural diversity represented in our schools. Your field experiences and student teaching will no doubt bring you into contact with some aspects of this diversity. But as we focus on providing individualized instruction in this chapter, here is one word of warning: while appreciating the contributions of many cultural and racial groups, teachers must avoid the potential danger of overgeneralizing about a particular group. For example, all Latinos do not represent a single monolithic culture; instead they derive from many individual places, communities, and cultural groups in Latin America. Teachers must be sensitive to diversity both *among* and *within* such groups.

As another example, consider the breadth of peoples encompassed by the term *Asian American*. People with origins in places as diverse as Vietnam, Japan, the Philippines, the Pacific islands, and India can all be described as Asian American. They speak a variety of languages and observe different traditions. Also, minority groups such as African Americans should not be lumped into one undifferentiated category. Social class lines and socioeconomic backgrounds affect minority students' educational needs and concerns. Though they may share many attributes, an African American child from the inner city may need different learning experiences than would a middle-class African American child. Also, long-held definitions of ethnic and minority groups are challenged as new immigrants continue to enter our country; the spectrum of differences that teachers deal with in the classroom is always in a state of flux.

As you consider ways to individualize instruction, discerning these fine distinctions within broader categories of ethnic and racial groups will make your planning and teaching more effective. Gender, race, socioeconomic status, religion, language, and ethnicity contribute to the uniqueness of each student and enrich learning for everyone, but they do present challenges to educators. Recognizing, valuing, and striving for a deeper understanding of individual differences will definitely enhance your work as a teacher. Excellent teachers care about the full range of students—the average, the gifted, and those with exceptionalities—and hold high expectations for all of them.

■ Educational equity and excellence for all children in the United States are unattainable without the incorporation of cultural pluralism in all aspects of the education process.

—**Geneva Gay**

In this chapter we discuss practical suggestions for meeting this challenge. Ways to identify needs, set attainable expectations, modify instruction to accommodate different students, manage time and supervision issues, and assess outcomes in terms of students' abilities will be offered, along with suggestions for meeting these goals specifically in social studies instruction. These ideas can be modified to address the needs of particular students.

■ Finding Support and Assistance

A common remark among student teachers facing difficulty in the classroom goes something like this: "I don't know what to do for Johnny or Susie." Fortunately, a good deal of expertise and services is available to teachers who wish to better address the needs of all kinds of learners. All schools and school districts provide a range of professional help. Colleagues, department chairs, counselors, special education teachers, community experts, and others offer guidance and support to teachers. In many cases, students with special needs have already been identified by the school, and procedures will be in place to help teachers address the needs of these students. In other cases, specialists, when invited, may come to your classroom to help you identify students with special needs. In other cases, professionals will give you background information on a particular group of students and pedagogical suggestions that have proved successful with this group. Teachers can take the initiative in this process. It is one more way to demonstrate to all students that they are valued and an important part of the class.

It is entirely normal for beginning teachers to seek some extra support in this area. It takes experience and expertise to identify students in need of help and to choose pedagogical strategies that will help them. For example, say that a recent immigrant from Kosovo was assigned to your classroom. How would you communicate with the student? What information would you need to identify whether his or her only difficulty is language? How would you determine the student's learning needs? How would you measure your success in providing appropriate instruction for the student? Using a combination of the following suggestions would set you on the right path.

Identifying the Needs of Students Who Speak a Language Other than English

- Identify an individual in the school or community who speaks the student's language.
- Learn phrases in the student's language.
- Become familiar with the student's culture.
- Familiarize yourself with the educational experiences of other students who speak the student's language.
- Speak with a community specialist in your school, and meet the student's parents.

- Contact the curriculum specialist to help you develop instruction that will provide opportunities for the student to experience success in your classroom.
- Where applicable, incorporate the student's cultural experiences into social studies instruction.
- Contact the ESL teachers or other support staff to initiate diagnostic procedures.
- Using this support system, begin addressing the needs of the student.
- Continue communicating to the student that you care and want him or her to succeed in your classroom.

Another strategy is to turn to experts on the education of particular groups of students. For example, a number of special education strategies exist to help teachers with inclusive classrooms. Teachers meet with special education educators and help plan the Individualized Education Plans (IEP). In social studies, the IEP for each student scheduled for inclusion includes objectives, activities, materials, and evaluation procedures. The assistance of a variety of specialists is available to teachers.

Accommodations for Students with Exceptionalities

As you begin planning instruction for students with exceptionalities, think about this general guideline: all students needs well-rounded instruction, and individual adjustments can improve learning. Gifted students should not focus entirely on creative activities and neglect basic social studies learning. Students with learning disabilities should not be overburdened with drill work and remedial studies; they also should have opportunities to exercise critical and creative thinking in their schoolwork. Also, students do not benefit from being isolated in groups according to their exceptionalities. Individual instruction can be provided while making sure that each student is vitally involved in the class as a whole.

Though a broad spectrum of exceptionalities exist, some planning strategies can be applied to all. Development of self-esteem, positive attitudes toward differences, respect for others, and prosocial behavior should be woven into the instruction of all these students. Building on students' strengths and supporting well-rounded growth (intellectual, social, emotional, and physical) are also universally applicable. Teachers should help students identify their particular talents and likewise look for discrepancies between students' potential and their achievement.

Another part of your planning as you individualize instruction will involve gathering information. You can gain background from IEPs and school records (be careful to maintain confidentiality!) and consult school psychologists, special education experts, reading specialists, and other professionals. The student's family is another important factor in gaining information and shaping successful instruction. With the family's cooperation you can plan individualized home study and, if appropriate, connect the family with libraries, service agencies, and other organizations that may be recommended by the experts whom you consult.

- Individualized instruction means that children are provided with personally meaningful learning experiences that will help them achieve the goals of the curriculum.
—**Walter C. Parker and John Jarolimek**

As you read the following sections, think about how to use a number of the ideas as you adapt instruction to address student needs. These ideas are not meant to be prescriptive for all students in a given category. Customizing instruction to the student's unique attributes is the essence of individualized instruction.

Gifted and Talented Students

Though it will be clear that certain students possess special abilities and talents, teachers need to be keenly observant to identify all such students. Look for a variety of abilities among students of different backgrounds and personalities; they may be gifted in the realms of math, science, creative writing, music, interpersonal and intrapersonal understanding, mechanical ability, art, and so on. Teachers can encourage the development of these talents in many ways, and many such abilities can enhance the social studies classroom.

Give these students chances to extend their learning in a variety of ways. They may engage in critical thinking relating to a particular topic studied in class, such as formulating new hypotheses about it, drawing inferences, stating generalizations, synthesizing information, and evaluating ideas. They can also benefit from individual study, using library and community resources. Encourage them to read widely and to pursue in-depth knowledge of selected topics. After gaining such knowledge, they might let their creativity flow in challenging activities such as taking on the role of a historical character in a class presentation, writing a booklet on citizenship, giving a multimedia presentation on Native American art, or working with other students to present a classroom "newscast" set in 1945.

Individual achievement should not be the sole focus, however. Gifted students can contribute to the class in areas of leadership and initiative, and they will gain both skills in teamwork and empathy for others by engaging in group activities. Development of positive attitudes and appreciation for the contributions of all students should be significant features in the education of gifted and talented students. Creative teachers can find many ways to involve these students in full-class and group activities while recognizing that gifted students may not need the review, drill, and reteaching experiences that support the education of many other students.

Students with Mental Retardation

In inclusive classrooms, students with mental retardation may form part of your student community. You can provide a number of supports to assist them in approaching the social studies curriculum. The number and complexity of concepts to be taught may need to be adjusted; aim for enough material to challenge the student, but not so much that the student experiences frustration. Give regular feedback on the student's progress, commending achievement and effort and helping the student find ways to evaluate his or her own progress. This feedback and attention can keep the student motivated and excited about learning.

For individual activities, guide students with mental retardation by offering concrete, specific questions or directions. Think of ways to simplify the worksheets or study guides that you provide for the class; pictures, charts, and diagrams may make the information more accessible to these students. Extra opportunities for review and practice will ensure learning, and extra study time can be helpful too.

Whenever possible, students with mental retardation should experience a range of classroom activities that enhance learning. Creative work, such as the projects described in Chapter 12, will both motivate learning and give these students a chance to enjoy the pleasure of self-expression. Call on them in class discussions. Find ways for them to share their talents and interests with other class members. As members of a team, these students can help gather data, prepare reports, use computer programs, make maps, and so on. Such activities should be customized to account for a student's strengths and needs.

Students with Learning Disabilities

Learning disabilities cover a range of difficulties that some students experience in school. Problems in reading, writing, math, organization, and concentration may characterize these students; some struggle with just one problem, whereas others experience a combination of them. Presence of a learning disability says nothing about a student's intelligence or overall ability; learning disabilities are present in students of widely varying intelligence and all kinds of backgrounds.

Consultation with specialists in the school system and review of the IEP will guide your planning for individualized instruction of these students. In one way or another, you will adapt the social studies curriculum to approach reading, writing, and other activities. The student's unique strengths and deficits will inform this planning.

For all students with learning disabilities, it is important to give precise directions and make clear the standard of work that is expected. Help students keep their study materials and work areas well organized to facilitate learning. You may need to shorten reading assignments, break assignments into smaller segments, or provide tape-recorded material, depending on how a student best processes information. Computer programs related to a given unit may help those who have difficulty getting information strictly from textbooks and other reading materials; working with a partner might also be beneficial. Students who have difficulty in math may need extra support in dealing with graphs or tables with numeric data.

As educators come to learn more about learning disabilities, no doubt new ways of addressing these challenges will emerge and enhance the education of this group of students.

Students with Emotional Disturbance

Again, teachers whose classrooms include students with emotional problems will work together with other school personnel to create a positive learning environment and specific plans for supporting these students. In general, an environment that provides structure, stability, and consistency in behavioral expectations will benefit a student with emotional disturbances. This includes daily routines and clear standards of work and conduct, which teachers explain in terms of why they must be followed and how they benefit students. Teachers reinforce these standards by providing immediate, on-the-spot feedback that rewards improvement in self-control and other positive behavior.

Of course, on certain days, routines have to be changed. Perhaps a special speaker is coming to class or a field trip has been planned. Students with emotional problems will adapt to these situations more smoothly if they receive advance preparation. Let them know what behaviors are expected on these occasions and give reasons to support your expectations. You might pair these students with a compatible partner for such activities. Working with a partner, and gradually advancing to cooperative work with three or four students, is an opportunity for growth in the area of interpersonal relationships. Social studies provides many such opportunities for positive group work.

Other practical suggestions include providing a space where a student with emotional problems can work quietly, without distractions. You might set aside a cubicle or learning station for this purpose. As you get to know specific students, you'll be able to anticipate the situations that cause them to feel frustration, over-stimulation, or hostility. Preventing such situations or intervening before they escalate requires that teachers be skilled in observation and classroom management.

Meeting the challenge of teaching these students can be very rewarding, but teachers should not hesitate to ask for help if problems become unmanageable. Seek assistance from the principal, the school psychologist, or other professionals whenever you need it.

At-Risk Students

Teachers give special attention to at-risk students—those who for a variety of reasons show signs of failing at school, who may later drop out, who feel inadequate, or who suffer from low self-esteem. Teachers may use a variety of the strategies and activities already described to encourage and support these students as learners. In addition, good after-school programs run by the school or other local organizations can help these students tackle homework and form positive relationships with adults and other students. Also, extracurricular activities in sports, music, or clubs may give these students a greater sense of belonging at school.

Students with Physical Impairments

Over the course of your teaching career, you may work with students who have a variety of physical impairments. Despite the legal and societal gains made by people with disabilities over the past few decades, they still face some forms of discrimination. The inclusive classroom can be a wonderful workshop in facing down this problem. Appreciation of differences and the contributions of all can enhance everyone's education and their later participation as citizens in a society that values and supports all its members.

What accommodations are schools making for students with exceptionalities? How have these accommodations improved social studies instruction?

Basic goals for all such students include providing meaningful instruction customized to their needs, building their self-esteem, and providing opportunities for them to share their talents. To support these goals, we provide a number of practical suggestions tailored to specific impairments.

Students with Hearing Impairments

Hearing loss may be minor or severe, but a hearing problem of any degree can cause problems in classroom learning. Teachers can make instruction more accessible to students with hearing problems by following these guidelines:

- If applicable, encourage the student to properly use a hearing aid.
- At the chalkboard, avoid writing and speaking simultaneously.
- Get a student's attention by lightly touching the student or making an inconspicuous gesture.
- To aid speech reading, speak in a normal voice with clear enunciation. Face the student, and keep your hands away from your face.
- Introduce new vocabulary both orally and in writing.
- Give the student detailed written instructions for assignments.
- Make use of visual materials, closed caption TV, and audio loops.
- When the student cannot hear a speaker or a recording, have another student provide assistance.

Students with Visual Impairments

Students who experience problems with seeing may have quite different levels of impairment: those that are minimal and those that establish the student as legally blind. These students can function well in the classroom when teachers provide a helpful environment and special supports.

A basic guideline for students with some visual ability is to reduce and prevent eye strain. Avoid exacting and extended tasks with a visual orientation, and offer rest periods too. Here are other suggestions:

- Provide good lighting, and eliminate glare and shadows.
- Arrange seating so that a student with a visual impairment can see and hear the teacher or members of a discussion group.
- Adapt art activities or map activities to account for the student's visual ability.
- As needed, offer paper with wide spaces and heavy lines, books and worksheets with large type, maps with raised relief, globe magnifiers, and computers with voice-synthesis software.

Students who are blind need other supports in the classroom. They include the following:

- Orient the student to the layout of the classroom, including seating arrangements, work centers, and the teacher's desk.
- Provide "talking books," braille translation software, and braille materials as needed. Find resources by consulting with the special education teacher and the library.
- During activities with a visual component, let a classroom aide serve as an interpreter who transmits information to and from the student.
- Provide learning materials that the student can feel, touch, and manipulate. These include models, artifacts, and raised relief maps and globes.

Students with Movement Impairments

Students who need assistance in movement may have a variety of particular impairments: injury from an auto accident, spina bifida, muscular dystrophy, cerebral palsy, or other conditions. These students can learn and participate in the classroom when adaptations such as the following are made:

- Seat the student in a place that provides easy entrance to and exit from the classroom. The location should also facilitate class participation.
- Encourage correct use of equipment such as crutches, braces, and wheelchairs, and support the student's independent use of them.
- Assist the student in using materials or equipment that causes difficulties. These might include scissors, globes, or large reference books.
- Provide a computer modified for the student's use, or appoint another student to act as a computer buddy.
- Modify group activities so that the student can participate.
- When certain activities require physical capabilities that the student simply does not have, provide an appealing substitute activity.

Students with Communication Disorders

Students with speech difficulties also need support in the classroom. Whether the problem stems from a poorly formed palate, a tendency to stutter, a breathing difficulty, or a different disorder, teachers can use a number of techniques to accommodate the student.

Discussion with the student's speech therapist is essential and will provide you with many ideas to use in class. Let the student practice speaking in nonthreatening situations, such as choral reading. Before such students become more confident in speaking, they can share their ideas with other students through "chalk talks" or by using puppets. As they gain skill, call on them in discussion, and give them plenty of time to respond, without pressure or interruption. Support the student by avoiding situations that seem to create feelings of insecurity.

■ Planning for Individualized Instruction

■ Parent Patch **http:// parentpatch.com** offers parents and teachers information on special needs topics.

Individualized instruction has three major components: needs assessment and diagnosis, selection and implementation of instructional strategies, and evaluation of learning (see Chapter 14 on assessment). For some students, such as those with learning disabilities, this will take the form of developing and carrying out the IEP, in consultation with the other members of the IEP team. For others, such as recent immigrants, it will involve meeting language-related needs, helping the student adjust to a new culture and classroom, and making use of the student's special abilities and experiences to contribute to everyone's learning. Teachers think of ways to individualize instruction for all students, even those who easily succeed at school; some students need only minor adaptations to the curriculum.

Teachers don't lay out a plan at the beginning of the year and then follow it step by step as the months go by. They constantly observe students and adjust the strategies and activities that comprise individualized instruction. They gather additional information and ideas from their colleagues. Thus the planning of individualized instruction is an ongoing task.

This challenging task can indeed seem overwhelming! How does the teacher meet the general goals of classroom teaching while attending to the individual needs of students? Here's one way to get the big picture. A helpful tool to use in preparing individualized instruction has been suggested by Fuller and Stone (1998). Figure 6.1 presents the planning pyramid that they developed to teach social studies to eighth-grade learners with diverse learning needs. You might refer to this model as you plan units that take into account the needs of all your students. Stone and others offer the following suggestions for using the model:

1. Present the same information to all of your students, though you may need to vary the presentation to address individual needs.
2. Make use of students' abilities, interests, prior knowledge, and experiences.
3. Develop activities that are creative and engaging.

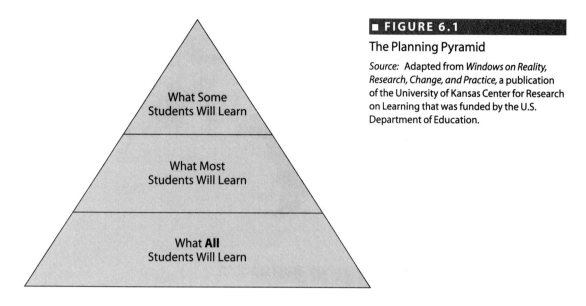

■ **FIGURE 6.1**

The Planning Pyramid

Source: Adapted from *Windows on Reality, Research, Change, and Practice,* a publication of the University of Kansas Center for Research on Learning that was funded by the U.S. Department of Education.

Needs Assessment

You can evaluate individuals' needs by observing them, using rating devices, reviewing portfolios of work, and giving tests. Review cumulative records, and informally diagnose needs during classroom activities. For example, as children engage in group planning, discussion, and evaluation, the teacher can identify interests, difficulties, language skills, and levels of understanding. As children interpret pictures, maps, graphs, and other resources, the teacher can identify those who need special help and those who have attained adequate achievement levels; interests, needs for further study, and misconceptions can also be determined.

Data obtained from tests should always be interpreted with caution. It is well known that intelligence tests do not accurately assess the ability of students from low socioeconomic backgrounds. The tests have also been proved culturally biased. Because tests and inventories designed to measure personality, attitudes, and social adjustment are even less reliable than achievement and intelligence tests, their data should be interpreted in light of the teacher's continuing direct study of children as they work in the classroom.

Another pitfall to avoid is the misuse of labels and classifications that define students' learning difficulties or intelligence levels. These labels can limit the educational experiences offered to students if they are understood as rigid categories. Don't presume that a student with learning disabilities (1) has all the "standard" traits used to define this category or (2) is gravely limited in learning ability because of this categorization. Likewise, don't presume that a low score on an achievement test reflects the overall ability of an at-risk student. All students should be challenged to learn. Instruction should not be shaped to fit a diagnostic classification or a test score; it should fit the student's unique profile of ability and background.

As you assess a student's needs, think about a whole range of characteristics. Do consider the student's background in terms of cultural heritage and socioeconomic group. You might note the student's strengths, needs, and achievements in the following areas:

prior knowledge	attitudes	reading ability
skills	interests	writing ability
talents	learning problems	speaking ability
type and amount of participation in class	social problems	learning style

Assessment of learning styles is informed by Gardner's theory of multiple intelligences. Gardner has postulated a number of intelligences including linguistic, musical, bodily–kinesthetic, and spatial. Teachers observe the ways in which students solve problems and produce work, and then teachers provide direction and activities reflecting students' approaches to learning. Learning styles may also be identified by using inventories and by questioning students. Some teachers use systems specially designed to accommodate learning styles. For example, the *4MAT System* (McCarthy, 1990) includes four major types of learners: imaginative, analytic, common-sense, and dynamic. Attention is given to the use of both hemispheres of the brain—the analytic, serial, and rational left, and the global, visual, and holistic right. Concrete experience, reflective observation, abstract conceptualization, and active experimentation are included in the program.

You can also encourage students to evaluate their own learning styles, expand their learning styles, and develop a broad range of skills. The following ideas may help.

Why is providing for individual differences one way of improving instruction for all *students? How do K–8 social studies teachers provide for individual differences?*

 *Learning Styles*

➤ As one aspect of developing metacognitive skills, encourage students to think about their own preferred ways of learning. You might provide a worksheet like this one to stimulate their thinking.

What Is My Favorite Way of Learning?

Circle the numbers of your favorite learning activities.

1. Looking at pictures
2. Watching demonstrations
3. Making drawings and diagrams
4. Listening to a speaker
5. Listening to a recording
6. Noticing sounds
7. Making things with my hands
8. Touching and holding objects as I study them
9. Putting models together or taking things apart
10. Reading books
11. Finding information in the library
12. Studying written materials

Answer key:

Items 1–3: visual learner   Items 7–9:   kinesthetic learner
Items 4–6: auditory learner   Items 10–12: verbal learner
Mixed items: combination learner

➤ You can urge students to expand their range of learning styles by reflecting on a variety of learning activities in social studies. A chart like this one might help them get started.

Expand Your Learning Style!

Be a visual learner!

- Get ideas from photographs, paintings, sculpture, textiles, and graphic design.
- Watch demonstrations, either in person or by viewing videos.
- Instead of writing notes, draw your thoughts and ideas.
- Pay attention to cartoons, company logos, international signage symbols, and other ways in which visuals are used to communicate.
- When you present a report, think of ways to use art or graphics to enhance your written or oral work.
- Focus on visual elements as you watch documentaries or movies.

(continued)

Be a listening learner!

■ Focus on listening skills. Notice how spoken words express thoughts and feelings. Think about tone of voice and the tempo of talk. How do they help shape communication?

■ Make use of recordings of speeches, poems, work songs, African American spirituals, and other listening experiences as you study all kinds of subject matter.

■ Focus on aspects of sound as you watch movies or TV. Try experiencing a video by listening only. What do you notice that you might have otherwise missed? How do sound effects, music, silences, or other auditory effects influence the message?

Be a kinesthetic learner!

■ Construct models or dioramas.

■ Participate in a litter clean-up project or help reconstruct a neighborhood park.

■ Cultivate plants, measure their growth, and note the stages in their development.

■ When possible, hold artifacts to better understand their use and the craftwork that formed them.

■ Use a recipe to make a food reflective of a culture or time period.

■ Offer to help in a local archaeological dig or in an oral history project.

Be a verbal learner!

■ Use written materials as a source of knowledge.

■ Get a variety of reading experiences by delving into textbooks, magazines, biographies, poems and stories, historic documents, and newspapers from different time periods.

■ Use writing to communicate your ideas in a variety of modes: persuasive writing, creative writing, reporting, and so on.

Be a cooperative learner!

■ Participate in group activities.

■ Brainstorm ideas with other students.

■ Notice how others think of ideas and get answers to questions.

■ Hone your listening and speaking skills.

■ Share parts of a task and participate in bringing the parts together.

Be an independent learner!

■ Set your own goals for learning and achieving.

■ Research topics and complete projects in areas that really interest you.

■ Stick to tasks that you set for yourself.

■ Be resourceful. Get help from people and from learning materials.

■ Evaluate how well you do. Make plans for improving your skills.

➤ As students think about learning styles, it's natural for them to notice skills that come easily to them and to take note of skills they lack. You might provide a skills inventory for students to use as they think about the skills they still need to develop. Then, of course, you'll provide opportunities for them to actually develop the skills! A skill inventory might look like this:

What Skills of Mine Need Improvement?

listening	making charts and graphs
speaking	using the dictionary
reading	using the thesaurus
reflecting on what I read	using the atlas
writing	studying effectively
reviewing what I've learned	working individually
using the computer	thinking critically
using the library	understanding drawings and diagrams
following directions	understanding numerical data
discussing problems	completing hands-on projects
investigating problems	keeping up with the news
working in groups	appreciating the arts
making maps	understanding different viewpoints
making outlines	expressing myself artistically
taking notes	expressing my own thoughts and feelings
reporting information	building cooperative relationships
interviewing	

➤ Thinking about learning styles and multiple intelligences often highlights the importance of aesthetic awareness and expression. To keep alive students' natural creativity and to refine their appreciation of the arts, it makes sense to focus on this area from time to time in social studies instruction. Here are assorted ideas to use as springboards for highlighting aesthetic topics in your classroom:

Textile production is a rich area to explore, and students can undertake their own simple projects in weaving, knitting, and needlework as well. You might focus on the stunning weavings of the Inca, Navajo rugs, Hmong embroidery, knotted rugs of Iran, Amish quilts, early American embroidered samplers, Scandinavian knitting, Irish crochet, or West African kente cloth. The tactile nature of handling fiber and the potential visual effects will be a natural magnet for students with visual and kinesthetic leanings. Students can reflect on the practical uses and aesthetic values embodied in these works.

Studying and making mosaics is another avenue for understanding artistic expression in certain cultures and for giving students opportunity for creative expression. Learning about mosaic design in sculpture, architecture, jewelry, and religious art can help bring various historical periods to life, and the medium's emphasis on recycling bits of pottery, glass, and other materials shows students how artists can be resourceful in finding materials to work with. Challenge students to find materials that they can recycle into their own mosaics.

Focusing on material culture and interior design in a given historical period gives students a window on the lifestyles and values that prevailed at the time. What does the interior of Mount Vernon tell about Washington's life and times? What do Versailles and the Taj Mahal tell about their respective cultures? What sorts of craftworkers were involved in the production of the materials that comprise these structures? Explorations at the other end of the socioeconomic spectrum can be just as rewarding. What does the simple housing at Plimoth Plantation tell about the experience of the Pilgrims? What do shanty towns tell about black African experience in South Africa?

Photography is another rich area to explore. This medium combines the painter's eye for composition and interesting visual elements with the immediacy of current social conditions, news events, and individual experience. Fine photography can present geographic and cultural detail in a gripping way. Once students understand the potential of this medium, they can find ways to document their own celebrations, local geography, school and family events, field trips and public service, and individual self-expression in photography. Low-cost cameras and funding from local organizations can support this activity. Students can also explore how photography is used in newspapers and magazines and on the Internet.

Wherever you begin teaching in the United States, you will find unique aesthetic expression. Every region is host to artists, local museums, and historical associations; you may have to seek them out, but it could be well worth it. Folk art, basketry, woodworking, textile production, sculpture, unique toys or games, calligraphy, collage, pottery, glass making, cabinet making, paper making, book binding, floral arts, building webpages, and tool making are just some of the crafts that may flourish in your own back yard. Many such artisans would be delighted to give demonstrations in the local school; others may give lessons to students. Students can gain both aesthetic enrichment and knowledge of part of the economy by interacting with such workers.

Instructional Strategies

Assessment of students' learning needs is reflected in the range of strategies and plans for instruction that the teacher develops. These may include classroom setup, selecting and developing study materials, arranging small-group and individual learning experiences, and techniques for supervising students and charting their progress.

Classroom Setup

At a basic level, the teacher determines the optimal classroom setup to accommodate students' needs. This arrangement, of course, can be readjusted as the year passes. Seating arrangements, learning centers, listening posts, areas for individual study, computer stations, viewing centers, the class library, and interest centers are just some of the possible physical components of the classroom. Teachers don't choose them randomly; they plan them to meet the needs of students.

Learning centers can change as you move from unit to unit. A social studies learning center may feature materials about Asia at one point in the year; later, the focus may switch to Africa. Teachers should introduce students to the materials at each center and post procedures for using them. Figure 6.2 shows a poster from a learning center that gives students directions for using it.

Gathering Materials

Another element of planning consists of gathering the learning materials suited to various members of the class. These materials may include texts at a variety of levels of reading difficulty (some, perhaps rewritten by the teacher to meet a student's needs), learning kits, study guides and modules customized to meet different needs, activity cards, computer programs, practice worksheets, learning games, and so on.

One of the best sources of information is the list of materials in school district units of study and teaching guides. Some media centers provide kits of materials on varying readability levels that have been assembled for different units. Catalogs from local media centers and the list of additional reading materials in social studies textbooks and accompanying teacher's guides are other good sources of information. School and community libraries are excellent sources of reading materials for both

■ **FIGURE 6.2**

Using the Social Studies Learning Center

Follow these rules:

1. *Choose the materials you want to use.*
2. *Use one item at a time.*
3. *Write down the ideas that you want to share.*
4. *Return the item to its proper place.*
5. *Choose another item.*

Where to put things:

TOP SHELF: materials for the transportation committee

MIDDLE SHELF: materials for the urban renewal committee

BOTTOM SHELF: materials for the pollution committee

ON THE TABLE: city map for the mapping committee

students and teachers. Many teachers share their room libraries with each other, thus making books on different levels available. Guides to books and free and inexpensive materials are listed in the references at the end of Chapter 9.

Planning for Group Work

When teachers discover that a group of students share a need for practice, review, or reteaching, they may use small groups to meet this need. Groups may be organized on the basis of the following:

Special needs: Students are given instruction in basic skills such as using an index or interpreting a map.

Assigned topics: Students are given a topic or a problem to investigate in depth.

Common interest: Students who have chosen a particular topic or problem read materials related to it.

Partner or group-leader study: One student assists a partner, or two or three children, in reading selected materials.

A form for making a block plan for three groups is presented in Figure 6.3. Notice that provision is made for each group to work with the teacher, to read an assignment, and to do a worksheet or independent study. The teacher moves from group A to group B and finally to Group C.

■ FIGURE 6.3

Planning for Group Work

Group A	Group B	Group C
Instruction by teacher: _____ _____ _____	Worksheet or independent reading: _____ _____ _____	Reading by students: _____ _____ _____
Reading by students: _____ _____ _____	Instruction by teacher: _____ _____ _____	Worksheet or independent reading: _____ _____ _____
Worksheet or independent reading: _____ _____ _____	Reading by students: _____ _____ _____	Instruction by teacher: _____ _____ _____

Teachers may also assemble groups for creative work or to develop skills in co-operation. Projects such as constructing a map or functioning as a committee (for example, the class's current events committee) are two possibilities for these types of group work.

Guidance and Supervision

Teachers provide different levels of guidance and supervision, based on student needs and the demands of the subject matter. Teachers may vary the amount of time a student is given to complete work and may provide different kinds of assistance. For example, one student may need help in settling down to work, another may need help in completing an outline, and a group working on a map may need help locating certain features. By moving about the room and observing children at work, a teacher can give guidance when it is needed. Because each child is unique, the teacher should tailor his or her approach to fit emotional as well as intellectual needs. A smile, an encouraging comment, or an understanding nod may be just right for one child, whereas another may need a thought-provoking question, a specific suggestion, or direct assistance on a problem.

At times a student may need and should receive a direct answer to a question—how to find a booklet, how to complete an outline, or where to locate particular items on a map. At other times the best answer is another question—Have you checked the study guide? Will the outline form on the chart be useful? Do you think the atlas will be a good source? If a student needs to move ahead, then direct assistance may be given. If the objective is to improve thinking skills and help students become more self-directive, then a question or a comment may actually be more helpful.

Accommodating Different Cognitive Levels

Differences in cognitive levels are apparent in the ways that students raise questions, interpret readings, draw inferences, and state generalizations. Some students may describe obvious features or relationships they observed in reading a passage. Others may explain complex relationships and hypothesize reasons for them. In class discussion, teachers can expect questions and answers that point to different levels of understanding, ranging from simple observation and recalling to higher-order responses that interpret or classify information. To encourage the participation of all students, teachers can ask questions suited to a variety of cognitive levels. Finding ways to challenge all students is the key.

Students will vary in the depth and breadth of their understanding of social studies concepts, concept clusters, and generalizations. Teachers can nudge students a step forward in developing their knowledge of this content. For example, a student may move from an understanding that (1) people in the home have different jobs, to the more refined judgment that (2) work is divided among people in the home and in the neighborhood, to the big-picture generalization that (3) division of labor helps to get more work done. The teacher can affirm and support each level of understanding while encouraging the student to move ahead into greater complexity and subtler judgment.

For example, the following questioning strategies will help move students from noting the obvious to making finer distinctions and judgments.

Interpreting the Map of Mexico

- What does each symbol in the key stand for?
- Where is the capital? What is its name?
- Where are other large cities located?
- Where are the main roads?
- What relationships might exist between the locations of cities and roads?
- How are the locations of cities, roads, and mountains interrelated?

Mexican Industries

- What data can you find about each industry?
- What generalizations can you make about these industries?
- How did you arrive at these generalizations? How did you group facts and ideas?
- Do your generalizations fit the facts?
- Do you need to adjust the generalizations in any way? Why?
- How important is each industry? Rank them in order.

Providing Different Learning Activities

- Among the tools that social studies teachers have found especially useful for developing instruction that takes into account individual differences are computers, multilevel reading materials, learning contracts, and learning centers.

—Peter H. Martorella

Choose among the learning activities presented in Chapter 5 to accommodate individual differences. First, provide activities that students can handle successfully in group work, making contributions to planning, discussion, and evaluation. Second, provide a variety of independent and team activities to meet special needs. Too frequently some students do a single activity over and over because they are good at it. Students who always choose drawing and painting, for example, may miss other needed learning activities. A cardinal rule to follow is to develop challenging activities. If necessary, challenging activities may be modified during instruction to meet the individual needs of students.

Developing Learning Contracts

One practical means of meeting individual needs is to develop learning contracts. A learning contract is an agreement between a student and a teacher, stating what the student will do and when it is to be completed. Different formats of the learning contract are shown in Figure 6.4.

Learning contracts may be prepared cooperatively by a student and a teacher, prepared by the teacher to meet a particular need, or prepared by a student to pursue a special interest. Whichever procedure is used, the student should fully understand what is expected, and the teacher should be sure that the activities of the contract have value for the student and are not merely busywork.

■ **FIGURE 6.4**

Learning Contract Forms

Option A

We do hereby agree that you will do the following by _____.

1. _____

2. _____

3. _____

_____   _____   _____
    Student's Signature   Teacher's Signature   Date

Option B

I, _____ , agree to do the following by _____.

1. To find information on shipbuilding in Japan in *Japan,* by Cuban and
   Greenblatt; *Japan,* by Pitts; and *The World Almanac*

2. To prepare a report on shipbuilding in Japan

3. To present the report to the class

_____   _____   _____
    Student's Signature   Teacher's Signature   Date

Option C

1. My objectives are (state specific things you plan to accomplish).

2. I will use these materials (list textbooks, references, and other sources).

3. I will find answers to these questions (list questions you plan to answer).

4. I will complete these activities (list mapping, chart making, interviewing,
   and so on).

5. I will complete the contract by _____.

Signature: _____

Individualizing Worksheets and Activity Cards

As you plan worksheets and activity cards for social studies units, you may need to vary them somewhat to accommodate the needs of students. Some may provide more challenging activities that call on higher-order thinking or creative work. Some may reinforce key concepts, review important information, and address a given student's difficulties. These activity card ideas will give you a range of choices in developing these materials for students.

ACTIVITY IDEAS ▶ *Social Studies Activity Cards*

➤ The following selection of activities can be used by students as they read or respond to selections in the textbook or other sources. They can be adapted to suit various grade levels and unique student needs.

Jobs at Home

Who does each job at home?

cooking _____   putting toys away _____

dusting _____   mowing the lawn _____

vacuuming _____   cleaning the clothes _____

making beds _____   washing the dishes_____

Communication

Which of these forms of communication are shown on page 32?

_____ television   _____ newspapers   _____ telegraph

_____ radio   _____ magazine   _____ signs

_____ telephone   _____ speech   _____ e-mail

_____ satellite   _____ signals   _____ website

Where Are They Located?

Look at the map on page 103. On what streets are these located?

bank _____   city hall _____

park _____   hospital _____

school _____   library _____

synagogue _____   post office _____

fire station _____   church _____

Compare our community and our state capital in the following areas:

Features	Our Community	State Capital
Population	_____	_____
Area	_____	_____
Industries	_____	_____
Recreation	_____	_____

Read pages 62–63, and then complete these sentences.

Adaptation means _____.

An artifact is _____.

Archaeologists study _____.

Customs are _____.

Traditions are _____.

Choose the best answer.

Archaeologists find artifacts by	The first Americans came from
(a) asking inhabitants about them.	(a) Africa.
(b) using maps.	(b) Asia.
(c) reading books.	(c) Europe.
(d) digging in ruins.	(d) Mexico.

Use each of these words in a sentence.

landforms	elevation	slope	altitude
plain	incline	province	longitude
plateau	region	country	latitude

Interpret a Graph

Study the graph on page 97, and then answer these questions.

1. What is the wettest month in San Francisco? in Los Angeles?
2. What is the driest month in San Francisco? in Los Angeles?

More detailed than activity cards, worksheets may present a task or objective, directions, and materials to use, as shown in Figures 6.5 and 6.6 (pp. 200 and 201). See Table 6.1 (pp. 198–199) for the wide variety of tasks that students can accomplish using activity cards and worksheets.

■ **TABLE 6.1**

Activities for Worksheets and Activity Cards

Writing
- Name of school, community, state, country, and places studied
- Descriptions of people, objects, activities, rural and urban scenes
- Answers to questions
- Main ideas, details, and conclusions
- Notes, outlines, and definitions
- Letters, editorials, and reports

Labeling
- Places on community, state, regional, country, and world maps
- Oceans, continents, and mountain ranges on maps
- Poles, equators, and other features on hemisphere maps
- Features on drawings and diagrams
- Travel routes on maps
- U.S. territorial acquisitions on maps
- Dates or events on time lines

Copying
- Basic rules such as those for a fire drill
- Portions of documents such as the Declaration of Independence and the Constitution
- Dates of important events

Rewriting
- Putting ideas into one's own words
- Recasting false statements to make them true
- Putting main ideas and details in the correct order

Listing
- List of community workers and the services they provide
- Resources and the products made from them
- Steps in a process, such as making bread or making steel
- Dates of historical events in correct time sequence
- Putting items in alphabetical order

Outlining
- Ideas for a report
- Main ideas and related details from a reading
- Causes and effects
- Alternative solutions to a problem and their consequences

Filling in the Blanks
- Blanks in statements and paragraphs
- Names of places on maps
- Blanks in outlines
- Names of states and capitals
- Blanks in stories
- Blanks in charts, graphs, and tables

Crossing Out
- Cross out the incorrect answer
- Cross out items that don't belong in a group
- Cross out a step that does not belong in a process

Underlining
- Underline the best answer
- Underline your preferred position on an issue
- Underline items in a list that belong together
- Underline the word needed to correctly complete a statement

Circling
- Circle the best answer
- Circle items that belong together
- Circle pictures or words that depict goods, services, or other items

Questions and Answers
- Essay questions
- Multiple-choice questions
- True–false questions
- Who am I? questions

Finding Information
- Using the atlas
- Using the dictionary
- Using the thesaurus
- Using the encyclopedia
- Using the glossary
- Using the Internet
- Using almanacs and yearbooks
- Reading bus, train, or airline schedules
- Using directories

Making Computations
- Determine distances by using a map scale
- Find length of great circle routes on a globe
- Determine population density
- Figure per capita income
- Find out the time that passed between certain events
- Determine the travel time between two places via air, bus, train, or ship

Matching
- Workers with goods or services that they provide
- Words with definitions
- People with their achievements
- Branches of government with their activities
- Map symbols with what they represent
- Type of information with the best source in which to find it

Classifying
- Goods and services
- Resources and products
- Needs and wants
- Causes and effects
- Duties of executive, legislative, and judicial officials
- Places according to climate
- Crops by region
- Past events and present events

Numbering in Order
- Sequence of steps in a process
- Events in chronological order
- Cities, states, or countries by area or population

Drawing Pictures
- Food, shelter, clothing, and other needs
- Wants
- Changes in season and seasonal activities
- Modes of transportation
- Map symbols and what they represent

Constructing
- Maps
- Charts, graphs, diagrams, and tables
- Time lines
- Models

Tracing
- Maps
- Travel routes
- Dot-to-dot tracing to make letters, words, maps, or names of places
- Equator, prime meridian, and other lines on hemisphere maps

Solving Puzzles
- Riddles
- Word searches
- Crossword puzzles
- Scrambled words and phrases

■ FIGURE 6.5

Worksheet on Explorers

Objectives	To use the index to locate information		
	To summarize information on explorers		
Materials	Textbook		
Directions	Use the index of your textbook to find information on the explorers listed below. Complete this worksheet by filling in the blanks as shown for the first explorer.		

Name of Explorer	Sponsoring Country	Year(s) of Exploration	Area Explored
Jacques Cartier	France	1534–1535	St. Lawrence River
Samuel de Champlain			
Henry Hudson			
William Baffin			
Robert de la Salle			

Providing Modules

■ World Council for Gifted and Talented Children **http:// worldgifted.com** provides researcher and teachers with recent developments in the area of gifted education.

Modules are more extensive than worksheets (see Chapter 5). They enable students to work at varying rates and to achieve specified objectives. The lesson plan on page 202 may be modified to develop skills such as finding main ideas and related details in reading materials and interpreting maps, tables, diagrams, and other media.

■ Planning for Differences in Reading and Other Skills

The wide range of reading ability that exists in every class calls for the same care in planning for reading in the social studies as in the developmental reading program. Information on children collected as part of the developmental reading program can be used to individualize reading in the social studies. It may be supplemented by observation of students as they read social studies materials. Particular attention should be given to students' ability to read maps, time lines, graphs, diagrams, and reference

■ **FIGURE 6.6**

Worksheet on U.S. Territories

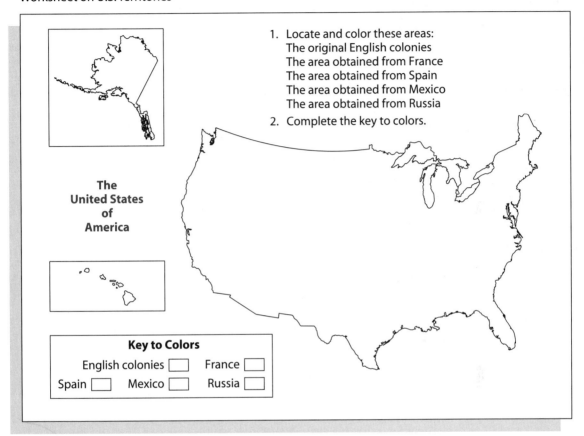

1. Locate and color these areas:
   The original English colonies
   The area obtained from France
   The area obtained from Spain
   The area obtained from Mexico
   The area obtained from Russia

2. Complete the key to colors.

The
United States
of
America

Key to Colors

English colonies ☐   France ☐

Spain ☐   Mexico ☐   Russia ☐

materials such as atlases and encyclopedias. Teachers should also observe students'
use of the table of contents, index, and glossary in social studies textbooks. Social
studies tests and study skill assessment also provide useful data.

Using Self-Directed Reading Strategies

The self-directed reading strategies that follow are designed to help students in upper
grades read on their own. A widely used one is SQ3R.

S *(Survey):* Get an overview; check the organization; read headings.
Q *(Question):* Develop questions to answer based on heading or topic sentences.
R *(Read):* Find answers to questions.
R *(Recite):* State or write answers to questions.
R *(Reread):* Clinch key ideas, check answers, reread key parts.

LESSON PLAN   *Identifying Features on the Globe and Global Maps*

Objective   To identify and name hemispheres, continents, and oceans shown on the globe and global maps

Directions   Go to the map center, and use the globe and global maps in folder A to complete this module.

Part A: Western Hemisphere
Take the global outline map that shows the Western Hemisphere, and place it by the globe turned to show the Western Hemisphere. Do the following:

1. Find the North Pole on the globe. Print North Pole on the global map.
2. Find the South Pole on the globe. Print South Pole on the global map.
3. Find North America on the globe. Print North America on the global map.
4. Find South America on the globe. Print South America on the global map.
5. Find Antarctica on the globe. Print Antarctica on the global map.
6. Find the Pacific Ocean on the globe. Print Pacific Ocean on the global map.
7. Find the Atlantic Ocean on the globe. Print Atlantic Ocean on the global map.
8. Find the Arctic Ocean on the globe. Print Arctic Ocean on the global map.

Part B: Eastern Hemisphere
Take the global outline map that shows the Eastern Hemisphere and place it by the globe turned to show the Eastern Hemisphere. Do the following:

1. Find the North Pole on the globe. Print North Pole on the global map.
2. Find the South Pole on the globe. Print South Pole on the global map.
3. Find Europe on the globe. Print Europe on the global map.
4. Find Asia on the globe. Print Asia on the global map.
5. Find Africa on the globe. Print Africa on the global map.
6. Find Australia on the globe. Print Australia on the global map.
7. Find Antarctica on the globe. Print Antarctica on the global map.
8. Find the Atlantic Ocean on the globe. Print Atlantic Ocean on the global map.
9. Find the Pacific Ocean on the globe. Print Pacific Ocean on the global map.
10. Find the Indian Ocean on the globe. Print Indian Ocean on the global map.

A helpful and creative activity is to guide students to create their own self-directed reading strategy (Prove), as illustrated by the following example:

Prove

P   *(Purpose):* Set a purpose or questions to guide reading.
R   *(Read):* Achieve your purpose or answer your questions.
O   *(Organize):* Place details under main ideas.
V   *(Vocabulary):* Note new concepts and words you mastered.
E   *(Evaluate):* Did you achieve your purpose?

How have recent technological innovations helped teachers? What are some ways teachers make use of technology to improve reading and writing in social studies instruction?

Encouraging Independent Reading

Provide individualized reading so that students can select and read unit-related materials on different reading levels, keep logs of their reading, share ideas related to unit topics, and recommend favorites to others. Guide them to volumes available from children's book clubs, articles and stories in children's magazines, and library resources.

Arrange special times for all students and the teacher to read silently, using DEAR (Drop Everything and Read), SSR (Sustained Silent Reading), WIERD (We're Involved in Enthused Reading Daily), DIRT (Daily Independent Reading Time), or SQUIRT (Super Quiet Undisturbed Reading Time) for students' reading of literature related to social studies instruction. Provide time for conferencing, in which children share ideas, read selected parts orally, raise questions, respond to questions raised by the teacher and others, and make plans for future reading (Wiseman, 1991).

Preparing Reports

Oral and written reports are an effective means of individualizing instruction in accord with differences in expressive skills. Students may work on a topic of special interest or on an assigned topic at a pace and a level consistent with their capabilities. The variety of topics is vast indeed, as the following sampling from a few social studies units shows.

Home and Family: How Work Is Divided; Care of Pets; How Our Family Saves Energy; How Our Family Has Fun; How Families Have Fun in Other Cultures

Our Community: How Our Community Got Its Name; The First Buildings; The First School; Our Water Supply; Parks with Playgrounds for Children; The City Center Renewal Projects; The Future of Our Community

Our State: The First Americans; The First European Settlers; The First Town; Early Travel Routes; Main Transportation Routes Today; How the Capital Was Chosen; Our State's Nickname; The Story of Our State Flag; Products We Send to Other States; Our State's Largest City; Our State Parks; Environmental and Pollution Problems; Future Plans to Meet Problems

Living in Early America: The Plymouth Colony; Town Meetings; What Early Schools Were Like; Games Children Played; Help from Native Americans; How Clothing Was Made; Candle Making; Some of Ben Franklin's Inventions

Living in Other Cultures: Family Life; Foods They Eat; Family Recreation; A Day in the Village of _____ ; Places to Visit; Special Customs and Holidays; Ways That We and the People of _____ Are Alike; Their Schools; Art and Music; Main Problems They Are Facing; Future Plans

Other topics for reports may be found in students' textbooks and identified in discussions of unit topics. Because developing a report can be quite challenging, the following ideas may be useful as you assist students.

 *Helping Students Create Reports*

➤ Choosing and narrowing a topic can be challenging. To help students make a positive start in writing a report, you might provide a worksheet like this one. The questions will help them focus and refine the topics they have chosen.

> **My Report Topic**
>
> I would like to write a report on _____ .
> Why is this topic important?
> How is it related to our unit?
> What makes it especially interesting to me?
> Why will others find it interesting?
> Can I find information about this topic? Where?
> Is this topic too big for one report? How can I narrow it?

➤ Once students have selected and narrowed a topic, they might develop a series of questions they'd like to answer in the report. The questions should include all the main ideas the student will research. Since the questions will guide the student's study, it's important to check the list to make sure the questions can be reasonably answered with the resources on hand and that the student is asking enough questions but not more than can be answered in a single report.

➤ As students move through the upper elementary and middle school grades, they typically begin creating outlines to use as they write their reports. The social studies classroom is a good place to teach and reinforce this procedure. For younger students or those who need a different approach, however, you might want to provide a simplified outline form that they can fill in as they organize their ideas. Here's an example.

My Social Studies Report

My topic is _____.

My sources of information are _____

_____.

I will write about the information in this order.

Introduction _____

First main idea _____

Second main idea _____

Third main idea _____

Conclusion _____

➤ Encourage students to enhance their reports with visuals. They might include flow charts, photocopies of photographs (crediting the source), drawings, charts, graphs, tables, diagrams, maps, time lines, or political cartoons. Students can create such visuals by hand or on the computer.

➤ Once they have completed their reports, help students think of creative ways to publish them. Reports about local history might be displayed in a store window downtown. Students might make oral presentations such as speaking as a newscaster, a tour guide, a public official, or a historical character. Students might gather their reports in a classroom encyclopedia or put them in separate booklets.

Independent Study Habits

Good study habits are essential to the completion of learning contracts, activity cards, reports, and other individual activities. Because of the variety of opportunities for individual study, the social studies program is particularly well suited to developing effective study habits and encouraging their use at home and in the library. The foundations for good study habits are established in the early grades and are refined as students advance.

As mentioned in other parts of this chapter, teachers help students internalize effective study habits by providing them every opportunity to practice these skills in the classroom and while completing individual activities that require the use of the library and other learning resources. When students are asked to complete assignments that require the use of sources outside of the school, teachers may wish to assess more carefully students' independent and study habit skills.

The following ideas may help you find ways to support good study habits among your students:

 **ACTIVITY IDEAS** ▶ *Building Good Study Habits*

➤ Good study habits include listening well to instructions, clarifying misunderstandings about an assignment, and carrying out work in a well-organized fashion. You might give students a list like the following to help them remember the steps in fully completing a study assignment.

Good Study Habits

Know your purpose and keep it clearly in mind:

Stop: Stop other activities so that you get clear directions.
Look: Watch the teacher so that you understand each point.
Listen: Note the details on what to do.
Ask: Raise questions if you do not understand any part.
Proceed to do it:
Organize: Arrange materials and plan the steps to take.
Concentrate: Stick to your job and ignore distractions.
Finish: Complete the job before starting other activities.
Check: Review your work to be sure it is complete and well done.

➤ To support students as they complete work at home, you might give them a set of guidelines to follow. It is easy to forget these steps in a busy atmosphere at home. Such guidelines will also help students internalize the conditions and methods that produce valuable study.

Improving Home Study

Know exactly what you are to do.
Be sure to take needed materials home.
Plan study time so that you will not have to stay up late.
Study in a place where you can work without interruption.
Arrange the study materials so that you can use them effectively.
Finish the job once you have started it.
Do your own work. (You may get advice on hard parts.)
Review your work and make any changes that will improve it.
Be ready to ask questions the next day on any parts you need help on.
Get more tips from *Homeworker, The Homework Solution, Deskmate,* or *A-Plus* in the computer center.

Helping Students Individualize Their Own Learning Activities

Students can learn how to choose materials, activities, individual work, group work, and performance standards that match their needs. This is another aspect of "learning how to learn," a goal for all students. When both the teacher and the student are working to individualize instruction, the student will make even greater gains in learning.

Encourage students to help themselves learn by raising questions when something seems unclear, asking for help when it is needed, using a variety of learning materials, and focusing on instructions for activities and study assignments. Help them learn how to take the initiative when they have free time on their hands: will they work on an individual project, listen to recordings or view a video related to the unit, practice a skill, find ideas in the picture file, study other readings related to the unit, or review what is available in the social studies learning center? They can become more independent in making these choices if they understand how to find materials in the classroom and library, use equipment in the learning center, and know when an especially challenging task requires quiet and extended concentration.

Students can improve in making such judgments, but they certainly need the teacher's input too. Teachers can also help when students become confused or frustrated by the fact that some students complete assignments quickly, other students work more slowly, and still others have their work modified to cover fewer concepts or to involve less reading. Here again, educators can help students understand such differences by making points such as these:

Because We Are Different . . .
- We vary the time spent on some activities.
- We work as a class on some projects and in small groups on others.
- We have projects that each of us can do alone.
- We find materials we can use in our work.
- We give help on some things and get help on others.

Conclusion

Diversity is a trademark of American schools, and in every classroom differences among students are quite evident. Diversity comes in all shapes and sizes and enriches the classroom. At one level, teachers incorporate the diversity found in their classrooms to enrich instruction. At another level, they identify the differences students bring to the classroom and tailor instruction to help students experience school success.

The teacher and the students can use numerous strategies and activities in the diverse classroom to facilitate instruction. They make curriculum modifications to help children and young adults with exceptionalities; those who speak a language other than English; those who experience difficulties in studying, reading, and initiating and completing assignments; and those who have low self-esteem. The key to addressing these student needs is the teacher. Caring and taking the initiative can go a long way in helping diverse students learn.

 Questions, Activities, and Evaluating

1. Visit a middle school and note the following:
   a. Identify the diverse student groups attending the school.
   b. Identify the languages you hear being spoken by the students.
   c. Speak to the special education teacher about the needs of students with exceptionalities.
   d. Speak with the principal or a teacher about expertise and services available to meet the needs of students.

2. Visit an elementary classroom and note the following:
   a. Differences among children in the use of language, work habits, involvement in activities, and the like
   b. Techniques and activities used by the teacher to accommodate individual differences and to include special students in social studies
   c. Learning centers in the classroom and materials that might be used to accommodate individual differences
   d. Forms used to prepare an IEP

3. How might the basic strategies and techniques for accommodating individual differences be put to use in a unit you are planning? Which are easiest to use? Which are hardest?

4. Prepare the following for use in a unit of your choice:
   a. A learning contract, an individual activity card, or a module
   b. A plan for teaching a self-directed reading strategy to students
   c. A plan for teaching students to individualize learning for themselves
   d. Adaptations you might make in a unit for gifted, or other exceptional students discussed in this chapter

References

Bristow, D. et al. (1990). Technology reaching out to special education students. *Media & Methods 26*, 38–40.

Cox III, C. C. (1993). The field trip as a positive experience for the learning disabled. *Social Education, 57*, 92–94.

Crosslin, R. (1994). Mainstreaming, *Learning, 22*, 56.

Cullata, R. A., & Tompkins, J. R. (1999). *Fundamentals of special education: What every teacher should know.* Upper Saddle River, NJ: Prentice Hall.

Dunn, R., Dunn, K., & Perrin, J. (1994). *Teaching young children through their individual learning styles: Practical approaches for grades K–2.* Boston: Allyn & Bacon.

Fuller, C., & Stone, M. E. (1998). Teaching social studies to diverse learners. *The Social Studies, 89*, 154–157.

Gallagher, J. J., & Gallagher, S. A. (1994). *Teaching the gifted child.* Boston: Allyn & Bacon.

Guide to special education resources. (1990). *Electronic Learning, 9*, 26–27. Media for exceptional students.

Hoge, R. D., & Renzulli, J. S. (1993). Exploring the link between giftedness and self-concept. *Review of Educational Research, 63*, 449–65.

Margolis, H., McCabe, P. P., & Schwartz, E. (1990). Using cooperative learning to facilitate mainstreaming in the social studies. *Social Educations, 54*, 111–14.

McCarthy, B. (1990). Using the 4MAT system to bring learning styles to schools. *Educational Leadership, 48*, 31–37.

The project approach. (1994, March). *ERIC/EECE Newsletter.* Urbana, IL: ERIC Clearinghouse on Elementary and Early Childhood Education.

Short, D. J. (1994). The challenge of social studies for limited english proficient students. *Social Education, 58*, 36–38.

Stainback, S., & Stainback, W. (1994). *Curriculum considerations in inclusive classrooms: Facilitating learning for all students.* Cited in "The Bookshelf" in *Education Week*, Vol. 13, Number 3, May 11, 1994. Also see *Inclusion Times: For Children and Youth with Disabilities*, a newsletter in many libraries.

Tampole, E. S., Mathews, F. N., & Konopak, B. C. (1994). Academically gifted students' use of imagery for creative writing. *The Journal of Creative Behavior, 28*, 1–15.

Van Cleaf, D. W. (1991). *Action in elementary social studies.* Englewood Cliffs, NJ: Prentice-Hall.

Vaughn, S., Bos, C. S., & Schumm, J. S. (1997). *Teaching mainstreamed, diverse, and at-risk students in the general education classroom.* Boston: Allyn & Bacon.

Winebrenner, S. (1994). Strategies every teacher can use: Meeting the needs of your high ability students, *Instructor, 104*, 60–63.

Winebrenner, S. (1992). *Teaching gifted kids in the regular classroom: Strategies and techniques every teacher can use to meet the academic needs of the gifted and talented.* Minneapolis: Free Spirit Publishing Inc.

Wiseman, D. L. (1991). *Reading instruction: A literature based approach.* Englewood Cliffs, NJ: Prentice-Hall. See the chapter on independent reading.

Chapter 7

Planning and Guiding Group Learning Activities

Chapter Objective

To present guidelines and strategies for whole-group and small-group learning activities

Focusing Questions

- What are the values and limitations of group learning activities?
- What growth in skills may be noted as students move through the K–8 social studies curriculum?
- What guiding principles are helpful in improving discussions?
- How can questions be used to guide and enrich discussion?
- What guidelines are helpful in improving learning in small-group activities?
- How can study guides be prepared and used to improve learning in small groups?

■ Why Use Group Learning Activities?

If you skim the *Curriculum Standards for Social Studies* and read the sections entitled "Focus on the Classroom: Standards into Practice" under each standard, you will quickly notice that more than a few of the classroom vignettes describe students involved in small-group activities. Why is this so? Why do K–6 teachers include group activities in their social studies programs? Why do middle school teachers do the same? The answer can be found in Chapter 1 by reviewing the definition and purpose of social studies. One purpose of social studies is to acquaint students with the responsibilities of citizenship for people living in a democracy. One of those responsibilities is learning to live and work with other members of society.

Review our history, and you will find numerous instances of Americans working together. The American Revolution would not have happened if colonists had not banded together to fight the British; the westward movement would not have occurred if people had not formed groups that eventually culminated in the movement of thousands of people across the country. Working together is also important because we are a "nation of immigrants" and value diversity. To foster harmony in our communities, we need to demonstrate to students the importance of getting to know their neighbors and learning to work with them.

Working together also is valued in schools because Americans are committed to equality. In America's schools, inclusion has become a reality as students with exceptionalities have been integrated into the general classroom. Group activities are

■ Most basically, the work of democracy requires citizens who can work well together in task oriented groups.
—**Walter C. Parker and John Jarolimek**

211

part of a strategy to address the intellectual and social needs of all students. In social studies, teachers group students to give them the opportunity to appreciate the abilities of others and to bring their abilities together to accomplish tasks.

Much of social studies instruction is provided in whole- and small-group activities. The quality of social studies learning is directly related to the skills with which teachers provide instruction for groups. They know the value of small-group instruction and, whether in the early grades or in middle school, work at fine-tuning these skills. In group activities, teachers introduce students to skills, provide opportunity to practice these skills, and extend the skills in a variety of ways.[1]

■ Whole-Group Activities

In whole-group activities, the class works together as a single group. In many cases whole-group work is the prerequisite to successful small-groups activities. That is, teachers succeed in small-group activities because of their expertise in single-group instruction. Teachers organize students as a whole group to accomplish tasks such as those noted in Table 7.1.

■ Small-Group Activities: Advantages and Limitations

Whereas whole-group activities build a spirit of community in the classroom, small-group activities provide firsthand learning about interpersonal and group participation. It offers a more supportive climate for learners who have difficulty in expressing themselves in large-group settings. Being part of a group fosters feelings of belonging, mutual respect, and responsibility. Interaction with others stimulates thinking. Attitudes and behavior patterns such as openmindedness, responsibility, cooperation, creativity, and concern for others can be developed in small-group settings.

■ The object of education is to get experience out of ideas.

—George Santayana

Small-group activities should be viewed as one of many tools available to the K–8 social studies teacher. As part of a teachers' lesson plan, these activities include instructional objectives, questions to be raised, concepts to be clarified, problems to be discussed, and tasks to be completed. This tool is sometimes overused at the expense of other instructional strategies. At times a short lecture, individualized reading, or a demonstration by the teacher may be more appropriate than small-group activities. Groups such as panels and roundtables should be avoided until students have developed the prerequisite skills. Group activities should be limited to those (1) that are guided by objectives shared by all group members, (2) that can be done better by a group than by individuals, (3) that lend themselves to constructive working relationships, and (4) that take advantage of the diverse talents in the classroom.

1. Grateful acknowledgment is made to Dr. Ruth Grossman, City University of New York, City College and Dr. Victoria Mui, California State University, Hayward, for suggested revisions in this chapter.

■ TABLE 7.1

Tasks Suited to Whole-Group Work

Planning Tasks

For example, planning for these activities:

- Dramatizations
- Things to make
- Displays
- Murals
- Maps
- Storytelling
- Simulation games
- Interviews
- Field trips
- Group projects
- Evaluation standards

Observation Tasks

- Watching a demonstration
- Viewing videos
- Listening to a speaker
- Watching a program on a field trip
- Listening to committee reports

- Listening to announcements
- Watching a role-playing activity
- Listening to a minilecture

Discussion Tasks

- Sharing observations
- Making interpretations
- Making generalizations
- Classifying information
- Making inferences
- Testing hypotheses
- Making predictions
- Analyzing information
- Synthesizing information
- Evaluating data

Giving Instruction

- Clarifying concepts or themes for students
- Presenting background information
- Giving directions for an activity

- Introducing a unit
- Presenting graphic organizers for information
- Explaining and demonstrating a procedure (such as making an outline or preparing a bibliography)
- Giving analysis of issues, problems, events, or situations
- Giving feedback to the class as a whole
- Suggesting improved procedures for accomplishing a task
- Introducing worksheets
- Guiding whole-class collaborative learning activities
- Providing instructional cues such as suggestions, questions, and nonverbal cues

Small-group activities both carry out work planned by the whole class and meet special needs and interests of students. Here are some examples:

Investigation Activities

studying assigned topics
solving problems
raising questions
setting hypotheses
carrying out interviews
doing library research
using study center materials

Collection Activities

gathering pictures
finding articles on a topic
gathering postcards
finding objects related to study
getting props for a dramatization

Construction Activities

making maps
creating charts or graphs
adding labels
painting murals
working with clay
making props for role playing
designing booklets
setting up displays
making a group report

Small-group activities are usually coordinated so that each group makes a contribution to the work of the class. On field trips, for example, the class may be divided into four or five groups to obtain information on different questions. Several groups may be set up to interview different individuals. Parts of murals, time lines, bulletin board arrangements, scrapbooks, and other projects may be handled by designated groups.

■ Discussion Guidelines

One of the most valuable group activities is discussion. Discussion is used to clarify objectives, introduce topics, answer questions, make plans, formulate work standards, analyze issues and problems, make decisions, and evaluate learning. Students learn courtesy, share thoughts and feelings, delegate responsibilities for individual and group work, and learn to respect the rights of others to express themselves. Teachers can observe originality of contributions, sharing of ideas, respect for the opinions of others, consideration of differing points of view, and tendencies toward shyness or boldness. Teachers can give special help as individual needs arise.

In middle school social studies, students are naturally inquisitive and seem to have an opinion on just about every topic. Unfortunately, students may also behave in a self-centered manner and may be reluctant to listen to others or act courteously during a discussion. Middle school teachers spend considerable time at the beginning of each semester in reviewing discussion guidelines—especially before initiating activities such as panel discussions, debates, and other activities calling for verbal interactions. Some teachers begin each discussion by reviewing guidelines to remind the students of proper behavior.

Teachers employ a variety of tools in the classroom. What are some of the ways teachers use wall maps and bulletin boards to enrich discussion in social studies instruction?

You might emphasize the following as you help students participate appropriately in a discussion.

- Focus on the topic.
- Raise your hand it you can't hear.
- Note points made by others.
- Speak up when you have something to contribute.
- Show respect for everyone.
- Listen to others as you want them to listen to you.
- Don't interrupt.

The teacher has a crucial role in group discussion. A supportive atmosphere is essential so that all students will feel that their contributions are valued by the teacher and the group. Shy children should be encouraged, and students who tend to monopolize the discussion should be guided to share discussion time with others.

The discussion topic should be clarified and kept in focus. The teacher should also call for questions, illustrations, and comments as particular items need clarification, and should allow adequate time for thinking. The group should avoid pitfalls such as not sticking to the point, failing to clarify the topic, wasting time on side issues and repetitious comments, failing to listen, embarrassing participants by rejecting their contributions, and allowing a few individuals to dominate discussion. The following guidelines are useful at various grade levels.

> ■ A teacher's method of grouping can sometimes make the difference between a student who feels neglected and who believes himself or herself to be a vital part of the group.
> —**Murry Nelson**

Grades K–3

1. Take turns.
2. Help make plans.
3. Listen to others.

Grades 3–6

1. Help state the problem.
2. Give your ideas.
3. Consider other students' ideas.
4. Listen carefully.
5. Help make a plan.

Grades 6–9

1. State problems clearly.
2. Stick to the point.
3. Be a good listener.
4. Make a contribution.
5. Weigh the evidence.
6. Ask questions about issues.
7. Help in making decisions.
8. Help in summarizing.

Discussion should not be limited to interaction between the teacher and a few individuals. In Figure 7.1 (p. 216), the first example illustrates a pattern of discussion-limiting interaction. The teacher raises a question and a student responds. The teacher comments or raises another question and calls on another student. The same question–answer recitation pattern continues. Although this pattern is useful at times—for eliciting information, reviewing key ideas, or achieving other objectives that require close teacher direction—it should not be used all the time.

■ FIGURE 7.1

Patterns of Discussion

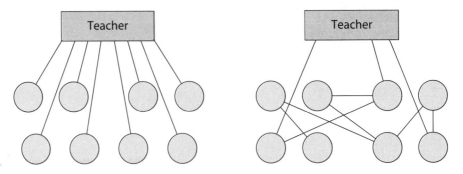

In sharp contrast is discussion characterized by interaction among group members, shown in the second example in Figure 7.1. Here the teacher or discussion leader raises a question or makes a comment, and several participants respond before the leader intervenes. This pattern brings out a variety of ideas and stimulates questions. It encourages initiative and enables students to build on each other's contributions. You might increase participation by seating students strategically, encouraging each to contribute to the discussion.

Students need to develop skill in leading and taking part in small-group discussions, particularly in middle school. The objective may be to brainstorm ideas, explore an issue in a buzz session, plan a panel or roundtable presentation, or find ways to solve a problem.

Using Questions to Improve Discussion

When you raise a discussion question and call on a student, you hold the class's attention. You might rephrase the question or ask another student to provide the answer if the first student can't respond. Consider individual differences as you engage students in discussion, so that each student is challenged to think, but no one is pushed beyond his or her capabilities.

In discussion, call on as many students as possible, and encourage interaction among the class members. If you plan a sequence of questions in advance, you'll be less likely to be sidetracked as tangential issues arise during the talk. Strike a balance between responding to students' questions and concerns and keeping the discussion moving in the right direction.

You can use a variety of expressions to acknowledge students' contributions. Excessive praise after each response dulls its effect. Too much of "Excellent!" and "Very good!" seems artificial. Teachers also use cues to assist students who have provided a partial answer to a question or who have lost track of what they were saying. Cues may include a hint, a synonym for the desired word, pointing to a chart or map, or asking a student to recall a similar event. Giving students time to think often improves the quality of the responses they give.

Teachers use small groups to improve discussion in social studies instruction. What other techniques do teachers employ? What strategies will you use?

As they plan sequences of questions to use in discussions, teachers often organize them by cognitive level, beginning with the simpler tasks of identification and description, and proceeding to higher-order thinking. The following questions exemplify this sequence:

Knowledge: What do you recall about early settlements in Ohio?

Comprehension: Who can summarize the main features of early settlements?

Application: How can we use this information to study western settlements?

Analysis: What are the main parts of this reading on western settlements?

Synthesis: How can we portray western settlements on a mural?

Evaluation: What were the best and poorest features of western settlements?

Three types of questions should be used to guide discussion, as shown in Table 7.2 (p. 218). Questions related to *content* are basic in the sense that they address concepts and main ideas under study. Questions related to the *structure* of discussion guide concept formation, interpretation of data, and use of high-level thinking skills. Questions related to *students' comments* develop a positive classroom climate and give support and encouragement to students.

Evaluating Discussion

Both the teacher and the group should evaluate discussion, giving specific attention to points and problems as they arise. The teacher should keep in mind both the essential elements of effective discussion and the maturity of students. The discussion itself can be appraised in terms of the earlier discussion in this chapter. Evaluation can be sharpened by videotaping a discussion and having students watch the playback.

In addition to group evaluation, the teacher should do ongoing evaluation and follow-up that includes individual guidance. Figure 7.2 includes key points to keep in mind in appraising students' discussion skills. Many students in the middle grades can use the checklist for self-evaluation.

■ **TABLE 7.2**

Types of Discussion Questions

Questions Related to Content	**Questions That Help Structure Discussion**	**Questions Related to Students' Comments**
Open-ended questions invite participation and elicit divergent responses:	*Focusing questions* guide thinking step by step:	*Accepting questions* or comments help students who repeat information or wander off the topic:
■ What do you remember about _____?	■ What did you find?	■ Have we already listed that?
■ What parts of this unit will be most interesting? Why?	■ Which items can be grouped together?	■ Could we come back to that question later, Ben?
	■ What is a good name for the group?	■ So you agree with what Jane said?
Specific questions focus attention and elicit convergent responses:	*Refocusing questions* bring students back to the topic:	*Supporting questions* help shy children and those who have difficulty:
■ What steps were taken to _____?	■ What is the point that we are discussing?	■ Can you tell us more about _____?
■ How are _____ and _____ alike? How are they different?	■ What is the focus of this discussion?	■ What is your own feeling about _____?
■ What were the main causes of _____?	■ Can someone give me more examples of _____?	■ Can you give an example of that?
Probing questions call for explanations, alternative solutions, and deeper thinking:	*Lifting questions* shift thinking from recalling to higher cognitive levels:	*Encouraging questions* bring silent students into the discussion:
■ What is another possible explanation for _____?	■ What do you recall about _____?	■ Can someone who hasn't had a turn give another example?
■ What might this person's motives have been?	■ What is likely to happen if _____?	■ Who has a question about any of the points we've made so far?
■ What are other possible reasons for _____?	■ What is your evaluation of _____?	■ Does anyone else have something to say about _____?
Clarifying questions focus on the meaning of terms and statements:		
■ What do you mean by _____?		
■ Who can state this information in his or her own words?		
■ What are examples of _____?		

■ **FIGURE 7.2**

Evaluating Discussion Skills

Note: Check each student two or three times during the term to see if growth is taking place.

Behaviors	Names of Students			
Helps define the topic				
Sticks to the topic				
Is an interested and willing listener				
Interjects ideas at appropriate points				
Considers ideas contrary to his or her own				
Tries to clarify, not "win," arguments				
Does not repeat ideas given by others				
Gets to the point without delay				
Speaks so all can hear				
Uses appropriate language				
Uses concepts accurately				
Helps evaluate discussion				

■ Growth in Group Work Skills

Group work in social studies refers to small groups of students assembled to accomplish a particular task. It might be the development of a visual report on community leaders, constructing sets for a dramatization, or painting a series of murals depicting the 1960s. The growth and development of group work skills from the beginning level to an advanced level is shown in Table 7.3 (p. 220). Items in the beginning level should be emphasized in the early grades with all students and in later grades with students who are inexperienced in group work. Students should be guided to move to the advanced phases by receiving skill instruction. By the time students reach the middle school, they should be able to work at the advanced level.

Group work of all types is most productive when space arrangements can be made to accommodate groups of varying sizes. Open-space schools provide an unlimited number of arrangements. Single classrooms with moveable furniture can also

■ **TABLE 7.3**

A Continuum of Group Work Skills

	Beginning Level	Intermediate Level	Advanced Level
Objectives	Brief, specific	Longer, yet directed	Long, more complex
Planning	Planned primarily by the teacher	Planned jointly by the teacher and pupils	Planned primarily by pupils
Duration	Short, one or two days	Longer, several days	Several days to several weeks
Materials and Sources of Data	Single source or few sources	Varied sources and materials	Variety of media and materials
Organization, Interaction	Informal, parallel activities, little interaction	Chairperson selected, tasks varied and assigned, some interaction	Chairperson or coordinator, much interaction in all phases
Reports	Parallel reports, or one student reporting with others filling in	Each member reports, or pupils share in reporting pooled information	Synthesis of information in one report; planned and given by the group
Evaluation	Informal, emphasis on sharing of best ideas	Attention to both content and procedures, self-evaluation	Emphasis on self-evaluation of activity in greater depth

Source: Grateful acknowledgment is made to Dr. Ruth Grossman, City University of New York, City College, for this chart.

provide a high degree of flexibility, as Figure 7.3 shows. Notice the spaces provided for learning centers, storage of unit materials, and group activities. Teachers appraise the physical makeup of their classroom before initiating group arrangements. Optimum use of the physical space and strategies to maximize instruction and learning are the criteria that teachers employ when arranging their classroom.

Guidelines for Initiating Small-Group Activities

Follow these guidelines as you organize committees and form other small working groups:

1. Before starting group work, first identify individuals who can work well together to make the first attempt at group work successful and a model for others. Sec-

■ **FIGURE 7.3**

Space Arrangements for Group Work

ond, identify specific needs for productive small-group work directly related to the unit under study. Provide sufficient materials that each member can use, including audio and pictorial resources for those unable to use reading materials.

2. Review small-group work skills with the students. Be sure they are proficient enough to begin a small-group activity. If needed, spend some time discussing the work skills that students may have forgotten or that are unclear to them.

3. Begin with one group. Clarify their task, directions to follow, materials, and working space. Select a recorder whose role is to note the group's task and what each member is to do. At the end of the work period the recorder should note what was accomplished and what still needs to be done. By reviewing the recorder's notes the teacher can monitor progress and identify which students are staying on task, how materials are being used, and other observations.

4. After the rest of the class is busy at work, take the small group to the work area, clarify their task, and see that they are off to a good start. Provide supervision as needed during the work period.

5. After the task is completed, guide the sharing of the group's efforts with the class. Discuss procedures used as well as outcomes, mentioning any problems that arose and ways to prevent them in the future. Summarize standards that similar groups can use.

6. Make plans for other working groups in a similar fashion. Move from one group to two or more as needs for group work arise and children are ready for such responsibilities. Have worthwhile independent activities ready for students who become overstimulated in small-group work and are not ready to assume a role in group activities.

7. Move from group to group as needed to supervise and direct. Note ideas that will provide more effective ways of working together for the follow-up evaluation.

■ Grouping children as a means to deal with individual differences can be a major contribution to the successful social studies program.

—**George W. Maxim**

8. As the class members develop group work skills, allow them more freedom to work on their own. Arrange groups so that students who are advanced in group work skills can assume leadership in helping others and in keeping the group moving in profitable directions. Give close supervision to any students who continue to have difficulty working with others.

■ Types of Group Work

You can try a variety of configurations for group work to help students develop a range of skills. Each type brings a different set of verbal, nonverbal, research, and social skills into play. The following types are commonly used in the social studies classroom. Most of these involve group research and study, followed by ways of presenting the results to the class.

Committees

Students may be grouped in committees to study and present an area of information to discuss and suggest policy changes in the community or at school, or to solve problems. Students may play different roles, such as chair, recorder, and time keeper. Committees should be congenial working groups interested in the job to be done and balanced in terms of needed abilities and talents. Some teachers describe the task at hand to all students to foster exemplary small-group behavior; others select one or two students who can lead and work well in groups to help select committee members. Standards for group participation should be developed and posted; examples are shown in Table 7.4. The leader may be selected by the group or the teacher. The committee may have a spokesperson who reports progress to the class, or committee members may take turns doing this.

■ **TABLE 7.4**

Responsibilities in Committee Work

Committee Members	Committee Leaders	Committee Reports
1. Know what to do.	1. Keep the main job in mind.	1. Stick to the questions.
2. Divide the work.	2. Get ideas from all members.	2. Use pictures, objects, and maps.
3. Do each job well.	3. See that each member has a job.	3. Be ready to answer questions.
4. Discuss problems quietly.	4. Be fair and do not talk all the time.	4. State ways to improve.
5. Plan the report carefully.	5. Urge everyone to do his or her best.	
	6. Say *our* committee, not *my* committee.	

Groups Focused on Making Presentations

As students gather information, develop viewpoints, and learn about discussion in small groups, they may report their findings and argue their perspectives in a number of forums. The symposium, the panel discussion, and the roundtable discussion are possible alternatives. Each demands an increasing sophistication in presenting information, stating disagreements inoffensively, courtesy in discussion, and respect for all participants.

The Symposium

This group prepares a presentation in which each group member speaks on one area of information. In the presentation itself, the chair introduces the topic and each of the speakers (usually five or six in number). Each speaker spends three to five minutes on one aspect of the topic. After all are finished, the audience is invited to ask questions.

The Panel Discussion

This group also prepares a presentation, but the format is somewhat different from that of the symposium. The role of the chair is more challenging, and participants speak not only from prepared notes but contribute to the flow of the discussion.

The chair explains the topic, identifies the issues involved, calls on panel members to contribute, directs the discussion, and summarizes ideas. The chair makes sure that all panel members participate, keeps track of time, and ensures that the topic is fully dealt with. Each panel member informally presents ideas on the problem and a point of view on each issue raised by the chair. After summarizing key points and different views, the chair invites questions from the class.

The Roundtable Discussion

This mode of presentation adds another layer of complexity and requires that students do more "thinking on their feet." The chair introduces the topic, invites discussion, and summarizes main ideas and differences in viewpoint. The participants (usually three or four) talk about the problem or issue, challenge each other in differences of opinion or conviction, and state their own positions. The chair may ask members to clarify certain points and requests evidence and reasons for holding a given position or arriving at a certain conclusion. The audience is then invited to question the participants on the topic at hand. Roundtable discussions can be quite lively!

Buzz Groups

In this arrangement, the class is divided into five or six groups to discuss a question, analyze a problem, brainstorm ideas, or clarify an idea or issue. Each member of the group speaks freely and informally, expressing thoughts and feelings. Students must, however, speak quietly and take turns. Later, a member of each group is selected to present to the class the group's ideas.

Brainstorming activities can be helpful in generating alternative solutions to problems, different points of view on an issue, steps to take in completing a task, ideas to study further, and so on. Sometimes enthusiasm can cause these sessions to spin out of control; it helps to provide brainstorming and buzz group guidelines such as these:

- State whatever pops into your mind.
- Do not criticize any ideas.
- Be brief and to the point.
- Listen to others, and do not repeat their ideas.
- Stick to the topic.
- Obey the group leader.
- Help summarize the best ideas.
- Think of ways to improve.

Cooperative Learning Groups

To organize groups that work together to meet learning goals, the teacher must consider not only the assigned task but also development of students' skills as leaders and followers, students' readiness for the activity, and compatibility among students. Many teachers, therefore, assign students to small groups. However, students should be allowed to select their own groups when interest in an activity is a key factor and students are ready to handle group tasks. When special topics are to be researched in reading materials, it is wise to use reading groups and to provide materials at different reading levels.

Teams may be used to serve purposes such as helping each member of the team, preparing and sharing reports, having periodic tournaments, and motivating learning through constructive competition. Emphasize positive team rewards, individual accountability, and equal opportunities for all team members to succeed. Examples of cooperative learning groups are as follows (Slavin, 1990):

Students Team-Achievement Divisions (STAD): Students complete worksheets and are tested; the team scores are determined by each student's performance.

Teams-Games-Tournament (TGT): This is like STAD except that weekly tournaments replace quizzes.

Jigsaw: Students become "experts" on a topic and teach it to others; team members are tested individually.

Group Investigation: Members plan, complete, and report on a topic.

Learning Together: Assignment sheets are completed.

Coop-Coop: Cooperation between groups as well as within groups is emphasized in completing assigned tasks.

Taking Turns: Members take turns in making written or oral reports.

After the whole class meets to plan the activities to be completed in cooperative learning groups, check to see that each student understands what to do, where to do it, how to proceed, materials to use, work standards to follow, and how to get help if needed. Then the groups assemble and get to work. As you monitor the groups, you might use these guidelines:

1. Encourage everyone to take part. Mention that the best ideas of each member are needed, and urge everyone to take responsibility for completing the activity.
2. Consider problems and questions expressed by students. Bring to their attention any problems they have overlooked.
3. Make constructive suggestions for work standards, use of materials, and roles of group members. Redirect negative comments into positive suggestions.
4. To ensure success, anticipate difficulties that may arise, and clarify what each member is to do, as necessary.
5. Support group work by providing charts of work standards, directions, worksheets, study guides, and diagrams.

As children engage in group learning activities, the teacher should gather information to use in group evaluation. Take note of acceptance of responsibilities, cooperation, courtesy, and self-control. During group work the teacher has many opportunities to move about and to give help. One student may have difficulty locating material in a given reference; another may have difficulty using tools and materials. By giving judicious assistance, the teacher can make sure that effective learning takes place. Observe students' proficiency levels in the use of materials, skills that need to be improved, and misconceptions or erroneous ideas that arise. For example, in a unit on pioneer life, a teacher noticed during a research period that several youngsters were having difficulty using the table of contents; others were not sure of the topics to locate in the index. The teacher planned a later discussion focused on locating information.

Teachers use cooperative learning groups to improve social studies instruction. With which cooperative learning groups are you familiar? Which are your favorites?

The teacher should also note how students meet the work standards that they have helped to set. Commend those who carry out standards and who help others to do so. Occasionally the teacher will have to ask a student to stop an activity for a few minutes and consider whether his or her behavior conforms to the group standard. Now and then, a student must be excluded from the group until ready to accept all the responsibilities involved in the activity. Following the work period, let students consider the group standards and how well each member helped maintain them.

Several techniques may be used to manage conflicts that may arise. Standards of work and conduct can be reviewed, explanations can clarify misunderstanding of rules or roles, and direct suggestions can correct obvious infractions. Time may be taken to discuss a difficulty, to role play or negotiate a "fair" solution, or to work out a compromise. In serious cases, a "cooling-off" period may be needed during which students do independent work. The group activity is not resumed until the conflict is resolved.

Teachers may find it challenging to manage group work with those students who experience difficulties working cooperatively, those with exceptionalities who may need special attention, and students who are new arrivals to this country and are not accustomed to small-group activities. For the first group, the teacher should plan carefully with these students in mind and, during the work period, observe their behavior and provide direction when needed. Planning collaboratively with the special education teacher is an excellent strategy for addressing the needs of exceptional children. Students unfamiliar with U.S. schools should be socialized into school culture, and an effective method for achieving this is to use the "buddy system." Many students would like to show new classmates "the lay of the land." The use of a buddy should be of short duration, however, so that the new student does not become overly dependent on one or two students for his or her school success.

Group Self-Evaluation

Group evaluation is essential, from initial definition of problems to appraisal of the effectiveness of group work. During evaluation, the group answers such questions as these:

- Is each individual doing his or her part?
- Are the plans effective?
- Are leadership responsibilities being carried out?
- Are our objectives being achieved?
- Are additional resources needed?
- What steps should be taken next?

In making appraisals, the group may use discussion charts or checklists, a log or diary of activities, assistance from the teacher, work materials, or other evaluative aids. Committees and other small groups may use "quality circles" to evaluate participation, suggest improvements, and develop self-evaluation skills.

Here is a list that an individual student might use to evaluate his or her participation:

Do I share leadership?	Do I stick to standards?
Do I take turns?	Do I take responsibility?
Do I help set standards?	Do I encourage others?
Do I cooperate?	Do I consider feelings?
Do I help clarify points?	Do I stick to the task?
Do I compromise as needed?	Do I help evaluate?

■ Study Guides for Cooperative Learning

Study guides enable cooperative learning groups to be more productive. Several types of study guides can be used, ranging from those that contain questions on a single source of information to those created by students themselves.

Here is a selection of study guides and ways to use them in small-group work.

ACTIVITY IDEAS ▶ *Study Guides for Group Work*

▶ Study guides may follow a question-and-answer format typical to other worksheets. For group work, it's helpful if the guide includes instruction for evaluating the answers as a group. In the following example, groups were studying the acquisition of territories such as Louisiana, Florida, Oregon, and so on.

> **Study Guide for the Acquisition of Louisiana**
>
> A. Answer the questions listed below as you read pages 114–17 in *The Country*.
>
> 1. Who had claimed the territory first?
> 2. Who had it when the United States wanted it?
> 3. Why did the United States want it?
>
> Does the group agree on each member's answers to the above questions? If so, proceed to the next questions. If not, reread the section and find out who is right.
>
> B. Discuss these questions in your group, and write the answers that members agree are the best.
>
> 1. Why did some people support acquisition of this territory?
> 2. Why were some people against it?
> 3. How was the territory finally acquired?
> 4. Was it a "good deal" for the United States? Why or why not?

▶ Students may also benefit from arranging the information they learn in semantic or cognitive webs. The web may be based on a theme, a concept, a question, and so on.

▶ The retrieval chart is another helpful study guide. Each group is responsible for finding a portion of the information needed to complete the chart. For a chart

■ Structured group settings that include diversity also afford students an opportunity for social dialogues that can stimulate cognitive growth. They offer the promise of environments where youngsters can explore alternative perspectives.

—**Peter H. Martorella**

like the following one, groups of three to five students gather information on each country; the work could be divided up in other ways as well, to accommodate special needs in the classroom or to give students a chance to study the topic they enjoy most.

Retrieval Chart on Countries in the Middle East						
	Egypt	Iran	Iraq	Israel	Saudi Arabia	Syria
Topics						
Population						
Area						
Main Regions						
Agriculture						
Natural Resources						
Religion						
Trade						
Transportation						
Education						
Art						
Music						
Form of Government						
Capital						

Teachers can also find ways to combine independent work and small-group study. A study guide can come in handy here as well. Students can work on a portion of the guide independently, then get together with group members to compare and synthesize information. The facing lesson plan shows how this process can work.

Models of decision making, problem solving, case-study analysis, and other sets of processes may be used by committees set up to consider proposals, solve a problem, analyze a case, or tackle a particular issue. The use of models in groups is most effective after students have considered them in class discussions directed by the teacher. Examples of decision-making and case-analysis models follow. They outline the procedure for a group to follow, focus discussion on key points, and serve as guides for preparing oral and written reports. They may be applied to a variety of issues, proposals, problems, and dilemmas that arise in social studies units.

Decision-Making Model
- Clarify the issue or proposal.
- Discuss and list values (justice, equality, etc.) that are important in this issue.

LESSON PLAN *Lifestyle*

Objectives
To state the meaning of *lifestyle*

To describe the effects of one's lifestyle on the environment

To state changes that may be made in one's lifestyle to improve the environment

Materials
Read one or more of the books and articles in the learning center. Use the index and table of contents to find the pages on which lifestyle is discussed. Take notes on the video *Using Our Forests Wisely* when it is shown in class.

Questions and Activities

1. What do you think *lifestyle* means?
2. Find and write the meaning of *lifestyle* in one of the readings. How is the meaning similar to and different from yours?
3. Describe your own lifestyle by completing the following:

   Foods I eat are _____

   Clothes I wear are _____

   Things I do to have fun are _____

   The way I treat other people is _____

   Other aspects of my lifestyle are _____

   Things I do that cause waste pollution are _____

   Things I do that cause noise pollution are _____

   Other things I do that hurt the environment are _____

   Things I do that do not hurt the environment are _____

4. How is your lifestyle like the lifestyle of people described in the reading material? How is it different?
5. Which changes in lifestyle noted in the reading materials do you think are most important to help the environment? Why?
6. Which changes in lifestyle do you think are most important in the video on forests? Why?
7. What changes in your lifestyle should be made to help the environment? Why? Do you think that you will make them? Why or why not?

Follow-up Activity
During the next three days keep a record of your activities, following the form below. (Examples are given in the first box.)

Activities	Energy or Resources Used	Helps the Environment	Hurts the Environment	Type of Pollution
Family picnic	Car and food	No	If we litter	Waste
1.				
2.				
3.				

- Discuss alternative decisions and reasons for them.
- Discuss the consequences of each alternative.
- Select the best alternative in terms of consequences and values.
- Summarize reasons for the decision. If there is disagreement, make a minority report.

Case-Analysis Model

- Discuss the issue to be resolved.
- Determine the facts (evidence) in the case.
- Double-check reliability of the facts.
- List the facts, pro and con (for and against).
- Make a decision or judgment after discussing pros and cons.
- List reasons for the decision—how justice will be served.

The lesson plan on page 231 illustrates one way to guide students to consider alternatives as a part of decision making.

Guides Prepared by Students

A most valuable learning activity is to have students develop their own study guides. Before students begin, the general plan should be discussed with the class; then teams go to work to develop their own detailed plan. Each team answers the questions listed in Table 7.5, then presents the resulting study plan to the teacher or the class for review and improvement. Think of the skills that students must use and the extra learning they may achieve as a result of sharing ideas and creating their own guide!

■ TABLE 7.5

Planning a Study Guide

Beginning	**Collecting and Organizing Information**	**Sharing and Reporting Findings**
1. What is the topic of study?		
2. What questions should be answered?	1. How may note taking and outlining be used?	1. What are the main parts? Can the report be based on questions stated at the beginning?
Identifying Sources of Information	2. What information should be put on charts?	
	3. What information should be put on maps?	2. In what order should the parts be placed?
1. Which reading materials in the classroom may be used?	4. What other ways of organizing information may be used?	3. What ideas should be put on cards for an oral report?
2. What library materials may be used?		4. How can pictures, maps, or other items be used to improve the report?
3. What people may be interviewed?		
4. What other sources may be used?		

LESSON PLAN   *Charting Alternatives*

Objective   To describe ways to reach a goal by charting alternatives

Introduction   Present a problem that can be solved in different ways, such as playground litter cleanup, collecting materials for recycling, or reduction of noise pollution. After the problem is clarified, ask the group questions such as these: How can a problem such as this be handled in different ways? Why should different ways be considered?

Development   Select one problem and write it on the chalkboard. Draw a chart such as the one shown below. Ask students to fill in the chart by describing different ways the problem may be solved, evaluating each suggested option and concluding with the expected results.

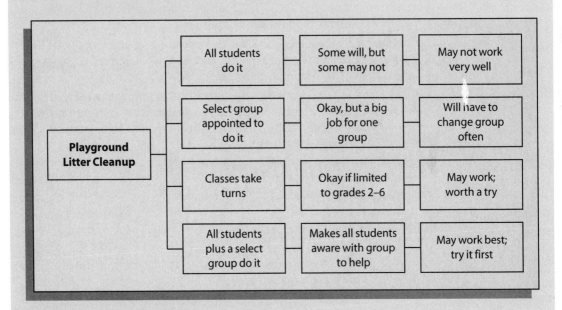

Conclusion and Evaluation   Discuss the value of considering alternative ways to solve problems. Ask students to suggest other problems that might be handled in a similar way. Observe to assess learning.

Follow-up   Ask individual students or committees to apply the procedure to a new problem.

■ Conclusion

Small-group activity is at the heart of elementary and middle social studies instruction. K–8 social studies teachers know that part of social studies is developing citizenship—learning to work with others toward a positive end. When developing their instructional programs, teachers provide opportunities for student to examine issues, problems, and personalities in discussion groups, committee work, and group work activities. In addition to promoting citizenship, small-group activities also provide students the opportunity to practice and extend skill development and to develop a positive disposition toward social studies.

 Questions, Activities, and Evaluation

1. Which of the values and the limitations of group work skills do you believe to be most significant? Why? What might be some dangers in overemphasizing them at the expense of independent study skills?

2. Note four or five whole-group skills you might use in a unit prepared for primary instruction. Then note some for middle school instruction. Do the same for small-group or committee activities.

3. Visit a K–3 and a middle school classroom, and use the following questions to observe and analyze the teacher's role in guiding discussion. Were the initiating questions clear? How did they give focus to discussion? Note how each of the following types of questions was used:

    a. Open-ended, specifying, clarifying, and probing questions related to content of the discussion

    b. Focusing, refocusing, and lifting questions related to the structure and flow of discussion

    c. Accepting, supporting, and encouraging questions related to students' comments

    On what level(s) was the discussion held? How did students respond to any shifts that were made to raise the level?

4. Select one small-group activity and make a plan for using it in a unit of your choice. Specify how you would select students, initiate the activity, guide it, and evaluate it.

5. Make a plan for a study guide that you might use to improve learning in small-group work, relating it to a unit of work.

6. Assume you are either a primary, elementary, or middle school teacher and mark your position on the following by writing A if you agree, D if you disagree, and ? if you are uncertain. Discuss your views with a colleague and explore reasons for any differences.

    _____ a. Small groups used for instruction in reading should also be used in the social studies.

_____ **b.** Students who do not follow group standards for committees should be given individual assignments.

_____ **c.** In general, a teacher should assign students to groups to ensure compatibility among members.

_____ **d.** The chair for a committee should be chosen by committee members.

_____ **e.** A teacher should have good discipline and control of whole-class activities before starting small-group work.

_____ **f.** The same care that is given to planning lessons based on textbooks and other materials should be given to planning group activities.

_____ **g.** Teachers who are serious about "back to basics" should give little or no time to small-group activities.

References

Beck, C. R. (1999). Francine, Kerplunk, and the Golden Nugget—Conducting mock trials and debates in the classroom. *The Social Studies, 90,* 78–84.

Bernagozzi, T. (1993). Cooperative learning. *Learning, 22,* 33.

Cohen, E. G. (1994). *Designing groupwork: Strategies for the heterogeneous classroom.* New York: Teachers College Press.

Davis, J. E., & Davis, S. (1994). *Citizen handbook.* Clarks Summit, PA: Educational Extension Systems, P.O. Box 259. Practical activities.

Johnson, D., Johnson, R., & Holubic, E. (1994). *The new circles of learning: Cooperation in the classroom and school.* Washington, DC: Association for Supervision and Curriculum Development.

Joyce, B. R. (1991). Common misconceptions about cooperative learning and gifted students. *Educational Leadership, 48,* 72–74.

Kreidler, W. J. (1994). *Conflict resolution in the middle school: A curriculum and teaching guide.* Cambridge, MA: Educators for Social Responsibilit, 23 Garden St., 02138. Write for catalog.

Lampe, J. R., Rooze, G. E., & Tallent-Runnels, M. (1996). Effects of cooperative learning among Hispanics students in elementary social studies. *Journal of Educational Research, 89,* 187–191.

McMillan, E. P. (1998). Building the George Washington Bridge: A first-grade experience. *Social Education, 62,* 222–226.

Meloth, M. S., & Deering, P. D. (1994). Task talk and task awareness under different cooperative learning conditions. *American Educational Research Journal, 31,* 138–65. Effects on discussion and metacognitive awareness.

Passe, J. (1998). The best museums for kids? The one they build themselves! *The Social Studies, 89,* 183–186.

Sharan, S. (Ed.). (1994). *Handbook of cooperative learning methods.* Westport, CT: Greenwood Publishing Group.

Slavin, R. E. (1990). *Cooperative learning: Theory, research, and practice.* Englewood Cliffs, NJ: Prentice-Hall. Guidelines for various groups.

Soto, B. (1998). Walking on the wild side: Geographic field study for fifth graders. *The Social Studies, 89,* 236–240.

Stoneham, R., & Vansickle, R. (Eds.) (1994). *Cooperative learning in the social studies classroom.* New York: NCSS Publications, c/o Maxway Data Corporation. Guiding principles and approaches.

Wheelan, S. A. (1994). *Group processes: A developmental perspective.* Boston: Allyn & Bacon.

Chapter 8

Developing Communication and Language Skills

Chapter Objective

*To describe principles, procedures, and teaching strategies for
integrating language arts into the social studies*

Focusing Questions

- What strategies and learning activities can apply and improve reading,
  listening, speaking, and writing skills?

- What techniques and learning activities are helpful in developing social
  studies vocabulary?

- What techniques and learning activities are used to develop comprehension
  of social studies content?

- What reading study skills do students need in order to locate information,
  do research, and "learn how to learn" social studies?

■ The Importance of Communication and Language Skills

How many times have you heard teachers say that if children don't learn to read,
write, and speak with confidence in the primary grades, they will experience difficulties in the upper elementary grades? Have teachers told you that if students come to
the middle school unable to read or write, they will have problems doing the required
academic work? Regardless of grade level, all teachers point to the relationship between communication skills and school success. Reflect on your K–8 experiences,
and think of the communication skills you used when exploring science, mathematics, health, social studies, and other subject areas. It is difficult to think of school success without mastery of communication and language skills.

Most Americans believe that K–8 instruction should include teaching students
basic language skills, both receptive (reading and listening) and expressive (writing
and speaking). This emphasis on reading, writing, listening, and speaking is commonly referred to as the literacy movement, and most states across the country have
developed K–8 standards integrating these skills into all areas of the curriculum.

Social studies in the K–8 curriculum is a *specialized* area of study and requires
the development of skills that can be characterized as functional (mastery of basic
concepts), informational (gaining knowledge of many topics in social studies), and
literary (experiencing the range of social studies literature and producing one's own

written and spoken expression). These skills develop as students gain an understanding of this area of study, learn to express themselves in a "social studies frame of mind," grow to value the rich literature of social studies, and seek a deeper understanding of human relationships and the development of responsible citizenship in a democracy.

■ There is more to treasure in books than in all the pirate's loot on Treasure Island.
—**Walt Disney**

These skills develop across all grade levels as students learn individual concepts, discover how related concepts can be grouped into clusters, and create generalizations based on concept clusters. For example, on the level of functional skills, students might first build an understanding of basic vocabulary related to community (e.g., core words such as *role, values,* and *interdependence*). They also learn about specific concepts (such as *family, local government,* and *community institutions*) and how these concepts are interrelated. Eventually, generalizations such as the following can emerge: Laws are nonviolent means of resolving community conflicts. Every community has special features that make it different from other communities. Elections and town meetings are two different ways by which individual citizens can affect the governance of their community.

Beginning in the primary grades, students year by year gain more understanding of functional concepts, concept clusters, and generalizations. This understanding lays the foundation for acquiring informational skills, allowing students to apply basic social studies concepts as they encounter new information. Thus students can learn to read a ballot and understand how it is used, interpret maps of increasing complexity, discuss geographic features of a region, describe important events in the history of a country, and imagine what it was like to travel the Silk Road or the Trail of Tears. They build richer concept clusters and can develop more refined and complex generalizations. As they "learn how to learn" social studies, they gain confidence and experience success.

Social studies comes to life for students when they discover that their own personal experiences relate to the subject matter. For example, children living in Kentucky can integrate their knowledge of their geographic region, local lore, and family history into a unit on frontier living in the 1800s. Students living in Chicago can enrich a unit on the diversity of American cities by using and extending their knowledge of their own city. Such a unit might include taking a tour of downtown Chicago, listening to a local poet read Chicago poems at a bookstore, writing a fictional short story based on an actual event in the city's history, or making a mural of the city skyline. A variety of reading, writing, speaking, and listening activities could be incorporated in such a unit.

As they build more complex webs of information, students can develop literary skills in social studies. By building solid reading, listening, and study skills, they can access a variety of information. Instead of sticking to the textbook, they can reach into autobiographies, diaries and journals, government documents, transcripts or recordings of speeches, poems, songs, posters, letters, and so on, to enhance their understanding. This depth and dimension will be reflected in the work that students produce: oral reports, book reviews, research papers, persuasive essays, class debates, written summaries, and so on.

Functional, informational, and literary skills are not built in sequence; instead, they overlap. In all grades, students can experience multiple levels of understanding of topics in social studies and can take part in a variety of listening, speaking, writing, and reading activities. For example, in K–3 classrooms, students could study immigration by reading children's nonfiction books about immigrants from a variety of backgrounds, especially those featuring children. Local immigrants might speak to the students about their experiences. Students might present written or oral reports on immigrants who have contributed to U.S. society. In grades 4–8, a unit on immigration might include study of census data, reading current newspaper and magazine articles on the subject, interviewing recent immigrants, giving persuasive speeches about changing current U.S. immigration policy, making annotated maps that show patterns of immigration, conducting team debates on immigration policy, or writing a short story about an immigrant, incorporating historical detail in the imaginative writing. At all grade levels, students can build core knowledge by using the textbook.

In this chapter we provide a host of suggestions on integrating communication and language skills into social studies.

■ Reading Skills

To improve reading in the social studies, three areas need attention: building vocabulary, developing comprehension, and developing reading study skills. The following section provides several activities to support the development of these skills.[1] Whenever students prepare to read, it is wise to remind them that reading is not a passive skill. Readers are instead actively engaged in building meaning.

Building Vocabulary

This section presents procedures and activities for developing concepts and the vocabulary used to express them.

Building Social Studies Vocabulary

To succeed in reading a variety of social studies texts, students need to understand vocabulary words from several categories. *Core words* include terms that arise in many contexts and across grade levels in the social studies curriculum. Generally speaking, core words denote broad concepts. *Technical social science terms* are more specific and relate to particular disciplines within social studies (such as geography or sociology), though they may occur in units on a variety of topics. *Unit words* are terms that

---

1. Acknowledgment is made to Dr. Ruth Grossman, City University of New York, Dr. Haig Rushdoony, California State College, Stanislaus, and Dr. Victoria Mui, California State University, Hayward, for comments on this chapter.

typically appear in units on particular topics. Specific *names* are proper nouns denoting places, people, events, time periods, and so on. Special *quantitative terms* express measure of time, distance, and other amounts. You will find these types of vocabulary words mixed together in vocabulary lists in textbook units. Here are examples from each category.

Core Words	Technical Social Science Terms	Unit Words for a Civil War Unit
adaptation	alliance	abolitionist
chronology	basic needs	antislavery
civilization	dictator	emancipation
culture	frontier	overseer
diversity	market	plantation
value	peninsula	secession

Names	Quantitative Terms
the Alamo	altitude
Elizabeth Dole	average
the Great Depression	decade
the Indian Ocean	longitude
the Roaring Twenties	per capita
the Vietnam War	population

Other Challenging Vocabulary

A good deal of figurative language is used in social studies vocabulary in the middle and upper elementary grades. Students will need special help understanding terms such as *rush hour, hat in the ring,* and *cold war* when they first encounter them. Other common uses of figurative language include *hot line, closed shop, breadbasket of the country,* and *avalanche of votes.*

Words with multiple meanings also present a challenge to students. Be sure to explain the various usages of words such as *bank, belt, bill, cabinet, land, line, range,* and *run.* Help students use context clues and the dictionary to determine which meaning is intended in a particular text.

Also, different words that look or sound alike can cause problems. Students may need help in distinguishing homophones (words pronounced alike but with different spellings and meanings) such as *loan* and *lone,* homographs (words spelled alike but different in meaning and sometimes in pronunciation) such as *bow* (that shoots an arrow) and *bow* (bending at the waist), and homonyms (words with the same pronunciation and spelling yet different in meaning) such as *well* (the noun) and *well* (the adjective or adverb). In addition, some words are easy to confuse because their spellings are similar. *House* and *horse, conservation* and *conversation,* and *illegal* and *illegible* fall into this category.

Students will also encounter acronyms and abbreviations, which, though usually defined in the textbook, should eventually become part of the students' working vocabulary. Help students learn what common acronyms and abbreviations stand for.

U.S.	NAACP	NOW
NY	AFL-CIO	USSR
OPEC	NASA	UN

Prereading: Introducing Vocabulary

As you plan for social studies units, how can you determine which vocabulary words your students have already mastered and which ones they need to learn? To begin, review textbook material for upcoming units. Check the teacher's manual for lists of key words and ideas for introducing them. The following activities may help you discover which words your students need to learn and ways to learn them.

■ For more information on reading and social studies, visit the International Reading Association's website at **http://www.reading. org**

 **ACTIVITY IDEAS** ➤ *Assessing and Building Vocabulary*

➤ Write each new social studies term on a large card. For example, words for a unit on community might include *worker, firefighter, producer, manager, services, goods, nurse, baker, teacher,* and *clerk*. Show the cards one at a time to the class, and ask students to raise their hands to tell the meaning of each term. Spend time discussing terms that are unfamiliar to students.

➤ Hand out a list of social studies vocabulary words to students. First, let them write the meaning of each word that they know; then let them find the others in the textbook glossary and write them in. They then will have a complete list of words and meanings.

➤ Have students write each new social studies vocabulary word on an index card. After each word, they can draw a picture clue or write a context clue that will remind them of the word's meaning. Or they can use the textbook glossary to find the definition.

➤ Provide a fill-in-the-blank form for students. Give the definitions of key terms in the text, and let the students fill in the correct terms. Here is an example.

The _____ branch of government makes the laws.

The _____ branch of government carries out the laws.

The _____ branch of government makes judgments about the meaning of laws.

➤ Locate instances of figurative language in the text. Discuss terms such as *cunning as a fox, a square deal, ruled with an iron hand,* and *window of opportunity,* asking students how the figurative language helps express the idea.

➤ Scan the text for words that may be mistaken for other words with similar spellings, pronunciations, or meanings. Write such words on the board, and discuss them with students. For example, talk about the distinctions between the words *rain, rein,* and *reign.*

➤ At the middle-school level, it can be valuable to study a word that has different shades of meaning. You might use a list like the following to discuss such a word.

The judge made a *fair* decision.	*(just)*
Fair shares will be given to each person.	*(equal)*
The hearing will be *fair.*	*(impartial)*
The final report was *fair.*	*(unbiased)*
Paul did the *fair* thing.	*(right)*
Tomorrow will bring *fair* weather.	*(good)*

Prereading: Building Background

Activities that build background are an important part of learning vocabulary as well as the broader concepts associated with a word. It is more than finding the dictionary meaning of a word and memorizing it; rather, it refers to enriching experiences that provide a broader conceptual context for understanding a word.

Concepts that are entirely new to students should be introduced before the reading begins. This requires planning on the teacher's part. Though it is impossible to anticipate all problems that students may have in understanding a text, important basic concepts should be identified and presented to spark interest and build understanding.

Hands-on activities or experiences with a visual emphasis are effective ways to introduce new concepts. Students might discuss pictures of places, objects, or structures (such as *corral, silo,* and *stall*) as presented in the textbook or other books. Even better, you might bring to class models of items, such as candle molds or different types of grain, which students can handle or use. A trip to a museum could introduce students to real models of Conestoga wagons, Ford Model T cars, birchbark canoes, or colonial furniture. Demonstrations of processes discussed in the unit (especially demonstrations that include student interaction) make light work of learning concepts that can seem abstract and complicated when presented in text. Candle dipping, weaving, and other craftwork might be demonstrated by a local expert or on video.

Students can also create visuals that they can refer to later, as they read. Large maps that show regions, natural resources, travel routes, or other items can be created and displayed in the classroom. Students can add labels, symbols, and legends as needed. Other interesting visuals include murals, panoramas, and exhibits of objects. These projects build background knowledge and support students as they read.

Here are additional activities that can help build background and meaning before students delve into a text.

 *Building Background*

➤ Invite students to collect and label pictures of related items and display them on the bulletin board. For example, labeled pictures of rivers, lakes, gulfs, and oceans could be grouped under the heading *Bodies of Water*. Students can use clippings from magazines and newspapers, graphics downloaded from the Internet, or their own drawings.

➤ As a class, listen to stories, poems, or songs that contribute meaning, stir feelings, or create a mood related to vocabulary words such as *courage, bravery, hardship, responsibility, cooperation,* and *celebration.*

➤ Use analogies to relate a new term to a known term. For example, you might say that a governor is like a mayor except that he or she is the chief administrator of a state instead of a city. Encourage students to think of their own analogies.

➤ As a group or individual activity, give students a broad category and a list of terms. Have them distinguish terms that belong in that category from those that do not.

Which are examples of natural resources? Which are not? Circle the natural resources.			
suburb	bricks	workers	plastic
forests	farms	mountains	glass
houses	oil	clay	minerals
spring water	paper	lumber	

During the reading experience, students may need support as they grapple with concepts. The reading study skills and strategies described later in this chapter will help them construct meaning, raise questions, and interpret the text on various levels. As postreading activities, teachers may use specific ideas from the sections on speaking and writing, which follow later in this chapter.

What techniques are you familiar with that help students build their language skills in social studies instruction? Which are quite successful in the elementary grades? middle school?

Building a Sight Vocabulary

A reader who can recognize words on sight, without stopping frequently to decode them, has a definite advantage in reading fluency and comprehension. Such a reader can concentrate on meaning without getting bogged down in figuring out particular words. But since students will find it necessary to stop and decode words, we do provide such word-recognition techniques in this section. However, they should be considered a waystation en route to developing a sight vocabulary, not a crutch to use again and again when encountering the same word.

Since a sight vocabulary is so important, social studies teachers should provide activities that encourage its development. Labeling items in the classroom, which students will see every day, is one way to encourage word recognition. In the early grades, new social studies words can be matched with pictures to strengthen that association. Before reading a selection on clothing, pictures can be labeled with words such as *shirt, skirt,* and *raincoat*. A selection on water transportation could include pictures with the labels *canal, harbor,* and *pier.* These labeled pictures could be presented in picture dictionaries, booklets, charts, or scrapbooks. Here are more ideas.

■ To acquire the habit of reading is to construct for yourself a refuge from all the miseries of life.

—Somerset Maugham

ACTIVITY IDEAS ▷ *Developing a Sight Vocabulary*

➤ Make a card file of key vocabulary words in a given unit. For example, a unit on northern lands might include the words *arctic, climate, deciduous, taiga, evergreen, fjord,* and *ice age.* Provide opportunities for students to refer to the file.

➤ As a class, keep a list of compound words used in social studies. Note those words that are often combined with other words in compound words, such as the word *land* in *landform, landslide, landfill,* and *landowner.* Ask students if they know of other compound words using that word. They can check in the dictionary to find whether such compounds should be two words, hyphenated, or closed up as one word.

➤ Note words in a selection that have similar spelling patterns, such as *bake, cake, lake, take,* and *thought, though, through.* Also, discuss words that have unusual spellings.

➤ As a class, keep a variety of word lists, such as lists of synonyms, antonyms, and words with related meanings (such as *place, site, location, area,* and *region*). Give students opportunities to add words to the lists.

➤ Make a hidden word puzzle. First, list several social studies words to put in the puzzle. Next, write them in a grid, with some running horizontally, some vertically, and/ or some diagonally. Then fill in the remaining spaces with randomly chosen letters. Here is a hidden word puzzle ready for students to solve.

Find the Hidden Words

Draw a line around the economics words hidden in the puzzle.

You may go across or down.

BARTER   BUY   BUYER

CAPITAL   CASH   COMPETE

CONSUMERS

DEBT   DIVISION OF LABOR

DIVERSIFICATION   DUE

GOODS   INTEREST   INVESTOR   JOB

LABOR   LEASE   LEND   LOAN   LOSS

MARKET   MIXED ECONOMY   MONEY

NEEDS   OWE   PAY   PRODUCERS

PROFIT   RENT   RETOOL   SCARCITY

SELL   SELLER   SERVICES

SPECIALIZATION   TOOL   TRADE

VALUE   WANTS

I	D	I	V	E	R	S	I	F	I	C	A	T	I	O	N
N	E	N	S	E	L	L	L	A	B	O	R	S	A	V	E
V	B	T	E	B	U	Y	W	C	A	P	I	T	A	L	E
E	T	E	L	U	W	A	N	T	S	A	C	O	R	E	D
S	N	R	L	Y	R	G	O	O	D	S	L	O	A	N	S
T	Q	E	E	E	D	B	A	R	T	E	R	L	N	D	S
O	F	S	R	R	E	R	E	S	O	U	R	C	E	S	P
R	E	T	O	O	L	D	J	O	B	O	P	A	Y	V	E
D	U	E	C	L	P	R	O	F	I	T	L	O	S	S	C
W	A	G	E	S	F	P	S	P	F	R	I	S	C	K	I
M	A	R	K	E	T	S	E	R	V	I	C	E	S	A	A
D	I	V	I	S	I	O	N	O	F	L	A	B	O	R	L
C	A	S	H	X	P	R	O	D	U	C	E	R	S	C	I
O	W	E	Z	C	O	N	S	U	M	E	R	S	B	I	Z
M	G	M	I	X	E	D	E	C	O	N	O	M	Y	T	A
P	O	V	A	L	U	E	R	T	R	A	D	E	I	Y	T
E	E	N	T	E	R	P	R	I	S	E	P	A	Y	E	I
T	I	N	F	L	A	T	I	O	N	M	A	R	K	E	O
E	L	E	A	S	E	M	O	N	E	Y	R	E	N	T	N

Applying Decoding Skills

To help in decoding words, students may use picture clues, context clues, phonics, and structural analysis. These techniques may be used separately or together.

Picture clues are derived from illustrations, photographs, and other visuals provided with the text. You can use picture clues in prereading activities to prepare students for the new words they will encounter. You might direct attention to pictures in the selection and present the related words on cards or on the board. Or discuss a picture in a selection and then have children skim the text to find the related word.

Context clues are found in the text surrounding the word to be decoded, in definitions, examples, descriptions, and so on. Alerting students to such clues will help them master new words. You can reinforce these associations by using riddles such as the following:

- What is it? It is found on a farm. They store hay in it. They milk cows in it. (*barn*)
- What is it? It is found in very cold regions. It is a huge mass of ice. It moves slowly. (*glacier*)
- All people have basic needs for food, shelter, and what else? (*clothing*)
- Major landforms are plains, hills, plateaus, and what else? (*mountains*)

Phonics involves decoding words by "sounding them out"—it requires an understanding of letter–sound correspondences and phonemic awareness, the ability to recognize the separate sounds within a word. You can improve students' facility with phonics by giving them practice in activities such as the following.

 **ACTIVITY IDEAS**   *Working with Phonics*

➤ In a given unit, label objects or pictures of objects with words that begin with the same consonant, such as *pot, pan,* and *picture;* the same consonant blends, such as *grass, grain,* and *granary;* or the same consonant digraphs, such as *shoe, ship,* and *sheep.* Give students opportunities both to write the words and to say them aloud.

➤ Identify and list examples of consonants that have more than one sound, and include examples of words. You might point out *c* in *city* and *capital, s* in *increase* and *cause,* and *g* in *gold* and *general.*

➤ Keep a chart of words in a unit that have a long vowel sounds signaled by a final *e,* such as *lake, space, time, trade,* and *zone.* Contrast these with words in which the final *e* does not indicate a long vowel, such as *income, climate,* and *justice.*

➤ Maintain a "silent letter list" in the classroom. On this list, group words with the same silent letter(s), and circle those letters in each word. Have students add to this list as they find more words with silent letters, such as *sack, might, lake,* and *knot.*

Structural analysis is the study of the Greek or Latin roots, base words, prefixes, and suffixes that make up words. As students become familiar with these parts of words, they can use them to infer the meaning of new words. The following activities will help students use structural analysis in decoding.

 *Using Structural Analysis*

➤ After defining the meaning of a suffix or prefix, ask students as a class to think of as many words as they can that begin or end with that word part. For example, ask, How many words can you think of that begin with *anti-?* How many words can you think of the end with *-ment?*

➤ After students generate a list of words with particular suffixes or prefixes, you may put the list to use later by asking students to write sentences using those words. This activity could be done individually, in small groups, or as a class.

➤ Discuss word roots that occur frequently in social studies vocabulary. For example, you might point out liber, meaning "free" (in *liberty, liberal,* and *liberation*); *civ,* meaning "citizen" (in *civic, civilian,* and *civilization*); *tele,* meaning "distant" (in *televise, telephone,* and *teleconference*); and *graph,* meaning "write" (in *autograph, cartography,* and *telegraph*).

➤ When studying long words, have students break the words into prefixes, suffixes, roots, and base words, and then discuss the meaning of each word part. Compound words can also be studied in this way.

➤ When a foreign word is used in text, send students on an "archaeological dig" to discover its origins. English dictionaries, foreign language dictionaries, and other reference works may be used. Encourage students to provide a rich definition of the term, including the word's history, connotations, or contexts in which it is used.

➤ On a worksheet, give students a list of suffixes. Then provide sentences that they must complete by filling in the correct suffixes. Here is an example.

> Complete each sentence by adding the correct suffix: *-or, -er, -ment,* or *-al.*
>
> A govern_____ is the head of the state govern_____.
>
> In the mayor_____ election, voters choose the lead_____ of their city.
>
> The town meeting reached a settle_____ about education_____ goals.

Developing Comprehension Skills

Reading comprehension can take place on four levels: the literal, the inferential, the applicative, and the appreciative. At the literal level, the reader gains factual knowledge, which forms the foundation for all other levels. At the literal level, the reader is basically "reading the lines"—building a basic understanding of the text.

At the inferential level, the reader goes a step farther, asking questions and assessing the text in ways that yield a richer understanding. The reader may identify the writer's purposes and motivations and the undisclosed assumptions that underlie certain passages. Thus, the reader "reads between the lines."

At the applicative level, the student relates the reading material to concepts or situations that lie beyond the reading assignment. This may include using the information to solve problems in the student's own life, to understand issues important to the community or nation, or to become motivated to learn more about a topic. In other words, at the applicative level, the ideas in a reading are put to use. The reader "reads beyond the lines."

At the appreciative level, the reader responds to a text in creative, empathic, and subjective ways. New insights or convictions may be generated by the reading experience. Individuals or groups of students may want to respond to a reading through artistic expression, such as writing a poem, creating a collage, performing a dramatic interpretation of the text, or writing a song. The reader "creates new lines."

Taken together, these levels of reading comprehension draw students into active involvement in the text, resulting in a rich learning experience. How can teachers ensure that students will attain each of the four levels of reading comprehension? One way is to encourage metacognition—the student's active monitoring of the reading experience. Thinking about the reading task while performing it helps students succeed in understanding a text. Students with good metacognitive skills may ask themselves questions like these as they read:

- What is my purpose in reading this?
- What is the main idea of this section?
- Is there something I don't understand? How can I get some help?
- Should I review this section before I move on to the next one?
- How does this relate to the chapter we read last week?
- What strategy can I use to help me understand this section?

Selecting strategies is an important part of metacognition. A number of time-tested comprehension strategies can help students tackle difficult material in an organized way, leading to better comprehension and avoiding frustration. You can teach strategies, show which are suitable for particular types of text, and make sure students get ample practice in using them. The following strategies are discussed in this section: finding the main idea and supporting details, asking questions, summarizing, classifying information, understanding relationships, drawing inferences, predicting outcomes, forming sensory impressions, and making critical evaluations.

Finding the main ideas in a text—determining what is the most important information to be learned—will help students' reading comprehension immensely. Here are ideas for helping them focus on main ideas and the details that support them.

 *Finding Main Ideas and Details*

➤ For a challenging passage, ask students to write down the main idea of each paragraph. Model this procedure with a couple of sample paragraphs.

➤ Ask students to preview headings and subheadings in a reading assignment. Note that each one gives clues about the content. Ask the class to brainstorm what kinds of information they think will follow each heading and subheading. After they read the passage, have them check the accuracy of their predictions.

➤ Have students make semantic webs to break a topic into main ideas and details. Challenge them to create the web as they read. Figure 8.1 gives an example.

Summarizing information is another way of expressing what is most important in a passage. A summary includes no trivial or extraneous information, but rather gives a condensed statement of the main ideas. The student makes accurate generalizations about the content. While writing a summary, students can refer to the passage and double-check any concepts that aren't yet fully understood.

Asking questions before embarking on a new reading can help focus the reading experience. Students can answer the questions as they read. Teachers can provide a list of questions to precede reading, but having the students generate the questions themselves will help them master this strategy independently.

Classifying information is an effective strategy to help students organize different categories of objects or ideas, steps in a process, or complicated data. For example, to support comprehension of a reading selection on natural resources and products, students could keep two lists: one of resources and one of products. Graphic organizers can help students classify information: outlines, flow charts, tables, or story maps can be filled out as students read or as they review material. Match the organizer to the type of text; for example, flow charts are helpful in defining the steps in a process, and story maps are helpful in noting the events in a narrative.

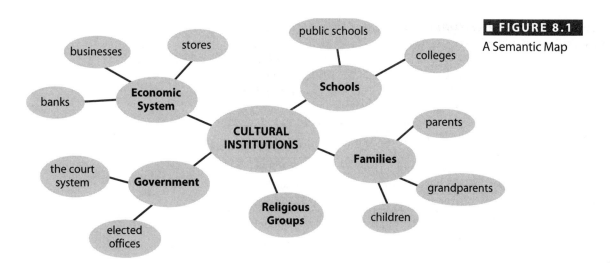

■ FIGURE 8.1

A Semantic Map

Understanding relationships that are described in text will assist comprehension as well. Give students practice in identifying these types of relationships:

Cause–effect relationships: In the social studies curriculum, causes and effects of individual behavior, group action, and historical events frequently surface in textbooks and other readings. You can also discuss cause and effect in the context of family and community problems, seasons and climate, the economy, and other topics.

Part–whole relationships: Help students analyze part–whole relationships in the context of topics like these: contributions of members of the family to the family's overall well-being, the interdependence of communities and states, and the relationship between lower and higher courts within the judicial system.

Analogous relationships: Understanding one concept in terms of another will stretch a student's comprehension of reading material. Examples of analogous relationships to explore include similarities and differences in family life within different cultures, in the work of governors and presidents, and in the modes of transportation used in different time periods.

Quantitative relationships: Raising students' awareness of quantitative relationships will promote comprehension of text involving time periods, distances, area, population, budgets, and numerical data.

Sequential relationships: Analyzing a series of events, such as those leading up to the American Revolution, or steps in a procedure, such as getting a bill passed in Congress, will give students a framework for approaching certain types of reading selections.

Place relationships: Pointing out relationships between the location of the school and the neighborhoods it serves, between large cities and waterways, or between a certain region and the equator can help students make sense of information in a selection.

In *drawing inferences,* students use what they already know to enhance what they learn from a text. They fill in additional information based on what seems implied in the new information or raise questions if the new text seems to conflict with what they already know. For example, in reading a passage about citizenship, the student discovers that a U.S. citizen is required to pay taxes, obey the law, and serve on a jury when called. The requirements did not list voting. The student already knew that citizenship has both requirements and privileges. Thus the student infers that voting is a privilege but not a requirement.

■ Books are friends that never fail.

—**Thomas Carlyle**

Predicting outcomes is another way to intensify students' engagement in a text. After reading a current news report, you might ask students to predict the eventual outcome of events, citing reasons from the text to support their predictions. Later, the class can discuss the outcome and how well it matched the prediction. For example, a news report on a candidate's presidential campaign or on a referendum concerning an environmental issue could be discussed in this way. Or, part way through a narrative of historical events, you may ask students to predict the final outcome. They can review their predictions after reading the end of the assignment.

Forming sensory impressions before or during a reading can draw students into the atmosphere of a selection. You might discuss questions like the following to enhance students' involvement in the text:

- Have you ever seen a roaring river? Where? What was it like? How might it be similar to the one in this chapter?
- What do you think Paul Revere might have felt during his midnight ride? What do you think the trip was like? What might he have seen or heard? What sentences in this selection help you understand Revere's experience?

Making critical evaluations includes distinguishing fact from opinion, recognizing the use of persuasive techniques, and evaluating the soundness of arguments and generalizations. Because opinions can be dressed up to look like facts, persuasion can glitter without being substantiated by reasons, and faulty arguments and generalizations can appear sound, students need practice in identifying such techniques. Students can ask questions like these as they evaluate a given text:

- Is this a fact or an opinion?
- Does this text use persuasive techniques such as name calling, bandwagon appeals, or testimonials to influence readers?
- Are strong reasons given to support this viewpoint?
- Is this argument based on sound reasoning? Does it account for opposing viewpoints? Is it fair?
- Is this generalization based on adequate information? If not, what additional information is needed? Where might it be found?

Understanding Visuals

In both the social studies curriculum and in the wider world, students are bombarded with information presented visually. To comprehend, interpret, and evaluate such information, students need to study it as thoroughly as they study text. Here are some questioning strategies to use in discussion of visual information:

For Maps
- What is the title of the map? What is the map meant to show? What information is left off this map, and why?
- What does each symbol in the key stand for? What does the compass rose show? What do the different colors represent?
- What might it have been like to travel along this route? What might have made the journey difficult? easy? interesting?
- Describe this region. What are its main landforms? products? resources? What might you see if you took a trip here?

Research skills are at the heart of social studies instruction in the upper elementary grades and middle schools. What skill is this teacher demonstrating to the class?

For Posters

■ What is the purpose behind this poster? What main idea does it present?

■ How do lines, shapes, space, and color contribute to the main idea?

■ What feelings does the poster arouse? What action does it motivate you to take?

■ What does this poster add to your understanding of the text?

For Cartoons

■ What is the title or caption? What event or issue does the cartoon highlight?

■ What is the purpose of the cartoon? Is it meant to ridicule? to explain something? to reveal an injustice? to present a point of view?

■ What symbols can you find in the cartoon? What is the meaning of each symbol?

■ What ideas or things are exaggerated or distorted? What is your reaction to this?

■ Describe a viewpoint that differs from the one expressed by the cartoon. Which viewpoint is more compelling? Why?

For Tables

■ What information is presented in the table?

■ What questions can be answered by data in the table?

■ What changes or trends are shown?

■ What are the largest, average, and smallest amounts included?

■ What conclusions can you draw after studying this table?

■ How is the information in the table related to the text?

For Graphs

- What type of information is presented in this graph?
- What changes, trends, amounts, or predictions are shown?
- What symbols are used? What do they represent?
- If it is a bar graph or line graph, what is the scale?
- What conclusions can you draw after studying this graph?
- How is the information in the graph related to the text?

For Figures and Diagrams

- What items are identified in this visual?
- What relationships or processes are demonstrated?
- What questions can you answer by looking at this visual? What conclusions can you draw?
- How does this information relate to the text?

The a lesson plan on page 252 is focused on learning the information presented in a diagram.

Developing Study and Research Skills

No subject offers more diverse opportunities for developing study skills than does social studies. The rich variety of texts, visuals, and other learning materials gives students many entry points into planning for reading, organizing learning activities, doing research, and preparing to present information in spoken and written form.

Making a Study Plan

Whatever students' purposes in reading—gaining background information, gathering information to present in a research report, preparing for a test, building arguments for a debate, or getting ready for a small-group discussion—students benefit by having a study plan. Here are ideas that students can use on their own to get the most benefit from the time spent in study.

Before Reading

- Preview headings and subheadings.
- Read the introduction and conclusion to the selection as an overview.
- Determine the purpose for reading and study. Is it to gain a thorough understanding of the material in order to succeed on a test? to get a general overview to see if the text will be helpful in a research project? to look for specific information without reading everything? to locate opposing viewpoints to help in preparing for a debate?
- Think about prior knowledge you already have of the subject. How will this selection add to it?

LESSON PLAN   *Reading a Diagram*

Objectives	To interpret a diagram of the three branches of government and to use information in the diagram to answer questions
Materials	Diagram on Branches of Government, in textbook, page 198
Introduction	Ask students to name the three branches of government. State that today we are going to identify the main activities of each branch and the people who work in each branch.
Development	Ask students to study the diagram on page 198 of their textbooks. Ask the following questions: What branch is listed first in the diagram? What people work in this branch? What are the main activities of this branch?
	Repeat the above question for the second and the third branches.
Conclusion and Evaluation	List the following questions on the board and ask students to write answers to them. What workers are in the executive branch? What are the main activities of the executive branch?
	Repeat the above questions for each of the other branches.
	Which branch has veto power? Which branch can approve or disapprove treaties? Which branch decides if laws are constitutional?
	Ask the students to rank the branches of government in order of importance. Which branch carries on the most governmental activities?
Follow-up	Ask students to find and share diagrams published in their weekly news periodicals or in magazines and newspapers.

During Reading

- Find a place for study where distractions will not interrupt you.
- Keep in mind your purpose for reading.
- Have note-taking materials at hand. Tailor note taking to the task at hand. Brief jottings are fine to support a general understanding of the text. To gather information for a research report, more detail must be noted, including documentation of sources.
- Make sure you understand all special terms and concepts. Look up unfamiliar terms, or make a note to look them up later.
- Use reading comprehension strategies suited to the type of text you are reading. Graphic organizers may help you organize information.

- Note questions that arise as you read.
- Study any visual aids included with the text, such as charts, maps, or artwork.
- Consider using a study technique, such as SQ3R (survey, question, read, recite, reread), to ensure an in-depth learning experience.

After Reading

- Evaluate whether you achieved your purpose in reading.
- Review any questions that you raised during study. Can you find answers in reference books, class discussion, or other resources in your textbook or classroom? You may check your textbook's glossary or index to find helpful information.
- For textbook readings, make sure you can answer questions at the end of the chapter or section. Review the text as necessary.

Using Library Resources

As part of developing solid study skills, student should become familiar with the library resources available for research and further study. Print resources and electronic resources offer a wealth of information to students.

- A book is a garden carried in the pocket.
  —**Arabian Proverb**

Print resources include books (fiction and nonfiction) that can be found in the library catalog and reference books in the reference area. Give children a chance to explore the variety of reference books available in the library, such as the following.

- multivolume general-reference encyclopedias such as the *Encyclopaedia Britannica* and *World Book*
- specialized encyclopedias on topics such as music, science, and U.S. presidents
- dictionaries and thesauruses
- almanacs
- atlases
- anthologies of different types of literature, such as haiku and folk songs
- yearbooks
- directories

As part of a social studies curriculum, students should become familiar with the parts of a book so that they can quickly access its information. Give students practice in working with the table of contents, the index, the glossary, and appendixes. Students can also find information in magazines and newspapers by using library indexes or the Internet.

Electronic resources offer students another means of accessing information. Many libraries offer reference works on CD-ROM as well as computer equipment with Internet access. See Chapter 9 for more information on using technology to enhance students' studies.

Teachers integrate reading skills in their K–8 social studies programs. What skills are these students demonstrating?

Skimming and Scanning

Because students may encounter a wealth of texts related to a topic of study, it is important for them to quickly evaluate each to decide whether to study it closely or put it aside. Developing skimming and scanning skills will help students select material appropriate for in-depth study.

Skimming gives a quick overview of a selection. Students read the title, any headings, the first and last paragraph, and the first sentences of other paragraphs. Taking note of visuals and captions is also part of skimming. *Scanning* involves looking for key words, dates, or other specific details. Both techniques can show whether close study of a selection will yield the information the student is seeking.

Note Taking

Taking notes while reading is a worthwhile skill to develop. Notes will help students understand the text during reading, can be used later for review, and will come in handy as practice for other learning activities, such as taking notes from resources in order to write a research report and taking down the main points while listening to a presentation. Coaching students to keep notes brief, to paraphrase, and to use quotations correctly will help them build this skill.

Using People Resources

Reading isn't the only way to find information. Students may use people resources as another means of researching social studies topics. Helping students to select qualified interviewees and to conduct an effective interview opens up a vital source of information that may not be available in any print source. Speaking and listening skills are developed in interviews, and such one-to-one interaction can make social studies projects personally relevant to students.

■ Listening Skills

Students use listening skills as they participate in discussions, attend to directions for class activities, and listen to oral reports. Far from being a passive activity, listening calls upon many skills: attending to content, sensing the mood or tone of the discussion or speech, critically evaluating the soundness of argument, and so on.

Many of the activity ideas in the preceding sections of this chapter can be adapted for use as listening activities. Here are ways to begin listening tasks:

- Listen as I read this paragraph. What is the main idea?
- Here are the directions for completing the outline. Listen carefully!
- Listen to this description of the Amazon jungle. How does it make you feel?
- Listen to this tape recording of our class discussion. Which parts went well? What can we improve in our next discussion?
- Now that you have read about Teddy Roosevelt, listen to this recording of a speech he made. What is his tone of voice? What does he feel about this topic? How can you tell?

Tape-recorded material can be especially helpful in developing listening skills. Analyzing a tape-recorded class discussion can yield a good deal of helpful information: whether students interrupted each other, failed to follow up on a question, repeated themselves unnecessarily, or communicated quite effectively. Students might privately listen to audiotapes of their own oral reports to note their strengths and weaknesses. A listening center in the classroom can facilitate such learning experiences. Here are additional ideas for fostering good listening skills.

ACTIVITY IDEAS ➤ *Listening Skills*

➤ To help students in the primary grades get ready for a listening experience, you might provide a simple checklist of things to focus on while listening. Discuss each item.

_____	I pay close attention.
_____	I listen for the main ideas.
_____	I try to picture the descriptions.
_____	I take notes.
_____	I summarize what I learned.

➤ With the class, brainstorm ideas for getting ready to listen to a speech, to enhance learning while listening, and to follow up after listening. The result may be a worksheet like this one, which could later be distributed to the class. Items on the sheet listed can be customized to suit the speeches—student reports, talks given by community leaders, or videotaped political speeches delivered by the president.

Before Listening

What is my purpose for listening? _____

_____

What is the speaker's purpose? _____

Am I prepared for listening? Do I have note-taking materials? Have I completed any required background reading? _____

_____

During Listening

What is the topic? _____

What are the main ideas? _____

What details support the main ideas? _____

Which ideas are new to me? _____

What is the conclusion? _____

After Listening

Was the speaker's purpose achieved? _____

Did I achieve my purpose in listening? _____

What additional questions do I have? _____

What were the strengths of the speech? the weaknesses? _____

_____

➤ Prepare students to critically evaluate the material they listen to by helping them understand fact versus opinion, bias, typical persuasive techniques, and the need for evidence and sound reasoning to support a speaker's argument. To prepare for listening to a particular speech, you might give students a list like this one, focused on problems that may emerge in the speech you have chosen.

> **Critical Evaluation**
>
> Is the speaker biased? What is the bias?
>
> What assumptions does the speaker state?
>
> What assumptions are unspoken?
>
> Does the speaker rely on stereotypes? Which ones?
>
> Does the speaker use clichés?
>
> Does the speaker give good reasons? What are they?
>
> Are there flaws in the speaker's argument? What are they?
>
> What facts and evidence does the speaker give? What opinions?
>
> What is the speaker's conclusion? Is it logical?

■ Speaking Skills

Building confidence and proficiency in speaking can be smoothly integrated into social studies. Here is a sampling of speaking activities that students can take part in.

■ For more information on language and social studies, visit the National Council of Teachers of English's website at **http://www.ncte.org**

show-and-tell	readers' theater
role playing	debates
giving a "radio report"	plays
dramatic readings	giving instructions
choral reading	impersonating a historical character
interviews	persuasive speeches
oral reports	retelling the events in a narrative
extemporaneous speaking	describing a personal experience
panel discussions	

For all speaking activities, it is important to maintain a supportive and positive atmosphere; make sure students feel support when they take the risk of speaking in front of a group. No hint of ridicule should be allowed. For more formal speeches, emphasize that preparation is the key to success. Encourage students to look up the pronunciation of unfamiliar terms, discuss their ideas with peers, and gather information from reliable sources. The following activities can help.

ACTIVITY IDEAS ➤ *Speaking Skills*

➤ To prepare students for speaking in front of a group, you might provide a checklist of guidelines like this one. It can be scaled down or elaborated to suit the grade level.

Speak Up! Speak Well!

_____ I speak so that everyone can hear.

_____ I do not rush. I take a breath when I need one.

_____ I stay on the topic.

_____ I glance at my notes when I need to. I don't stare at them.

_____ I make eye contact with my audience.

_____ I let my voice rise and fall naturally. I don't speak in a monotone.

➤ To prepare students for taking part in discussions, you might discuss and post a set of rules for discussions. Here is an example.

Rules for Classroom Discussions

Think about the discussion topic.

Raise your hand when you have something to say.

Listen carefully to what others say.

Speak tactfully when you disagree with someone.

Do not interrupt.

Ask questions when you don't understand something.

Don't talk all the time. Give someone else a chance.

Don't stay silent all the time. Contribute your thoughts.

Be polite and friendly to everyone.

■ Books are the fit inheritance of generations and nations.

—Henry David Thoreau

➤ Discussions are especially helpful for solving problems. You might follow these steps to lead a class discussion focused on solving a particular problem.

1. Define the problem.
2. Break the problem into parts, if necessary.
3. Clarify terms and questions that have been raised.
4. Brainstorm possible solutions.
5. Discuss each solution, noting its strengths or weaknesses.
6. Choose the best solution.
7. Discuss ways to implement the solution.

■ Writing Skills

Social studies can provide opportunities to write in several different modes. As well as sharpening students' writing skills, these opportunities can help foster critical thinking, reasoning, observation, and expressiveness. Writing projects can vary in length and intensity, from simple jottings to elaborate reports. This list shows the variety of writing projects that social studies students can engage in.

fact sheets	interview questions
scripts for newscasts	survey forms
class newspapers	editorials
outlines	case studies
summaries	historical vignettes
research reports	captions for photo essays
fictional letters	annotated bibliographies
book reviews	"you were there" scenarios
scrapbooks	poems
descriptions of geographic features	fictional stories
speech reviews	plays
directions	riddles and puzzles
biographical sketches	songs
opinion pieces	checklists
learning logs	analogies
records of data	databases
journals	fictional interview with a
minutes of meetings	historical character

Writing Reports

For good reason, writing reports is a typical assignment in the social studies class. It encourages students to undertake research, to synthesize information, and to present the results in a clear, engaging way. Students can gather information for reports by using techniques discussed in the section on reading study skills; they may also find out more from interviews, visuals, and their own observations.

In the primary grades, teachers can help students write reports by recording the text as dictated by the students. This can be done by hand, but it is easier to type the text on a computer. Students can then get a printout of their report text. In the upper grades, students can produce word-processed or handwritten text. At every grade level, visuals—such as drawings, charts, and maps—can be added if they will enhance the report.

Because writing a report can be somewhat complex, here are suggested ways of approaching each step. These steps can be simplified or elaborated according to grade level.

Prewriting
- Choose a topic.
- Determine what is already known about the topic.
- Develop further questions to be answered about the topic.
- Gather facts from good sources to answer the questions.

- Sort the facts. Decide what to include in the report.
- Create an outline.

Drafting

- Draft the report without worrying about small errors.
- Write one paragraph for each main idea.

Revising

- Have a writing conference to find ways to improve the draft.
- Look for more facts if needed.
- Reorder the information if needed.
- Think of creative, interesting ways to state things.

Proofreading

- Check spelling, grammar, punctuation, and capitalization.
- Check paragraphing.
- Make sure the report has a title and a list of sources that were used.

Publishing

- Think of an interesting way to share your report.

Other Writing Activities

Social studies also can tap into students' imaginations. Writing assignments can challenge students to use their knowledge in creative ways: imagining what it was like to experience a moment in history from past centuries as well as imagining future events. The lesson plan on page 261 gives students practice in thinking about future scenarios.

See Chapter 12 for more information about encouraging creativity in the social studies classroom. The following tips will help you as you incorporate a variety of writing experiences into the social studies curriculum:

- As they write, encourage students to incorporate social studies vocabulary by using social studies word lists, word cards, or other aids.
- Provide a variety of writing opportunities—some informal ones and others that are more demanding. You may ask that students take certain assignments through the five steps of the writing process: prewriting, drafting, revising, proofreading, and publishing.
- Make sure that dictionaries and thesauruses are available to students as they write. Urge them to use dictionaries to check spellings and specific meanings and to use thesauruses to explore shades of meaning and enrich their vocabularies.

LESSON PLAN *Writing Scenarios*

Objective   To write scenarios related to a future event

Materials   Paper and pencil

Introduction   Explain that a scenario is used by futurists, military personnel, policy planners, and others to help them think about the future and various alternatives. Although it is an imaginary account, efforts are made to project situations as the writer thinks they will happen.

Development   Ask students to respond orally to a question of this nature: If you were to advise a writer of scenarios on what to include about schools 50 years from now, what would you say?

After discussion of contributions and any questions about scenarios, ask students to write a scenario for one of the following or for a topic of their choice:

A twenty-hour workweek	Education by television and computer
New energy technologies	Robots replace factory workers
Underwater cities	Cooperation replaces competition
Living in a space colony	Ideal city of the future

Conclusion and Evaluation   Ask students to share and discuss their scenarios, encouraging them to give reasons for their views.

Evaluate written scenarios, with emphasis on imaginative thinking and projection of alternative views.

Follow-up   Encourage students to write other scenarios and to get ideas from the following sources: Dickson, *Future File;* Kahn, *The Next Two Hundred Years;* and such journals as *Science News* and students' news periodicals.

■ Give students encouragement by commenting on the positive features of their writing as well as indicating areas to improve. Both holistic evaluation and assessment of specific skills can be combined in feedback.

■ For some assignments, allow time for writing conferences between peers as well as student–teacher writing conferences.

■ Encourage students to use the computer for writing assignments. Programs such as *Publish It!, Bank Street Writer, Kidwriter, Story Tree, Storymaker, First Draft, Multiscribe, Children's Writing and Publishing, Once Upon a Time,* and *The Write Connection* are good choices. See Chapter 9 for more information on technology in social studies instruction.

■ Conclusion

Basic language and communication skills are fundamental to a social studies program. Using a developmental approach, teachers at all grade levels can integrate reading, writing, listening, and speaking activities into the curriculum to provide students with comprehensive literacy skills. Over time, students will move from a basic to a more sophisticated understanding of social studies concepts and generalizations. In addition, command of communication skills helps students enjoy reading, writing, and speaking about social studies. In the end, this understanding and appreciation of social studies can lead to a deeper understanding of human relationships and the development of responsible citizenship in a democracy.

 Questions, Activities, and Evaluation

1. Read a chapter in a social studies textbook and the notes to the teacher in the accompanying manual.
   a. List the vocabulary that should be developed.
   b. Note techniques for vocabulary development suggested in the manual.
   c. Review the vocabulary development techniques suggested in this chapter and add useful ones to those noted in the manual.
   d. Note examples of questions and activities that you might use to guide students to (1) interpret the meaning of a section, a graph, a table, or some other item; (2) find main ideas and related details; (3) find relationships; and (4) formulate a generalization, draw an inference, predict an outcome, or form a sensory impression.

2. Plan an activity that students might do in a unit to find needed information and develop the following reading study skills:
   a. Locating information in a textbook index
   b. Using an encyclopedia
   c. Using a glossary, a dictionary, or a thesaurus
   d. Finding up-to-date information in periodicals, newspapers, and an almanac

3. Select one of the activity ideas in this chapter, and adapt it to fit a unit for a grade level of your choice.

4. Note examples of ways you might use the following in a unit:
   a. Listening to evaluate or to achieve another objective
   b. Oral reports, buzz sessions, or some other speaking activity
   c. Questions and comments to guide discussion of a topic
   d. Three of the writing activities noted in this chapter

5. Make a lesson plan for a writing activity. Use the plan on page 261 as a model.

References

Anntonacci, P. A. (1991, March). Students search for meaning in the text through semantic mapping. *Social Education, 55,* 174–55, 194.

Davis, B. H., et al. (1992, November/December). Writing-to-learn in elementary social studies. *Social Education, 56,* 393-97.

Devine, T. G. (1981). *Teaching study skills.* Boston: Allyn and Bacon.

Dunthorn, T., & Woods, L. (1993, Fall). Making connections in the elementary curriculum: The Florida K–5 social studies plan of study. *International Journal of Social Education, 8,* 33–40.

Durkin, D. (1993). *Teaching them to read* (6th ed.). Boston: Allyn and Bacon.

Fielding, L. G., & Pearson, P. D. (1994, February). Synthesis of research—reading comprehension: What works. *Educational Leadership, 51,* 62–68.

Fry, P. G., et al. (1996, March/April). Halliday's functions of language: A framework to integrate elementary-level social studies and language arts. *The Social Studies, 87,* 78–80.

Kincade, K. M., & Pruitt N. E. (1996, Fall). Using multicultural literature as an ally to elementary social studies texts. *Reading Research and Instruction, 36,* 18–32.

Kornfeld, J. (1994, September). Using fiction to teach history. *Social Education, 58,* 281–86.

Martorella, P. H. (1991, May/June). Strategies for aiding students in comprehending social studies subject matter. *The Social Studies, 81,* 131–34.

Notable children's trade books in the field of the social studies. (annual review, April-May issue). *Social Education.*

O'Day, K. (1994, January). Using formal and informal writing in middle school social studies. *Social Education, 58,* 39–40.

Rieckein, T., & Miller, M. R. (1990, March/April). Introduce children to problem solving and decision making by using children's literature. *The Social Studies, 81,* 59–64.

Tindall, L. C. (1996). *A comparison of teaching social studies using a traditional textbook versus using a literature-based approach.* Unpublished master's research project. Mercer University.

Viadero, D. (1995, December 13). Americans land in the middle of international literacy scale. *Education Week, 15,* 6.

Zarnowski, M. (1990). *Learning about biographies: A reading and writing approach for children.* Urbana, IL: National Council for Teachers of English.

Zarnowski, M., & Gallagher, A. F. (Eds.). (1993). *Children's literature & social studies.* Dubuque, IA: Kendall/Hunt Publishers.

Chapter 9

Identifying and Using Instructional Resources and Technology

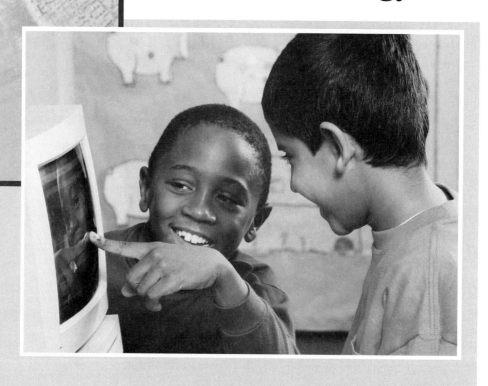

Chapter Objective

To present principles and strategies for identifying, evaluating, and using instructional resources to improve teaching and learning

Focusing Questions

- ■ What criteria are used to select instructional resources?

- ■ How can textbooks, charts, databases, literary selections, and practice materials be used to provide the maximum educational benefit?

- ■ How can computers, videos, and other technology be used to improve teaching and learning?

- ■ What community resources are most useful? How can they contribute to learning?

- ■ What guidelines are helpful in planning, guiding, and evaluating all resources?

- ■ How can teachers find materials that are not available at school?

■ Materials Galore!

Have you attended an annual meeting of the National Council for the Social Studies (NCSS)? One of the reasons why teachers attend national meetings of professional associations is to visit the exhibit area. Here, publishers display the latest materials they have developed. It is a teacher's delight! These exhibits present the latest K–8 social studies series, teachers' edition textbooks, and ancillary materials; maps, globes and accompanying teacher materials; specialized offerings in areas such as multicultural education, global education, civic education, and women's studies; technology of all kinds, reflecting all areas of the social studies; and displays of trade books, news magazines, and periodicals designed for K–8 learners. Teachers leave the exhibit area with bags of materials, which they store in the hotel room until they are ready to depart. The flow of material is so heavy that small businesses that specialize in packing and shipping are on hand to help teachers who cannot possibly squeeze all the new materials in their suitcases! When teachers unpack and review these items, they begin the process of deciding which will become classroom instructional resources.

Whether or not you've attended such a conference, as a college student interested in teaching, you've no doubt experienced "information overload." Another example of this "overload" is the stream of material available on the Internet—it is boundless. The school library contains another array of materials, including

■ We conclude with a potpourri of learned thoughts from an assortment of learned sources. Enjoy!
—**Anonymous**

children's trade books. Community resources add to this inventory of educational material. How do teachers transform this "stuff" into valuable instructional resources?

These materials do not become instructional resources until teachers decide to consider them for classroom use. The most important person in the selection, evaluation, and use of materials is the social studies teacher. In this chapter, we look at an array of materials and provide methods of evaluating and using these materials in K–8 classrooms.

■ Selecting Instructional Materials

With the wealth of material available to teachers, it is important to use a critical eye in choosing which items to use in teaching. Despite how many "bells and whistles" a particular educational product may offer, it won't be suitable for the classroom unless it fits the definition and purpose of social studies as defined by your school and by you, your goals and objectives for social studies learning, and your standards of quality. Resources shouldn't be used indiscriminately.

You might ask these questions as you review materials from instructional media centers, community agencies, the library, and other sources:

- Does this item contribute to social studies goals and objectives?
- Does it contain authentic, relevant content?
- Does it treat the spectrum of societal groups fairly?
- Does it present a positive view of cultural diversity?
- Does it include gender, racial, or ethnic stereotypes? Is bias evident?
- Does it fit well with the current curriculum?
- Will students find it significant and meaningful?
- Is it sturdy and well made?
- Does it include helpful supports such as a teacher's manual?
- Does it treat issues fairly, providing a variety of viewpoints?
- Is it suitable to the students' age group and maturity level?

Free or inexpensive material can interest teachers because it takes only a little bite out of the budget. There are some precautions to exercise in considering it, however. Make sure the material has a reputable sponsor and does not contain objectional advertising. Also, check that using the free material does not obligate you to make purchases or other commitments. It should, of course, meet all other criteria that you apply in selecting instructional materials.

As technology products continue to increase in number and variety, care must be taken in choosing which items to use. When selecting software, check that it is easy for students to use. Does it have interactive components that will challenge students? Are the rate and presentation of material easy to control? Also, good support materials will help you make the best use of such products.

Being choosy will benefit your students!

■ Reading Materials

Reading materials are among the most widely used instructional materials in social studies. Why? Their rich content, illustrations, graphics, and other features make them a convenient and effective tool of instruction. Reading materials are widely varied, and you may find a number of the following types useful in a given unit, module, or lesson.

Textbooks, including interdisciplinary ones and those that focus on geography, history, civics, or other disciplines

Teacher-prepared materials, including charts, rewritten material, and worksheets

Literary materials, including biography, fiction, folklore, short stories, poetry, trade books, travel books, and read-along books on cassettes

Booklets on a variety of topics, ranging from family life and community workers to ethnic groups and daily life experiences in other countries

Reference materials, including almanacs, anthologies, atlases, dictionaries, thesauruses, directories, encyclopedias, government bulletins, scrapbooks, yearbooks, and databases

Fugitive materials, including bulletins, clippings, folders, leaflets, simulation games, pamphlets, and free or inexpensive materials

Current events materials, including children's weekly news publications, adult and children's magazines, and daily newspapers

Source materials, including ballots, diaries, directions, logs, maps, minutes of meetings, recipes, and timetables

Self-help materials, including charts, checklists, directions, outlines, study guides, teacher-prepared practice materials, and workbooks

Textbooks

Textbooks serve as the core of instruction in many social studies programs, but they do not dominate instruction as they once did. It seems that they are used less in the primary and elementary grades but more in the middle grades. Although a multimedia approach is currently favored, textbooks are used in several ways in K–8 classrooms. Some teachers use the adopted textbooks as the basis of instruction, employing teaching procedures similar to those used in the reading program. Other teachers use a basic textbook as a general guide but supplement various chapters of the text with additional reading materials, audiovisual media, and other resources. This approach provides opportunities to use multiple data sources. In classrooms where multimedia and unit approaches are used, the textbook is one component of instruction along with a variety of other resources, all of which are viewed as sources of data for achieving instructional objectives.

No matter which approach is used, teachers may use social studies textbooks to achieve objectives such as these:

To introduce a unit through photo essays and introductory sections that set the stage or give an overview

To develop new concepts and related vocabulary as students use picture and context clues, phonics, and structural analysis

To find main ideas and details related to topics and problems

To apply and extend learning, provide practice, and reinforce learning

To provide a background of ideas that students can use to make comparisons as they study media that present different information

To answer questions and "prove" points by having students locate and report relevant information

To improve skill in reading, interpreting maps, charts, diagrams, illustrations, tables, and graphs, and in using the table of contents, glossary, and index

To sharpen the ability to draw inferences, derive generalizations, predict outcomes, and use other thinking skills

To foster positive feelings and attitudes toward others as students read about other groups and cultures

Although textbook instruction has its advantages, some weaknesses are associated with it. Textbooks, for example, may lack depth and breadth, presenting only one perspective on topics, issues, and events. Students may view them as dull and not related to their interests or needs. They also represent a lockstep approach to learning. Teachers at all levels avoid heavy reliance on the textbook in their social studies programs.

Teacher-Prepared Material

One of the most useful materials is text that has been rewritten by the teacher to fit students' reading abilities. In the early grades teachers use these materials to gauge reading abilities and to identify students' ability to gain understanding of social studies concepts from the materials. A sound approach is to imagine that you are writing a letter or telling an exciting story to a child, keeping in mind that every idea must be expressed as simply and as clearly as possible. Choose vocabulary, phrasing, and sentences similar to those used by children, and keep sentences and paragraphs short, as they are in children's periodicals.

Other teacher-prepared materials include charts, vocabulary lists and card files, practice exercises, and activity cards that may be adapted for use with a variety of materials (see Figure 9.1).

Booklets may be made of pictures and articles related to a topic, and folders may be organized to include materials on topics in a unit. Reports and scrapbooks prepared by students may be edited and revised for use by future classes.

■ **FIGURE 9.1**

Sample Reading Activity Card: Wind Power

Directions. Find the folder on wind power in the reading center. Answer the following questions as you read the one-page article entitled "What About Wind Power?"

1. What is the main idea in the first paragraph?

2. What is the main idea in the second paragraph?

3. What is the main idea in the third paragraph?

4. Complete the following:

   a. Three of the best places for using wind power are

      _____ , _____ , and _____ .

   b. Three problems that are hindering the use of wind power are

      _____ , _____ , and _____ .

5. What is your view of the future of wind power? Write a paragraph in which you include two or more reasons for your view.

Making and Using Charts

Charts are useful in units at all levels of instruction. They are especially helpful in developing reading ability in social studies. For example, as concepts and generalizations and the related vocabulary are developed and used to make charts, children construct the meanings needed in a whole-language approach to reading and writing in social studies.

Charts are also useful in the upper grades because they provide students with examples of ways of organizing and presenting content. Students in the elementary and middle school levels should begin appreciating the advantages of presenting information both graphically and in prose.

For variety and to achieve different purposes, we can choose among several chart formats. Here are some ideas:

Experience charts: These can be based on field trips, interviews, and other activities.

Direction charts: Use these to guide field trips, map making, and other activities.

Question charts: The charts guide individual and group study of topics.

Vocabulary charts: These list special terms to be learned in a unit.

Classification charts: Students can record specific items under headings such as *fruits, vegetables, natural resources,* and *modes of transportation.*

Retrieval charts: Students can record data about cities, countries, and other topics.

Organization charts: These show committees, structure of government, economic or political systems, and organization of other groups.

Sequence charts: These show a series of events, processes, or steps in producing various items, and the flow of materials from farm to city.

Group standard charts: These are used to guide and evaluate discussion, committee work, role playing, and other activities.

Progress charts: These record the completion of individual and group work.

The format of charts should make them easy to use. Make the lettering large enough for group use, use standard paragraph form, and leave adequate space between words and lines. Balanced placement of illustrations, consistent use of standard letter forms, and margins similar to those on picture mats are other important elements of good charts.

Teachers who use teacher-prepared materials are aware of the potential weaknesses associated with this approach. For example, such materials may be slanted toward a particular perspective on issues, events, or people. They may stray away from the goals and objectives of the program. By using a variety of materials and constantly reflecting on the overall goals of the program, teachers can avoid these problems.

Literary Materials

Perhaps because of the emphasis on whole-language learning, the number of trade books available to teachers at all grade levels has increased significantly. Teachers will not find it difficult to infuse literature into their social studies programs. In many K–3 programs, literary materials are the mainstay of social studies programs, and in the elementary and middle grades, they support textbooks and teacher-prepared materials. These works are extremely powerful in helping students gain an appreciation for social studies.

Children's literature provides a wealth of material for motivating students, enriching and individualizing instruction, and achieving effective objectives. Literary selections can heighten interest, deepen understanding, create mood and atmosphere, stimulate imagination, give colorful background, promote identification with others, create sympathy for the problems of others, improve attitudes toward others, build appreciation for other cultures, provoke creativity, and give vivid impressions of different ways of living. Factual material rarely kindles a feeling for the joys, sorrows, and problems of others; hence the importance of poetry, stories, biography, fiction, letters, legends, and travel literature to take children beyond facts to the spiritual and aesthetic qualities and values involved in human relationships. The following examples illustrate the ways in which literature can enrich the social studies program:

A primary group that had been studying regions around the world was fascinated by the extreme weather conditions described in Wheeler's *Greetings from Antarctica.*

A group examining natural disasters asked their teacher to read Simon's books—*Tornadoes, Earthquakes, Volcanoes,* and *Wildfires*—over and over again.

A group being introduced to countries near and far enjoyed reading Illsley's *Mexico: Food and Festivals* and having the teacher read *Tibet* (Sperling and Garfunkel, editors).

Children found Kimmel's *When Mindy Saved Hanukkah* a favorite when learning about religious holidays.

Young children learned to separate myth from reality when their teachers read Marshall's *A Giant Cutaway: Inside the Titanic.*

In an elementary classroom, *The Way People Live* series published by Lucent Books was a big favorite.

Streissguth's *Life among the Vikings* served as core knowledge for students learning about early explorers to America.

Dean and Thomson's *Life in the American Colonies* served as one of the major sources when students collected information about early colonial America.

Students exploring the 1960s civil rights movement found Duncan's *The National Civil Rights Museum* extremely informative.

Wells's *Streets of Gold* provided students with the experiences of one immigrant group that arrived in Boston in the early 1900s.

Hill's *Denzel Washington* was a popular choice for students who put together a short biographical sketch of their favorite movie star.

■ There is no limit to the availability of materials for social studies instruction! Visit the Mariner's Museum **http://www.mariner.org** to learn about the heritage of the sea and its tributaries.

In the middle grades, the literature is equally rich. You might find the following ideas helpful; other sources are noted at the end of the chapter. See also "Bookwatching" in *Language Arts* and the April/May issue of *Social Education*, which lists trade books.

Students looking into murder plots in American history enjoyed reading Zeinert's *The Lincoln Murder Plot.*

Students who studied World War II found a fresh perspective by reading Myer's *The Journal of Scott Pendleton Collins.*

Students exploring a unit on tales and myths were pleasantly surprised by the variety of information found in McFarlane's *Sacred Myths: Stories of World Religions,* Crossley-Holland's *The Young Oxford Book of Folk Tales,* and Curry's *Turtle Island: Tales of the Algonquian Nations.*

A favorite among students learning about famous athletes is Freedman's *Babe Didrikson Zaharias,* known as the greatest woman athlete of all time.

Other than the textbook, what additional instructional resources do teachers employ when planning and implementing instructing? What resources will you use in your classroom?

A variety of activities can enhance the study of literature. Book reports, card files of favorite poems and stories, choral reading, dramatization of scenes from a book, independent reading, oral reading (by children or the teacher), programs or pageants based on a book, puppet shows, listening to stories on audiocassette, and storytelling are just a few ideas.

As you guide students in reading literary works, let them discover the work's meanings, moods, and values; teachers should not foist their interpretations on students nor moralize about the story. Share and discuss the parts of the story that children especially like—enjoyment should be the emphasis. If you analyze parts of the work, do so in a way that increases the enjoyment. Let students share their subjective experience of the reading; do not test them on the content as you would for factual material. Also, you might help students distinguish between fact and fiction as they read works of historical fiction.

Databases

Databases may vary in size from "minibases" kept in the classroom and software on states, countries, and other topics, to large ones in libraries and media centers, and to even larger ones, such as *America Online, CompuServe, Delphi, FrEd Mail, Learning Link, Prodigy, Sprint, Library of Congress,* and others. Accessible local databases can provide pictures, fact sheets, articles, summaries, reports, and other material for use in various units. When supplemented with almanacs, encyclopedias, video encyclopedias on compact discs, and other references, they give students access to an abundance of information undreamed of a few years ago. The Internet offers even more options in finding all kinds of information.

Making databases builds skill in locating, organizing, indexing, retrieving, and analyzing information. Databases may be made to organize information on students and their families, the community, states, regions, countries, careers, notable people, and other topics. Children in primary grades can make mini databases that include drawings, pictures, charts, and local maps related to topics of study. Materials may be kept in folders or envelopes clearly labeled with titles such as *Food, Shelter, Clothing, Workers,* and *Transportation.* Students in the middle grades can create more detailed databases with card file and cross-reference systems. Computer software for making databases and filing data can be used, and you might place information on disks for storage.

A practical approach is to involve students in making a database for a particular unit, guiding them in activities such as the following:

Collect pictures, news reports, and articles related to a topic.

Prepare data sheets or cards on particular countries under study—for example, geography (physical features, climate, resources), people (population, urban centers, ancestry), economy (agriculture, manufacturing, mining, trade, transportation, communication), culture (education, traditions, customs, festivals, arts, values, religion), and government (national, other levels, branches, form, capital).

Make data sheets or cards that contain information on topics in a unit, such as achievements of members of minority groups, the views of W. E. B. DuBois, and the Freedom March.

Make a chronology of key dates in a period or set of events, such as the settlement of the West, African Americans in historical perspective, civil rights acts, and the struggle for gender equality.

Prepare biographical sketches of men and women included in a unit.

Prepare book reviews that may be used as guides to supplementary materials.

Make charts, diagrams, graphs, and tables on topics in a unit.

Make reference cards that indicate where to locate information in almanacs, encyclopedias, and other sources.

Practice Materials

Practice materials for individual and group use can develop reading, mapping, and other skills. Multilevel materials that match students' reading levels and provide immediate feedback are helpful. Individualized practice is as necessary in social studies as it is in reading and other subjects. Excellent sources of practice materials are the teacher's guide that accompanies social studies textbooks, the end-of-chapter activities listed in textbooks, and the workbooks that accompany textbooks. Other sources are children's weekly news periodicals, booklets and instructional kits from publishers, computer programs, and activities in magazines for teachers such as *Instructor, Teacher Magazine,* and *Learning.*

■ Audio, Visual, and Audiovisual Resources

In addition to the wide variety of reading materials available for social studies instruction, audiovisual resources can provide meaningful learning experiences for students. You may obtain these materials from the school, the library, local and county school district offices, and other community sources. Realia (and representations of realia) and many different technology products can enhance your social studies program at any grade level. Table 9.1 shows the many options available; perhaps more will be available as soon as technology further develops!

■ TABLE 9.1

Audio, Visual, and Audiovisual Materials

■ Realia and Representations of Realia

Tools	Utensils	Documents	Costumes	Dolls
Art objects	Coins	Textiles	Stamps	Models
Exhibits	Instruments			

■ Audio and Visual Resources

Television programs	Videotapes	CD-ROM	DVD	Audiocassettes

■ Computer Resources

Software	The Internet	Network databases	Directories

■ Pictures and Pictorial Representations

Photographs	Drawings	Transparencies	Postcards	Albums
Scrapbooks	Collages	Murals	Storyboards	

■ Symbolic and Graphic Representations

Maps	Globes	Atlases	Charts	Cartoons
Posters	Diagrams	Graphs	Chalkboard	Bulletin board
Flannel board	Time lines			

■ Equipment for Viewing and Listening

Slide projector	Tape player	Overhead projector	VCR	Television
DVD player				

■ Devices for Producing Media

Lettering devices	Map outlines	Transparencies	Tape recorders	Photocopiers
Duplicators	Camcorders	Cameras	Scanners	Art supplies
Digital cameras	Computers			

Realia, Exhibits, Dioramas, and Panoramas

Realia are artifacts or real objects, including models, items in exhibits, dioramas, and panoramas. Children cannot go back in time and space, but they can have experiences with real things or replicas of them. For example, colonial living can be enriched by studying candle molds, muskets, cooking utensils, a spinning wheel, and clothing of the period. Questions for analyzing realia might include the following:

1. What is it made of? What might it be used for? How does it resemble and differ from other objects we have studied?
2. Who might have made it? How was it used? What can we infer about the environment, work, and values of the people who made it?
3. Do the materials or the design suggest a relationship between this culture and other cultures? Why or why not?

Social studies exhibits may include realia along with pictures, maps, and other items organized around a concept or theme, such as modes of transportation or communication.

Dioramas show scenes such as Boonesboro or the setup of a log cabin in three-dimensional perspective. Panoramas depict a scene in broad scope, such as depictions of production of lumber or recreational activities in an area.

Demonstrations, Films, and TV Programs

For today's visually sophisticated students, demonstrations, films, and TV offer compelling means of enhancing social studies instruction.

Demonstrations show how to complete an activity, step by step. Demonstrating how to make a map, use a globe, operate the classroom computer, or prepare an ethnic meal are some examples of demonstrations in the social studies classroom. Teachers often present the demonstrations, though other school staff or community helpers could do so as well.

Films and television programs portray historical events, present and analyze news items and political issues, and introduce students to places and people around the world. With the advent of the VCR, showing parts of films or informative TV programs has become simple. It's easy to review or reshow segments that students have not understood clearly. Students also benefit from analyzing the messages embodied in such audiovisual media. You might have them discuss examples of cooperation, responsibility and other democratic behavior that they observe in a film, a documentary, or another video program.

One activity idea involves assigning students to watch an upcoming show on TV. One approach is to use a forum technique: ask one set of students to view the show, while the others prepare questions to ask them about it.

Demonstrations, films, and television offer opportunities for developing listening, viewing, and critical thinking skills. You can give students specific guidelines to follow during these activities. The following is just one example:

1. Be alert, and note the most important points.
2. Be ready to state the main points and to raise questions.
3. Note any points with which you agree or disagree.
4. Note ideas we can use and ideas we need to learn more about.

Video Resources

Videodiscs, videocassettes, and DVDs can be used as needed and are available on a variety of topics. For example, units on communities can be enriched by video materials on great cities such as Rome, London, and Athens. Camcorders can be used to make videotapes of resource persons and places in the community, thus reducing the need for field trips and interviews. To locate videos on all subjects, see publications by Bowker, NICEM, and the American Library Association.

Computer Resources

The advent of computers and social studies software has made possible electronic instruction that includes skill practice and tutorials, educational games and simulations, and creative expression. Among the benefits are providing quick feedback and self-pacing, developing linear thinking ability, individualizing instruction, and developing problem-solving and decision-making skills. Reading and expressive skills also can be improved, as noted in these comments of elementary students: "You had better read and follow directions, or you will get all fouled up" and "You can create maps, charts, graphs, drawings, puzzles—you name it." The following list shows more ways of using the computer in social studies instruction:

1. Make outlines, databases, and spreadsheets.
2. Write, illustrate, edit, and revise reports.
3. Practice map, globe, study, and other skills.
4. Use tutorials to learn new content and skills.
5. Use simulations to improve decision-making skills.
6. Create graphs, posters, puzzles, and other visual materials.
7. Use integrated instructional and learning systems.
8. Use desktop publishing to present information.
9. Use online services, networks, and bulletin boards.

Make sure that social studies computer work is integrated into lessons and units. The computer itself should not be the primary focus. The growing array of social studies software includes programs on map concepts and skills, time and seasons, exploration, colonization, states, countries, continents, notable men and women, and American history, making it easy to keep the emphasis on social studies and content skills. Among the available simulations are navigating to find the Americas, sailing from New York to California, traveling to Oregon, fur trading, ruling an ancient kingdom, competing for a profit, living in ancient civilizations, and making governmental decisions. Examples of online information services that may be accessed are *America Online, CompuServe, Prodigy,* and others noted in the section on databases.

Programs are available for creating social studies word puzzles, dictionaries, task cards, posters, tables, graphs, drawings, charts, databases, test items, music, and other materials. Word-processing, desktop publishing, and programming software is usually available for classroom use. Integrated software contains several programs with one set of commands for easy coordination—for example, database, word processing, and graphics for preparing illustrated reports. Hypermedia (such as Hypercard) can be used to link text, pictures, and other materials.

Computers can be used for collaborative writing; sharing information via networks and bulletin boards; integrating text, sound, and graphics; using a scanner to display images on a monitor and to add images to reports; linking a computer and videodisc player to provide interactive learning systems; putting images from video cameras, photographs, and other items onto a computer; making slides; sending and receiving e-mail; and making multimedia presentations.

PowerPoint is a comprehensive program used by teachers and students to develop presentations. The program features a help system, graphics tools, linking and embedding, and full integration with Microsoft Word and Excel. It is popular among

What are ways you might employ classroom computers to enhance social studies instruction? What other resources might be used with the computer?

teachers and upper elementary and middle school students, regardless of their experiences with technology, because it includes text-editing tools, full graphing and charting capabilities, toolbars that can be customized, and an array of other features. The program can enhance lectures, teacher-directed discussions, and demonstrations.

Students with special needs may be aided by a computer supplied with a voice synthesizer, powerpad, touch window, other devices, and selected software.

The following sources contain information on useful software: *Instructor, Social Education,* and directories or catalogs from Bowker, Scholastic, Social Studies School Service, and other distributors. Check with local schools to find out which computer network services are available.

Combining Microcomputer, CD-ROM, and Video Technology

■ Education is a matter of building bridges.

—Ralph Ellison

Linking these technologies makes possible the creation of a single package that may include films, slides, text, video, audio, and other elements. With available videodiscs that can store thousands of frames of visual material and other information that can be readily accessed, the computer can be used to retrieve single pictures, a set of pictures, text, and other items as needed for decision making, problem solving, reporting, or other purposes. Interactive video lessons can be created to achieve various objectives. Original video and CD-ROM discs can be created, containing text, images, animation, graphics, and other features. Encyclopedias on CD-ROM are also available. A digital camera can be used to take photographs that can be reproduced.

Audio Recordings

Recordings are made and used for many different purposes in social studies. They provide background and sound effects for dramatic activities, programs, choral readings, and rhythmic expression. You may tape-record speeches, talks with school visitors, students' reports, interviews, and songs related to a unit. Recordings of students' reports may be played back to encourage self-evaluation and help identify ways to improve.

You may also share with students recordings made before video equipment had been invented. Political speeches and music are two options.

Pictures

Of all visual materials, pictures are the most widely used in K–6 classrooms. Pictures and study prints can introduce topics, raise questions, clarify concepts, illustrate reports, show steps in sequence, and be made into collages and scrapbooks. They can also clarify map symbols, show how tools are used, and develop visual literacy—

recognizing, naming, interpreting, and analyzing the objects and activities that are portrayed, as well as inferring the feelings of people who are shown.

You might develop questioning strategies to help students scrutinize pictures more carefully. For pictures of landscapes, you could ask questions like these:

- Where is this scene located?
- What features stand out? Do you see hills? valleys? rivers? other features?
- How high, large, or small are the features?
- Is there any natural vegetation? What kind?
- Are crops or gardens shown? If so, what is being raised?
- Can you tell what the weather is like? Do you see signs of wind? heat or cold? rainfall or snowfall?
- Do you see roads? canals? railroads? buildings?

Pictures of human activities are also common in social studies instruction. As your students study such images, you might raise questions like these:

- Where is the activity taking place?
- What are the people doing?
- Does the picture show individual work or group work?
- What tools and materials are being used?
- How are these ways of working like ours? different from ours?
- What homes or other buildings are shown?
- How are activities and buildings adapted to the climate?
- What values does this picture seem to show?

Slides and Overhead Projections

These materials are used to cover a variety of topics in all grades. Many are accompanied by helpful manuals. They are popular among teachers because it is easy to stop and discuss the images for as long as desired. Teachers can write on transparent plastic and point to items on maps, diagrams, and the like while facing the class. Relationships can be shown by using overlays, for example, placing a population map transparency over a relief map transparency to show settlement–landform relationships.

The Bulletin Board

The bulletin board is useful for starting new units, stimulating new interests, clarifying problems, posting student work, and displaying materials. In initiating units, display materials that evoke interest and stimulate questions about those topics that come first in the unit. By changing and rearranging materials to stimulate new interests, the teacher can guide the development of the unit in sound directions. Related materials, such as posters, drawings, charts, maps, or graphs, should be posted as needed. Student work may be displayed to share and summarize learning.

Interactive bulletin boards that invite student participation may be arranged by providing captions, questions, and space for students' contributions. Students may bring pictures, postcards, clippings, and other items to share on the bulletin board. You might give students a chance to describe an item they contribute and to answer questions that other students have about it. You can vary the layout of the board, as shown in Figure 9.2.

■ **FIGURE 9.2**

Sample Bulletin Board Arrangements

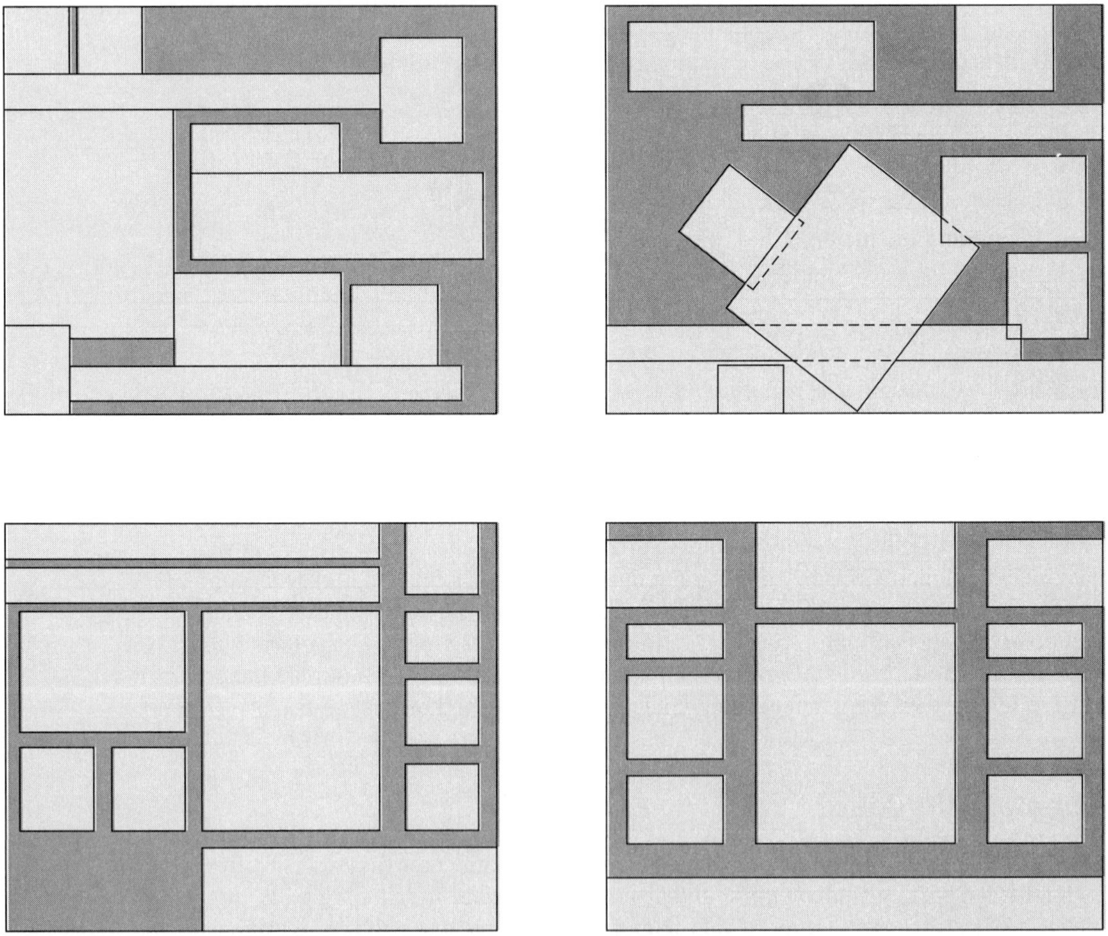

The Storyboard

Storyboards are used to first brainstorm and then arrange the elements in a story, film, photo essay, or other form of expression. Each event or idea is sketched out, using hand-drawn cartoons, pictures that have been taken, or handwritten text. These items are arranged on a flannel board, a bulletin board, or some other surface. A storyboard is created by a team of workers, thus providing an opportunity for creative interaction. It also increases students' visual literacy.

You can use storyboards to plan projects in social studies. A photo essay, videotape, audiotape, or classroom dramatization can be approached in this way. Follow these steps:

1. Select a topic and a product to make.
2. Brainstorm ideas, write or draw each one, and post them on the storyboard.
3. Rearrange the items until you come up with the best sequence.
4. Add notes to clarify details.
5. Make the product.
6. Evaluate the product and the storyboarding experience.

The Chalkboard or Whiteboard

The chalkboard or whiteboard is a basic and versatile visual tool. Teachers use it to list suggestions during group planning, sketch illustrations, list reading materials, note assignments, copy suggestions for charts, note facts under main ideas, summarize a discussion, record group-dictated stories or letters, and give "chalk talks." Many teachers add simple stick figures to illustrate points, work with colored chalk or pens to emphasize key ideas, and use rulers, compasses, and stencils to create neat, artistic effects. Carefully select materials to place on the board, remembering that slides, charts, and duplicated materials are more effective when large amounts of information or detailed data are to be presented.

Symbolic and Graphic Materials

Making and interpreting graphics is a valuable experience and especially attuned to social studies instruction. Posters, tables, graphs, and cartoons are just some of the kinds you might focus on.

Posters   Posters convey a single idea in a way that can be grasped at a glance. They are used to sway people to favor a course of action and are often used in campaigns for safety, energy conservation, or other concerns. Space, line, form, and color direct attention to the desired action. Making posters acquaints students with ways of presenting a single idea simply and forcefully.

Tables   Tables summarize data on population, resources, products, exports, and other topics in succinct form. The first tables interpreted by students may simply be a list of figures headed by a title—for example, *Classroom Attendance* or *Population Growth in Our Community.* Tables with two or more columns are then introduced, and the teacher directs attention to the title, the column headings, comparisons between columns, and changes and trends.

Graphs   Graphs are visual presentations of data. In the early grades they are used to show information such as daily temperature, enrollment, attendance, books read, and other items familiar to children. In later grades they are used to show trends in population growth, resources, exports, and other data. In all grades the interpretation and construction of graphs must be related to instruction in the mathematics program.

Cartoons   Cartoons convey an idea by means of caricature, humor, stereotype, oversimplification, exaggeration, and satire. Symbols such as Uncle Sam, John Bull, and the dove of peace may be used. The meaning of the symbol must be clear and an understanding of the situation, issue, or problem must be developed if students are to interpret a cartoon. This is why so many cartoons that amuse adults have little or no impact on children. When cartoons are encountered in reading and other materials they must be analyzed to help students understand the symbols used, the situation or problem portrayed, and the purpose of the cartoonist.

Learning activities and questions that help students learn to interpret symbolic and graphic material are presented in Chapters 8 and 9.

Time Charts and Time Lines

Time charts and time lines clarify time relationships, relate events to major time periods, and relate events in one country to those in another. In the early grades, charts may be made to show events of the day, major events during the week, events related to the growth of the community, changes in transportation, changes in farming, and changing ways of providing food, shelter, and clothing. In later grades charts and time lines may be used to show events during major periods of the history of the state or the nation, the development of transportation or communication, and the like.

Time charts and time lines take many different forms. The most common form is simply a sequence of events with space between the events scaled to show elapsed time. A wire can be strung across the room and cards representing events hung at appropriate intervals. Large envelopes can be attached to the wall under a line showing time periods, and children can place appropriate pictures or names of events in them. Events in two or more regions or countries can be arranged in parallel form, either vertically or horizontally, to show what occurred in different places at the same time. Figure 9.3 shows four different formats.

Working with time lines can help students develop an overall temporal frame of reference for interpreting time periods and time relationships. Have students look at examples in *Timelines of the Ancient World,* published by the Smithsonian. Many

■ **FIGURE 9.3**

Formats for Time Charts and Time Lines

Time Line of Early Settlements (Students fill in the rest)

Jamestown

1607

Community Events			
1985	1990	1995	2000

Major Events in the Western Hemisphere

	1700	1750	1800	1850	1900	1950	2000
United States							
Canada							
Mexico							

Major Events in the United States, 1970–2000

Decade	Social	Political	Economic
1970			
1980			
1990			
2000			

teachers have children use their own age as a touchstone for understanding time periods. For example, the following list was made by a group of ten-year-olds:

Decade: 10 years, equal to my age, about one third my parents' age

Generation: 33 years, a little more than three times my age, about the same as my parents' age

Century: 100 years, ten times my age, about three times my parents' age

The following lesson plan illustrates how future time lines may be introduced to students.

LESSON PLAN   *Future Time Lines*

Objective   To make personal and community (or state or nation) future time lines

Introduction   Review time lines in students' textbooks that show past events. Tell the class that they are going to learn to project a time line into the future.

Development   First, ask members of the class to make a personal time line on a time horizon of their choice, explaining that "time horizon" refers to the period of time to be used. Make sure it projects into the future. Discuss possible events that may be included, such as birthdays, promotion to a higher grade, completion of elementary school, and other events of special interest, such as a trip or a vacation.

After completion and discussion of the personal time lines, ask students to make one for their community (or state or nation) over the same time period. Discuss possible events to include, such as legal holidays, elections, new buildings, renewal projects, or technological advancements.

Conclusion and Evaluation   Share and discuss time lines, with attention to events students think will actually happen and to those they hope will happen. Evaluate by observing students in discussion and by checking their time lines.

Follow-up   Ask students to continue to add to and revise their time lines.

Learning Centers

An effective way to make instructional materials available for individual and small-group use is to set up learning centers. A variety of focuses are possible. Here is a sampling:

   *Setting Up Learning Centers*

➤ Arrange a community learning center for students. Decorate it with photographs of prominent places, such as the school, governmental buildings, the fire station, stores, banks, and so on. Include a simple map of the community, with labels that students can add to it. Provide reading materials on your community and other ones. Worksheets might include matching activities that match workers with workplaces, names of buildings with pictures of the buildings, and so on.

➤ Create a dramatic play area that can be adapted to different topics in social studies. For example, for a unit on the family, the play area may contain a small table and chairs, dolls, a crib, and other role-playing props. For a unit on the community, you might set up the area as a store, with counter, shelves of canned goods, and shopping bags. For a unit on transportation, provide toy airplanes, spaces marked as the runway and the control tower, and baggage trucks.

➤ Set up a U.S. history learning center, featuring books on explorers, colonists, pioneers, and other leaders. Include a wall map and atlas, as well as worksheets and outline maps to note data. You might change the focus of this center from time to time; for example, you might feature U.S. presidents and supply books with information on and pictures of them. Provide task cards that direct students to find term of office, political party, main achievements, and other information about particular presidents. You might add a listening aspect to the center by providing tapes of speeches made by some presidents.

➤ At some point in the year, your classroom reading center might focus on literature related to social studies. Choose texts at a variety of reading levels that also deal with the current social studies unit. Provide trade books, both fiction and nonfiction, and a selection of articles and other suitable readings. You might provide worksheets like this one to help students interpret and evaluate their readings:

> Read a book or an article, and then answer these questions.
>
> 1. What did this reading add to your understanding of our social studies unit?
> 2. What new things did you learn?
> 3. How did you feel about the story or the information?
> 4. What new ideas did it give you?
> 5. Would you rate this reading as good, fair, or poor? Why?
> 6. Would you recommend this book to your classmates?

➤ You might offer a learning center focused on map and globe skills. Include a large globe, a wall map, and an atlas for use as a reference. Set up a file of other maps, including local, state, and regional maps and maps developed for special purposes, such as topographical maps. Supply students with task cards, outline maps, and research and mapping assignments.

➤ Consider setting up a world cultures center. Organize clipping files, picture files, books, maps, and other resources that focus on particular cultures. Try to find slides or videos that bring to life different places in the world. Provide worksheets. You may wish to assign each student a brief oral presentation based on the information they've gained in the world cultures center.

Learning centers offer students an alternative to teacher-directed instruction. What are the advantages of using learning centers in social studies instruction? disadvantages?

■ A teacher is one who brings us tools and enables us to use them.
—**Jean Toomer**

For all work in learning centers, make sure students understand the proper procedures for using materials and being considerate to others. When students engage in collaborative learning in these centers, you may need to give them additional guidelines for behavior.

■ Community Resources

By taking classes into the community or encouraging students to examine their community, you allow them to move beyond their immediate neighborhood, to appreciate the complex nature of community living, and to think about communities in other parts of the world. Learners can study changing conditions as they take place and the factors that produce them. Changes in the makeup of neighborhoods and new buildings, parks, or memorials can be interesting to study. Students can experience holidays, special events, and commemorations. Field trips, interviews with local experts, and visits to historical sites can enhance students' learning and motivation to learn. To explore the resources in your community, you might compile a list like the one shown in Figure 9.4.

The Community Survey

In many social studies programs the community is the focus of study, and study topics are determined by the curriculum and the maturity of the students.

Many educational benefits can be gained from a community survey. A community survey conducted in a social studies classroom represents the physical sites, individuals, and topics that the teacher and students wish to explore. Many aspects of community life can be the focus. Surveys will differ from class to class and year to year. If the social studies program focuses on the community, the teacher may want to select survey topics closely related to the curriculum and take into account the maturity of the students.

As students conduct their survey—perhaps checking safety hazards, types and locations of residence, housing conditions, the business and industrial sections, or museums—their observation skills are sharpened. As they talk with old-timers, business people, school workers, public officials, and other community workers, they improve their interviewing techniques. As they examine pictures, letters, newspapers, reports, and other local documents, they develop skill in content analysis.

Topics can include the following:

communication	societal groups	education	resources
museums, theaters	future plans	social services	utilities
health services	geography	mass media	ecology
sanitation services	government	conservation	pollution
sports facilities	residences	transportation	history
urban renewal	population	recreation	occupations

■ **FIGURE 9.4**

Exploring the Community

Study (or field) trips (to cultural centers, museums, local businesses, and so on):

Field studies (of housing, pollution, transportation, and so on):

People to interview (police officers, government officials, and various professionals):

Resource visitors (panel or individuals):

Service and other organizations (Red Cross, clubs, and so on):

Service projects (safety, cleanup, and so on):

Local current events (campaigns, drives, celebrations, and so on):

Recreational resources (parks and marinas):

School resources (collections, teachers):

Publications, visual media (newspapers, bulletins, and so on):

Television, radio (travel programs, news programs, and so on):

Daily Experiences

Everyday experiences in the community constitute one of the student's most valuable resources. As children see buildings under construction, watch changes in the season, see workers in action, observe holidays and celebrations, enjoy radio and television, hear and discuss current events, buy articles in stores, use the transportation system, attend public meetings, and engage in a host of other activities, they make discoveries and raise questions. Sharing, discussion, individual reporting, and journal writing may be used to capitalize on daily experiences.

Study Trips

Listed here are examples of study trips. As a substitute, videotapes can be made and used as needed.

airport	cultural center	library	police station
bank	dairy	mission	post office
city hall	historic homes	museum	television station
courtroom			

Short, informal walks taken in the immediate neighborhood are valuable study trips. Children may see a neighborhood fire station or library, a historic home, soil erosion, or various people at work. Also useful are trips with parents to places in the community, especially when guided by questions raised in class. Informal walks and trips with parents require a minimum of organization and make students more critical observers of their environment.

The difference between a study trip and just going somewhere is that a study trip has educational objectives. Points to consider when planning a study trip are given in Table 9.2.

It is helpful to summarize plans on charts, the chalkboard, or duplicated sheets of paper so that each student clearly understands objectives, procedures, and behavior standards. When the study involves many questions, divide them into sets and assign sets to committees. Each committee member may pose one question to the teacher or tour guide.

People as Resources

Community studies are enriched when students interview fire fighters, police officers, journalists, and other workers, or these workers meet with the class to discuss problems and questions. More people to invite to the classroom or to videotape at work include the following:

airport employees	house builders	retired persons
authors	industrial workers	social workers
business people	librarians	traffic safety specialists
city officials	merchants	travelers
consuls of foreign nations	musicians	

■ **TABLE 9.2**

Planning a Study Trip

First Considerations

_____ Have adequate backgrounds, ideas, and objectives been developed?

_____ Are related materials—videos, books, pictures—available?

_____ Are there profitable follow-up activities?

Preliminary Arrangements

_____ Has administrative approval been given?

_____ Has the approval of parents been secured?

_____ Are eating and restroom arrangements satisfactory?

_____ Has the time schedule been prepared?

_____ Have students been assigned partners?

_____ Has the guide been advised on problems, needs, and maturity of the group?

_____ Have travel arrangements and expenses been arranged?

_____ Are assistants needed to help supervise the group?

_____ Has a list been made of the students' names, telephone numbers, and addresses?

Group Planning

_____ Are study questions prepared and understood?

_____ Are recording procedures and assignments clear?

_____ Have behavior standards been developed?

_____ Have safety precautions been considered?

_____ Have the time schedule, travel arrangements, and expenses been clarified?

_____ Has attention been given to appropriateness of dress?

_____ Are monitorial assignments clear?

Follow-Up

_____ Do follow-up experiences contribute to objectives?

_____ What summaries and records should be made?

_____ What misconceptions may need to be addressed?

_____ Are letters of appreciation to be sent?

_____ How is learning to be evaluated?

In units about foreign countries such as Mexico or Japan, individuals who are natives of the country or who have visited it can share their experiences with the class. Showing realia, pictures, and videos along with discussion enhances the contributions of resource visitors.

You can organize a file of resource people who can contribute to the social studies program. A simple card system can be used by noting the following information on index cards (see Figure 9.5, p. 290).

■ FIGURE 9.5

Sample Card for Resource File

Contribution _____

Name _____   Telephone _____

Hours available _____   E-mail _____

Will come to school? _____

Children may visit at home or office? _____

Comments _____

_____

Conducting Interviews

When a resource person cannot come to school, when essential materials must be kept on the job, or when seeing the person in a working situation is more beneficial, a student or a small group can interview the person at work. Interviews require planning. You might recommend guidelines like these:

1. Introduce yourself. State questions clearly, and listen attentively.
2. Let the expert talk. Ask questions on any points that are not clear.
3. Take notes on difficult ideas or technical points.
4. Do not waste time. Express thanks when finished.

■ Making Critiques of Resources

■ NativeWeb **http:// nativeweb.org** is a popular site on the Internet for social studies teachers interested in learning more about indigenous nations and people and organizations around the world.

Students as well as teachers should critique media to note strengths, weaknesses, bias, and other elements. Such critiques might focus on purpose, underlying values, motives, feelings that were aroused, images of people, stereotypes, emotional appeals, use of persuasion and propaganda techniques, logical fallacies, and the impact on thinking and acting. To appraise TV, film, or video media, questions like these may be used:

- What is the central theme, purpose, or motive?
- What positive, negative, or mixed feelings were aroused?
- What images of people were presented? Are any of them stereotypes?
- What special effects were used—music, color, or lighting?
- What is the text message—factual, opinionated, explicit, implied?
- What should be changed—images, special effects, text, other?

The following ideas may help you guide students in making judgments about sources of information.

 **ACTIVITY IDEAS** *Detecting Bias and Stereotype*

➤ After viewing a video, ask students to evaluate how women and girls were depicted in it. Since stereotyping can be done quite subtly, students may need initial guidance in detecting it. You might use a worksheet like this one to focus their critique.

> Are women shown in a variety of activities and jobs? What are they?
>
> Are women shown as making a variety of contributions to society?
>
> Are girls portrayed as passive, fearful, or unable to make up their minds?
>
> Are boys portrayed as more active, more mature, and larger than girls?
>
> Are boys shown making things and earning money while girls are shown sewing, cooking, or playing with dolls?
>
> How could this video be improved to treat women and girls more fairly?

➤ To explore how a book or documentary treats groups other than middle-class white Americans, you might have students complete a worksheet like this one.

> Are other groups shown as making a variety of contributions to society?
>
> Are members of other groups depicted in a variety of roles and jobs?
>
> Are other groups portrayed as lazy, savage, dull, lacking intelligence, primitive, or a burden to society?
>
> Is diversity valued in this work?
>
> Are discrimination, prejudice, and stereotyping portrayed as negative and counterproductive?
>
> Are equality, justice, and concern for other people highly valued?
>
> How could this work be improved?

Evaluate instructional materials after you use them. Did they meet your expectations? Did students gain valuable learning experiences by using them? Noting the items that worked well and those that didn't will assist you in future instructional planning.

■ Sources of Information

When resources you need are not available at your school, check the following sources. Most can be found in instructional media centers and college libraries.

1. The catalog of materials in the school system's media center.

2. Catalogs and lists from the county school's office, the state department of education, state universities, colleges, and other agencies from which your school district obtains materials.

3. Center for Media Education, 2120 L Street, Suite 200, Washington, DC 20037, Phone 202-231-7833. An organization interested in the quality of media culture available on the Web and in other sources to children and young adults.

4. Social Science Education Consortium, P.O. Box 21270, Boulder, CO 80308-4270, Phone 303-492-8154. A long-standing organization offering K–12 teachers a variety of social studies materials and services.

5. Guides to free or inexpensive materials (also check special sections in the magazines listed in item 9): *Find It Fast: How to Uncover Expert Information on Any Subject* (1994); *Resources for Teaching U.S. History: TeachERIC Resource Series, no. 1* (1980); *Educators' Grade Guide to Free Teaching Aids* (1995); *Educators' Guide to Free Social Studies Materials* (1995); *Let's Discover Computers: Ready-to-Use Computer Lessons & Activities for Grades K–3* (1997); *Guide to Free Computer Materials (1992); Index to Elementary Instructional Materials* (1964).

6. "The History Channel," National Council for History Education, 26915 Westwood Road, Suite B-2, Westlake, OH 44145, Phone 440-835-1776; National Council for the Social Studies, 3501 Newark Street NW, Washington, DC 20016, Phone 202-966-7840.

7. ERIC Clearinghouse, Social Studies/Social Science Education, 2805 East Tenth Street, Suite 120, Bloomington, IN 47408-2698, Phone 800-266-3815; E-mail ericso@indiana.edu; website http://indiana.edu/ ~ ssdc/eric_chess.htm. ERIC offers teachers a variety of services. Arizona Educational Information System offers teachers packets of educational information on a variety of topics. Write to College of Education, Arizona State University, Box 872611, Tempe, AZ 85287-2611.

8. Latest editions of guides to reading materials: *The Young Adult Reader's Advisor Vols. I & II* (1992); *Children's Book Review Index Vol. 24* (1998); *What Do Young Adults Read Next?: A Reader's Guide to Fiction for Young Adults* (1994); *Children's Books in Print* (1999); *Resources for Middle-Grade Reluctant Readers* (1987); *A Selection Guide to Basic Books for Children: Reading in Series* (1999); *Literature and the Child* (1989); *This Is Our Land: A Guide to Multicultural Literature for Children and Young Adults* (1994).

9. Periodicals: *AIT Newsletter, Booklist* (American Library Association*), Bulletin of the Center for Children's Books, Teacher Magazine, Learning, Textbook Letter, Instructor, Social Studies, Social Education, Social Studies and the Young*

Learner, The Reading Teacher, The Mailbox Magazine. Computer journals and magazines: *Electronic Learning, Choosing Children's Software,* and *Multimedia Schools.*

10. Information on materials related to racial and ethnic groups: All Ethnic Groups http://www.ops.org, Anti-Defamation League of B'nai B'rith, Department JW, 823 United Nations Plaza, New York, NY 10017, Phone 212-490-2525; Social Studies School Service, 10200 Jefferson Boulevard, CA 90232, Phone 800-421-4246; USC Center for Multilingual, Multicultural Research, University of Southern California, Rossier School of Education, Waite Phillips Hall, Suite 402, Los Angeles, CA 90089-0031, Phone 213-740-2360, E-mail cmmr@usc.edu lists resources on a number of racial and ethnic groups; African American Collections at UC Berkeley http://www.lib.berkeley.edu/Collections/Africana offers teachers a rich array of materials including electronic journals on African and African American history; AskAsia http://askasia.org a website of the Asia Society, is an excellent site for materials on Asian Americans; Association for the Study of African-American Life and History, 7961 Eastern Avenue STE 301, Silver Spring, MD 20910, Phone 301-587-5900 and the Avery Research Center for African American History, College of Charleston, 125 Bull Street, Charleston, SC 29424, Phone 843-953-7609 offer teachers materials on African Americans.

 Questions, Activities, and Evaluation

1. Visit an elementary or middle school and ask permission to "roam" the media center to identify resources available to teachers. Select materials for use in a unit of your choice using the guidelines provided in this chapter.

2. Examine a textbook, and make notes detailing how you might use it in a unit. Which of the objectives noted in the first part of this chapter might you achieve?

3. Make a sketch of a chart you might use in a unit. Indicate what type of chart it is and how you would use it.

4. Select and preview a film or a video. Make a plan for using it in a unit, following the guidelines given in this chapter.

5. Examine one or more of the guides to free or inexpensive materials listed at the end of this chapter. Request materials that appear suitable for a unit you plan to teach. Appraise items that you receive in terms of the criteria in the first part of this chapter.

6. Examine a K–6 social studies series or a middle school U.S. history textbook for its treatment of a specific societal group. Note what material (e.g., prose, illustrations, tables, and graphs) is included and where it appears in the text. How effective is the material at providing a broad and comprehensive depiction of the group?

7. Identify two community resources you might use in a unit, and note the objectives you would hope to achieve.

8. Obtain magazines that contain pictures related to a unit you plan to teach. Cut out and mount useful pictures, and organize them in a picture file. Indicate how they may be used to develop interpreting, classifying, and other thinking processes as well as concepts and related vocabulary.

9. Visit a computer store, and ask an attendant to show you the social studies materials in stock. Review some software packages by reading the descriptions. How might this software be integrated into units of instruction?

10. Write to three or more of the following to obtain materials.
    a. ABA Division of Public Education, 541 N. Fairbanks Court, Suite 1500, Chicago, IL 60611-3314
    b. American Federation of Teachers (AFT), 555 New Jersey Avenue NW, Washington, DC 20001
    c. National Education Association (NEA), 1201 16th Street NW, Washington, DC 20036
    d. Center for Human Rights and Constitutional Law, 256 S. Occidental Blvd., Los Angeles, CA 90056
    e. Center for Civic Education, 5146 Douglas Fir Road, Calabasas, CA 91302
    f. Constitutional Rights Foundation, 601 S. Kingsley Dr., Los Angeles, CA 90005
    g. Council for the Advancement of Citizenship, 44 Canal Center Plaza, Suite 600, Alexandria, VA 22314
    h. Films for the Humanities, P.O. Box 2053, Princeton, NJ 08543-2053
    i. Foreign Policy Association, 470 Park Avenue South, New York, NY 10016
    j. Global TeachNet, 1900 L. Street NW, Suite 205, Washington, DC 20036
    k. International Technology Education Association, 1914 Association Drive, Suite 201, Reston, VA 20191-1539
    l. National Geographic Association, 1145 17th Street NW, Washington, DC 20036-4688

References

Bennett, C. T., & Dawson, K. (1998). Software reviews: 3-D Atlas 97 and America Rock. *Social Education, 62,* 161–164.

Catalog Connection. (1996). *Education Week, 15.* Description of free catalogs and informational brochures.

Denton, K. L., & Muir, S. P. (1994). Making every picture count: Ethnicity in primary grade textbook photographs. *Social Education, 48,* 156–58.

Dunthorn, T., Nelson, E., & Woods, L. (1995). Redefining instructional materials: Social science 2000 connections, challenges, choices. *Social Studies and The Young Learner, 7,* 17–18.

Educator's World Wide Web tour guide. Cited in "The Bookshelf" in *Education Week*, Vol. 15, Number 38, June 12, 1996.

Ellsworth, J. H. (1996). *Education on the Internet: A hands-on book of ideas, resources, projects, and advice.* Cited in "The Bookshelf" in *Education Week*, Vol. 15, Number 38, June 12, 1996.

Hepburn, M. A. (1998). The power of the electronic media in the socialization of young Americans: Implications for social studies education. *The Social Studies, 89,* 71–76.

Notable children's trade books in the field of social studies. Annual review in the April/May issue of *Social Education.*

Pierce, J., et al. (1994). The educational research list (ERL-L) on BITNET/INTERNET. *Educational Researcher, 23,* 25–28. Computer networks and uses.

Ponessa, J. (1996). Working the Web. *Education Week, 16,* 36–37.

Porter, P. H. (1995). Keeping up with technology. *Social Studies and The Young Learner, 7,* 22–23, 30.

Realizing the promise of technology. (1994). *Educational Leadership, 51,* 4–82. How to use computers, multimedia, and other technology.

Rose, S. A., & Fernlund, R. M. (1997). Using technology for powerful social studies learning. *Social Education, 61,* 160–166.

Sembor, E. C. (1997). Citizenship, diversity, and distance learning: Videoconferencing in Connecticut. *Social Education, 61,* 154–59.

Singleton, L. R., & Giese, J. R. (1998). American memory: Using Library of Congress online resources to enhance history teaching. *Social Education, 62,* 142–144.

Splaine, J. E. (1991). The mass media as an influence on social studies. In J. P. Shaver (Ed.), *The handbook of research on social studies teaching and learning* (pp. 300–309). New York: Macmillan.

Sunal, C. S., Smith, C., Sunal, D. W., & Britt, J. (1998). Using the Internet to create meaningful instruction. *The Social Studies, 89,* 13–18.

Thomas, D. F., Creel, M. M., Day, J. (1998). Building a useful elementary social studies website. *Social Education, 62,* 154–157.

West, P. (1995). New crop of CD-ROMs focuses on Vietnam War, conflicts at home. *Education Week, 15,* 8.

White, C. S. (1997). Citizenship participation and the Internet: Prospects for civic deliberation in the information age. *The Social Studies, 88,* 23–28.

Wilson, J. (1995). Social studies online resources. *Social Studies and The Young Learner, 7,* 24–26.

Wilson, J. (1995). Potential for diversity projects abound on the Internet: Yet go unrealized in the commercial world. *Social Studies and The Young Learner, 7,* 28–30.

Chapter 10

Developing Globe and Map Concepts and Skills

Chapter Objective

To present guidelines, strategies, and activities for developing the concepts and skills essential to effective use of globes and maps

Focusing Questions

- What concepts and skills related to maps and globes are emphasized in current programs in the elementary and middle grades?

- What general guidelines are useful at all levels of instruction?

- What practical activities can be used to teach concepts and skills related to maps and globes, symbols, location, orientation and direction, scale, distance, comparisons and inferences, and map projections?

- What principles and procedures should be used in mapping and mapmaking activities?

■ Concept and Skill Development, K–8

Where is Seattle, Washington? Manchester, New Hampshire? Belfast, Northern Ireland? Recently, events taking place in these cities were front-page news in the *New York Times*. These stories, and others appearing each day in newspapers across the country, are of interest because they can connect the event (such as protest against the World Trade Organization, Republican presidential debates, or the challenges of forging a workable government in Northern Ireland) with a place on a map or a globe. That is, the reader knows where the event occurred.

Social studies programs for K–8 students, especially in the early grades, devote considerable time to showing students how to make connections between time and place. The sequence of instruction is geared to students' developmental stages and the experiences they bring to the classroom. Map and globe concepts and skills introduced in the K–2 block are tied closely to children's daily experiences, familiar landscape features, and neighborhood and community studies. Those in the 3–4 block are embedded in studies of communities, the state, and regions. In the remaining grades, study of maps and globes is focused on our country and other lands. Adaptations may be made to accommodate individual differences, provide review and reteaching, and maximize use of available learning resources. This sequence is typical in current social studies textbooks and curriculum guides. It is summarized in Table 10.1 (pp. 298–299).

Much overlap exists among the concepts and skills presented at various grade levels, and concepts may be presented in various combinations. For example, symbols must be used to locate places, find distances between and directions to places, and make comparisons and draw inferences. Direction and distance may be used to state the relative location of a place as "ten miles north of Albany."

■ Instructional Guidelines

Globes and maps are enormously useful in school studies and everyday life. You can emphasize their practical value to students by showing how these resources can help to answer a whole range of questions: *Where is this place? In what direction is it from here? How far away is it? How big is it? What features does it have?* Questions like

■ TABLE 10.1

Scope and Sequence of Globe and Map Learning, K–8

■ Symbols

Grades K–2	Grades 3–4	Grades 5–6	Grades 7–8
models; pictorial and semipictorial symbols for familiar features; lines for streets and roads; colors for land and water; direction labels and arrows	symbols for towns, cities, and other features; letter–number coordinates, such as A–3, on road maps; how symbols differ on maps; map legend; compass rose	symbols on special feature maps; colors to show relief, elevation, and other features; uses of hachures, shadings and dots, contour lines, legend	variety of symbols on maps in atlases and other sources; international color scheme; isobars, isotherms, and other isolines; legend

■ Locations

Grades K–2	Grades 3–4	Grades 5–6	Grades 7–8
familiar places in neighborhood and community; nearby communities; land and water areas; state, country, continents, and oceans on globe	communities studied in other lands; main cities and capital in state; resources, cities, and other features in regions studied; current events	regions of United States; countries in North America; explorers' routes, colonies; westward expansion; other lands; latitude and longitude; high, middle, and low latitudes; relative to selected places	Prime Meridian; International Date Line; time zones around the world; historical and current events; natural and cultural features in places studied; analysis of distributions of population, resources, and other features

■ Orientation and Direction

Grades K–2	Grades 3–4	Grades 5–6	Grades 7–8
left, right; up, down; north, south, east, west; direction related to familiar places; sunrise in east, sunset in west; shadow at noon; orientation of community map	cardinal and intermediate; relation to poles and equator; grid lines as direction lines; orientation of maps; directions to places by compass rose	parallels as east–west lines; meridians as north–south lines; habit of orienting maps correctly; directions to places studied	directions on various map projections; changes in directions on great-circle routes; systematic orientation of maps in atlases and other sources

these surface in students' work in a variety of subject areas but also arise during travel, while watching the news and reading the newspaper, and when talking to someone from a different part of the country.

Students can learn about several concepts that will help them understand and interpret maps and globes. One category of concepts deals with natural and physical features, including landforms, bodies of water, types of terrain, and climate. The category of cultural features encompasses concepts of population, transportation net-

■ Scale and Distance

Grades K–2	Grades 3–4	Grades 5–6	Grades 7–8
larger, smaller; scale on classroom and neighborhood or community maps; globe as small-scale model of earth; near, far; blocks to familiar places; miles and kilometers; relative distance to familiar places	inch to block and mile; centimeter to kilometer; graphic scale to measure distance; scale on highway, textbook, and state maps; distance related to travel time	comparison of maps of a given area on different scales; selection of scale to make a map; distance on great-circle routes and in degrees from equator	interpretation of fraction and graduated scales; analysis of large- and small-scale maps of the same area; relative and exact distance to places

■ Comparisons and Inferences: Understanding Relationships

Grades K–2	Grades 3–4	Grades 5–6	Grades 7–8
comparison of pictures and symbols for features; distance and time between familiar places; relative size of neighborhoods, continents, and oceans	relative size of communities, states, and regions; comparison of size and shape of areas on maps and globes; relationships between location and climate, between land use and terrain, and between other features	relative size of countries; climate in relation to latitude, elevation, coastal location, and wind currents; industries in relation to resources and technology	comparison of old and modern trade routes; distortion of areas on various map projections; factors related to location and growth of urban centers; distributions of resources, population, and other features

works, and urban and rural areas. Yet another group of concepts includes the symbols and other visual elements that make maps readable: the compass rose, the scale of miles or other units of measure, patterns of color, hachure lines, and so on. Students need to gain proficiency in working with all these concepts.

As they build this conceptual framework, learners will deepen their understanding of the five geographic themes noted in Chapter 2: location, place, human–environment interaction, movement, and regions. Maps of the community, state, and other areas can broaden students' understanding of *location*—their own location, as well as those of familiar places and ones that they are beginning to learn about. Maps that show a community's layout at different time periods can also help students understand their own location in time.

An understanding of *place* develops as students focus on both the physical and human features of an area—how buildings and roads coexist with hills and valleys, for example. At another level, students also discover *human–environment interaction* as they study maps. This interaction includes the ways in which humans adapt to the environment and the ways in which they modify it. Building igloos is one way in which the Inuit adapted to their environment. Making caves in cliffs is one way in which the Anasazi modified their environment.

Study of human *movement* is enriched by using globes and maps. Students can trace trade routes, transportation networks, migration patterns, exploration routes, and the spread of ideas. Globes or maps can enhance the discussion of the physical features that made such passages difficult or convenient, the length of travel time, and the impact of such travel on the physical environment. Such discussion and activities help students connect knowledge of historical developments with the geographical settings in which they took place.

Finally, understanding of *regions* can be deepened by using maps and globes. Whether physical regions (such as those characterized by deserts, mountains, or other physical features) or cultural regions (those characterized by human activity, such as the Corn Belt, mining zones, and industrial areas) are the focus, using maps to identify and explore them will give students a visual reference point for each region and a sense of how regions are connected. All told, maps and globes help students get the "big picture" in social studies education.

As a general guideline, begin your instruction with familiar features and concrete activities, and then move to unfamiliar features and more abstract concepts. For example, instruction about map symbols should begin with simple pictures that represent familiar features of the students' community or state. Later, students can manage less pictorial symbols that still contain some hints; they will eventually progress to understanding standard map symbols.

Plan instruction in maps and globes at points in the program when students can really put these resources to use in a meaningful way. Use a map of Canada when your class really needs to know the features of this country to understand a lesson. Try using this three-step instructional pattern: demonstrate, practice, and apply. For example, demonstrate how to use the scale of miles by using a wall map; then have students practice this skill using a textbook map; later, challenge students to apply this skill as they encounter other maps.

■ Journey over all the universe in a map, without the expense and fatigue of traveling, without suffering the inconveniences of heat, cold, hunger, and thirst.

—Miguel de Cervantes

As you instruct students in using and understanding maps and globes, help them move from the simpler tasks, such as identifying places and describing locations, to tasks that involve higher-order thinking. Encourage them to *compare* features based on size, location, population, distance, and other factors. Challenge them to *make inferences and hypotheses* concerning the location of cities and transportation routes, how resources in an area might be used, and why some regions support urban development whereas others remain rural. They might *analyze* the zones of a particular city or the regions of a country. They might *synthesize* their knowledge of an area by completing an outline map that includes the area's main features and its connections with other regions. You might also ask students to *evaluate* travel routes, land use, types of map projections, and maps given in textbooks. Such activities teach the lasting value of these resources.

Learning activities related to maps and globes tend to fall into two categories: (1) systematic instruction on concepts and skills and (2) use of the globe or map in the context of study (of a unit, of current events, and so on). The following activities are just a sampling of ways to involve students in working with maps and globes.

ACTIVITY IDEAS *Introductory Map and Globe Activities*

➤ Assign small groups of students to find and bring to class a variety of maps. Each group can show their maps to the class and tell what each kind is used for. You might ask them to find the following:

- maps of major cities
- physical relief maps that show surface features
- political maps of states and countries
- historical maps showing the location of notable events
- maps of state or national parks
- pictorial maps showing resources or plants and animals
- world maps with different projections
- comparison maps that show relative size or population
- maps of towns or neighborhoods
- maps showing travel routes
- maps showing weather and climate
- oceanographic maps

➤ To introduce students to a globe, you might use a series of questions to familiarize them with the globe's features. Here are sample questions.

What do the colors tell us?
How can you tell what is north? south? east? west?
How do you find the shortest distance between two points?
How can you locate time zones?
Where is the equator? the North Pole? the South Pole?
How can you measure distance from the equator?
Can you find and name each continent?

➤ Students (and adults!) can make errors in interpreting maps and globes. Be aware of typical problems, and help steer students away from them. Here are common mistakes to avoid:

The same symbols stand for the same things on all maps.
North is always at the top of a map.
Up is north, and down is south.
The shortest distance between two points is along a parallel.
Areas in the same color have the same elevation.
The size and shape of physical features are the same on globes and maps.

➤ Present maps to students in a variety of ways—the textbook shouldn't be the only resource they use. Also, mapmaking activities help students internalize map concepts and attend to the details that comprise a good map. (Specific ideas are given later in the chapter.) Computer programs and videos add variety and interest. Students might work in pairs using programs such as the following:

Unlocking the Map Code	*Road Rally U.S.A.*
The Language of Maps	*Journey into the Unknown*
MapMaker	*One World Countries Database*
*Atlas*Draw*	*European Nations & Locations*
World Atlas Action	*Where in the World is Carmen Sandiego?*
Game of the States	*Direction and Distance*
Uncle Sam's Jigsaw	*Latitude and Longitude*

Here is a list of topics that you may wish to include in your plans for map and globe instruction:

Community: streets, buildings, parks, zones, neighborhoods, airport

Travel: highways, state and national parks, cities, railroads, recreational and historical sites

Political: cities, states, regions, countries, alliances, boundaries

Physical: landforms, water bodies, terrain, elevation, vegetation

Climate: precipitation, temperature, wind and ocean currents, types of climate

Population: distribution, density, migration, rural, urban

Economic: resources, products, crops, industries, land use, trade

Historical and cultural: explorations, colonization, territorial changes, events, religions, languages; sites related to art or literature

What are ways of using globe and map concepts and skills in social studies instruction? What concepts and skills are these students practicing?

■ Skill-Building Activities

To familiarize you with ways of guiding students in using maps and globes, there's nothing like a set of practical examples. This section of the chapter gives hands-on activities and instructional strategies that you can put to use in the classroom. A wide range of concepts and skills are covered, including initial instruction for the primary grades and advanced instruction for the upper elementary and middle school grades. Whatever grade you teach, select activities that meet students' learning needs.

Learning about the Globe

Use a globe in early grades to develop concepts of the roundness of the earth and major land and water areas. Present the globe as a model of the earth after clarifying the concept of a model. You can do this by discussing toy cars, dolls, and other models familiar to children. Point to the land and water areas of the globe and ask children to tell the colors that show them.

> ■ Every social studies classroom should have a globe and use it often.
>
> **—Walter C. Parker and John Jarolimek**

Show the area on which we live. Point to North America, and state that this is the large land area called *North America.* Point to the location of the United States and the students' home state. Use a globe to locate places encountered in the study of families and communities in other lands, in reading instruction, and in other subjects.

Identify the North Pole, and demonstrate that *north* means "toward the North Pole." Use a washable crayon to draw lines from the home state and from other places to the North Pole to the north–south lines (meridians), and describe how they converge at the North Pole. Do the same for the South Pole. Explain that the terms *north* and *south* must not be confused with the terms *up* and *down*. Show that up is away from the globe and down is toward the globe. For young students, you may want to include items from the fact sheet shown in Figure 10.1.

Point to the equator, show that it encircles the globe, and explain that it is midway between the poles and divides the globe into hemispheres. Show the Northern Hemisphere and explain that it includes the area north of the equator. Do the same for the Southern Hemisphere. Have students point to continents in the Northern and Southern Hemispheres. Discuss the following questions:

- Where is the most land?
- Why is the Northern Hemisphere sometimes referred to as the land hemisphere?
- Why is the Southern Hemisphere sometimes called the water hemisphere?

Show the Western and Eastern Hemispheres. Ask, What continents are in the Western Hemisphere? What continents are in the Eastern Hemisphere? In which hemisphere is the continent on which we live? In which hemisphere is the largest continent? the smallest one?

Demonstrate day and night by shining a flashlight on the globe in a darkened room and slowly turning the globe from west to east. Place a piece of Plasticene on the home state, and ask students to tell when day begins and ends as you turn the globe. Stop rotating the globe, and ask students to point to the day and night hemispheres. Demonstrate directions north and south along the meridians (lines of longitude) and east and west along the parallels (lines of latitude). Ask students to point to places as they respond to these questions:

- What north–south line crosses British Columbia, Washington, Oregon, and California?
- What states are south of Montana?
- Which states are directly west of Ohio?
- Which states are east of Texas?
- What is the first country east of New York across the Atlantic Ocean?

Demonstrate how parallels and meridians form a grid that can be used to locate places. Have students locate places in response to questions like these:

- What state is approximately 40° N, 90° W?
- What city is located at 30° N, 90° W?
- What is the approximate location of Washington, DC?

Develop the concept of great circles by showing that the equator and the meridians are circles that divide the globe into hemispheres. Demonstrate that a great circle

■ **FIGURE 10.1**

Globe Fact Sheet for Younger Students

Our Globe

It is a model of the earth.

It is round like a ball.

It shows land and bodies of water.

The Earth

It is a large sphere.

It turns once each day, causing day and night.

It has more water than land on its surface.

Colors and Lines

Blue shows bodies of water.

Other colors show land.

Lines show directions, boundaries, and rivers.

Bodies of Water

The largest ones are called oceans.

We live on land between the Atlantic Ocean and the Pacific Ocean.

Two other oceans are the Arctic Ocean and the Indian Ocean.

The Poles and the Equator

The North Pole is the farthest point north.

The South Pole is the farthest point south.

The equator is midway between the two poles.

Large Land Masses

The large land masses are called continents.

We live on the continent of North America.

There are six other continents.

They are South America, Europe, Asia, Africa, Australia, and Antarctica.

Up, Down, North, South

Up means away from the earth.

Down means toward the earth.

North means toward the North Pole.

South means toward the South Pole.

is the shortest distance between places, and compare the distance on great-circle and other routes. For example, hold a tape along the 30° N parallel, and measure the distance from New Orleans to Cairo. Hold the tape tightly against the globe and measure the great-circle distance. Ask students to describe the areas over which an airplane would fly on each route. Ask them to describe the shortest route by ship. The lesson plan below shows how to do this, step by step.

Point to the Tropic of Cancer and the Tropic of Capricorn. Turn the globe slowly, and explain that these parallels are 23½° N and 23½° S, respectively, and that places

---

 LESSON PLAN   *Teaching Great-Circle Distance*

Objectives
To demonstrate understanding of great circles as the shortest distance between two points

To show the great-circle distance between selected places

Materials
Globe

World wall map

Textbook that shows great-circle distances

Introduction
Direct attention to a wall map of the world, and ask students to state the shortest distance from New York to Tokyo. Repeat the activity, using a globe.

Development
Ask students to look at the section in their textbook that describes and shows great-circle routes. Ask:

What are great-circle routes? How can they be shown, using a string or tape on a globe?

Why are they shown as curved lines on world maps? Why are they shown as straight lines on polar projections? Why are they the shortest distance between places?

Demonstrate how to use a tape on a globe to show great-circle distance.

Conclusion and Evaluation
Ask a student to show great-circle distance from New York to Tokyo on a globe. Follow by having a student point to the route on a world wall map.

Follow-up
Ask students to find great-circle routes on a globe between Atlanta, Denver, Los Angeles, and other cities to Delhi, Moscow, Singapore, and other foreign cities.

Have students draw freehand sketch maps to show the above.

between them on each side of the equator are in the low latitudes and most have tropical climates. Identify the middle latitudes, which include places with temperate climates, by pointing to the area between the Tropic of Cancer and the Arctic Circle in the Northern Hemisphere and the Tropic of Capricorn and the Antarctic Circle in the Southern Hemisphere. Point to the high latitudes, which include places with polar climates, between the Arctic Circle and the North Pole and between the Antarctic Circle and the South Pole. State that these are sometimes referred to as *torrid, temperate,* and *frigid zones,* but that the preferred terms are *low, middle,* and *high latitudes.* Give students a worksheet on which lines are drawn to represent the parallels, and ask them to complete it by labeling each of the following: equator, Tropic of Cancer, Tropic of Capricorn, Arctic Circle, Antarctic Circle, low latitudes, middle latitudes, and high latitudes.

Demonstrate revolution of the earth around the sun; explain changes in the seasons and the meaning and dates of the solstices and the equinoxes. Follow with a discussion of diagrams in students' textbooks that show earth–sun relationships on June 21 or 22, September 22 or 23, December 21 or 22, and March 20 or 21. Use questions such as these:

- When are the sun's direct rays north of the equator? on the equator? at the Tropic of Cancer? south of the equator? at the Tropic of Capricorn?
- When is there sunshine all day north of the Arctic Circle? south of the Antarctic Circle?
- When do summer and winter begin in the Northern Hemisphere? in the Southern Hemisphere?

Compare time zones on a map to meridians on a globe, and explain why each zone represents about 15 degrees of longitude ($360° ÷ 24 = 15°$). Point to the Prime Meridian, and explain that it is in the center of the zero time zone. As one goes westward, time is one hour earlier in the next zone, two hours earlier in the following one, and so on. Rotate the globe to show how time changes, why noon is one hour later at 15-degree intervals, and that when it is noon in places on one side, it is midnight in places on the opposite side. Discuss the time zones in the United States, beginning with Eastern Standard Time at 75° W longitude. Have students describe deviations from meridians. Point to the International Date Line, and explain that this is where each new calendar day begins. Travelers add a day crossing it to the west and subtract a day crossing it to the east.

You might use items from the fact sheet in Figure 10.2 (p. 308) as you work with students in the upper elementary and middle school grades.

Learning about Symbols

Have students in early grades use models, pictures, and blocks to stand for real things on floor maps. Ask them to tell what is represented and how the models, pictures, and blocks differ from what they stand for. As the broader community is studied,

■ FIGURE 10.2

Globe Fact Sheet for Older Students

Find Your Way around the Globe!

Direction Lines

The equator and other lines of latitude, called *parallels*, are east–west lines.

The Prime Meridian and other lines of longitude, called *meridians*, are north–south lines.

Latitude and Longitude

Latitude is the distance in degrees north or south of the equator.

Longitude is the distance in degrees east or west of the Prime Meridian.

High, Low, and Middle Latitudes

The high latitudes, near the poles, have cold climates.

The low latitudes, near the equator, have tropical climates.

The middle latitudes, between the high and low latitudes, have temperate climates.

Important Meridians

The Prime Meridian is the 0° line of longitude, from which time and east–west distances are measured.

The International Date Line is drawn close to 180° longitude and determines change in date: one day later going west, one day earlier going east. When it is Tuesday on the west side, it is Monday on the east side.

Important Parallels

The Arctic Circle, 66½° N	The Tropic of Cancer, 23½° N
The Antarctic Circle, 66½° S	The Tropic of Capricorn, 23½° S

Time Zones

There are 24 time zones.

Each zone covers about 15 degrees of longitude.

In the United States, there are seven zones: Eastern, Central, Mountain, Pacific, Yukon, Alaska–Hawaii, and Bering.

As you move between zones, the standard time changes by one hour: an hour earlier to the west, and an hour later to the east.

Great Circles

Great circles divide the globe into hemispheres.

The meridians and the equator are great circles.

A great-circle route is the shortest distance between two points.

have students use semipictorial symbols to show houses, the school, a hospital, and other objects. Show aerial photos, pictures, and slides to help students visualize what symbols represent. Discuss colors that students may use to show a nearby lake, a city park, the parking area around a shopping center, and other familiar features. Have students use arrows to show directions on floor and other maps.

Discuss three perspectives from which features can be viewed: ground-level or profile view, combination of profile and aerial view, and consistent aerial view as used on maps and globes. Take students on a walking trip, and have them compare the ground view with that of an aerial view of the same area or to the view from a high building. Discuss the shape of objects as seen from the ground and as seen from above—for example, from the front of a house and from the roof. Have students place tissue paper on an aerial photo and trace a map of selected features, such as streets and buildings. In middle and upper grades, compare maps of specific areas with aerial and satellite photos.

Develop concepts of features represented by symbols. Begin with familiar landscape features in the neighborhood and community. Show pictures of hills, lakes, and other features. Direct attention to wall charts and to drawings or pictures in textbooks.

Direct attention to textbook and other maps students are using. Discuss new uses of symbols and colors, and guide interpretation of the legend or key. Point to examples of the use of symbols on the map. Check students' understanding by asking them to explain the meaning of symbols and to point to examples on the map. Compare symbols on new maps with those on familiar ones, and discuss differences in the use of symbols, such as dots for communities of differing size on one map and dots for population density on another. Stress the importance of always examining the legend! As a student said, "The legend is really a key. It opens the door to maps."

■ Nystrom **http://www. nystromnet.com** offers teachers a variety of resources in the area of maps and globe concepts and skills.

Ask students how each of these items is shown:

airports	lowlands	population	resources
boundaries	mountains	products	rivers
capitals	plains	railways	roads
cities	plateaus	rainfall	seaports

Explain that elevation and altitude refer to height above sea level and may be shown by colors and by contour lines. Discuss the shades of color used to show elevation on maps in textbooks and atlases. Show a map with contour lines, and point to the highest and lowest elevations, the steepest area with lines close together, and gentle-sloping areas with lines farther apart.[1] Have students use layers of clay or balsa wood to make a model of a mountain with one steep side. They should color each layer. Direct them to view the models from above and draw contour lines on graph paper. Follow by having students draw a simple contour map of a hill 600 feet high, using a contour interval of 100 feet.

---

1. A topographic map of any area can be obtained from U.S. Department of the Interior/U.S. Geological Survey, 1220 Sunrise Valley Drive, Reston, VA 20192.

Compare the use of colors to show elevation on a relief map and on a wall map. Point out that gradual changes in elevation are shown on the relief map in contrast to seemingly abrupt changes on the wall map. Ask students to identify sloping areas on the relief map and then point to the same areas on the wall map.

Guide students' interpretation of maps that show special conditions or features. For example, as students in upper grades encounter isolines that show where temperature, rainfall, water depth, and other items are the same, have them describe and trace with a finger the area over which the same condition or feature is shown.

Here are additional ideas for helping students understand map and globe symbols.

ACTIVITY IDEAS ➤ *Using Map and Globe Symbols*

➤ To help students become familiar with a particular map, you might give them a worksheet like this one to fill out. It will help them analyze the information in the legend.

Answer each of the following questions about the map legend.

1. What does each color stand for? _____

2. What do the thick lines represent? _____
   the dotted lines? _____

3. What does each symbol represent? _____
   _____
   _____

4. What do different shadings stand for? _____
   _____
   _____

5. What date is given for the map? _____
   Why is this important? _____

6. What other information is given? _____

7. What questions do you have? _____
   _____
   _____
   _____
   _____

➤ When you ask students to complete outline maps, it's helpful to give them a set of symbols to use. The following is an example; note that the symbols will be quite easy for students to draw.

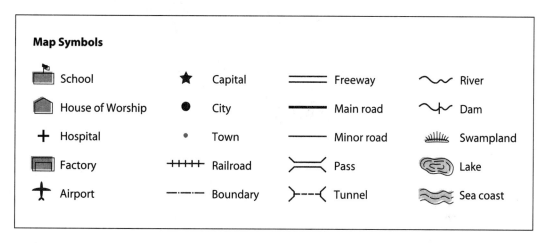

➤ To help students analyze the elevations shown on a given map, you might provide a worksheet like this one.

Each color on your map shows a certain elevation. Fill out the elevations on this sheet. The first one has been done for you.

Red	10,000 feet and higher
Dark brown	_____
Light brown	_____
Yellow	_____
Light green	_____
Dark green	_____
Grayish green	_____

Learning about Location

Ask students in early grades to describe the relative location of objects in the classroom and of buildings around the school by using terms such as *to the right, to the left, next to, in front of,* and *behind.* Ask, Is my desk to your right or to your left? What building is in front of our school?

Have students locate streets, the school, and homes around the school on floor maps and simple neighborhood maps. Have them locate the airport, factories, and other features as the broader community is studied.

Photographs of familiar locations are an excellent resource in social studies instruction. What globe and map concepts and skills might you introduce or reinforce using this photograph?

Distribute worksheets with lines that form a grid, and ask students to mark the location of their desks and other objects in the classroom. Repeat the activity for rooms in the school and for buildings around the school.

Have students make simple sketch maps that show streets and buildings around the school and in the neighborhood around their homes.

Point to the location of the community, state, and country on the globe and on hemispheres and world maps. Do the same for oceans and continents.

In studies of the state, ask students to use the number-and-letter system to locate places on road maps. Direct attention to the index of places, and guide students to find the point on the map where the given numbered and lettered lines meet. Later, this skill can be transferred to the use of the index in atlases.

If the community is shown on an insert on the road map, have it enlarged. Eliminate unnecessary detail to create a large map that can be used to refine skill in locating places in the community.

As regions and countries are studied, extend the concept of relative location of places by discussing the impact of mountains, terrain, and waterways on accessibility to places. Point out how improvements in transportation and the construction of roads and canals have helped to overcome barriers—for example, polar flights on great-circle routes, tunnels through mountains, the Panama Canal, and the tunnel connecting England and France.

Show that parallels are east–west lines and meridians are north–south lines that form a grid that can be used to locate places. Guide students to use parallels to identify places north or south of their community or state and to find places nearer to or farther from the equator. They can use meridians to identify places east or west of their community or state and to describe the location of places on the same meridian as directly north or south of each other.

Show upper elementary and middle school students how to use degrees of latitude and longitude to locate places. For example, after indicating that Denver and

Philadelphia are on or near 40° N, ask, How can we use degrees of longitude to indicate the location of these cities? Show that Philadelphia is 75° W and Denver is 105° W (30° farther west). Combining degrees of latitude and longitude, we have these approximate locations: Philadelphia 40° N, 75° W, and Denver 40° N, 105° W.

After finding the latitude and longitude for given places, reverse the procedure and have students find places when latitude and longitude are given. For example, ask students to find the capital of a country located 20° N and 100° W (Mexico City) or to find the city located 30° N and 90° W (New Orleans). The following lesson plan shows how to teach these concepts.

 LESSON PLAN *Latitude, Longitude, and Time Zones*

Objectives
To state how latitude and longitude are numbered

To describe how latitude and longitude are used to locate places

To identify time zones and state how they are determined

Materials
Video, *Latitude, Longitude, and Time Zones*

Textbook, pages 20–21

Introduction
Ask: Who can tell what the lines that circle the globe from east to west represent?

Who can tell what the lines that circle the globe from north to south represent?

Who knows how time zones are determined?

Watch the video, and be ready to discuss each question.

Development
Show the video and discuss each question, including attention to the following:

What is the heavy dark line around the center of the globe? How are degrees of latitude numbered, starting with the equator?

What are the lines that circle the globe and run through the North and South Poles? What is the Prime Meridian? How are degrees of longitude determined, starting with the Prime Meridian?

How can places be located precisely by using latitude and longitude?

How are time zones determined? What time is it in New York when it is 4:00 in the afternoon in London?

Conclusion
Have students point to lines of latitude on the globe and on a large wall map. Do the same for lines of longitude.

Discuss the map of time zones on page 21 of the textbook.

(continued)

LESSON PLAN   *Continued*

Follow-up   Have students read pages 200–21 of their textbook.

Have students fill out the following worksheet as homework.

Location by Latitude and Longitude

Use the map of North America in your textbook to complete the following:

1. Write the latitude and longitude in appropriate degrees for:

   Sacramento ____ ____   Winnipeg ____ ____   Fairbanks ____ ____

   Maui ____ ____   New Orleans ____ ____   Montreal ____ ____

2. Write the name of the city at each of the following approximate locations:

   33° N, 87° W _____   33° N, 97° W _____   40° N, 112° W _____

   52° N, 97° W _____   48° N, 122° W _____   40° N, 77° W _____

3. Write the name of the city that is closest to a ship that sends an SOS from 30° N and 120° W.

   _____

4. Write the name of the gulf that is located between 20° N to 30° N and 80° W to 100° W.

   _____

In addition, show middle school students the division of degrees into minutes and seconds, as is done in some atlases and in *The World Almanac.* Follow by directing students to note the precise location of cities for which they have noted approximate locations.

Direct students to show the location of features being studied on outline maps—for example, cities, states, countries, routes of explorers, colonies, westward expansion, high, middle, and low latitudes, climate regions, landforms and water bodies, resources and products.

Identify time zones on maps of the United States and the world, and explain how they are related to longitude, the Prime Meridian, and the International Date Line.

Learning about Orientation and Direction

Review and use concepts of directions to objects and directions from one's position, such as *over, under, in front of, in back of, toward, away from, left,* and *right.* Ask questions and direct students to do things that employ these concepts:

- What is over the bookshelves?
- Who is sitting in front of Ben?
- Is Juan's desk to the right or to the left of Mary's?
- Watch while I walk. Am I going toward or away from the classroom door?
- What street is in back of our school?
- Point to the object under the picture on the wall to your left.
- Take one step to your right.
- Turn left and describe what is in front of you.

Clarify the terms *up* and *down* by asking students to respond to the following questions:

- Point directly over your heads. What do you see when you look up in our classroom? outdoors?
- Now, point to the floor. What do you see when you look down in our classroom? outdoors?
- Is up always away from the earth?
- Is down always toward the earth?

Use a globe to demonstrate *up* and *down* and *toward* the earth. Call on students to show up and down from various positions on the globe. Conclude by asking, Is up always away from the earth? Is down always toward the earth?

Have students stand with their backs to the sun at noon. Explain that they are facing north. Ask, In what direction is your shadow pointing? What direction is to your right? What direction is to your left? What direction is behind you? Explain that where we live, the sun is always in the south at noon.

Place signs NORTH, SOUTH, EAST, and WEST on classroom walls. Ask, What do you see when facing north? east? west? south? Direct students to do the following:

- Take one step north.
- Take one step south.
- Point east.
- Point west.
- Turn to face toward the east.
- Turn to face south.
- Point north.

- Learning to read maps, like learning to read the printed word, depends upon a student's ability to attach arbitrary labels to something in the environment for the purpose of communicating ideas to others.

  —George W. Maxim

Print the cardinal directions on the sides of a large piece of paper. Draw lines on it to represent rows of desks. Ask students to state how the paper should be placed on the floor or on a table so that each side is in the correct position. Next, have students place either pictures they have drawn of themselves or name cards in the correct position. Ask, Whose desk is north of Betty's? Whose desk is east of Ben's? Is Leticia's desk west or south of Paul's?

Distribute worksheets with direction arrows that form a cross, with NORTH labeled. Direct students to print EAST, WEST, and SOUTH by the correct points of the other arrows. Have students orient their worksheets, with the NORTH arrow pointing toward the NORTH sign on the classroom wall.

Make a floor or tabletop map of the area around the school, and place direction arrows on it. After a walking trip, have students name the streets around the school, guided by such questions as these:

- What street is north of our school?
- What street is east of our school?
- What street is south of Elm?
- What street next to our school should we take to go west?

Ask students to name familiar places that are north of the school. Follow by asking them to name places that are east, south, and west of the school.

Show students how to use a compass outdoors to identify cardinal and intermediate directions. Ask them to tell the direction to various objects on the playground and near the school as you point to them.

Direct attention to a compass rose on a textbook map. Ask students to state the direction from one place to another on the map, referring to the compass rose as needed to identify the direction. Follow by having students state the direction to various places as you point to them on a wall map.

Play a game called "What Direction Am I Going?" Make statements such as those listed next, and after each one ask: What direction am I going? Students may refer to a wall map.

1. I am walking toward the rising sun.
2. I am walking north and turn left.
3. I am flying from Denver to Chicago.
4. I am flying from St. Paul to Miami.
5. I am flying from Los Angeles to Tokyo on a great-circle route.

Review with upper elementary and middle school students how to find directions by using a compass and their shadows at noon. Explain that their shadows at noon show north because at places north of the Tropic of Cancer (where the sun's rays are overhead only on June 21 or 22) the noonday sun is always to the south.

Demonstrate how to use parallels and meridians to identify places east and west and north and south of each other. For example, Los Angeles is east of San Francisco and Reno, the southern tip of Ontario is south of the state of Washington, and nearly all of South America is east of the United States. Show that places on the same parallel are east or west of each other because parallels are true east–west lines, and that places on the same meridian are north or south of each other because meridians are true north–south lines. Show how the pattern of grid lines differs on Mercator, polar, and other projections. Use a globe to show directions on great-circle routes.

Provide practice in orienting maps correctly as students complete outline maps and interpret maps in textbooks and other sources.

Learning about Scale

Have students describe relative size of objects as larger or smaller; compare the size of models, photos, and drawings with the large objects they represent; and draw pictures to represent trees, houses, and other large objects.

Have students use blocks or boxes of varying size to make a floor map that represents the school, houses, and other buildings on the streets next to the school. Discuss how small objects are used to stand for large ones.

Discuss the following as representations of large objects: maps of the classroom, neighborhood, and community; the globe as a model of the earth; and drawings and maps in textbooks. Ask questions such as these:

- How high is a building if a model of it is ten inches high and the model is made to a scale of one inch to twenty feet?
- What is the scale if a rowboat eighteen feet long is shown in a drawing as three inches long?
- If one inch is used to stand for one block, how many inches should be used to show a street that is eight blocks long?

Demonstrate how an inch or a centimeter can be used to represent a block, a mile or a kilometer, or some other distance. Have students use one inch to stand for a yard, or one centimeter to stand for a meter, and draw a map of the classroom. Repeat the activity later by having students use one inch or one centimeter to stand for a block on a neighborhood map and for a mile or a kilometer on a community map.

Direct attention to the scale on textbooks and other maps and discuss the following: graphic or bar scale with segments numbered to show miles and kilometers, and a statement of inches-to-miles and centimeters-to-kilometers. The Worksheet shown in Figure 10.3 (p. 318) can help students develop skill in figuring distances.

Have students compare an area shown on maps with different scales—for example, a textbook map and a wall map of the United States. Also, compare maps of a given area with different scales as students use atlases, encyclopedias, periodicals, and other sources.

Have students complete outline maps of the community, the state, and other areas, using maps with different scales.

Direct attention to the use of small-scale maps to show large areas and large-scale maps to show small areas in textbooks, atlases, and other sources. Have students describe the features and greater detail shown on large-scale maps that cannot be shown on small-scale maps. As a student stated, "The larger the scale, the more detail."

███ **FIGURE 10.3**

Using the Scale to Determine Distance

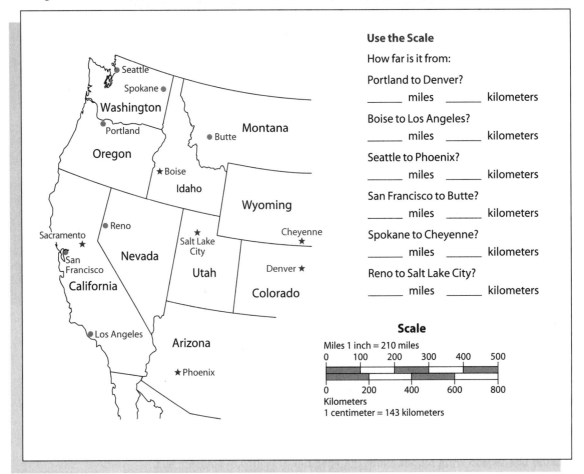

Use the Scale

How far is it from:

Portland to Denver?

_____ miles   _____ kilometers

Boise to Los Angeles?

_____ miles   _____ kilometers

Seattle to Phoenix?

_____ miles   _____ kilometers

San Francisco to Butte?

_____ miles   _____ kilometers

Spokane to Cheyenne?

_____ miles   _____ kilometers

Reno to Salt Lake City?

_____ miles   _____ kilometers

Scale

Miles 1 inch = 210 miles

0   100   200   300   400   500

0   200   400   600   800

Kilometers

1 centimeter = 143 kilometers

Discuss profile drawings of mountains, plains, and other landforms. Point out that the vertical scale is different from the horizontal scale and that elevation is distorted; for example, mountains are shown to be relatively higher than they really are. Do the same for relief maps, which show mountains to be higher above sea level than they would be shown if the horizontal scale were used.

Explain the representative fraction scale (1:1,000,000) and graduated scales as students in the middle grades encounter them. For example, on a scale of 1:1,000,000 one unit on the map represents the given number—1,000,000 units on earth. Explain that a graduated scale is used to show how the scale varies with latitude and is important on polar maps and on some world maps.

Learning about Distance

Have students use the terms *nearer* and *farther* to describe relative distance to objects in the classroom and familiar places near the school.

Have students use centimeters, inches, yards, and meters to measure short distances between objects in the classroom and on the playground.

Ask students to count and report the number of blocks from home to school and to familiar places in the neighborhood. Follow by having them count the blocks between the same places on a neighborhood map.

Take students on a walking trip of one mile (or one kilometer) around the school, and have them count the blocks and record the time it takes. Trace the route, and count the blocks on a school-neighborhood map. Show students how the scale can be used to measure distance between familiar places.

Demonstrate how to use the scale on other maps to figure the distance between places. Follow by having students figure the distance, as illustrated in Figure 10.3. Repeat the activity, using state, highway, country, and other maps.

Ask students to compare distances between places on great-circle routes and other routes, using a globe and illustrations in their textbooks. Have them estimate distances north and south of the equator, using 1 degree of latitude to represent approximately 69 miles.

Have students use the globe and appropriate maps to estimate the distances to places being studied in units and current events. Have them compare the distance across selected states, countries, and continents, and relate distance to travel time by various modes of transportation.

Show students how to use parallels to identify places farther north or south of one another and meridians to identify places farther east or west of one another. Follow by having students use the globe or a map to answer questions such as these:

- Which is farther north, Seattle or Toronto?
- Which is farther east, Los Angeles or Reno?
- Which is farther south, Hawaii or Florida?
- Which is farther north, Spain or Mexico?

Making Comparisons and Inferences

Students can practice this thinking skill in many ways by using maps and globes. They can make comparisons between the following items:

- distance and travel time between familiar places
- the relative size of communities, states, countries, continents, rivers, lakes, and oceans
- area and surface features of regions
- climates, resources, and products of regions

Compare two maps of the same area, and describe relationships. For example, compare a map of the United States that shows landforms to one that shows population to discover that few people live in mountainous areas. Later, find out if this is true in other areas.

Infer conditions in an area on prior knowledge. For example, what conditions would one expect to find in a desert area? in a tropical rainforest?

Infer the relationships that exist between various features, such as elevation and growing season in areas located in high, middle, and low latitudes; ocean currents, winds, and location on a continent and weather and climate of a particular area; highlands and grazing; lowlands and farming; travel routes and surface features; industries and natural resources and level of technological development; natural vegetation and rainfall, type of soil, and elevation; temperature at places near the equator and temperatures at high and low elevations; location of cities and access to oceans and large rivers; industrial centers and natural resources and transportation systems.

Make a habit of double-checking inferences by consulting other sources of information, analyzing cause–effect and other relationships, and using critical thinking skills as suggested in Chapter 11. The following activities will help students develop such thinking skills.

 **Using Thinking Skills with Maps and Globes**

➤ Have younger students review a map of their community—one that they have made or one that you have provided. To help them get a sense of relative distance, have them estimate approximate walking time between sites, based on their everyday knowledge. Students can then test these hypotheses and discuss why they were accurate or inaccurate.

➤ Ask students to list physical features and cultural features that exist in a given area and then make inferences based on their discoveries. They might use maps in their textbooks or other maps that you provide. A worksheet like the following one may help them organize their thoughts.

> Look at the map on page 60 of your textbook. Then fill in this sheet.
>
> The four physical features shown on this map are _____ ,
>
> _____ , _____ , and _____ .
>
> The four cultural features shown on this map are _____ ,
>
> _____ , _____ , and _____ .

The cultural feature that is farthest north is _____.

The physical feature that is farthest south is _____.

List ways in which the physical and cultural features might affect each other.

_____   _____

_____   _____

➤ To do careful interpretation of a map that shows climate, provide a worksheet like the following that students can complete on their own or in small groups. To extend this activity, you might ask students to infer how climate affects the activities of the people who live in each region.

Climates in the United States

Study the map on page 18. Then write the regions of the country that have each type of climate listed here.

1. Cold and dry year-round _____

2. Hot and dry year-round _____

3. Hot and rainy year-round _____

4. Hot summer, cold winter _____

5. Dry summer and mild rainy winter _____

➤ As a means of studying and interpreting a historical map, you might provide an activity card like this one. Then ask students to discuss any broad historical trends that they can infer from looking at the map.

Look at the map on page 289, and write the names of the states that became part of the United States during these time periods.

1. 1810–1819 _____

2. 1820–1839 _____

3. 1840–1859 _____

4. 1860–1869 _____

5. 1870–1919 _____

6. after 1920 _____

➤ As a class, work together to interpret a time zone map. Ask students to identify the time zone for each state you call out.

➤ To locate and compare mountains, you might have students complete a worksheet like this one as they review a map.

1. What mountain ranges are in Alaska?
2. What mountain range extends from Canada, through the United States, and into Mexico?
3. Between what mountain ranges is the Great Basin?
4. Between what mountain ranges are the Great Plains?
5. Look at each mountain range. How do they compare in height? in area?

Learning about Map Projections

The globe shows land masses and water bodies accurately in terms of area, shape, distance, and direction. Distortion is introduced when the surface of the globe is transferred to a flat map. Students in upper elementary and middle school grades should become aware of different projections and their distortions. To do this without presenting technical cartographic details, provide activities such as the following:

Demonstrate how difficult it is to flatten a sphere by peeling an orange and flattening the peeling.

Place tissue paper on a globe and trace a small area, such as a state, and a large area, such as North America. Discuss how much more the paper is distorted when a large area is traced.

Examine and discuss the illustrations in textbooks and other sources that show how distortion is introduced when the globe is flattened to make a map.

Compare the size and shape of large areas on world maps with the same areas on the globe—for example, Alaska and Greenland on a Mercator projection and on a globe.

Compare the shape and area of North America and other continents as shown on various projections and on the globe. Have students describe where the distortion is greatest on different projections.

Compare recent National Geographic world maps based on the Robinson projection to earlier ones based on the Van Der Grinten projection. Direct attention to how much more the size of Alaska, Canada, Greenland, and Russia is exaggerated on the Van Der Grinten.

Discuss the purposes for using different projections as students encounter them in textbooks and other sources: equal-area and interrupted projections to compare size and shape of areas; Mercator projection, which shows correct directions and is used in navigation; and polar projections, which show shortest distance or great-circle routes and are used to plan long flights.

■ Mapping Activities

Students apply and extend concepts and skills when they make maps related to topics of study. The focus in early grades is on familiar features in the immediate environment. In later grades the focus shifts to topics related to studies of the state, regions, the country, and other lands. A great variety of maps may be made:

- Floor or table maps have blocks, models, and drawings to represent objects.
- Maps on wrapping paper represent features with paper cutouts or drawings made by pencil, crayon, or tempera paint.
- Pictorial maps show objects in the neighborhood and community, resources and products in selected areas, and other features.
- Specimen maps show the location of real items such as wheat, corn, and cotton.
- Mural maps have strips of paper or tape for streets and drawings or cutouts for buildings, parks, and other features.
- Relief maps can be made of papier-mâché, clay, moistened sand, or other modeling material.
- Large wall maps can be made by projecting a small map or by using a pantograph or proportional squares to enlarge a map.
- Jigsaw puzzle maps can represent states, countries, and continents.
- Maps made on slated globes, flat maps, and outline maps can show air routes, trade routes, early explorations, and other movements.
- Transportation maps with line-and-dot patterns show air, railway, interstate highway, and major pipeline routes.
- Historical maps depict patterns of exploration, early settlements, colonization, westward movement, and territorial expansion.
- Special interest maps show national and state parks, major cities, seaports, river systems, and states in the Sunbelt, the Frostbelt, and the Heartland.
- Transparent maps show resources, population, transportation networks, and other distributions to superimpose over base maps to show relationships.

The following sample lesson plan for making a classroom map can be adapted for making neighborhood, community, and other maps.

LESSON PLAN   *Making a Classroom Map*

Objective   To make a map that shows the location of objects in the classroom

Materials   Large piece of wrapping paper to represent the classroom
Construction paper cutouts to represent desks and other objects
Drawing paper without a grid for students' use
Drawing paper with a grid for students' use

Introduction   State that today we are going to make maps that show the location of desks and other objects in the classroom.

Development   Place the wrapping paper on the floor or on a table, and explain that it represents the classroom.

Show the cutouts, and explain that they stand for objects in the classroom.

Show the cutout that represents the teacher's desk, and place it in the proper position.

Show the cutouts that represent students' desks, and ask where they should be placed. Begin with those nearest the teacher's desk, and ask each student to show where the cutout for his or her desk should be placed.

Show the cutouts for other objects, and call on students to show where they should be placed.

Hand out the drawing paper without a grid, and tell students to make a drawing that shows the location of objects in the classroom.

Discuss any difficulties students had in positioning objects accurately.

Hand out the drawing paper with a grid on it, and ask students to make a drawing that shows the location of objects.

Conclusion   Discuss the advantages of using paper with a grid to map objects.

Follow-up   Give students paper with a grid, and ask them to make a map of a room at home and bring it to class on the following day.

Outline Maps

Outline maps are useful at all levels to map features related to topics of study. For example, a simple outline map of the streets around the school can be used to locate features as students take a short walk or "mapping trip." Outline maps of the neighborhood and community can depict students' homes, the school, the central business district, and other features. Outline maps of the state, the country, and other areas are used extensively in the upper elementary and middle grades.

When you need an outline map that is not furnished by the school district, you can make one. Maps on slides and videos can be projected and traced. Proportional squares can be used to enlarge small maps. Draw small squares over the small map, draw the same number of squares on wrapping paper, and mark the outline in the matching squares on the wrapping paper. The outline of a map can be traced on a sheet of paper or stencil and then duplicated. Students should use these techniques to make outline maps needed for individual and small-group projects.

Guidelines for students to follow as they complete outline maps are as follows:

1. Collect and check information on features to be mapped.
2. Select symbols and colors, and note them in the legend.
3. Use the grid to locate features accurately.
4. Print the names of places in parallel form.
5. Make a north arrow or a compass rose to show directions.
6. Print the title in capital letters at the top.
7. Print the date under the title.
8. Print your name in the upper right-hand corner.

Modeled Relief Maps

Modeled relief maps are helpful in many ways. They can help show why people settle in certain places, why highways are built in certain places, where mountain passes are located, how mountain ranges cause certain areas to be dry and other areas to receive much rainfall, how climate is affected by terrain, how areas are drained by rivers, and a host of other information related to distance, travel, elevation, and topography. Relief maps enable children to visualize surface features and conditions in the areas they study.

Remember that the vertical scale on relief maps is different from the horizontal scale. For example, Pike's Peak, which may be prominent on a relief map, is only a tiny pinpoint on the earth's surface when its elevation (under 3 miles or 4.8 kilometers) is considered in relation to the circumference of the earth (25,000 miles, or 40,225 kilometers). Nevertheless, one child who had seen it said, "It was no pinpoint from where I saw it," thus indicating that relief on smaller areas stands out dramatically and realistically. By mapping a smaller area, less distortion is introduced. When

■ Many teachers turn to The George F. Cram Company, Inc. **http:// georgefcram.com**, for ideas and resources on effective approaches to the teaching of map and globe concepts and skills.

large areas are mapped, however, considerable distortion is introduced and should be considered as children grow in their understanding of map scale. One technique is to draw a long line on the chalkboard to represent the distance across the area being mapped. Then draw vertical lines to show the relative height of mountains, plateaus, and other features to be shown. Thus, if a mountain approximately 3 miles high is located in an area 300 miles long, the vertical line would be 3 inches, while the baseline would be 300 inches. (Corresponding metric measurements would be mountain, 4.83 kilometers high; length of area, 483 kilometers; vertical line, 7.6 centimeters; and baseline, 760 centimeters.) After such a demonstration, one fifth grader said, "That mountain isn't so high when you think of how long the ground is." When distortion exists, the teacher should explain that features appear relatively higher than they really are.

Table 10.2 gives recipes for modeling materials that students can use to make relief maps. If the maps will be used for only a short time, use simple and inexpensive recipes: finishing the surface with paint and shellac is unnecessary. If the maps are to be used often, they should be well made and shellacked to protect the surface. The outline on which the relief map is made should be carefully prepared. A wise procedure is to make two outline maps and to use the second one as a working guide while the modeling material is being placed on the relief map. Then, when one layer is in place, the second outline map is available for easy reference. Make a list of the features that are to be shown, show pictures illustrating them (the jagged Rockies, long flat prairies, great valleys), and guide children to find them on physical maps—either wall maps or maps in atlases.

Make the map outline by means of a projector or one of the other methods discussed under outline maps. Sketch in rivers, mountains, other features, and contour lines. After the outline is mounted on a base board, drive in brads and small nails to show relative height and position of peaks, mountain ranges, and hills; these serve as guides during the modeling process. Anticipate and discuss common errors, such as gross distortion of features (hills and mountains too large), omission of significant features (lakes, valleys, dams), inaccuracy of slope (rivers running uphill), and errors in relative height of features (Appalachians and Rockies same height). Plan for gradual inclines from plains to hills to mountains where appropriate. Some teachers also find it helpful to show and discuss relief maps made by classes of preceding years.

Many relief maps can be made and used without coloring them in any way. The features will stand out clearly and the surface will speak for itself as children use the map. In other instances, the surface can be painted to highlight features and to show contrasts. Tempera water paint works very well; the surface can be protected by shellacking after it has dried. Enamel can also be used if the surface is first shellacked. Another effective technique is to place sawdust in a can or jar of powdered paint and to shake thoroughly. After coating the areas to be colored with glue, sprinkle the sawdust on and allow the glue to dry. Brush off any loose particles. Clean sand can be used in a similar manner. Be sure to plan carefully for the use of different colors on appropriate sections of the map so that they will be clear in contrast and consistent with standard uses of color on maps. You might add tiny sticks to signify trees or other similar details.

■ **TABLE 10.2**

Recipes for Modeling Material

Paste and Paper	Tear paper towels or newspapers into 1½-inch pieces. Put paste on one piece at a time, wad it or shape it with your fingers, and stick it on the map outline. Build up hills and mountains as desired. Paint with tempera paint after the paste has dried.
Paper Strips and Paste	Begin with crumpled paper to build up terrain, holding it in place with string or masking tape. Dip half-inch strips of paper towels into wheat paste, and place them on the crumpled paper form. After two layers have been placed on the map, coat the entire surface with paste and allow it to dry; secure the base of the map so that it cannot buckle. After the map is dry, paint with calcimine paint.
Sawdust and Paste	Mix any sawdust, except redwood or cedar, with wheat paste (from a wallpaper store); spoon paste into sawdust until it is well moistened and of good modeling consistency. Good proportions are 5 cups of sawdust to 1 cup of wheat paste. The mixture may be applied directly to wood or cardboard. Paint it after it is dry.
Papier-Mâché	This is one of the most popular modeling materials. Tear 20 to 25 newspaper sheets (or paper towels) into fine shreds, and soak them for 24 hours. Pulverize the soaked paper by rubbing it over a washboard or by kneading it. Add wheat paste (or 4 cups of flour and 2 cups of salt) until the mixture is of the consistency of modeling clay. Build up mountains, plateaus, and hills by applying papier-mâché mixture to the surface. After 3 to 6 days of drying, paint elevations, water, and other features.
Salt and Flour	Mix equal parts of salt and flour, using only enough water to hold the ingredients together. Apply to map outline, modeling the terrain according to plan. (Keep the map out of damp places because salt attracts moisture.)
Plaster and Sawdust	Mix 1 pint of plaster, 1 pint of sawdust, and one-quarter pint of paste that has been dissolved in water. Knead and apply to map outline. Paint after the mixture has set for 15 to 30 minutes.
Plaster and Papier-Mâché	Add 2 pints of plaster, one-half tablespoon of LePage's glue, and one-half pint of water to prepared papier-mâché. Be sure that the mixture is of modeling consistency. Paint after mixture has set for 30 to 45 minutes.

■ Conclusion

Globe and map concepts help young students understand their immediate world, and in the upper elementary and middle grades this knowledge is essential to gaining a better understanding of people, events, places, and relationships throughout the world. Students of all ages will be better U.S. and global citizens if they possess a firm understanding of these concepts and skills since they help to foster appreciation of the earth's complexity, the natural world, the setting of historical events, and the variety of peoples and cultures that are our distant or near neighbors. As you integrate this area of knowledge into social studies, you will find that it enriches your program while helping students understand concepts that will benefit many areas of study as well as life outside the classroom.

 Questions, Activities, and Evaluation

1. Which of the examples of map and globe use presented in this chapter might you incorporate in a unit you are planning? Can you think of additional uses of maps and globes in a social studies program? in other subject areas?

2. Study a recently published map, and check the legend, the use of colors, and the information presented. Can you find related pictures to illustrate items on the map?

3. Prepare a list of questions to direct students' attention to symbols and features on a map you plan to use.

4. Using what you have learned in this chapter, prepare a current events lesson integrating globe or map concepts and skills. How might you help students connect time and place? How might you help students see the significance of the highlighted current event?

5. Direct students to collect newspapers for a specific period of time, and then ask them to identify locations where the United Nations is involved in peace-keeping missions. Next ask students to identify the locations, using their map and globe skills.

6. Ask students to identify a friend or relative who lives nearby and to develop a neighborhood map and a set of instructions directing them to school. Encourage the students to use some of the terms presented in this chapter.

7. Examine two or three social studies textbooks that contain maps, and notice how they are discussed in the text. Note questions that can be answered by children as they use the maps. Refer to the accompanying teacher's manual for suggestions. Make an activity card based on one of the maps.

8. Review a local course of study or a textbook for a grade of your choice, or both, and make a summary of the suggested map and globe concepts and skills.

9. Visit a nearby media center, and preview computer programs, videos, and films on globe and map concepts and skills. Note how you might use them in a lesson or a unit.

10. Make a large chart of symbols for classroom use. Include three columns with commonly used symbols in the first column, pictures of what each symbol represents in the second column, and the name of the feature represented by the symbol in the third column.

References

Bennett, L. (1997). Geography and the national parks. *Social Studies and the Young Learner, 9,* 1 (pull-out feature).

Berson, M. J., Ouzts, D. T., & Walsh, L. S. (1999). Connecting literature with K–8 national geography standards. *Social Studies, 90,* 85–92.

Brown, R. G. (1995). Globally speaking, smaller can be better. *Social Studies, 86,* 231–233.

Cochrane, K. (1992). A case study in using geography to understand culture. *Social Studies and the Young Learner, 4,* 1 (pull-out feature).

Fernald, E. A., & Allen, R. F. (1989). Great circles and distance. *Social Education, 53,* 71–72. Specific teaching suggestions.

Forsyth, A. S., Jr. (1988). How we learn place location: Bringing theory and practice together. *Social Education, 52,* 500–503. Current methods; computer software programs.

Garvey, J. B. (1988). New perspective on the world. *National Geographic, 174,* 911–13. Examples of distortions on various projections.

Gilsbach, M. T. (1997). Improvement needed: Preservice geography teacher education. *Social Studies, 88,* 35–38.

Liebert, D. K. (1999). Millennium Island: Creating a storyline about geography and time. *Social Studies and the Young Learner, 12,* 6–7.

Metz, H. M. (1990). Sketch maps. *Journal of Geography, 89,* 114–18. Uses of freehand drawn maps.

Muir, S. P., & Cheek, H. N. (1991). Assessing spatial development: Implications for map skill instruction. *Social Education, 55,* 316–19.

Palmer, J., Berry, B., & Smith, B. (1991). Teaching location and some characteristics of place: Using South Africa. *Social Education, 55,* 58–60.

Pieranek, F. (1994). Using maps to teach note taking and outlining for report writing. *The Social Studies, 85,* 165–69.

Rallis, D. N., & Rallis, H. (1995). Changing the image of geography. *Social Studies, 86,* 167–168.

Rice, G. H. (1990). Teaching students to be discriminating map users. *Social Education, 54,* 393–97. Various map projections shown and reviewed.

Soto, B. (1998). Walking on the wild side: Geographic field study for fifth graders. *Social Studies, 89,* 236–238.

Sunal, C. S., Christensen, L., & Haas, M. E. (1995). Using the five themes of geography to teach about Venezuela. *Social Studies, 86,* 169–174.

Werner, R., & Young, J. (1991). A checklist to evaluate mapping software. *Journal of Geography, 90,* 118–20.

Chapter 11

Developing Thinking Skills

Chapter Objective

To present guidelines and teaching strategies for developing conceptual components, modes, processes, and skills essential to productive thinking

Focusing Questions

- What aspects of thinking are of central importance in social studies?

- What thinking modes, processes, and skills merit special attention? What are the key features of each one?

- How can metacognition—thinking about thinking—improve students' thinking?

- What questions and strategies can be used to develop concepts and generalizations—two key tools and outcomes of thinking?

- What questions and strategies help raise thinking to high cognitive levels?

- How can knowledge and thinking skills be unified in a model of teaching?

■ Asking the Right Questions

In your field experiences, have you observed a K–8 classroom in which students were excited about something they read, saw, or experienced? Did you count the many questions they directed at their teacher or classmates as they tried to understand an experience? Were you taken aback by the quality of the questions? Wasn't it exciting? Perhaps you remember a K–8 social studies experience in which you became captivated by something you read in your textbook, a current events lesson, or a document you brought from home to show your teacher. You might well remember that learning experience because you, your teacher, and schoolmates asked questions that helped you learn more about what excited you!

In teaching social studies, you will have many opportunities to help students develop thinking skills—that is, to develop thinking strategies, to learn how to ask questions, and to choose the best sequence of questions. Let's begin with some classroom examples to highlight the importance of thinking skills:

1. A child in the primary grades brings to the classroom an advertisement from a toy store. This store is going out of business, and all of its merchandise is marked down by 60 percent! Is this a good deal? Should the student shop at the store?

2. In the elementary grades a group of students are examining poverty in their community. They want to raise money to donate to a charity involved in helping poor and homeless people. How will the students decide which charity to select?

3. In the middle school a group of students and their teacher are collecting free and inexpensive social studies materials for their classroom. How will the students decide where to look and what to collect?

These examples illustrate the centrality of thinking skills in social studies. In this chapter we discuss strategies that will help students appreciate the value of thinking skills in school and all daily activities.

Keep the following guidelines in mind. As you integrate instruction on content and thinking skills into each social studies unit, consider students' intellectual growth. Would you judge them to be in the preoperational stage, the concrete operations stage, or the formal operations stage? Adapt various approaches (models of thinking, cognitive skills, logical reasoning) to your students' level of cognitive development, and help them transfer to social studies the skills that are taught in separate instruction on thinking.[1] Guide students to combine skills as appropriate. Engage students in thinking about their thinking (metacognition), activities that suit different learning or cognitive styles, and use of the left hemisphere of the brain (the verbal, logical center) and right hemisphere (the intuitive, creative center). Stress the importance of attitudes and behavior such as respect for evidence, sensitivity to differing views, open-mindedness, control of feelings, and freedom to inquire and to express ideas. Remember that each student's self-concept, learning style, motivation, attitudes, interests, values, knowledge, and skills will affect thinking.

A variety of terms are used to discuss modes of thinking, thinking processes, and thinking skills. In this chapter we try to keep them simple and straightforward; as you read other books and articles, however, you may see the terms *modes of thinking*, *ways of thinking*, and *forms of thinking* used interchangeably, and other terminology as well. This chapter highlights four forms of thinking (creative thinking, critical thinking, problem solving, and decision making), several thinking skills (such as interpreting and synthesizing), and metacognition. We then explore how thinking is used to organize data, learn concepts, and make meaningful generalizations.

■ Four Forms of Thinking

■ The function of education is to teach one to think intensively and to think critically. Intelligence plus character—that is the goal of true education.
  —**Martin Luther King, Jr.**

During thinking, we use symbols to represent concepts related to objects and events. Words, map symbols, and numbers are all symbols that help us manipulate ideas. We are drawn into thinking activities by questions, problems, and other stimuli. While thinking, we tap into prior knowledge and seek new information and insight. These abilities can be developed through practice and good instructional guidance. Growth in thinking skills is an educational goal for every student.

The four forms of thinking we discuss here—critical thinking, creative thinking, problem solving, and decision making—can be broken into two more precise cate-

---

1. For a description of programs designed to develop thinking, see Marzano et al. (1988), Paul (1990), and Costa (1991).

gories. Critical thinking and creative thinking are two modes of thinking. Decision making and problem solving are two processes, and each involves critical thinking and creative thinking.

Critical Thinking

In critical thinking, a person chooses criteria or standards to use in analyzing, evaluating, or judging a statement, an idea, a point of view, an action, a behavior, the quality of a group discussion, and so on. Analyzing information based on a set of criteria is involved in several of the activities that students encounter in the curriculum: distinguishing fact from opinion, determining cause and effect, detecting bias and stereotypes, and weighing evidence.[2]

Respect for facts and sound reasoning are generally accepted criteria used to judge merit. However, a person's beliefs and values also inform the standards they use in critical thinking. For example, standards of fairness and justice can be applied to judge the soundness of an argument or the value of a political action. Gaining an ever-broadening sense of the criteria people use to make judgments is an important part of social studies education.

The following steps define the process of critical thinking:

1. Define what is to be judged, analyzed, or evaluated.
2. Clarify the criteria that will be used.
3. Gather accurate, relevant data about the issue or topic.
4. Evaluate the data for bias, inconsistency, fallacies in reasoning, or persuasive techniques such as emotional appeals. Distinguish fact from opinion.
5. Complete the judgment, analysis, or evaluation based on evidence and reasons related to the criteria.

Those five steps are anything but simple. Each one can be quite exacting, depending on the complexity of the material being analyzed. Studying the data can call upon quite a few thinking skills (discussed later in this chapter). Here are concrete examples of social studies questions that can be answered only by using critical thinking skills.

- What rules are important in discussion? in the learning center? in group work? How do they help? Should any be changed? Why?
- What plans should be made in our state to conserve resources? What should individuals be required to do?
- Why did some settlers remain loyal to Britain during the American Revolution? What reasons were given for being a loyalist? a patriot?
- To what extent should immigrants keep their ethnic and cultural heritage? To what extent should they be "Americanized"?
- What problems faced by the country we are studying can be solved by outside help? by internal effort? by a combination of both?

2. For various models and comparisons, see Marzano et al. (1988), Paul (1990), and Costa (1991).

- What contributions of ancient civilizations do you believe to be most important in our lives today? Why?
- Was this book helpful to your study of Texas history? What were its strengths? its weaknesses?

The following activities will help you incorporate critical thinking practice into your social studies curriculum. You may scale down or complicate the activities based on your grade level and students' readiness.

 **ACTIVITY IDEAS** ▶ *Developing Skills in Critical Thinking*

➤ Give students a list of statements, half of which are facts and half of which are opinions. Have them mark *F* for facts and *O* for opinions. After students have finished this exercise, discuss with the class how they arrived at their answers.

➤ Challenge students to find and share examples of faulty reasoning. You might assign them to look for some of these types.

Single cause: identifying one cause when there are actually several

Weak generalization: generalizing without enough supporting evidence

Selected evidence: presenting facts that support a claim but leaving out others

Vagueness: using undefined terms or confusing terms

Personal attack: attacking a person rather than discussing an issue

Faulty assumption: basing an argument on an unrelated or wrong idea

Appeal to authority: basing an argument on someone's authority rather than reasons

False cause: assuming that because two events occurred simultaneously, one caused the other

➤ Creating and critiquing analogies is a good exercise in critical thinking. After working on analogies as a class, you might provide worksheets in which students complete some analogies and then create their own.

> What relationship is expressed in each analogy?
> 1. A mayor is to the city council as a governor is to the legislature.
> 2. Albany:New York :: Sacramento:California
>
> Complete these analogies.
> 1. New:Hampshire :: West: _____
> 2. Brazil:South America :: Canada: _____
>
> Create two analogies of your own.
> 1. _____
> 2. _____

➤ Give students practice in setting criteria to use in critical thinking. Choose a recent policy decision made at your school or in your community. Then have students set criteria to use in judging its merits. They might set standards in each of these areas.

safety	comfort	clarity of purpose	practicality
convenience	expense	long-term value	

➤ In the middle school you might help students analyze a persuasive essay, speech, advertisement, or other work in terms of three kinds of appeals: to reason and logic, to ethics, and to emotion. Stress that none of these appeals is bad or good by definition—it depends on *how* they are used and for what purpose. For example, Martin Luther King Jr.'s "I Have a Dream" speech makes all three types of appeals in a compelling way. However, an ad for anti-wrinkle cream may also use them. Students need to be aware of such appeals in order to judge their merits in particular situations.

➤ Help students understand the importance of clearly defining the terms they use when they communicate, as well as clearly understanding the terms used in material they read or listen to. To show how easy it is to use terms in a confusing way, you might give them a worksheet like this one, exemplifying how one word may mean many things.

■ The Center for Critical Thinking and Moral Critique **http:// criticalthinking.org** seeks to promote change in education and society through the cultivation of fair-minded critical thinking.

To an army general, *charge* means _____.

To a gas station worker, *charge* means _____.

To a store clerk, *charge* means _____.

To an electrician, *charge* means _____.

Creative Thinking

Creative thinking is the source of originality, divergent thinking, fluency, and new ideas. First, the new idea is conceived, efforts are made to express it, and finally the creative act is complete when the end product is shaped into a harmonious whole. Teachers may stimulate creative thinking in social studies by encouraging students to suggest new ways of doing things, to design learning centers and displays, to organize information in new ways on maps and charts, to express thoughts and feelings through oral and written language activities, and to engage in art, music, construction, and other expressive activities. Setting goals and choosing topics that stimulate students' imaginations is the best way to jump-start creative thinking.

Creative thinking may begin with building background: meanings, images, feelings, and expressive terms and phrases associated with the topic at hand. In the next phase, known as the illumination stage, students discover new insights and relationships and new ways of expressing them. Students may then proceed to express their discoveries through a mural, a dramatic skit, creative writing, or some other creative activity. Later, in this phase students may revise their projects and even start anew after evaluating the adequacy of expression of the original idea.

Review the previous activities and others in this chapter for ideas for projects and activities that encourage and develop creative thinking.

Have you thought of the many ways students might demonstrate learning in social studies? Can you connect the construction of masks with social studies learning?

Decision Making

In decision making, students make intelligent choices by identifying objectives and alternative ways of achieving them. This process is used in social studies when students make personal and group decisions and when they study the decisions made and alternatives available to the people discussed in unit and current events lessons. Students should use both critical thinking and creative thinking as they appraise alternatives and propose new ones. Clarifying the personal and social values that underlie decision making is an important facet of this process.

For example, after a series of lessons that focused on problems of poverty and homelessness, students in an upper elementary classroom may wish to participate in a community effort to address such problems. There may be a number of options at hand: volunteering at a local "soup kitchen," donating food to a food bank, gathering supplies such as coats and blankets, or participating in a letter-writing campaign to government officials regarding legislation affecting the homeless. To decide on a course of action, the class will get practice in each step involved in making a decision.

The following steps are typical of the decision-making process:

1. Define the issue or situation that requires a decision.
2. Set decision-making goals, and clarify the values that should inform the decision.
3. Brainstorm alternative ways to achieve goals and support the chosen values.
4. Evaluate each alternative and its consequences in terms of goals and values.
5. Rank the alternatives, based on positive and negative consequences.
6. Decide on the best alternative, and take the action it requires.
7. Evaluate the decision-making process, the final decision, and the way it has been carried out.

You may create charts or worksheets to help students complete each step. Small groups could be assigned to study the potential effects of each alternative; the groups could then report to the class.

Problem Solving and Inquiry

These thinking processes involve the rational and objective study of questions, issues, and problems in social studies, ranging from investigating ways of living in families, communities, and cultures around the world to studying contemporary issues and global problems. In problem solving and inquiry, students attempt to understand, explain, and predict human behavior. Creative thinking and critical thinking are involved in inquiry and investigation.

Investigation begins with defining a problem and posing questions or hypotheses to guide study. Then students identify study procedures and sources of information. Next, they appraise data sources and collect, interpret, and organize information in order to answer questions or test hypotheses. Finally, students draw conclusions and identify needs for further study.

One challenge in the problem-solving process is how to handle feelings that arise during discussion of a problem. For example, in analyzing problems and solutions concerning a town budget and allocation of money for education and for road repairs, some of your students might voice strong opinions and feelings for one priority or the other. How can you keep the discussion focused on significant data and the pros and cons of each potential solution? Sometimes political, economic, community, and other problems can cause an outpouring of emotion that may not be informed by critical or creative thinking.

Feelings should not be suppressed because they often point to the values that students hold dear. On the other hand, feelings should be expressed with a measure of control and with respect for those who disagree. In a problem-solving situation focused on gathering evidence and reasons, students may be instructed to put their feelings aside for the time being and attempt to weigh solutions by analyzing facts and reasons. This can be a good exercise in acknowledging feelings while encouraging critical thought, research, and creative solutions that address the full complexity of a situation.

The following list of steps in the problem-solving or inquiry process can be adapted to particular situations and to the grade level of your students:

1. Identify and define the problem.
2. If helpful, break the problem into parts.
3. State questions, hypotheses, or hunches to guide the process. Determine what is already known and what information needs to be gathered.
4. Choose procedures for gathering information and the sources to be used. Consider reading materials and interviews with specialists.
5. Gather the data, and decide which information is relevant and reliable.
6. Use the data to answer each question or to test each hypothesis or hunch.
7. Synthesize the information, and make a conclusion. If necessary, state the limitations of the conclusion and identify needs for further study.
8. Evaluate the conclusion. If relevant, take action based on the conclusion. Note ways in which the problem-solving or inquiry process could be improved in the future.

■ Metacognition

■ Learning is the discovery that something is possible.

—**Fritz Perls**

In addition to using various modes of thinking, students need to be guided to "think about their thinking" (metacognition) and to find ways to monitor and improve it. A helpful small-group activity gives each group member the opportunity to "think out loud" about how to solve a problem, create something, or do some other task. Group members observe the student who is thinking out loud and note the student's strengths in defining the problem, suggesting procedures and sources, and other aspects of thinking. The teacher observes and guides the group.

Students develop metacognitive abilities as they practice the four forms of thinking. As the student, the group, or the teacher evaluates the thinking process and the product that resulted from it, students reflect on their own thinking as it occurred during the task. The strengths and weaknesses that surface during such reflection will foster metacognition in future tasks.

Here are some concrete suggestions for improving students' metacognition.

 *Building Skills in Metacognition*

➤ To introduce a lesson on map skills, ask students to close their eyes to see the "mental map" that they already have of the area to be studied. Ask them to notice what is accurate about the map and what details or information is missing. Then guide them in filling in these gaps as they work through the lesson with you.

➤ Help middle school students think about their own biases, assumptions, or fuzzy thinking. You might have individual students analyze a persuasive essay or speech that they made and answer the following questions about their own work. (Such self-critical analyses do not need to be shared with others but can help students really ponder how they think through an issue and support their ideas.)

> Can you find any examples of the following in your work?
>
> ■ slanted definitions of terms
> ■ use of stereotypes
> ■ overgeneralizing
> ■ using just one example to support a generalization
> ■ withholding evidence that goes against my thoughts or feelings
> ■ making faulty assumptions
> ■ not really supporting my points with facts or reasons
> ■ mixing the real with the fanciful
>
> How can you correct these problems?

➤ Students can benefit from thinking carefully about their learning styles—particularly what they do well and what areas need improvement. You might provide an inventory like the following one for students to use as they consider their schoolwork overall or their performance on a certain type of task.

I set my purpose for learning by _____ .

I make a learning plan by _____ .

I begin my work by _____ .

I then proceed by _____ .

I get help by _____ .

I find main ideas by _____ .

I relate details to main ideas by _____ .

I summarize by _____ .

I check my work by _____ .

I work best alone on _____ .

I work best in a group on _____ .

➤ Since class and small-group discussions are such an important feature of social studies learning, you might help students develop metacognitive skills to use during discussion. A classroom chart or a handout with the following list can be helpful.

- Am I focusing on the topic of this discussion?
- Am I avoiding distractions?
- Are any terms or concepts unfamiliar to me? What questions can I ask to clarify them?
- What facts can I contribute?
- What questions can I raise?
- What creative ideas can I suggest?
- Do I focus on what each person says?
- Can I summarize information presented by different people?
- Do I express my ideas clearly?
- Can I give an example to clarify an abstract idea?
- Can I tell the difference between fact and opinion?
- Can I tell the difference between a good reason and a weak one?

➤ Reflecting on their mental processes over the course of a project that is now completed can help students improve their metacognition in future projects.

You might ask them to analyze their mental approach to the project by asking questions like these.

What questions did you focus on as you worked?
What overall purpose did you have?
What plans did you form?
What directions did you give yourself for finishing the project?
What materials did you choose? Why?
What difficulties arose? How did you handle them?
How well did you answer your questions?
What would you do differently next time?

➤ When studying events in history, students can become victims of "information overload." It's easy to become dazed by the rush of facts and ideas. Developing the mental habit of organizing information into main ideas and details and asking questions while reading can help students approach longer and more complicated study assignments. To study a historical event or trend, students might ask themselves questions like these as they read.

When did this happen?
Where did it happen?
How long did it last?
Why did it happen?
What causes and effects were involved?
How did this event relate to other events?
Was this event part of a major trend?
Should I consider this a major or minor event? Why?

■ Thinking Skills and Acquisition of Knowledge

All forms of thinking that we have discussed involve the use of knowledge and specific thinking skills. There are many individual thinking skills; some overlap, and some are referred to by different terms. Here is a typical sampling:

recalling	synthesizing	inferring	organizing
classifying	analyzing	generalizing	applying
comparing	predicting	interpreting	summarizing
evaluating	hypothesizing	concluding	observing

In this section we discuss several thinking skills and how they support the acquisition of knowledge. We begin with the most basic skills and progress to those requiring greater discernment and mental agility. Taken together, these skills help students develop concepts and make generalizations that together form the foundation of social studies learning.

Generating, Organizing, and Interpreting Data

Early on, students begin developing basic thinking skills such as recalling information, gathering data, interpreting data, making comparisons, and classifying information. Each is important to an understanding of social studies.

Recalling Information

To recall is to retrieve pertinent information that the student has already learned. It involves remembering facts, reasons, and feelings related to a topic. You can help students develop skills in memory and memory retrieval. Here are some hints.

- Remind students to retrieve information related to the topic at hand. Encourage them to focus on the topic as they tap into their memory.
- To help students remember a piece of information, use key words, acronyms, visual images, or rhymes or other sounds that have been used to reinforce the learning.
- Urge students to think of dates, places, or events as organizers for clusters of information.
- Encourage students to take notes, make outlines, or fill out graphic organizers to organize and reinforce important information.
- When students study a historical event, help them use story grammar to note the main characters, the problem, what happened, the outcome, and the main points.
- Some types of information can be organized in alphabetical or numerical order to assist students' memory.
- Frequently ask students to recall the definitions of important terms, the places on a map that have been studied, and other facts and concepts.

Collecting Data

Students gather information through many means: observing, listening, reading, doing research, choosing audiovisual resources, interviewing, and so on. Making good decisions in choosing resources is an important thinking skill in many learning activities. You can help students refine this skill in many ways—here are just a few ideas.

- Emphasize that when gathering information to serve a particular learning goal, it's important to stick to the topic at hand. Differentiate between tasks in which students simply browse available information to learn about available resources and tasks that require focus on a particular issue, problem, topic, or question.
- Show students how different kinds of information come from different sources. For example, a list of dates related to the Revolutionary War could be found in a reference book, a nonfiction history book, or a detailed time line. The process of making pottery might be found on a video, in a live demonstration by an expert, or in a detailed diagram. Also note the advantages of using different types of resources.

What thinking skills might this student be using? What is the relationship between thinking and reading skills? Why are these skills part of a social studies program?

- Through learning activities, demonstrate to students how research can be guided by questions or hypotheses and how such tools help focus research.
- Help students differentiate between main ideas and detail as they gather data. Also help them note the difference between relevant information and data that really has nothing to do with the topic at hand.
- Give students practice in checking the accuracy of the data they find. They might support their observations of nature by finding confirming facts in an encyclopedia. They might double-check information obtained in an interview by looking at a related newspaper article or almanac.

Interpreting Data

Students can use the information that they have gathered or recalled to engage in a more challenging thinking skill: interpretation. Interpretation can involve a number of activities: explaining the meaning of a text, the significance of an event, or the thoughts and feelings encoded in a speech. This skill helps students develop concepts.

It can, however, be challenging to interpret the gist of a message or event without straying into misconceptions. You can guide students by directing them to look for main ideas and supporting details, relationships between concepts, and definitions of terms. Having them state the main point in their own words will help you gauge the soundness of students' interpretations. Such summaries or conclusions are significant types of interpretation.

Making Comparisons

Identifying the similarities and differences that characterize various concepts, time periods, historical characters, political positions, and so on is an important thinking skill in social studies. These ideas will help you foster this skill.

- Have students clearly define the basis for comparison. Will they compare items based on size, use, behavior, time period, or some other element?
- Let students clearly describe each feature that is being compared.
- Urge students to first consider similarities thoroughly and then focus on differences. Then they can summarize them.

Classifying Data

Organizing information based on certain characteristics, uses, or relationships is an important skill and helps students in developing concepts. Grouping resources and products, physical features and cultural features of an area, or goods and services requires rigorous thinking and an understanding of the key features of certain objects or concepts. You can help students follow these steps as they classify items:

1. Select a basis for grouping the items.
2. Examine each item to identify its defining characteristics.
3. Identify which group the item belongs in.
4. Make sure that all items with common features are in the same group.

Developing Concepts

Concepts and concept clusters are key elements of schemata—the knowledge structures that guide perception, categorize information, interpret experience, draw inferences, and evaluate information.[3] Concept development goes hand in hand with development of a knowledge base. Interpreting, comparing, and classifying are three important components of concept development.

Students' understanding of concepts may be facilitated by providing both direct sensory and vicarious experiences, ranging from observing activities and examining realia to reading and doing research on a topic. Literature, art, and music are used to develop qualitative shades of meaning. Reading about Daniel Boone, for example, adds meaning to students' conceptions of scouts, wilderness, and the adventures of explorers. Teachers should control the number and difficulty of concepts to be learned in order to develop depth of understanding and to avoid misconceptions and mere "word calling." Because words are the labels for concepts, meaningful vocabulary development requires concept development.

Types of Concepts

Three main types of concepts may be identified: conjunctive, disjunctive, and relational (Bruner et al., 1962). *Conjunctive* concepts, such as legislator and taxes, are based on a conglomeration of characteristics. For example, taxes have all the following characteristics: they are a class of payments, are levied according to law, and are paid to the government. *Disjunctive* concepts have either/or characteristics—for example, U.S. citizenship may be obtained by birth, by passing an exam, or because one's parents were born here. *Relational* concepts, such as population density, per capita income, and area, are defined in terms of how one element varies in relation to another. A mathematical operation may define certain relational concepts; per capita income, for example, is determined by dividing income by number of people.

Concepts may also be categorized by level of abstractness, comprehensiveness, and other features. At a low level of abstraction and difficulty are concepts of *concrete* items, such as lake, island, and goods. More abstract and difficult are *defined* concepts, such as interdependence, justice, and cultural exchange; learning these concepts

---

3. For a discussion of schema theory see Marzano (1988) and Paul (1990).

requires precise definition, a variety of examples, and identification of relationships—for example, demonstration of interdependence among workers in a community. Students also need to recognize the *specificity* and *generality* of concepts used in social studies. Land, resources, and nation are generally applicable to any culture, area, or time period. Concepts such as New England colonies, muckrakers, and caste system (in India) are applicable only in designated time periods, cultures, or places. *Value-neutral* concepts, such as resources, role, and communication, do not usually arouse feelings. In contrast, *value-laden* concepts, such as prejudice, discrimination, and justice, can stir feelings. Teachers should recognize that feelings associated with value-laden concepts are among the "facts to be considered."

■ Genius means little
more than the faculty
of perceiving in an
unhabitual way.
—William James

Concept Development Strategies

Five strategies are used to develop concepts: defining concepts; distinguishing examples from nonexamples; listing, grouping, and labeling; problem solving or inquiry; and providing a series of learning activities.

Defining Concepts   Learning definitions contributes to both concept development and vocabulary development. Students learn definitions from teachers and find them in textbooks, glossaries, dictionaries, and other sources. Several types of definition are used, as illustrated in the following examples:

> ***Demonstrating:*** Watch while I show a great-circle route on the globe.
>
> ***Showing:*** This picture shows a tropical rain forest.
>
> ***Using analogies:*** A governor is like a president except she runs a state.
>
> ***Using synonyms or antonyms:*** Being loyal means being devoted; the opposite is being a traitor.
>
> ***Using glossaries or dictionaries:*** The glossary says that *urban* means having to do with cities.
>
> ***Stating behavior (behavioral definitions):*** A legislator campaigns for office, writes bills, votes on bills, communicates with constituents, and serves on committees.
>
> ***Stating operations (operational definitions):*** You figure population density by dividing the population of an area by the number of square miles in the area.

The model questions listed below highlight these different types of definition.

■ What do you mean by _____ (producer, goods, urban function)?

■ What does _____ mean?

■ What is a good way to define the meaning of this term—using an example, a picture, an action, or a symbol?

■ Who can define _____ (carpenter, judge, scout) by telling what he or she does?

■ Who can define _____ (average income per family, population density) by stating how it is figured?

■ Which meaning(s) of _____ (bank, pollution, democracy) should we use? Which one best fits the context?

An activity that is useful in defining concepts is concept mapping, or the making of a semantic web or map. For example, print PUBLIC SERVICES in a circle on the chalkboard or a chart and draw lines from it to education, police, and other services.

Distinguishing Examples from Nonexamples   This is a deductive (general to specific) concept-attainment strategy that begins with the name of the concept and moves to identification of examples; it is often used with the defining activities just noted.

1. State the concept to be learned, or pose a question: "Today we are to learn about peninsulas. What is a peninsula?"
2. Identify defining characteristics (critical attributes): "Look at this example on the wall map. Which parts are surrounded by water?"
3. Present other examples of the concept: "Look at the map on page 22. See the peninsula at the bottom. Find the one on the next page."
4. Present nonexamples: "Look at the island on page 22. Why is that *not* a peninsula? Find others that are *not* peninsulas."
5. Have students state or write a definition: "A piece of land nearly surrounded by water and connected with the mainland."

Listing, Grouping, and Labeling   This is an inductive (specific to general) concept-formation strategy developed by Taba et al. (1971) as one of three cognitive tasks. The classifying process is used to group items encountered in materials and activities:

1. Identify and list items to be grouped: "What did you see (hear, note)? What items are shown in this picture?"
2. Identify items that can be grouped together: "Which items seem to belong together?"

What kinds of hands-on activities can teachers use to help students develop thinking skills through social studies instruction?

3. State characteristics of items that belong together: "Why do they belong to-gether? How are they alike?"
4. Label the group: "What is a good name or label for the group? Why is that a good name (label)?"

Problem Solving and Inquiry   Concept development, extension, and enrichment may be fostered through inquiry and problem solving, particularly when the concepts being considered are ones like justice, equality, democracy, prejudice, and others that grow in meaning as they are encountered in differing contexts. The meaning of concepts is clarified in ongoing activities, put to immediate use, and used to pose questions, gather and process data, and state conclusions, as the following example from a unit on prejudice illustrates.

1. Define the problem: "What is prejudice, and how does it affect us?"
2. Pose questions (or hypotheses) to guide study: "What is prejudice? What causes it? What are different types of prejudice? What are the effects on oneself and on others? How can prejudice be reduced?"
3. Collect and process relevant information: "What information do we have on each question? How shall we organize it? Can we use the headings *causes, types, effects,* and *ways to reduce?*"
4. State a conclusion: "What can we conclude about causes, types, effects, and ways to reduce?"
5. Suggest needs for further study: "What new questions do you have? How can we find answers to them?"

Developing Concept Clusters and Themes   The strategies just described may be used to develop concept clusters and themes. Each concept in a cluster or in a theme must be given special attention. For example, the cluster of concepts included in *landforms*—plains, hills, plateaus, mountains—may be developed by identifying examples and nonexamples of plains, then hills, and so on. In addition, differences between plains and hills and between plateaus and mountains should be identified. Focusing attention on clusters of concepts allows meaningful comparisons to be made between pairs of concepts; moreover, meaningful examples and nonexamples are contained within the clusters. For instance, after identifying examples of plains, students may identify hills and plateaus as nonexamples. Another advantage is that relationships among the concepts in a cluster make for meaningful learning that promotes the ability to recall, recognize, and apply concepts. This may be illustrated by the comment of a student: "As you go across the plains you come to hills and then on to plateaus and finally to mountains—the Rocky Mountains."

Themes such as ways of living on the frontier, the westward movement, equality for minority groups, and extending civil rights to all groups call for concept development plus extending learning activities within a unit of instruction. For example, the theme of extending civil rights to all groups calls for initial instruction on civil rights, followed by a series of learning activities on the struggles of various groups to achieve them. Some teachers may employ a historical strategy, others may focus on the 1960s civil rights movement, and still others may focus on a particular group to illustrate the theme.

Providing a Series of Activities   This procedure, which makes use of many concept-development strategies, begins with concrete activities and moves to pictorial and symbolic activities. Table 11.1 (p. 348) shows such a sequence of activities for development of time concepts in the early grades. Figure 11.1 shows a diagnostic tool that teachers may use in the upper elementary or middle school grades to determine which time concepts students have mastered and which ones they need to develop.

Developing Generalizations

Generalizations are summarizing and concluding statements based on information and indicating a relationship among concepts. They have many uses in social studies: to generate questions or hypotheses to guide study, to explain human behavior and relationships, or to build a model or a theory. For instance, students who comprehend the generalization "people use resources to meet basic needs" may then ask, "How

■ FIGURE 11.1

Evaluating Students' Mastery of Time Concepts

Which Time Concepts Do You Know and Use?

Clock time:

____ hour	____ half-hour	____ quarter-hour	____ minute
____ second	____ morning	____ noon	____ afternoon
____ evening	____ midnight	____ A.M.	____ P.M.
____ time zones	____ Prime Meridian	____ International Date Line	

Calendar time:

____ day	____ week	____ month	____ year
____ decade	____ score	____ generation	____ century
____ millennium	____ calendar year	____ fiscal year	____ school year
____ seasons	____ holidays	____ period	____ era
____ epoch	____ A.D.	____ B.C.	

Chronology:

____ then	____ now	____ soon	____ before
____ after	____ next	____ yesterday	____ today
____ tomorrow	____ past	____ present	____ future
____ movement	____ trend	____ ancient	____ medieval
____ modern	____ prehistoric time	____ geological time	____ time line
____ time chart	____ chronology		

do people in other countries use resources to meet their needs for food, shelter, and clothing?"

Generalizations range from limited statements that apply to a particular culture, time, or place to statements that have universal applicability. For example, a generalization about the causes of the Civil War is bound by time and place, but the law of

---

■ TABLE 11.1

Activities for Developing Time Concepts

Clock Time

- Use a metronome or clock with second hand to demonstrate the length of a second and the seconds in a minute.
- Count the number of seconds or minutes it takes to complete activities such as walking around the classroom, writing one's name, reading an assignment, and drawing a picture.
- Count the number of seconds it takes for a second hand to go around a clock face and a minute sand timer to empty.
- Use a kitchen timer to demonstrate half-hour and hour and to set the amount of time allotted to various periods or activities.
- Discuss and compare the number of minutes in class periods, recess, lunch period, favorite TV programs, and home activities.
- Read and write time words and numerals such as *minutes, hour, two o'clock, 2:00 P.M.,* and *noon.*

Calendar Time

- Discuss hours in a day; major parts of a day including time spent in school, after school, and while sleeping; and time from noon to midnight and from midnight to noon.
- Keep a record of a unit activity each school day and a personal activity over the weekend, and arrange them in order to show activities for one week.
- Refer frequently to the classroom calendar posted on a bulletin board, using terms such as *yesterday, today, tomorrow, last Friday, two weeks ago,* and so on.
- Teach and review names of days, months, seasons, and major holidays.
- Make time lines that show events during a week, month, or year.

Chronology

- Discuss sequence or order of the daily class schedule, days of the week, months of the year, the seasons, holidays, events in the lives of children, and changes in the neighborhood or community.
- Arrange pictures of babies, toddlers, nursery and elementary school children, teenagers, and adults in order from youngest to oldest.
- Use, read, and write terms such as *first, second, past, present, future, before, after, next, later, sequence or order of events, yesterday, today, tomorrow, two years later,* and *time line.*
- Make time charts or time lines of events in the community.

supply and demand has universal application. Some generalizations are conditional and take an if–then form: "If the supply of an item increases, then the price will decrease (other things being equal)." A cause–effect relationship is implied in if–then generalizations.

Students should learn to distinguish between descriptive generalizations that are value-neutral and prescriptive generalizations that are valuative, just as they are expected to distinguish between statements of fact and opinion. Most generalizations in social studies are descriptive, as they are in the social sciences. They take a form such as "Population growth, industrialization, and urbanization are among the causes of environmental problems." Fewer in number but of equal importance are prescriptive, or value-laden, generalizations. They include a preference, demand, value, or value principle, such as "Population growth, industrialization, and urbanization must be controlled if the environment is to be improved." Notice that in descriptive generalizations the emphasis is on *what is;* in prescriptive generalizations the emphasis is on *what ought to be.* The implication is to clarify the basis or standards and related evidence for the prescription or recommendation.

Teachers may focus on the development of different types and levels of generalization by providing for three types of study. The descriptive and widely applicable (or universal) generalizations may be developed through studies that draw samples of data from selected times, places, or cultures. Students analyze the data to identify common elements that form a basis for generalizations. Descriptive and limited generalizations may be developed in units that focus on particular times, places, and cultures. Students bring together the particular features characteristic of places such as our community, Israel, or China, and they formulate appropriate time-, place-, and culture-bound generalizations. Prescriptive generalizations call for use of decision-making processes. Students consider alternatives and consequences and make a decision or a judgment regarding the best alternative in light of goals.

When designing instruction in making generalizations, teachers can take an inductive approach (moving from collecting of data to making generalizations about it) or a deductive approach (moving from a reasoned generalization to collecting data that supports it). Here is how each process can be approached:

Inductive Process

1. Collect, organize, and examine data.
2. Identify common elements and what is generally true for the data.
3. State a generalization based on common or general elements.
4. Check the generalization against all data to make sure that it is sound.

Deductive Process

1. Present the generalization to the group.
2. Present supporting data, cases, or evidence.
3. Refer students to additional sources of data, and ask them to find more support.
4. Test the generalization against all the data.

Generalizations can also be gained through activities in problem solving and decision making. These step-by-step procedures show how:

Problem-Solving Process

1. Define the problem to be investigated.
2. State a hypothesis or a question to guide the investigation.
3. Collect, organize, and evaluate data.
4. Using the data, test the hypothesis or the answer to the question.
5. State a generalization (a conclusion) based on the data.
6. Double-check the generalization to make sure it is sound.

Decision-Making Process

1. Define the issue that needs a decision.
2. Clarify the standards and values on which the decision will be based.
3. Consider alternative decisions.
4. Consider the consequences (positive and negative) of each alternative.
5. Select the best alternative in terms of the chosen standards or values.
6. State a prescriptive generalization based on the outcome of this process.

Providing a variety of activities related to one generalization enriches students' learning and provides a context in which meaningful generalizations take root. For example, to encourage students to generalize about how rules and laws protect and govern people, you might discuss familiar rules and laws that everyone follows in the students' community, have students gather information from their reading that pertains to rules and laws in other communities, show videos about rules and laws, and discuss particular rules and laws such as those designed to promote health and safety and to guard individual rights. This variety of learning experiences will prepare students to answer well when you ask, "In general, what can we say about rules and laws in communities?"

Generalizations can be broadened and refined as students gain more knowledge and skill. For example, a generalization about using resources to meet human needs may begin with local uses and move to state, national, and worldwide uses. Figure 11.2 shows how concepts and related generalizations progress over a typical K–8 course of study in social studies.

The meaning of concepts and generalizations should grow deeper and broader as students move from level to level and encounter them in new settings. For example, the concept of community may begin with one's own community, be expanded to include other communities, and eventually embrace the idea of national and world community.

Inferring, Predicting, and Hypothesizing

These three interrelated skills involve applying main ideas or principles. They are similar in that they emphasize going beyond the data at hand to identify and consider consequences, cause–effect and other relationships, supporting data, reasons, principles, and assumptions.

To *infer* is to draw a possible consequence, conclusion, or implication from a set of facts or premises; students often must read between the lines, since the inferred idea is typically not explicit. Inferring frequently follows interpreting a reading selection or

■ **FIGURE 11.2**

Development of Concepts and Related Generalizations, K–8

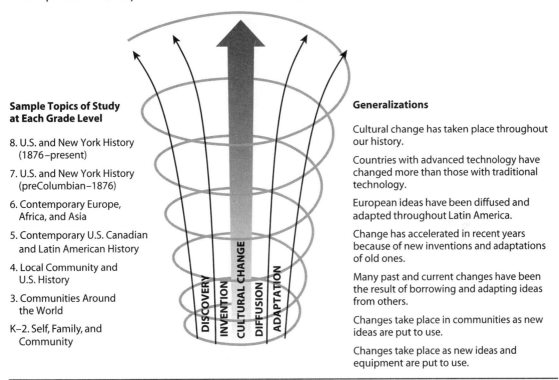

**Sample Topics of Study
at Each Grade Level**

8. U.S. and New York History
   (1876–present)

7. U.S. and New York History
   (preColumbian–1876)

6. Contemporary Europe,
   Africa, and Asia

5. Contemporary U.S. Canadian
   and Latin American History

4. Local Community and
   U.S. History

3. Communities Around
   the World

K–2. Self, Family, and
   Community

DISCOVERY   INVENTION   CULTURAL CHANGE   DIFFUSION   ADAPTATION

Generalizations

Cultural change has taken place throughout
our history.

Countries with advanced technology have
changed more than those with traditional
technology.

European ideas have been diffused and
adapted throughout Latin America.

Change has accelerated in recent years
because of new inventions and adaptations
of old ones.

Many past and current changes have been
the result of borrowing and adapting ideas
from others.

Changes take place in communities as new
ideas are put to use.

Changes take place as new ideas and
equipment are put to use.

other source of information. Inferences should be logical, reasonable, and applicable
in a given situation. Questions to ask students to guide inferring include these:

Why do you suppose _____ (that happened, they were surprised, they arrived at that conclusion)?

What do you suppose someone would do _____ (in that situation, if faced
by that problem)?

Why do you think that _____ (they felt happy, the writer is biased)?

To *predict* is to forecast or anticipate what may happen under certain conditions.
Like an inference, a prediction should be reasonable and supported by evidence, but
one must usually wait to see if it is accurate—for example, a prediction about an election or a change in population. Students may be guided by questions such as these:

What do you think will happen if _____ (more people move to suburbs,
acid rain is not reduced)?

What do you estimate the _____ (school enrollment, state population)
will be in ten years?

What do you think will happen if _____ (the school budget is cut, the
school day and the school year are extended)?

Why is concept development an exercise in using thinking skills? How does explaining different types of concepts encourage critical thinking?

A hypothesis is usually more general than an inference or a prediction and should apply to all similar cases; it should also be testable. To *hypothesize* is to state a tentative generalization or question that shows how two or more items are related. Hypotheses may be stated as questions, if–then statements, or declarative statements. The following are all examples of hypotheses:

- What is generally believed to be a good location for cities?
- If a place has waterways, then it is a good location for a city.
- Cities are usually located near waterways.

Notice that each example indicates a condition (location of cities) and related items (near waterways), and that each may be tested by gathering data. Questions to guide students' hypothesizing include these:

What are the main causes of _____ (urban growth, air pollution)?

What are generally believed to be _____ (the advantages of division of labor, the reasons people moved westward)?

If people live in _____ (deserts, mountains, cities), what problems can they expect?

In Table 11.2 we present a method for moving from procedure to illustrative questions for predicting and hypothesizing (adopted from one proposed by Taba et al., 1971). Select a topic, and develop your own set of questions. The lesson plan on page 354 develops the thinking skills of inferring, predicting, and hypothesizing. The plan illustrates how students can move to higher levels of thinking by predicting, and then analyzing consequences.

Analyzing and Synthesizing Information

Analyzing and synthesizing are high-level intellectual processes that go beyond the development of information, concepts, and generalizations. They are used in social studies to reorganize content and to bring it together in ways that are new to students. For

352

■ **TABLE 11.2**

Guiding Students in Making Predictions and Hypotheses

Procedure	Focusing Questions	Examples
State prediction. *or*	What will happen if _____?	What will our city be like in the year 2025 if urban growth continues at the current rate?
State hypothesis.	If _____, then_____? What usually happens when _____?	What usually happens to cities with rapid growth?
Give reasons or data that support the prediction or the hypothesis.	What is the basis for your prediction? for your hypothesis?	Why do you think our city will be like that? Why do you say that usually happens to cities?
State conditions necessary for prediction to occur. *or*	What conditions are necessary for your prediction to happen?	What conditions do you assume in saying our city will change in that way?
Identify needed data and data-gathering procedures to test hypothesis.	What data do we need to test the hypothesis? What procedures should we use?	What data do we need to show the usual effects of urban growth? How should we gather data?

example, students analyze environmental problems by breaking them down into causes and effects; they may then present the causes and effects in a new way, perhaps in a flow chart that relates each cause to its effects on people and other living things.

To *analyze* is to identify the parts, elements, relationships, or principles presented in reading materials, on maps, in audiovisual materials, and in other sources. Questions to ask students to guide analysis include these:

> ■ Curiosity is the one permanent and certain characteristic of a vigorous mind.
> **—Samuel Johnson**

What are the main parts of this _____ (story, picture, map)? How are they related?

What _____ (concepts, activities, regions, time periods) are used to organize this material?

What is the central idea? What ideas are organized around it?

To *synthesize* is to bring parts together into a meaningful whole, to create a new product, or to form a unified structure around a concept, a theme, or some other element. The synthesis may take the form of a model, report, map, chart, story, display, or dramatic presentation. Such questions as the following may be used to emphasize creativity while guiding synthesis:

How can we show the main _____ (regions, types of work) in a new way?

What _____ (concept, theme, main idea) can we use to organize the parts?

What form of presentation should we use? Booklet? Chart? Map? Mural? Other?

LESSON PLAN *The Impact of Innovations*

Objective
To identify recent technological innovations and describe their possible consequences

Materials
Magazines and books in the learning center and in the library

Introduction
Discuss past innovations such as radio and television. Ask students to describe what effects these innovations have had on them and on members of their families.

Development
Ask students to identify recent innovations. Guide discussion of such innovations as

cellular phones	digital cameras	e-mail
Internet	software programs	fiber optics

Discuss each innovation in terms of (1) what it is and (2) its effects on human activities.

Divide the class into groups to research the innovations, with primary emphasis on their effects or consequences and future uses.

Ask members of each group to report to the class. Record findings on a retrieval chart with the following headings: *Innovation, Uses in the Future,* and *Consequences.*

Conclusion and Evaluation
Ask students to summarize the future uses and consequences of each innovation.

Ask students to rank the innovations in terms of future usefulness and desirable consequences for human welfare, giving reasons for their ranking. If differences in ranking arise, organize teams to marshal evidence and present arguments for their position.

Evaluate students' learning by noting their contributions and the quality of their reasoning in projecting trends, noting consequences, and ranking the innovations.

Follow-up
Ask students to prepare individual reports on an innovation of their choice in which consequences are analyzed in terms of questions such as these:

What are possible benefits? What are possible negative effects?

How might the innovation affect family life? How might it affect you personally?

What effects might there be on the quality of life in our country? in other countries?

Will it lead to permanent or temporary changes in our lifestyles? Give reasons for your answer.

Finally, do you think the innovation is desirable or undesirable? Give reasons for your position.

Ask students to select an innovation or a trend and make a futures wheel.

To synthesize after an analysis has been made, one simply moves ahead to determine a new way to combine the parts identified in the analysis. For example, after major types of land use are identified, as shown in Table 11.3, the teacher may ask what new ways can be used to show major types of land use. After considering a map, diagram, mural, or other form of presentation, students may synthesize information by making a new map combining themes or items from the material they analyzed. A clear understanding of the parts to be synthesized is prerequisite to combining them in a new way.

Evaluating: An Ongoing Process

Evaluating is an *ongoing* (formative) process that continues from the beginning of an activity through its culmination, as one asks: How well am I doing? How can I improve? Evaluating is also a *capstone* (summative) process that occurs on a higher cog-

---

■ TABLE 11.3

Guiding Students in Analyzing and Synthesizing Information

Procedure	Focusing Questions	Application
Analyzing		
Identify useful ways to break the problem into parts.	How can we break the problem into parts? What main parts (types, reasons, causes) should be studied?	How can we break down our question on urban land use? What are the main types of land use in cities?
Define each part clearly.	What does each part include? Do any key terms need to be defined?	How can we define commercial, industrial, residential, and recreational land use?
Identify and organize data related to each part.	What information do we have about each part? How are these parts related?	What data can we classify under each type of land use?
State summary, conclusion, or explanation based on the analysis.	What does our analysis show? What can we conclude?	Who can summarize the types of land use in cities in order from greatest to least? How might we explain the differences?
Synthesizing		
Identify the organizing idea and the form of presentation.	How can we present our findings in a new way?	How can we organize our findings on urban land use?
Decide on a way to present findings, and proceed.	What plan(s) should we make?	What organizing idea is best? What form of presentation is best? Why?

nitive level than the processes discussed earlier. To evaluate is to make a judgment of the merit or worth of an activity or object in terms of selected criteria. Critical thinking is used to define criteria, apply them, gather related evidence, and make a judgment; without these steps, an opinion, rather than a reasoned judgment, will result.

Focusing questions are needed for two different types of evaluation. In the first type internal standards are used to appraise reports, reading selections, and other materials. Typical standards are accuracy, consistency in use of terms, soundness of arguments, and relation of conclusions to evidence. Guiding questions for internal evaluation are shown here:

How can _____ (our report, map; this graph, plan) be improved? Is it accurate? well organized? meaningful? useful for our purpose?

How accurate (adequate, useful, consistent, biased) is this _____ (document, diagram, flow chart, report)?

To what extent are the _____ (conclusions, generalizations, inferences) supported by evidence? What logical fallacies are evident?

In the second type of evaluation external standards are used. These may be objectives, criteria, or a recognized standard of excellence. Examples of external evaluation are (1) using objectives of urban renewal as criteria to appraise plans, (2) using freedom of speech to judge the conduct of a meeting, and (3) using one model conservation program as a standard to appraise another. Guiding questions for external evaluation are shown here:

To what extent will this _____ (plan, program, type of action) lead to the stated goals?

Which of the alternatives is most desirable in terms of _____ (individual benefits, group benefits, objectives)?

To what extent were standards of _____ (justice, freedom, personal security) upheld during this period?

How does this _____ (report, antipollution proposal, airport, political system) compare with the model of an outstanding one?

The strategy for evaluation presented in Table 11.4 begins by identifying and defining what is to be appraised, then determining the standards or criteria that should be used. In practice these phases may be joined together, providing students understand the focus of the evaluation. Next, evidence is gathered and interpreted to show the extent to which the defined standards are met. The next step is necessary if alternatives—different plans, materials, or proposals—are being assessed. Possible outcomes or consequences of each alternative are considered, and the one that is most desirable in light of the standards is identified. Finally, the quality or merit of the item(s) under appraisal should be judged and suggestions for improvement made as appropriate.

■ **TABLE 11.4**

Guiding Students in Making Evaluations

Procedure	Focusing Questions	Application
Identify and define the focus of evaluation.	What is to be appraised? Why should _____ be assessed?	What are the proposals for recycling waste materials?
Identify and define standards of appraisal.	What standards (values, criteria) should be used?	What standards can we use to judge goals? benefits? other?
Collect data related to each standard.	What is the evidence? What data can we find for each standard?	What evidence is available on the possible benefits or other standards used to judge them?
Identify possible outcomes (effects, consequences) of each proposal.	What are likely outcomes of each proposal? Which one will have the most desirable outcomes?	What effects or outcomes are expected?
Make a judgment, including suggestions for improvement.	Which one best meets the standards? How might it be improved?	In general, which proposal is best? Why? How can it be improved?

■ A Unifying Model of Teaching

This section presents a model that is useful in group work; it can also be used to generate individual activities. It incorporates a variety of thinking skills. Like any model, this one should be used flexibly, varying the steps or phases to guide creative study of the topic at hand and to avoid the pitfalls of a regimented, step-by-step procedure. The major phases are as follows:

1. Define questions and problems to guide study.
2. Recall information and hypothesize.
3. Clarify the steps of the procedure.
4. Find, interpret, appraise, and classify data.
5. Process information and make generalizations.
6. Evaluate procedures and outcomes.

Defining Questions and Problems

As you introduce or deal with problems that arise in a unit, you will spare yourself time and trouble by clearly defining questions and problems. Such questions and problems will help pupils recognize and understand what is to be studied. To begin a unit, select materials especially geared to stimulate thinking. Pictures, maps, objects, and other resources can highlight significant questions or problems. After the students have examined the materials, they should discuss the questions or problems to be attacked first. As initial problems are defined and clarified, they may be listed on the chalkboard or on charts, as illustrated in Table 11.5.

Recalling Information and Hypothesizing

This phase should be both systematic and creative. As the teacher asks questions, students may recall both previous information and information introduced during the initiation of the unit: "What can you recall about this topic?" "What have you learned before that we might use?" "How is it like other topics we have studied?" The teacher may next ask questions designed to elicit hypotheses: "What ideas do you have on this topic?" "What do you think we will find?" "What answers might we find to the questions we have listed?"

The objectives of these two sets of questions are to retrieve information related to questions posed by the group during definition of the problem, to get students to state hypotheses regarding what they may find, to identify misconceptions they may have, and to motivate the search for data. The following examples indicate the nature of students' hypotheses.

In a unit on the post office, students discussed the question "What happens to letters that are put in mailboxes?" Children's comments were as follows:

"A mail carrier picks them up. Then they are taken to the right place."

"Wait! They have to be sorted by somebody. I think they are taken downtown. Maybe they are sorted by workers or a machine."

"There must be a plan or a system. Then a mail carrier can deliver them."

In a unit on the westward movement, the group was considering this problem on travel routes: Check the relief map of the United States, and plan a route to California from St. Joseph, Missouri; then check to see if your proposed route is the same as one of those used by early settlers. The students made the following hypotheses:

■ TABLE 11.5

Sample of Introductory Unit Questions

Work at Home	Boonesboro	Community History
What jobs are there?	Why was it built?	Who were the first settlers?
What skills are needed?	Who built it?	What were the first buildings like?
What can children do?	Where was it?	Where was the first school?
What do others do?	When was it built?	Where were the first streets?
	How was it built?	When was the railroad begun?
	How did people travel to it?	What changes have taken place?

"Go straight across the plains and mountains to San Francisco. If you go this way, you have to find mountain passes through the Rockies and Sierras."

"Go along the Missouri to the Platte River and on to the coast across Utah and Nevada. If you would keep close to rivers, you could get water and there would not be many steep grades. I heard that some railroads and highways are built along water level routes."

"Go along south to Santa Fe and on to Los Angeles across New Mexico and Arizona. This would be a good route in the winter."

"Why couldn't we start our trip in St. Louis? Then we could use boats all the way to San Francisco."

A group of middle school students and their teacher, considering a study of the 1920s, decided to brainstorm topics that might lead to a hypothesis that could guide a three-week period of study. The teacher began the brainstorming by mentioning President Coolidge and laissez-faire economics—that business, if left alone, would act in a way that would benefit the whole country. A student blurted out that the 1920s concerned gangsters and alcohol. An avid sports fan wanted to mention the 1927 Yankees. A student who had recently become interested in cars thought that Henry Ford was significant. The class offered other ideas, some of which were not of the period; the teacher acknowledged these but placed them to the side as not pertinent. After some discussion the class developed the following generalization to use as a hypothesis: "For many Americans, the 1920s was a time of stable politics, economic prosperity, and changes in American culture." Although some students felt that their interests were not specifically addressed, they did agree that the hypothesis provided sufficient flexibility for a broad range of research and exploration.

Teachers sometimes ask, "Should hypotheses be proposed for every problem that arises in social studies?" No! When students lack the background for hypothesizing, the teacher should begin by studying the questions noted during definition of the problem.

Clarifying the Procedure

This phase, directed by the teacher or planned by the group, sets out ways to gather information, sources of information, and assignment of responsibilities. Questions such as the following are raised: How shall we proceed? What are the next steps? How can we obtain needed information? What sources of information should be used? Should any jobs be assigned to individuals or small groups? Does everyone know what he or she has to do?

Give students a sense of the wide range of resources that they can explore. They include the following:

newspaper clippings	the library	study trips	films
encyclopedias	magazines	textbooks	pictures
maps and globes	the Internet	interviews	lectures
videotapes			

As students gather and organize information, you can suggest several techniques to make their work more efficient and interesting. These techniques include the following:

asking questions	demonstrating	note taking	drawing
collecting objects	experimenting	observing	mapping
constructing	writing to learn	interviewing	outlining
gathering reading material			

Armed with resources and learning techniques, students can plan their learning activities.

Finding, Interpreting, Appraising, and Classifying Information

With a definite procedure in place, students gather and interpret data to answer questions, solve problems, or test hypotheses. They use observation and study skills to collect data. Terms are defined; pictures, maps, and other data sources are interpreted; comparisons and contrasts are made; and information is evaluated for accuracy and relevance. Students should develop the habit of cross-checking information in different sources. Sometimes facts can be difficult to pin down. At times a video may need to be shown again, a section of a reference reread, or one reference checked against another. An expert may be interviewed to resolve a contradiction in facts or problems in interpretation of data.

As students gather information, they might list it on the chalkboard or record it on retrieval. Directions for making something or steps in a sequence may be noted on a chart or on the chalkboard. An outline, a set of notes, or simply sharing and grouping information may be adequate. The objective is to organize information to make meaningful generalizations.

Generalizing

Generalizing frequently follows the previously discussed phases, although other concluding thinking processes may be used. For example, after interpreting data related to population growth in their city, students may draw and check inferences about possible environmental effects, state generalizations about the main causes of growth, make predictions about future growth and future ecological problems, and synthesize findings in graphs or maps. For example, in a unit on our changing community, one group moved beyond interpretations and made the following generalizations and predictions:

> *"Changes have been faster in recent years. Some changes were made to take care of population growth. Some changes were caused by inventions."*

> *"We predict that school enrollment will be 23,000 in ten years. Population will probably be around 112,000."*

In a unit on environmental problems, students proceeded to infer, generalize, predict, and synthesize as follows:

> *"Feelings about flood control and environmental problems seem to be high enough to get some action. Some people seem to be changing their ideas about what is important."*

> *"The proposed legislation on environmental problems will be passed. If it is passed, the dam will probably be constructed at point A on the map, because it is best for preserving wildlife."*

Students then made a map to show location of flooded areas, points at which damage occurred to wildlife and to people, and possible sites for a dam.

Evaluating Processes and Outcomes

Evaluation is important to each phase of instruction. For example, as problems are defined, the teacher may ask, Is the problem clear? Have main parts of the problem been considered? As procedures are discussed, the teacher may ask, Have good sources of information been noted? Does each individual know what to do? Similarly, the following questions may be asked during the classifying, interpreting, and further processing of information: Are facts related to main ideas? Are relationships shown? Have we selected the best means of summarizing information? Using clues from observation, the teacher raises questions and makes comments that help students appraise and improve their work. Table 11.6 gives points to consider in teacher evaluation and in student self-evaluation.

■ TABLE 11.6
Evaluation by Students and by Teachers

Questions for Appraising Sources	Questions for Appraising Information	Questions for Appraising Reports
Is it related to the topic?	Is it related to our questions?	Does the title describe the topic?
Is it recent enough for our purposes?	Is the source reliable?	Does the introduction set the stage?
Is it reliable? valid?	Is it consistent with related ideas?	Are the ideas in good order?
Is it published by a special interest group? Might this give the information a particular slant?	Is it supported by evidence?	Are main ideas supported by facts?
	Is it too general to be useful?	Are opinions distinguished from facts?
Does it contain enough information?	Is it advanced for a worthy cause?	Do conclusions tie ideas together?
Can it be checked against reliable sources?		

◾ Conclusion

Thinking skills are at the heart of social studies education. These skills help students understand, explore, and create knowledge. In both elementary and middle school classrooms, these skills are prerequisite to making advancements in critical thinking, decision making, creative thinking, and problem solving and inquiry. In addition to using various modes of thinking, students should be guided to "think about their thinking," that is, to learn how they think and how to become clear thinkers.

Social studies allows teachers to employ a teaching model that gradually develops and deepens the thinking skills that, over the course of a K–8 program, will enable students to make informed and reasoned decisions. This model lets students build thinking skills by generating, organizing, and interpreting data; forming concepts and developing generalizations; and further refining their thinking skills by inferring, predicting, hypothesizing, analyzing, and synthesizing information. In a capstone experience, students reflect on and evaluate their use of thinking skills.

 Questions, Activities, and Evaluation

1. Select a unit of your choice and note how you might encourage use of the following: (a) critical thinking, (b) creative thinking, (c) decision making, (d) problem solving or inquiry. Include specific examples of questions and activities that will emphasize the unique characteristics of each mode.

2. Review the section on generating, organizing, and interpreting data and note questions and activities you might use to build a solid base of knowledge. Which suggestions for recalling, collecting data, comparing, interpreting, and classifying might you use?

3. Select a concept of a concrete object, such as mayor, and a concept of an abstract quality, such as concern for others. Indicate the strategy you would use to develop each one. Explain why you selected the strategy.

4. Identify a main idea or generalization you wish to develop in a unit of your choice. Select a strategy for developing it, and outline how you would use it. Explain why you selected the strategy.

5. Review the sections on analyzing, synthesizing, and evaluating, and indicate how you might develop them in a unit. Use the suggested teaching strategies as guides to planning. What changes, if any, do you think might be made in the strategies? Why?

6. Present in outline form a plan for using the teaching model presented near the end of this chapter. What changes, if any, do you think should be made in it? Why?

7. Select any three activities presented in this chapter, and modify them to fit a unit you plan to teach. Explain why you chose them over the others.

8. Write to the following organizations to get information on activity booklets to develop thinking skills: Thinking Caps, Inc., P.O. Box 26239, Phoenix, AZ 85068; Critical Thinking Press and Software, P.O. Box 448, Pacific Grove, CA 93950.

References

Baer, J. (1993). *Creativity and divergent thinking.* Hillsdale, NJ: Erlbaum. A task-specific approach.

Blythe, T., & Gardner, H. (1990). A school for all intelligences. *Educational Leadership, 47,* 33–37. Seven intelligences discussed.

Bruner, J. S., Goodnow, J. J., & Austin, G. A. (1962). *A study of thinking.* New York: Wiley.

Costa, A. L. (Ed.). (1991). *Developing minds: A resource book for teaching thinking* (Vol. 1), and *Programs for teaching thinking.* Alexandria, VA: Association for Supervision and Curriculum Development. Skills, models, strategies, metacognition, and programs.

Dewey, J. (1910, 1933). *How we think.* Boston: Heath. Classic analysis.

Gardner, H. *How are kids? Multiple intelligences (MI) in the classroom* (Video). Cited in "The Bookshelf" in *Education Week,* Vol. 15, Number 37, June 5, 1996.

Levitt, G., et al. (1992). Columbus and the exploration of the Americas: Ideas for thematic units in the elementary grades. *Social Studies and the Young Learner, 4,* 19–22.

Lumpkin, C. (1992). Effects of teaching critical thinking skills on the critical thinking ability, achievement, and retention of social studies content by fifth and sixth graders. *Journal of Research in Education, 2,* 8–12.

Marshall, P. (1991). Critical thinking for primary learners in social studies. *Southern Social Studies Journal, 16,* 2–15.

Marzano, R. J., et al. (1988). *Dimensions of thinking.* Alexandria, VA: Association for Supervision and Curriculum Development. Processes and skills of thinking.

McKinney, C. W., & Edgington, W. D. (1997). Issues related to teaching generalizations in elementary social studies. *The Social Studies, 88,* 78–82.

Olsen, D. G. (1995). "Less" can be "more" in the promotion of thinking. *Social Education, 59,* 130–34.

Pellow, R. A. (1992). Using thinking skills to solve geographic riddles. *Social Studies Journal, 19,* 9–12.

Reissman, R. (1994). Thinking skills. *Learning, 22,* 47.

Shiveley, J. M., & VanFossen, P. J. (1999). Critical thinking and the Internet: Opportunities for the social studies classroom. *The Social Studies, 90,* 42–46.

Sims, R. R., & Sims, S. J. (Eds.). (1995). *The importance of learning styles.* Westport, CT: Greenwood Publishing Group.

Taba, H., Durkin, M. C., Fraenkel, J. R., & McNaughton, A. H. (1971). *A teacher's handbook to elementary social studies* (2nd ed.). Reading, MA: Addison-Wesley.

Torney-Purta, J. (1991). Schema theory and cognitive psychology: Implications for social studies. *Theory and Research in Social Education, 19,* 189–210. Procedures; concept maps.

VanFossen, P. J., & Shiveley, J. M. (1997). Things that make you go "Hmmm . . .": Creating inquiry "problems" in the elementary social studies classroom. *Social Studies, 88,* 71–77.

Wilen, W, W., & Philips, J. A. (1995). Teaching critical thinking: A metacognitive approach. *Social Education, 59,* 135–38.

Wright, I. (1995). Making critical thinking possible: Options for teachers. *Social Education, 59,* 139–43.

Chapter 12

Developing Creative Thinking through Expressive Experiences

Chapter Objective

To describe social studies teaching and learning strategies and activities that will develop students' creativity

Focusing Questions

- What expressive experiences are useful in developing students' creative thinking and their appreciation of creativity in our own and other cultures?

- How can creative writing be used to stimulate and nurture creative thinking?

- How can role-taking experiences—dramatic representation, role playing, simulations—be used creatively?

- How can experiences in music, arts, and crafts be used in social studies to foster creativity?

- What types of construction activities are useful in developing creativity?

■ Motivating Students through Creativity

Children and young adults enjoy expressive experiences. Effective teachers involve their students in expressive experiences throughout the school year. In the primary grades, students who are studying communities might use creative thinking to develop a diorama of an ideal neighborhood in the year 2100, complete with shopping malls, government buildings, theater complexes, schools, and so on. In the elementary grades, students who are studying world cultures might read about violation of children's rights and think of creating a world organization that facilitates communication among children and young adults. This organization might counter human rights violations against children by enlisting elementary school students around the world to write poetry about human rights issues to targeted political leaders. At the middle school, a group of students, after reading about the homeless in American society, might seek assistance from their social studies, language arts, and music teachers to write a series of songs describing the history of homelessness in America. This idea originated in social studies class as the students listened to songs about the Great Depression. These are but a few of the ideas generated by excited students expressing themselves creatively.

Given the cultural and ethnic richness of today's communities and classrooms, the opportunities for creative and expressive experiences are greater than ever. In classrooms with prominent cultural diversity, for example, teachers should encourage students to demonstrate facets of home culture in creative and expressive experiences. For example, a recent immigrant from Russia may enrich a particular social studies unit by demonstrating Russian folk dances. Also, when some children experience difficulties expressing themselves in writing, creative and expressive experiences can

■ What we have to learn
to do, we learn by doing.
—**Aristotle**

365

help them attain success as they acquire more knowledge and skills. Teachers find that students at all grade levels respond positively when asked to be creative. Teachers can encourage students to be creative by using creative methods of instruction themselves and by fostering a risk-free classroom climate in which expression is accepted as a valuable method of gaining social studies insights.

This chapter focuses on two dimensions of creativity—creative thinking and appreciation of creativity in human behavior. Creative thinking is nurtured as students make plans, put information to new uses, and express their thoughts and feelings in new ways. Appreciation for the creativity of others is developed as students discover the richness of aesthetic expression in their own and other cultures. Activities that highlight originality, initiative, and delight in discovery will add zest to learning. As a student exclaimed: "There really are a lot of ways to be creative!"

Creative writing, role playing, simulations, and other expressive activities bring the "doing" part of thinking into play. They also provide new insights into the hopes, aspirations, and feelings of others as students identify with people in their own and other cultures.

Expressive activities may be used to individualize and personalize learning. When students write stories, poems, and songs, when they paint pictures and construct objects, and when they take various roles and engage in simulation, they individualize their learning by expressing themselves in ways that fit their learning styles. And they personalize their learning by expressing their own thoughts and feelings.

Expressive experiences involve both *impression* and *expression*. Students form impressions as they learn about creative expression of the people being studied in a unit. Then they in turn express their thoughts and feelings in response to the learning experiences in the unit. To avoid distorted and stereotypic portrayals of individuals and groups, teachers provide rich classroom impressions before asking students to express themselves creatively.

Planning is essential to make creative and expressive assignments a successful part of the social studies program. Teachers enjoy inserting creative activities into the curriculum when they experience success; students enjoy them when they are learning and having fun.

■ Creative Writing

Once students have some background and understanding in the pleasures of literature, they can create and share poems, stories, and descriptions. In the early grades, children may dictate their ideas to the teacher for recording on the chalkboard, charts, or a word processor. Computers with word processing capability allow young children to watch the display as the teacher enters their sentences; changes can be made easily, and a printout can be made for immediate use (Braun et al., 1998; Hoot and Silvern, 1988). In later grades, students can write their ideas or use the word processor to express their thoughts and feelings directly, using software such as *Bank Street Writer, Compupoem, Story Tree, MECC Writer, LogoWriter, Word Vision, Word Perfect Jr., The Writing Workshop, MultiScribe, Write,* and *The Writing Connection.*

Why is creative writing one of many ways students can demonstrate learning in social studies? How might you employ creative writing in the classroom?

As children discover patterns in the poetry enjoyed by people in other cultures—such as Japanese haiku, with a five/seven/five pattern of syllables, and tanka, with a five/seven/five/seven/seven pattern—they can use the patterns to express their thoughts, as illustrated by these examples:

Lofty mountain peak,
   Rising above the plateau,
      With valleys below.

Blowing on our door,
   The westerly winds offshore,
      Blow forevermore.

The shimmering sea
   Extensive coral kingdoms
      Soft white sand shoreline
         Sea stars on the rocky reefs
            Nature's splendor everywhere.

The rocky Maine coast
   Natural unspoiled splendor
      Magnificent views
         A seascape panorama
            Exhilarating delight.

Both teachers and students find the writing of a cinquain—a five-line stanza—to be an activity that sparks creative expression in units at all levels.[1]

Write a Cinquain!

First line—2 syllables	Small town,
Second line—4 syllables	Quiet, cozy,
Third line—6 syllables	A great place for living,
Fourth line—8 syllables	May it always be neighborly,
Fifth line—2 syllables	My home.

1. For a variety of forms, see Padgett (1987), Tsujimoto (1988), and Perry (1997).

Try teaming up a student who is experiencing difficulties in English with a proficient student who is familiar with the student's home language. Working in pairs, they can create social studies written work, using both English and their home language.

Students' creativity can be sparked by making puzzles, as shown in Figure 12.1. A variety of puzzles can be created by using computer programs such as *Puzzlemaster, Crossword Magic, Wordsearch,* and *Super Wordfind.* Authoring programs that do not require programming skills can also be used.

Art and music activities can be coordinated with writing projects. The following activity ideas can be customized to your students' grade level, abilities, and interests.

ACTIVITY IDEAS ➤ *Creative Writing*

➤ In small groups, have students write scripts for classroom plays, videos, or radio programs. These scripts should be closely related to a social studies topic, interweaving facts from the unit and students' imaginative interpretations. They might write about an evening at a campsite on the Oregon Trail, a firsthand experience of seeing the Wright brothers' first flight, participating in a march for women's suffrage, or a typical day in a Chinese village. Here are some tips:

Encourage students to concentrate on a few characters, rather than a large cast.

Recommend that they portray only a few events, rather than create a complicated plot.

Discuss ways in which personality is shown through what a person says.

Give students materials that describe the setting of the script. Then urge them to imagine how things look, smell, taste, feel, and sound there. They can incorporate these details into the script.

Help them strike a balance between using imagination and creating a realistic script. Draw them back to the social studies content as needed.

➤ Challenge students to write "in character," imagining what it would be like to sign the Declaration of Independence, travel the Trail of Tears, hear a speech by Martin Luther King Jr., or live during the Mali Empire. They might compose a letter that the character might send to a friend or write a diary entry about an important event. Remind students to write in the first person.

➤ Students might write an entirely fictional story set in a particular historical period and place. They can make up characters and a plot while incorporating period details of clothing, buildings, occupations, issues of the day, and so on.

➤ Have students write a creative description of a geographical location, a city, a culture, a person, a historical event, or some other social studies topic. Encourage them to use vivid language and a variety of sentence structures as they depict the overall features of the topic as well as fascinating details.

➤ Invite students to create a future scenario. Help them choose a time and place to envision. Before writing, they should gather enough information about trends that may lead to the scenario they imagine. The scenario should combine both research and some flights of fancy.

■ **FIGURE 12.1**

Making Social Studies Word Puzzles

Make a Pyramid of States

1. First letter of leading dairy state
2. Abbreviation of Old Line State
3. Abbreviation of the first state
4. Capital is Salt Lake City
5. Capital is Austin
6. The island state
7. The peninsula state
8. Capital is Lincoln
9. Capital is Baton Rouge
10. Most populated state

Make a Pyramid of States or Capitals

1.
2.
3.
4.
5.
6.
7.
8.
9.
10.

■ Role Taking through Dramatic Representation

Students who are recent immigrants, culturally diverse, or experiencing difficulties in the classroom may experience success in role taking, a learning mode that makes use of the home language as a transition into social studies learning and English proficiency.

Role taking enables students to identify with others in a variety of situations. These activities range from taking a role in a discussion to playing a role in a value-laden situation. This section focuses on role taking through dramatic representation.

Dramatic representation is an excellent substitute for firsthand experience with people, events, and situations far removed from the classroom. Although children cannot direct activities in a control tower at the airport, a railway classification yard, or a space station, they can participate in dramatic representation and thus gain insight into how such activities are directed. They cannot be firefighters, post office workers, pilots, colonists, pioneers, scouts, or early settlers, but they can identify with such people through dramatic activities.

Children are familiar with dramatic representation. They have used it before entering school during make-believe and imaginary play—"being" a mother, father, teacher, bus driver, firefighter, or airplane pilot. On entering school, children are eager to act out activities that they are studying and to portray their impressions of people, events, and situations.

Dramatic representation in school, however, is different from make-believe play at home. At home, children engage in dramatic play on their own; in school, they are guided so as to achieve desired outcomes. At home, children base their dramatic play on ideas and impressions they have gathered in an incidental fashion; in school, they gather specific background information and make it the basis for dramatic representation of social studies experiences. At home, make-believe play keeps children occupied; in school, dramatic representation develops concepts, skills, attitudes, and appreciations.

Dramatic representation offers excellent opportunities to evaluate children's learning. As teachers observe children in dramatic activities, they can appraise how children use concepts, grasp main ideas, express attitudes, identify with others, and express themselves.

Guiding Dramatic Activities

An essential first step in guiding dramatic activities is to develop adequate backgrounds of understanding so that children will dramatize events and activities authentically and creatively. Next, group planning is guided by questions such as these:

- What shall we dramatize?
- What space do we need?
- What materials do we need?
- What characters do we need?
- Who should take each part?

■ Always aim for achievement, and forget about success.
   —**Helen Hayes**

By beginning with *what* to do, the children can open up many possibilities without undue concern about *who* will take each part. Decisions on who will take each part may well be left until the last stage of planning, after the scope of the dramatic activity is clear.

After plans are made, the group should try out different suggestions, discuss them, and make changes as needed. During dramatic activity, the teacher should note needs, problems, and suggestions for improvement.

Adjustments may be needed to improve the value of the activity. For example, during a unit on the harbor, one group developed the following standards after a dramatic activity ran into difficulties because of "wrong boat sounds," "boats clogging the harbor," and "fire boats tugging liners in."

Running the Harbor

1. Share the boats with others.
2. Remember how each boat sounds.
3. Keep the harbor open for liners.
4. Let the tugs pull the liner in.
5. Listen to the captain's signals.

Following a skit involving life in Boonesboro, another group listed the following standards because several children had failed to dramatize their roles authentically.

Protecting Boonesboro

1. Sentinels should keep a sharp lookout.
2. The gates should be closed on the signal.
3. Gun loaders should load guns and not shoot.
4. Scouts should sneak out through the little gate.
5. Get gunpowder out of the powder horns.

Forms of Dramatic Representation

Dramatic representation takes a variety of forms in social studies, including dramatic play, dramatic rhythms, and role playing.

Dramatic play is used frequently in the early grades to portray activities in units on the home, school, neighborhood, and community. Dramatic play allows children to stage an informal and creative portrayal of experiences without a set pattern, refined staging, costumes, or memorization of parts.

Dramatic rhythms involve the interpretation of activities and events by means of rhythmic bodily movement. Dramatic rhythms differ from dramatic play in that rhythmic movement is emphasized. Dramatic rhythms differ from creative dance in that the child is interpreting something learned in social studies. They resemble creative dance in that children give their own personal interpretations, not those of others. For example, students exploring a unit entitled Social Change in the Sixties might give their personal interpretations to the Twist, the Swim, and the Jerk, popular dance steps of the period.

Role playing develops insight into human relations, problems of others, a main idea, or the feelings and values of individuals in a critical situation. After the role is portrayed in different ways, questions such as these may be discussed: Which role did you prefer? Why? Which role was least desirable? Why? How did each role make you feel? How might individuals feel in the actual situation? What might be done to improve the situation?

Dramatic skits are more formal than dramatic play; they involve the enactment of a selected event or activity in which assigned roles are taken and lines are learned to portray a significant incident—for example, the signing of the Mayflower Compact or the landing on the moon.

Pageants are used to portray a sequence of incidents or activities related to unit topics such as the history of our community, the development of our state, the growth of America, and living in Mexico. Dramatic skits prepared by small groups within the class are easily arranged as a pageant.

Pantomimes may be used to portray simply and briefly an activity such as a plane landing, the movement of a boat into the harbor, or a scout blazing a trail through a mountain range.

Dramatization involves presenting a playlet or a play in which a script, costumes, and a stage setting are used.

Marionettes and puppets may be used for both creative dramatics and formal dramatization. Children may construct them, plan for their use, use them to present skits and plays, and use them in new situations by preparing new lines, staging, and costumes. Some teachers use them to build confidence in shy children as well as to provide a different form of dramatic expression for typical children.

Mock trials enable students to simulate courtroom activities, including the roles of the judge, plaintiff, and defendant and their attorneys, witnesses, and the jury.

Mock meetings may be planned and conducted in the upper grades to simulate New England town meetings, city council meetings, and legislative sessions.

Unfinished stories or *reaction stories* put students in hypothetical situations to find out what they would do. After hearing a story about problems such as fair play, helping others, carrying out one's responsibilities, respecting property, or minority group relations, students act out a solution and evaluate the enactment.

Students in the upper elementary and middle school grades are especially interested in mock trials, mock meetings, and unfinished stories. In this age group, many students move from making simple explanations to realizing the complexity of most issues, problems, and personalities; some are forming opinions that differ from those of their loved ones; others are simply confused by what they read and hear in school. These forms of dramatic representation provide them with not only the opportunity to explore social studies issues, problems, and personalities in a new way, but also a chance to use thinking skills and become clearer thinkers. Students at these grade levels are developing concern for justice and enjoy delving into court decisions and the twists and turns of history.

Dramatic activities require planning and can be difficult to coordinate. A teacher who has not observed or guided creative dramatic activities might first experiment with a play written for children. Next the teacher might plan short skits related to topics under study. This may be followed by longer dramatic activities, until finally the group has moved to a creative and informal approach to dramatization.

Sometimes a teacher may decide that a play written for students—for example, a program for a special occasion or the commemoration of a special event—is more appropriate than creative dramatics. If so, an appropriate play should be selected, rehearsed, and presented in a way that develops backgrounds and understanding, involves the students in planning and evaluation, and achieves other educational goals. Table 12.1 presents a complete list of planning, enactment, and evaluation questions that will help you develop meaningful learning activities that involve dramatization.

■ TABLE 12.1

Making Plans for Dramatic Activities

Teacher Preplanning

- What topics within the unit lend themselves to dramatic activities?
- Are materials available? What space is needed?
- Is additional information needed to enrich the activity? How should it be introduced?
- Which students probably will wish to participate first? Which should?
- What will others do?

Group Planning

- Have students chosen important material to dramatize?
- Have they considered all important aspects of the activity?
- Are materials on hand?
- Do individuals suggest meaningful roles to play?
- Do they incorporate new ideas and materials as they make plans?

During the Activity

- Are the students identifying with the person and the objects involved?
- Are they staying on topic?
- Are space and materials used effectively?
- Are the suggestions made during planning carried out in the activity?
- Does the activity show understanding of concepts?
- Are new needs emerging for any of the following?
  1. clarification of ideas
  2. authentic information
  3. group standards
  4. language expression
- Are any individuals confused or uncertain as to purpose, use of materials, or role?
- Are changes needed in space arrangements or materials?

Group Evaluation

- Does the group appraise the activity in terms of the roles discussed during planning?
- Are newly discovered needs and problems considered?
- Are inaccuracies and misconceptions clarified?
- What additional group and individual activities will extend knowledge and keep the unit moving forward?

 *Drama Activities*

➤ Younger students can benefit from acting out scenarios related to family life. Small groups might dramatize cleaning, gardening, washing and ironing, taking care of a baby, preparing and serving meals, or enjoying leisure activities.

➤ Individual students might dramatize the activities of particular workers in the community. You might assign these roles to students or ask them to choose; be sure they avoid sex-role stereotyping. You might use these ideas:

firefighter	aircraft pilot	florist
postal worker	carpenter	teacher
gas station attendant	bank teller	librarian
news broadcaster		

Encourage students not to generalize, but to portray the interesting specifics of each workers' tasks. For example, a drama on a day in a grocery store could depict jobs such as pricing, sorting, shelving, working at the checkout counter, making signs, weighing produce, assisting a customer, and so on.

➤ Farming activities can be an interesting focus for drama activities. Tasks such as pitching hay, feeding animals, planting and harvesting, and preparing produce for the market are lively and help students understand the challenges and importance of farming life.

➤ The topic of colonial life offers potential for dramatization. Students might play out the story of the Pilgrims, meetings with Native Americans (from the perspective of the new settlers, the Native Americans, or both), subsistence activities such as gathering food and building shelters, early games such as leapfrog and wood tag, the drama of a lively town meeting, a day in a colonial home, and so on.

➤ Have students enact the traditions of a particular festival. They might pick festivals related to a particular culture or place, such as China's New Year, Festival of the Lanterns, Festival of the Dragon Boats, and the Mid-Autumn, or Moon, Festival.

➤ Students might focus on dramatizing events in state history. They might choose the founding of a city, a person who played an important role in the state, significant economic activities, early history of the state, or important episodes in state government.

Dramatic Rhythms

Children are quick to respond to the rhythm in life around them. Grain swaying in the field, waves rolling in to shore, birds flying from tree to tree, people at work in the community, trains starting and stopping—all these will stimulate natural and spontaneous rhythmic expression. Similarly, rich experiences in the social studies lead to dramatic rhythms that are meaningful demonstrations of the students' impressions.

"Here comes a 777," said the child, who demonstrated a long glide and finally stopped at the end of the "runway."

"Wait until the runway is clear," said the traffic controller as another "plane" gracefully circled the airport.

"I'm landing my Lear jet now," said a third child, who glided in, stopped halfway down the "runway," and taxied away quickly.

Children often add rhythmic expression to other dramatic activities. For example, they may "catch the beat" and use rhythmic expression to portray activities such as digging, raking, and working in the garden; loading and unloading trucks; movement of freight trains as they start, gain speed, speed along, slow down, and stop; and activities of farmers as they ride horses, milk cows, and plow a field. When musical accompaniment is added, students can bring together dramatic, rhythmic, and musical modes of expression to enrich their interpretations of activities (music is discussed later in this chapter).

In addition, folk games and folk dances have a place in social studies. Many units would be incomplete if folk dances were omitted. For example, in units on Mexico "La Cucaracha" and "La Bamba" and in units on pioneer life "Old Dan Tucker," "Virginia Reel," and "Captain Jenks" are most appropriate. Other examples can be found in references listed at the end of this chapter.

Growth in dramatic rhythms progresses from simple interpretation of single episodes to more complete patterns of expression centered in a unifying theme. At first, children's responses to rhythm are short and simple. A single phase of an activity, such as the train starting, may be interpreted with real satisfaction. Other phases, such as gaining speed, slowing down, or going up a grade may be added later. Still later, several phases are brought together in a pattern of rhythm as the child portrays the complete activity. Finally, several children can cooperate in activities such as a train backing up to couple cars, starting up, traveling along, leaving cars at different places, and arriving at its destination. In this final stage, the group develops a creative synthesis of individual interpretations.

Role Playing

Role playing can develop empathy, concern for others, and other prosocial behaviors as students enact an incident or a problem and propose desirable solutions. Role playing may be an ideal strategy in culturally diverse classrooms where misunderstandings may arise among the children.

After a realistic incident has been chosen, students are asked to volunteer to play defined roles; the class observes and suggests other ways to enact the incident. Steps of procedure are illustrated in the lesson plan on page 377 (see Shaftel & Shaftel, 1982, for other examples). In such a lesson, the objective should note the value that is being developed. The introduction should introduce the subject and warm up the students for the activity. During the role playing itself, you might mix students who are confident in dramatic activities with those who are shy or reticent. Also prepare students to be careful observers as they watch other students' role playing.

*What do you remember
most about your K–8
social studies experiences?
Chances are you remember
a pageant, a dramatization,
or a mock trial. Why do we
remember these experiences
over others?*

Mock Trials

Mock trials help students develop concepts of justice, learn about courtroom procedure, analyze issues, interpret facts, and evaluate decisions. To carry out a mock trial,
students must learn the roles of judges, jurors, attorneys, and witnesses. They also
need to know courtroom procedures and rules of evidence. Visits to courts, interviews with judges and attorneys, study of materials for students, television programs,
and videos are useful sources of information. You might provide simple instruction
sheets with guidelines like these:

Small Claims Court
1. The plaintiff and the defendant appear before the judge.
2. The plaintiff states his or her case.
3. The defendant states his or her case.
4. The judge asks questions to clarify facts in the case.
5. The judge makes and explains the decision.

Civil Court
1. The court is opened and the jury sworn in.
2. Attorneys for the plaintiff and the defendant make opening statements.
3. Attorneys examine and cross-examine witnesses.
4. Attorneys present closing statements.
5. The jury receives instructions, deliberates, and gives a verdict.

An inexperienced group should begin with a simple mock trial in which a judge
hears the case and makes the decision with no attorneys present, as in small claims
court. After students have a background of knowledge and experience, a civil court
mock trial may be simulated. The main steps in a mock trial are briefing (prepara-

LESSON PLAN   *Concern for Others*

Objective   To demonstrate ways in which to show concern for others

Materials   Video

Introduction   Warm up the group by presenting a video that highlights concern for others.

Discuss other situations of significance to students in which they might show concern for others.

Select one in which they are interested for a role-playing episode.

Development   Select the role players. Provide time for the role players to plan, guiding them by asking questions such as these:

1. What different roles are needed? Who will play each one?
2. How will concern for others be portrayed?

Prepare the class to observe by making such suggestions as these:

1. Pay attention to the ways in which concern for others is portrayed.
2. Think about how you would show concern for others if you were one of the role players.
3. Be prepared to answer these questions after watching the role-playing episode: How did each player show concern for others? In what other ways might they have shown concern for others? How would one actually feel in this situation?

Provide for the role-playing enactment by the selected students.

Conclusion   Discuss the enactment. Ask students the following questions:

1. How was concern for others shown? How realistic was it?
2. In what other ways might it have been portrayed?
3. Have you ever actually shown concern for another person in one of these ways? in another way? Describe what you did. How did the person react?
4. What are some other aspects of concern for others that we might role play? Who will volunteer to enact them?

Provide for additional enactments and follow-up discussion.

Evaluation   Use these questions to evaluate learning:

1. What new ways of showing concern for others were shown?
2. What ways of showing concern for others that we have used in the past were shown?
3. In what situations could you use both new and old ways of showing concern for others?

tion), conducting the trial (simulation), and debriefing (evaluation). Briefing should be thorough so that participants understand their roles, the issue, and the facts. Debriefing contributes much to learning as students ask the following questions:

- How were the roles played?
- How might they be changed?
- What was the issue?
- Which facts were relevant?
- How effectively were they presented?
- How sound were the arguments on each side?
- How might they be improved?
- Why do you agree or disagree with the decision?
- Can you think of sound reasons for an appeal?

Mock trials are extremely popular with students. However, teachers should use good judgment when helping students carry one out. Similar to other activities described in this chapter, a mock trial should have educational value and promote the goals of social studies.

Simulations

Simulations are scaled-down or simplified models of situations, problems, activities, or systems. Students assume roles and make decisions according to specified rules. Simulations are more restricted and patterned than typical role playing because of the rules and constraints that help to portray the situation realistically. Some teachers prefer to use simulation games in middle and upper grades.

Simulations include games like Monopoly® (Parker Brothers), in which students simulate purchasing and selling property; role playing in which students act out a particular role following a format or set of rules, like learning how to drive a car using a simulator; and a combination of the two, in which students act out a role in a particular game.

The current social studies simulation games include *Dividing the Work, Market, The Barter Game, Making a Profit,* and *Roaring Camp.* A variety of computer programs may be used to simulate decision making in economic, geographic, governmental, and historic situations. Examples include *Sell Lemonade, Trading Post, President-Elect, Geography Search, Road Rally U.S.A., Oregon,* and *Lincoln's Decisions. Simulation Construction Kit* can be used to create simulations.

Teachers should anticipate and avoid problems that may offset the interest-building and motivating power of simulation games. Some simulations take so much time that other needed learning activities are neglected. Arguments may arise over rules and roles, or the desire to win may interfere with the attainment of stated objectives. Such problems may be avoided by following these guidelines:

1. Make a plan to clarify objectives, concepts, roles and rules, time limits, space arrangements, and role assignment.

2. Make sure that the objectives, rules, and other elements of the plan are understood by the entire group.

3. Provide direction as needed during the simulation to help students keep the objectives in mind and follow the specified rules.

4. Guide group debriefing and evaluation after the simulation, noting problems, effectiveness of strategies and decisions, needed modifications, and ways to make improvements.

Students may be guided to create their own simulations after they have gained experience with using simulations prepared by others. For example, a variety of simulations may be made by using procedures similar to those in Monopoly®. The main steps in creating a simulation are as follows:

1. Select an activity.
2. Choose the form of presentation.
3. Establish rules, and define roles.
4. Set guidelines for keeping the simulation realistic.
5. Decide how decisions will be made during the simulation.
6. Make plans for debriefing and evaluation. (Braun et al., 1998)

■ Music Activities

The world's musical heritage is a rich source of content and activities that help students understand people and their ways of living. Music that is familiar to students as well as music that is totally new to them can both be used to advantage in the social studies classroom. Teachers can identify the cultural groups represented in their classrooms and find out how each group has expressed customs, traditions, and values in music. They can reach beyond the classroom, beyond their communities, to other parts of the United States and elsewhere for examples that will provide a rich source of activities.

People at home and around the world have expressed their customs, traditions, and values in music. Patriotic music stirs feelings of loyalty, highlights great events, and celebrates festivals, ceremonies, and religious activities. Poems, stories, legends, and other literary works have been set to music. Folksongs and dances have evolved from everyday activities. Musical instruments have been invented to provide unique modes of expression. And as the music created in one part of the world has reached people in other parts of the world, cultural interdependence has increased.

Six types of music activity are used in social studies units of instruction: singing activities, listening activities, rhythmic activities, instrumental activities, creative expression, and research activities. By directing children's participation, a teacher can guide students to make meaningful cross-cultural comparisons, one of the main reasons for giving attention to music in the social studies.

■ Resources for the Arts **http://www.hol.edu/ main/TheArts.htm** offers K–12 teachers an array of materials in dance, music, and the other arts.

Singing

Singing is the most extensively used music activity in social studies. Children's music books contain many songs related to topics in each unit of instruction. Children's identification with others is increased as they sing songs about human experience and activities—working and playing at home, working on the farm, living in a hogan, trekking westward across the plains, and living in other lands. Feelings about and appreciation of events in our country's history may be stirred as children sing "The Star-Spangled Banner," "America the Beautiful," "Battle Hymn of the Republic," and "Columbia, the Gem of the Ocean." A feeling of kinship with others may be kindled as children sing the folksongs of different regions of America and of other lands.[2]

In social studies, building background is important before children learn and sing a song. Information about its historical and cultural context will enrich the students' experience. The questions that follow can guide study and discussion:

- What thoughts and values are expressed?
- What is the mood? the rhythmic pattern? the melody?
- Is this a song of work, play, worship, adventure, nature, fantasy, or patriotism?
- Is this song sung at festivals, ceremonies, or other special occasions?

Listening

Through directed listening experiences students can learn much about the folksongs, dances, instruments, festivals, holidays, patriotic events, composers, and performing artists significant to a given unit. Recordings of different types of music lend realism and authenticity to children's learning. Music is stunningly varied. To American ears, Chinese opera, Indian sitar playing, African drumming, and Laplander throat singing can sound quite startling. The trend in world music has broadened the listening experiences of many Americans, yet there is a great deal of room for informed and careful study of these varied types of human expression. Starting early can give students a deep appreciation for the many realms of music rarely represented in the popular mainstream.

Radio and television programs, community concerts, folk festivals, musicians invited to school, and students' own recordings can contribute to learning about music. Questions such as these may be used to guide listening and discussion:

- What feelings were aroused?
- Who can demonstrate the rhythmic pattern?
- Who can name the instruments that were played? Have you heard them before?
- What new tonal patterns did you hear?
- How is this music related to customs and traditions?
- What clues did you get about the cultural values behind this music?

2. For examples, see Kidd (1992) and Krull (1992).

Musical Rhythms

Four types of rhythmic activity may be provided in the social studies:

Informal rhythms allow children to express rhythmic patterns without direction from the teacher.

Formal rhythms are directed by the teacher, and students move to the rhythm (skip, gallop, and the like) as music is played.

Creative rhythms encourage children to express their responses in original ways.

Dramatic rhythms stimulate students to use rhythmic expression to interpret experiences they have had (see the earlier section on dramatic rhythms).

Grasping the concept of rhythm is also a component of students' singing and listening activities. Special rhythmic patterns characterize different musical forms: bouncy polkas, gently rhythmic folk ballads, the lively tempo used in playing steel drums, the stately rhythm of marches, the soothing sounds of lullabies, and so on. Analyzing rhythm gives students a deeper understanding of any music they encounter. The following activities can foster students' sense of rhythm:

 *Rhythm Activities*

➤ Ask students to look for patterns of rhythm in the world surrounding them and bring a list of them to class. Everyone can share their findings, and you might ask students to describe these rhythms in words, tap them out on the desktop, or express them in bodily movement. Here are some examples of what they might find:

bells ringing	motors revving	coins jingling
hammers pounding	trees swaying	trains chugging
horns tooting	a person sawing wood	rabbits hopping
horses trotting	a runner's feet pounding	

➤ To engage students in a fun rhythmic activity, teach them the steps of a simple dance. It might be a folk dance related to the culture of some of your students or a dance that characterizes a country, a region, or an era, such as the German polka, the Charleston of the 1920s, square dance steps, the eighteenth-century minuet, or Irish step dancing. Keep the patterns simple, and use the dance to complement study of the place, culture, or era.

➤ Young children can learn a lot about rhythm through simpler physical activities, such as skipping, galloping, slide-stepping, tiptoeing, marching, and hopping. With music in the background, you might call out different types of steps for students to make.

➤ Ask students to bring in examples of rhythmic music that they would like to share with the class, including an explanation of what it means to them. They might play a brief recording, give a short instrumental or sung performance, or invite a specialist to class (perhaps a relative or friend who is an accomplished musician).

Instrumental Activities

Musical instruments of various types may be used to extend children's learning. Rhythm instruments such as drums, sticks, blocks, bells, triangles, cymbals, gongs, rattles, and tambourines may be used to accompany rhythmic and singing activities, produce sound effects, and play rhythmic patterns. Chording instruments such as electronic keyboards, the Autoharp, and the harmolin may be used to accompany activities and to demonstrate harmonic and rhythmic patterns. Simple melody instruments such as melody bells, tuned bottles or glasses, song flutes, and recorders may be used to play tunes created by children as well as melodies discovered in the songs and recordings presented in units. Native instruments may be examined and played to give authenticity to music activities; examples include castanets, claves, guiro, maracas, cabaca, bongo, conga, antara or pipes of Pan, quena or flute, and chocalho in units on South America; and the bamboo xylophone, gong, temple block, and finger cymbals in units on Asian countries.

Creative Musical Expression

Creative musical expression can thrive in social studies as students develop insights and appreciation. The students' own poems may be set to music. As children hum tunes or play them on simple melody instruments, the teacher can record them on the chalkboard, a chart, or a tape recorder. You might ask these questions to guide students as they create a song:

- What moods or feelings shall we express?
- What words or phrases fit the mood?
- Shall we hum, play, or sing to create the melody?
- What rhythms shall we use?
- Shall we record the lyrics and the melody?

Students can create accompaniments for songs, rhythmic movement, choral reading, and dramatic activities suited to the mood and the thoughts expressed in the words. They can create special sound effects and background music for skits, plays, and pageants. They can make simple instruments from gourds, bamboo, bottles, glasses, and other materials. Creative expression through art, writing, dramatics, and rhythmic movement can be stimulated as children listen to recordings. A range of creative processes can be brought into play as children plan and develop concluding activities that include a script, lyrics and melodies, costumes, staging, musical accompaniments, and their own special effects. Computer programs such as *Music, The Music Machine, Music Shaper, Music Studio, Music Maker,* and *Song Writer* extend students' opportunities to create songs, tunes, and rhythms.

Research Activities

Individual and group research activities may be undertaken to find background information on the music emphasized in units of instruction. Take a trip to a nearby museum to examine instruments and to see costumes used in folk dances. Interview experts or invite them to the classroom to give demonstrations. Encyclopedias, library resources, and supplementary music books may be reviewed. The Internet can be a valuable source of music activities related to a particular unit of instruction. Notebooks, scrapbooks, and individual and group reports may be compiled to summarize information. Such research may be guided by questions like these:

Investigating Music in Another Land

- What are some of their best-known songs?
- What folk dances do they have? How are they related to festivals?
- What costumes do they wear?
- What music do they play at ceremonies and other activities?
- What folk instruments do they have? How are they made?
- What composers and artists live there?
- What influences have others had on their music? How has their music influenced ours?
- What customs, values, and beliefs are expressed through music?
- What events, deeds, and activities have been set to music?

The musical heritage of different cultural settings should be explored by the class. For example, in South America, Africa, Europe, Canada, and the United States, many different types of music are found, and as students study them they can discover the influences of diverse cultural backgrounds. Folk music, adaptations of music from other lands, music created by native composers, and famous performing artists may be studied as a part of units. For example, Argentina's music shows the Italian influence in "El Estilo," a melancholy song of the pampas. The tango shows Spanish influence, and the American Indian influence is reflected in folk music. Well-known songs in children's music books include "Sí Señor," "Palapala," "Adíos Te Digo," "Chacerera," "Song of the Pampas," "The Gaucho," "Vidalita," and "Ay, Zamba."

Brazil's music shows the influence of the Portuguese, who sang the "Modinha" to drive away homesickness. The African influence is shown in the samba. Children's music books contain songs such as "The Painter of Cannahay," "My Pretty Cabacla," "Tutu Maramba," "Cantilena," "Sambalele," "Bambamulele," "In Bahia Town," "O Gato," and "Come Here, Vitu."

Arranging a Classroom Music Center

A classroom music center may be changed as different units of instruction are developed. Songbooks, instruments, other music materials, and pictures showing musical activities may be placed there. The bulletin board in the music center might display news clippings about musicians in places under study, announcements of related programs on television and radio, a list of recordings for individual listening, and pictures showing native musical activities. The center might also include a listening post, maps showing the locale of songs and musicians, chording and rhythm instruments, and a flannel board for showing rhythmic and tonal patterns.

■ Art and Construction

Hands-on activities in creative art and construction can greatly enhance students' appreciation for artistic expression, the processes of construction related to a wide variety of products, and their knowledge of many social studies concepts and concept clusters. Ideas for such activities are inexhaustible; Table 12.2 gives a sampling of art and construction activities that may benefit your students.

Though the concepts of art and construction do overlap, we discuss them separately in this section to give each its due.

Arts and Crafts

From ancient times to the present, people have expressed their thoughts and feelings through various art forms. Artists and artisans of each generation have selected ideas and created forms that clarify, simplify, and interpret the ideals, beliefs, and customs of their times. Line, form, color, texture, space, and other elements have been unified to express the artists' visions. Touches of beauty have been added to dwellings, clothing, utensils, festivals, ceremonies, and other objects and activities.

■ All life is an experiment. The more experiments you make, the better.
　—**Ralph Waldo Emerson**

Art activities enrich students' learning as they discover the impact of art on homes, furnishings, transportation vehicles, buildings, and other objects. Subtle shades of meaning may be brought out as children consider the work of artists who have portrayed great events, heroes and heroines, landscapes, poems, songs, everyday activities, ceremonies, festivals, and holidays. Appreciation for the diversity of artistic expression may be kindled as students discover the concepts of nature in sand paintings of the Navajo, the simple beauty of the Puritan church, the delicate patterns in Japanese paintings, the search for harmony between people and nature in Chinese art, the recurring themes and patterns in Egyptian art, the stateliness of Roman architecture, and the desire for freedom boldly revealed by Mexico's mural painters. Cultural interdependence may be highlighted as the thunderbird, the cross, geometric forms, and other designs are discovered in the art of peoples in different lands.

As a general guideline, emphasize originality in both appreciative and creative activities. As the art of other people is studied, each individual, whether a child or an adult, will respond in unique ways. To be sure, children may have similar under-

■ **TABLE 12.2**

Types of Art and Construction Activities

Drawing and Painting
- backgrounds
- borders
- cartoons
- decorations
- friezes
- greeting cards
- illustrations
- landscapes
- murals
- painted fans
- pictures
- posters
- sketches
- stage scenery

Modeling, Sculpturing, Carving, and Whittling
- animals
- beads
- bowls
- candlesticks
- dishes
- figurines

- jars
- jewelry
- jugs
- plaques
- pots
- tiles
- trays
- utensils

Arranging
- artifact and object exhibits
- cornucopias
- displays
- driftwood arrangements
- flower arrangements
- fruit arrangements
- gourd arrangements

Print Design
- announcements
- booklets
- borders
- calendars
- greeting cards
- labels

- mats
- posters
- programs
- signs
- stenciling

Textiles (weaving, sewing, knitting, fabric collage)
- bags
- belts
- caps
- costumes
- headbands
- mats
- rugs
- wall hangings

Mixed Media
- chalk and paper sculpture
- collage
- combined recycled materials
- dioramas
- mosaic
- paper, cork, and wire
- shadow boxes

standings of background ideas about the culture in which the art product was created and certain common understandings about the processes involved. But the individual's reaction, response, and feelings are always personalized.

But what if a child has misconceptions and erroneous ideas about the people or the activities portrayed? Teachers can correct these problems through their own familiarity with the content and by encouraging students to do additional study; simply telling or showing a child how to draw something is not a substitute for developing backgrounds of understanding. You might direct students' study of ideas, art materials, and the process of working with certain media. But when children proceed to express the ideas, they must use their own techniques, hunches, and ideas if the experience is to be called an art activity. Otherwise it is mere copying, illustrating, or reproducing the technique of another person. It is not art.

Social studies instruction is not limited to the classroom. K–8 teachers explore their immediate surroundings and beyond to help students gain a broad and rich understanding of social studies.

Table 12.2 gives categories of artwork that students might create in the social studies classroom. You may also wish to try out some of the following activities.

 *Art Activities*

➤ You might organize students to create a mural related to social studies content. It may show an expedition attempting the Northwest Passage, the different people in a neighborhood, the story of how a town was founded, or the events in a cultural festival. You might use these questions to help students get started:

What main ideas shall we show?

What images will we use to show the ideas?

In what order shall we place the images?

What materials will we use?

Who will work on each section of the mural?

Should we use computer programs such as *Dazzle Draw* and *Blazing Paddles* to create images?

Where will we display our mural?

How can we evaluate our experience?

➤ In studying arts and crafts of a particular culture, you might focus on how different symbols, shapes, colors, and other features can express a great deal about the maker and the maker's cultural context. Ask students to discuss how these works tell about the following:

aspirations	freedom	ideas
beliefs	heroes	nature
customs	historical events	recreation
fears	hopes	religion
feelings	ideals	traditions

➤ In a given unit, you might want to give sustained attention to the arts and crafts of a particular culture or time period. Using the following activities in sequence will deepen students' experience of these works.

Study and discuss pictures in the textbook.

Look at other reproductions of these works.

Watch videos or slide shows about the crafts.

Visit a museum or gallery to see real examples.

If possible, examine and handle actual artifacts or models of them.

Interview people who know about the culture or the form of art being studied.

Conduct research on a specific area. Use art books, reference books, periodicals, and the Internet.

Write a report or create a bulletin board display as a culmination.

➤ As students study a given work of art or craft, you may want to draw their attention to formal aspects of the work. Define one or more of the following concepts, and use them in discussion of the work:

balance	movement	space
color	perspective	texture
design	repetition	unity
form	rhythm	variation
line		

The Classroom Art Center

A work center for art materials facilitates pupils' work and simplifies art activities in social studies. Materials should be changed as new topics are studied. Related pictures may be displayed on the bulletin board, and selected art objects may be exhibited on nearby shelves, window sills, or tables. Space should be provided to display children's completed artwork and to store unfinished work. Computer programs such as *Blazing Paddles, Delta Drawing, Paint, MACPaint, MousePaint, DeluxePaint, Easy 3D, AppleMouse II,* and various versions of LOGO may be used to create diagrams, sketches, posters, drawings, and other unit-related items. A Koala Pad can also be used for drawing.

Construction

Construction in social studies usually involves the use of tools and materials to make authentic objects to promote the growth of social concepts and understandings. The value of construction lies in its contribution to learning, not in the products that are made. Lasting values may be achieved only if construction achieves significant objectives, shows students the connections between activities and objectives, and motivates students' learning—a primary goal.

■ Young people need to feel that their ideas and skills are valued.

—Joe Nathan

These few examples indicate the variety of items students can make in the social studies.

> *Paper and cardboard construction:* albums, booklets, notebooks, scrapbooks; collages, montages, mobiles, stabiles; puppets, marionettes; dioramas, panoramas; shadow boxes, television and movie paper-roll programs; posters, graphs, maps; holiday decorations, containers, favors; table covers, wall hangings

> *Wood construction:* playhouse furniture for home units; barns, trucks, silos, other items for farm units; oil tankers, tugboats, piers, other items for a unit on the harbor; covered wagon, churns, butter ladles, benches, brooms for units on colonial and pioneer life; planes, gliders, wind sock, control tower, model airport for units on air transportation

The following questions may be used as criteria to select activities and to guide planning:

- What objectives can be achieved by this activity?
- How practical is it in terms of available time, materials, and tools?
- In what ways is it more effective than other activities?
- How can it be used to develop accurate concepts and appreciations?
- How can it be related to other activities in the unit?
- Do students have the necessary background and construction skills?

Construction may be closely related to dramatic activities. Dramatic representation of activities in units on the home, the farm, the harbor, the airport, colonial life, Mexico, and other lands creates needs for objects, models, props, and scenery. Students can plan and make essential items and thus relate the making of objects to stated objectives.

Materials and tools are available in most schools for paper and cardboard construction activities. Materials for making items of wood can be obtained from crates, boxes, scraps of lumber, lumber yards, and hobby stores. Doweling of various sizes can be used to make masts, funnels, and other cylindrical items. Wooden buttons can be used for wheels, and an awning pole can be cut to make tank cars and oil and milk trucks. Students themselves will think of creative uses of materials and can obtain wood and make items at home—with the permission and assistance of parents! Simple tools such as saws, C-clamps, hammers, and a T-square are adequate for most activities.

Safety first is the motto in all activities! Proper use of scissors, saws, and other tools should be taught systematically, and close supervision should be provided during construction activities.

Processing Materials

Processing materials is similar in many ways to construction, in that similar values, selection criteria, techniques of planning, instructional procedures, and skills are involved. Processing materials in the social studies may be defined as changing raw or semiprocessed materials (yarn, for example) into finished products. Typical examples are making cottage cheese, processing wool, dyeing fabrics, weaving, drying fruit, and making soap. As children engage in such processes, emphasize development of understanding and appreciation of creative ways in which people have met their needs without benefit of today's technology.

In early times, children helped process a variety of materials. They helped with churning butter, collecting berries and making dyes, using tallow to make candles, and washing, carding, spinning, and weaving wool. Today children see finished products in stores and lack firsthand opportunities to carry out the processes involved in making them.

The social studies program offers many possibilities for processing of materials in various units:

Home and Family: making popcorn, applesauce, and cornstarch pudding

Dairy Farm: churning butter and making cottage cheese

Colonial and Pioneer Life: weaving, quilting, candle making, soap making, sewing, and drying fruits

Communication: making and using ink, parchment, clay tablets, and books

Mexico: grinding corn with a metate, making candles, weaving, cooking Mexican foods, making adobe bricks, and sewing

The actual steps for some processes are given in Table 12.3.

The planning and guiding of construction and processing activities are similar in many ways to the planning and guiding of study trips, dramatic activities, and other "doing" activities in the social studies. Four basic steps are involved: (1) planning by the teacher, (2) planning with the class, (3) providing guidance during the activity, and (4) evaluating progress after the activity, as shown earlier in Table 12.1.

■ TABLE 12.3

Directions for Processing Materials

Making Butter	**Making Pumpkin Rings**	**Making Apple Leather**
Materials: ½ pint whipping cream, ¼ teaspoon salt, ice cubes, water, a spoon, a pint jar.	Cut a pumpkin crosswise into halves.	Peel some apples and cook them in water.
Pour cream into jar and seal it.	Remove seeds, and cut pumpkin into ½-inch thick rings.	After apples are cooked to a mush, spread the mush on a cloth to dry.
Shake the jar until butter appears.	Place rings on a pole to dry.	Let it stand for a day or two.
Pour off bluish liquid.		
Place butter in a bowl and add salt.		
Add a few ice cubes and water; work the mixture with a spoon.		
Pour off liquid and mold butter into a block.		

■ Conclusion

There are countless ways to develop creative thinking through expressive experiences. Students, young and old, can use creative writing to express their ideas on particular topics, issues, and people. Role taking enables children to identify with others in a variety of situations, whereas role playing may develop empathy, concern for others, and other prosocial behaviors. In the upper elementary and middle school grades, students use mock trials, mock meetings, and unfinished stories to learn about civics and to bring history alive, while giving their own creative twist to the learning experience. Musical content and activities help students understand people and ways of living, and arts and crafts study and work can develop appreciation for creative expression and ingenious design. In construction and processing of materials, students use tools and information to make authentic materials that promote the growth of social concepts and understanding.

Expressive experiences are an integral part of social studies instruction. Teachers who prize creativity set up risk-free classroom environments in which students are encouraged to express themselves, knowing that their efforts will be appreciated. Well-planned creative activities add breadth and depth to social studies instruction while enhancing students' creative thinking and their appreciation of creativity in our own and other cultures.

 Questions, Activities, and Evaluation

1. What two or three creative writing activities can you include in a unit of your choice? What makes them fit well?

2. Which forms of role taking through dramatic representation do you believe to be most useful in the social studies? Indicate ways in which you might use them.

3. Review a music book for a grade of your choice, and identify songs, rhythms, listening activities, and instrumental activities that you might use in a unit.

4. Make a brief plan to show how you might provide for creative musical expression and for investigating the music of a culture under study.

5. Review Table 12.2, and indicate specific ways in which you might use each major type of activity in a unit.

6. Select one construction activity and one processing activity, and note how you might use each in a unit.

7. Describe the importance of teacher planning when developing creative thinking among children and young adults. What major pitfalls should teachers avoid? What advantages do you see to the development of creative thinking among K–8 students?

8. Develop a rationale for the inclusion of expressive experiences in the elementary *and* middle grades.

9. What is the role of evaluation in expressive experiences? What information presented in this chapter offers suggestions on the merits of student expressive experiences?

References

Allen, M. G., & Stevens, R. L. (1998). *Middle grades social studies.* Boston: Allyn & Bacon.

Anderson, W. M., & Lawrence, J. E. (1995). *Integrating music into the elementary classroom.* (3rd ed.). Belmont: Wadsworth.

Ankeney, K., et al. (1996). *Bring history alive!* Los Angeles: National Center for History in the Schools, University of California.

Banks, D., & Gallagher, D. (1993). Teaching as a sensory activity: Making the Maya come to life. *Social Studies and the Young Learner, 5,* 11–12.

Bennett, J. P., & Riemer, P. C. (1995). *Rhythmic dances and dance.* Champaign, IL: Human Kinetics.

Braun, J. A. Jr., Fernlund, P., & White, C. S. (1998). *Technology tools in the social studies curriculum.* Wilson, OR: Franklin, Beedle, & Associates.

Chilcoat, G. W. (1995). Using panorama theater to teach middle school social studies. *Middle School Journal, 26,* 52–56.

Dhand, H. (1994). Global doers: A creative and challenging strategy. *Canadian Social Studies, 29,* 26–33.

Hoot, J. L., & Silvern, S. B. (Eds.). (1988). *Writing with computers in the early grades.* New York: Teachers College Press.

Kidd, R. (Ed.). (1992). *On Top of Old Smokey: A collection of songs and stories from Appalachia.* Nashville, TN: Ideals Children's Books.

Krull, K. (Ed.). (1992). *Gonna sing my head off! American folk songs for children.* New York: Knopf.

Levstik, L. S., & Barton, K. C. (1997). *Doing history.* Mahwah, NJ: Erlbaum.

Lindquist, T. (1997). *Ways that work: Putting social studies standards into practice.* Portsmouth, NH: Heinemann.

McKenzie, B. K., et al. (1996). Photography and the curriculum . . . More focus on learning. *School Library Media Activities Monthly, 13,* 32–33 + .

Myers, R. E. (1998). *Fireworks for igniting creativity in young minds.* Waco, TX: Prufrock Press.

Nichols-McGreevy, S., & Scheff, H. (1995). *Building dances: A guide to putting movements together.* Champaign, IL: Human Kinetics.

Padgett, R. (Ed.). (1987). *Handbook of poetic forms.* New York: Teachers & Writers Collaborative.

Perry, A. Y. (1997). *Poetry across the curriculum.* Boston: Allyn & Bacon.

Selwyn, D. (1995). Arts and humanities in the social studies. *Social Education, 59,* 71–77.

Smith, C. R. (1997). Using student monologues to integrate language arts and social studies. *Journal of Adolescent and Adult Literacy, 40,* 563–564.

Tsujimoto, J. I. (1988). *Teaching poetry writing to adolescents.* Urbana, IL: National Council of Teachers of English.

Zukowski, G., & Dickson, A. (1990). *On the move: A handbook for exploring creative movement with young children.* Carbondale, IL: Southern Illinois University Press.

Chapter 13

Developing Affective Learning

Chapter Objective

To identify affective elements and strategies for developing them

Focusing Questions

- What affective elements—interests, attitudes, appreciations, values, and related behavior—are included in many programs?
- What are core societal values? How do they differ from personal values?
- What strategies and teaching and learning activities can be adapted and used to achieve affective objectives in social studies?
- What strategies from various approaches to values education can be used to develop values and valuing processes?
- What strategies and activities can be used to develop democratic behavior that is consistent with core societal values?

■ Why Focus on Affective Learning?

When you think of social studies instruction, do the affective elements of learning come to mind? Some teachers take the position that affective learning occurs naturally as students listen to their teachers, learn from textbooks, or involve themselves in social studies activities. That is, students gain an understanding of core civic values as they learn about our country's history, clarify personal values as they interact with peers, and ease any tension between personal values and civic values in the social studies activities they experience. Although some of this may happen, we feel that the affective domain in social studies instruction is too important to be left to chance.

What are affective elements? First, they include the values binding us as Americans. A set of core values is found in the NCSS Standards located in the appendix of this textbook (i.e., "Democratic Beliefs and Values—Rights of the Individual, Freedoms of the Individual, Responsibilities of the Individual, and Beliefs Concerning Societal Conditions and Governmental Responsibilities"). According to leading social studies educators, these beliefs and values are essential to participation in sociocivic affairs. Second, the affective realm includes personal values, which are different from civic values. Personal values come into play as we make individual choices and decisions related to recreation, purchases, and other personal preferences. Third, in order to grapple with ethics in government, students must understand the importance of traits such as honesty, fairness, integrity, respect for rule by law, avoidance of favoritism, self-discipline, regard for the public good, humility, morality, rectitude, and diligence.

Learning in the affective domain is effective when students develop a solid knowledge base, understand and appreciate the cognitive elements of affective learning, and can effectively apply them in personal and public affairs. This solid base allows students to appreciate the complex nature of human behavior. Linked together, cognitive and affective traits help young people develop the ability to make informed and reasoned decisions for themselves and the public good.

There are a number of reasons teachers should incorporate affective elements into social studies instruction. They help children and young adults (1) value the differences between a democracy and other forms of government and the rights and responsibilities of living in a democracy; (2) appreciate those values that we as Americans feel are essential for participation in a democracy; (3) distinguish between personal and civic values and appreciate the tension that exists between personal and public actions and behaviors; and (4) appreciate and apply democratic values to personal and public affairs.

How should the affective elements be integrated in a social studies program? Although there is no set formula, many K–8 programs adhere to the following format: (1) In the primary grades, teachers introduce children to prosocial behavior by encouraging them to explore their personal values and learn to practice behaviors such as cooperation, responsibility, concern for others, creativity, and open-mindedness. The goal is to have a child explore self while learning and playing in an environment with other children and adults. (2) In the elementary grades, core societal values are emphasized as students explore the neighborhood, community, state, country, and the world. They become acquainted with core civic values as they read about the American experience and the American Dream. They read and hear about Americans who exhibit behaviors consistent with social values and those who fall short of the mark. They gain a greater understanding of cultural diversity in a democratic society and realizing the American Dream as they look at their actions and behaviors and those of others. (3) At the middle school, as adolescents learn how to make sense of personal values, the personal values of others, and living in a democratic society, teachers integrate into social studies programs activities focusing on self-control, self-discipline, respect for self and others, feeling of self-esteem, cooperation, constraints of pursuits of self-interest, and ways to find peaceful solutions to problems.

The affective elements should be addressed at all grade levels to help children and young adults understand diversity and the responsibilities of living "for the public good as citizens of a culturally diverse, democratic society in an interdependent world."

■ The human mind is our fundamental resource.
—**John F. Kennedy**

What is diversity? What are core civic values? What are the rights and responsibilities of individuals living in a culturally diverse country and world? What is the role of diversity in a democratic society? These and other questions need to be explored by children and young adults. And they can be successfully addressed when teachers integrate knowledge and skills with affective elements. Regardless of the approach used, affective learning should be well thought out and aligned with the goals of social studies education.

◼ Integrating Affective Learning into Basic Instruction

When teachers plan for social studies, they look at the cognitive, psychomotor, and affective elements of learning; content and skills they wish to teach; strengths and weaknesses of their students; and the availability of curriculum. Affective elements are integrated throughout the program and in special units of instruction when the need arises. The different elements (e.g., interest, civic values, personal values, appreciations) are introduced and systematically developed using a variety of instructional strategies. Most important, children and young adults can apply what they have learned in social studies and in other classroom settings.

Identifying Objectives

A first step is to note affective objectives in unit and lesson plans, as shown in these examples based on procedures suggested in Chapters 1 and 5.

> To list and demonstrate ways to show concern for members of one's family
>
> To show appreciation of the contributions of community workers by describing goods and services they produce
>
> To identify the attitudes and the values of women and men who led the struggle to obtain civil rights
>
> To explain the meaning of values in the Bill of Rights and give examples of their significance in current affairs
>
> To demonstrate interest in learning about human affairs by finding and sharing current events related to topics of study

Objectives may indicate various degrees of internalization of the affective domain (Krathwohl et al., 1964). Here are some examples:

> *Receiving:* to listen to a report on ways to show concern for others
>
> *Responding:* to state feelings aroused while listening to a story
>
> *Valuing:* to state why showing concern for others is important
>
> *Organization:* to show concern for others consistently
>
> *Characterization:* to show concern for others in all situations habitually

Choosing Learning Activities

A well-thought-out format should be used to select learning activities. One example appears in the first few pages of Chapter 5, and we're sure you can offer other methods. The selected activities should be used in ways that evoke positive emotional overtones because attitudes, appreciations, and values are rooted deeply in feelings.

The cognitive elements of affective learning need development because understanding the meaning and significance of attitudes and values is essential to effective application of them to human affairs. The following may be adapted for use in various units of study.

Introductory Activities

Show a video, arrange a display of pictures, or call attention to sections in reading center materials that highlight attitudes, appreciations, or values. Discuss a story, dilemma, incident, or news report related to affective objectives. Pose questions or elicit questions from students to focus attention on affective elements, as shown in these examples:

- How can we show respect for each other in discussion?
- What attitudes toward work do outstanding workers have?
- How were equality and justice extended by Martin Luther King, Jr.?
- What individual responsibilities go along with freedom of speech and press?
- What attitudes do outstanding leaders have toward the poor?

Developmental Activities

The following examples illustrate how affective and cognitive elements are related, activities that may be used, and the importance of the teacher's role.

Build a knowledge base that includes understanding of the concepts, beliefs, and appropriate behavior in situations selected for study. For example, justice as fairness and the belief that individual rights must be respected may be clarified and used to develop standards of behavior for use in discussion and in other activities. Knowledge of actions that harm others, the effects of discrimination, and denial of civil rights, along with information on needed corrective measures, may be used to make and weigh proposals for improvement. A desired outcome is reflected in such statements as "Knowing that, I must act differently" and "Is that so? Then we must do this."

Use questions that stimulate students to explore reasons for actions and to think about related feelings. Here are some examples:

Why must rules for discussion be followed? What happens when they are broken? How do you feel when they are broken?

Why was the Underground Railroad started? Who ran it? How must the "passengers" have felt? Why?

Why was the bus boycott started in Montgomery, Alabama? What did Rosa Parks do? How must she have felt? Why?

Who are the homeless in this country? How must it feel to be homeless? How do others treat the homeless? Why?

A series of questions may be used to move students to a higher level of commitment to a given value (Hannah and Michaelis, 1977). For example, after the students have read a selection or have seen a video that highlights responsibility (or some other behavior), you can guide group discussion to these deepening levels of commitment:

Responding level: What examples of responsibility did you find?

Complying level: Why should you carry out responsibilities?

Accepting level: Why should you carry out responsibilities on your own?

Preferring level: Why is it always better to carry out individual responsibilities than not to do so?

Integrating level: Why should you consistently be responsible in all home and school activities?

The discussion may be concluded by having students list specific home and school responsibilities and suggest ways to improve in carrying them out consistently.

Provide role models that students regard highly and can emulate. Teachers, students, community leaders, or notable women and men may serve as role models. Of key importance is the model provided by teachers. For example, references to minority groups should be made in positive terms, and facial grimaces, jokes, or other indicators of negative attitudes must be avoided. Focus on objectivity when examining people, issues, contributions, and problems. As students move from unit to unit, they may be guided to analyze role models that typify exemplary students, community workers, members of minority groups, and present and past individuals who worked for gender equality, civil rights, and fulfillment of other values.

Provide experiences that kindle the imagination and arouse positive feelings. Stories, legends, folk tales, poetry, and other unit-related literature are very helpful in stimulating desirable emotional responses and giving insight into the feelings of others. Also helpful are art and music activities, creative writing, and the making of murals, collages, and displays that reflect values and behavior. Guide students to find and share values and character traits reflected in unit-related art, music, and literary activities (see Chapter 12).

Provide dramatic activities and role playing in which students take defined roles, identify with others, express positive attitudes, and demonstrate desirable behavior. Guide students to try *new* attitudes and demonstrate ways to handle critical situations. Provide opportunities to analyze incidents that show negative attitudes; follow them with incidents that demonstrate positive attitudes.

Use community resources. Students might observe or participate in relevant community activities or events. For example, members of minority, ethnic, or affirmative action groups may be invited to discuss topics such as these: (1) values of special concern to them, (2) basic values they have in common with others, and (3) actions they are taking to achieve equality and justice for themselves and for others. Holidays, festivals, and commemorations may be observed to clarify customs, traditions, values, achievements, and contributions and the reasons why they are important and should be respected. Explore the significance of flag ceremonies, codes of ethics, the Bill of Rights, the Pledge of Allegiance, pageants, historical shrines and monuments, and special TV programs. Discuss items to include in a code of ethics for public officials, such as honesty, integrity, fairness, humility, open-mindedness, respect of all groups, and self-control.

Guide students to discover positive expression of attitudes and appreciations in daily activities and in instructional media. Help them analyze situations in which there is marked disparity between the real and the ideal, noting ways to move toward the ideal. Help them identify beliefs and ideals that were and still are important in daily living in the community, the state, the nation, or other lands. For example, students may analyze reasons for immigration in the video *Journey to Freedom: The Immigrant Experience* or in other media, comparing them to reasons for immigration today.

Have students find and discuss both positive and negative attitudes of characters in stories related to unit topics. Discuss the impact of attitudes on interaction with others.

Explore the impact of religious beliefs and values on ways of living in our own and in other lands from early times to the present (Haynes, 1990). For example, students may find and discuss the meaning of the Noble Eightfold Path of Buddhism, which includes right views, right resolve, right speech, right action, right livelihood, right effort, right mindfulness, and right concentration. Be descriptive, not prescriptive, in guiding discussion of religions and their impact on behavior; emphasize the point that instruction is *about* religion; and avoid imposition of any beliefs and other actions inconsistent with freedom of religion and separation of church and state.

Guide students to find, discuss, and apply values as they engage in class activities and study topics and issues—for example, in case studies and current events that focus on individual and group needs and actions and in discussions of the contributions of individuals from various societal groups who were guided by the ideal of equality for everyone.

Guide students to demonstrate democratic behavior in group activities, to observe examples in school and community activities, to find examples in textbooks and other materials, and to be creative and think of other examples.

Discuss negative examples, and have students propose actions that are consistent with high standards; for example, irresponsible behavior in group work should lead to a clarification of rules to guide future activities. Analyses of a lack of teamwork and concern for others can pinpoint specific ways to improve. Reviews of prejudice and bias can reveal the importance of being open-minded and fair in the treatment of individuals and groups.

Provide time for discussion of value conflicts such as environmental needs versus economic goals, individual rights versus the common good, comparable pay for comparable worth versus pay based on supply and demand. Also helpful are discussions of topics such as responsibilities that go along with individual freedoms, ways to eliminate stereotypes from our thinking, hardships and satisfactions of civil rights leaders, and the significance today of values expressed in the Declaration of Independence and other basic documents.

Develop understanding of the nature of prejudice and ways to avoid it. Consider stereotypes as they are encountered in units of study, instructional media, and students' experiences. The following two-day lesson plan may be used to guide individual, small-group, or class study.

LESSON PLAN   *Prejudice*

Objective   To define prejudice and state ways to avoid it

Focusing Questions   What is prejudice? How can it be avoided?

Materials   Dictionary, textbook *People in the Americas,* video *Exploding Myths of Prejudice*

Introduction   Place the following statement on the blackboard, and ask students to offer their opinions on it:

> "Professional athletes are selfish individuals who show little interest in being positive role models."

Ask students to comment on their experiences with professional athletes. Ask them why the statement on the board may be prejudicial. What makes it prejudicial?

In this two-day lesson, students will define *prejudice,* learn to detect it, and learn ways to avoid making prejudicial statements.

Development   Present the video.

Give students the following worksheet to fill out.

1. Write the meaning of *prejudge* as given by the teacher.
2. List three prejudgments you have made in the past—for example, a person, a food, or an activity you prejudged.
3. Write the meaning of *prejudice* as given in a dictionary. Note how prejudging is a part of prejudice.
4. After viewing the video *Exploding Myths of Prejudice,* complete the following:
   Examples of prejudging are _____.
   Myths about prejudice are _____.
5. List three things you can do to avoid prejudice.
6. You meet someone for the first time. List what you want to learn about this person while deciding whether or not to become friends. What prejudgments should you avoid? Why?
7. A person meets you for the first time. List what you want this person to learn about you while deciding whether or not to become friends. What prejudgments should this person avoid? Why?
8. List rules that you and other students can follow to avoid prejudice in the future.

(continued)

LESSON PLAN   *Continued*

SECOND DAY

List students' responses to these questions:

- What do you think Africans look like? What do they eat? How do they dress? What are their houses like?
- Where did you get your images or ideas of Africans?

View a video such as *Stereotypes: African Girl Malabi*. Then ask students to compare their responses to what they actually saw in the video. Which comparisons are radically different? How could such false ideas about Africans have been learned?

Conclusion   Conclude by discussing how oversimplified mental images of others can lead to wrong ideas. Ask students to think of ways they can find out if their images of other people are accurate—for example, seeing videos, reading about them, looking for individual differences, and evaluating statements for bias.

Evaluation   As a class, have students evaluate these statements in terms of fairness, equality, and concern for others. Ask students to explain their answers.

- Members of *that* group are not cooperative.
- Members of any group are not all the same.
- People in *that* country are not industrious.
- Housework should be done by women.
- Their standard of living would be higher if they worked harder.
- Some teachers like male principals better than female principals.
- Male principals handle discipline better than female principals.

Have students investigate and report on actions of women and men to advance civil rights and achieve gender equality; reasons people from diverse lands have come here and contributions they have made to our culture; and how human dignity and rights have been negated through discrimination, persecutions, the Holocaust, and apartheid. Include attention to discrimination related to age, ethnicity, national origin, race, and gender; the impact of discrimination on employment, housing, voting, and education; and progress that has been made and steps still needed to eliminate discrimination. Guide students to make booklets or scrapbooks that contain pictures, drawings, reports, and news items related to holidays, notable persons, issues of special concern, and other value-laden topics.

Use individual and group guidance techniques to help individuals overcome negative attitudes and to redirect their behavior into positive channels. Individual counseling and small-group discussion of ways to abide by class standards and demonstrate respect for others should be used as needed without hesitation. Make clear behavior that is expected and how the student must proceed to meet those expectations.

The following activities can be used to teach and reinforce positive values and appreciations.

ACTIVITY IDEAS *Affective Learning*

➤ Help students understand that certain positive behaviors need to be used at all times, in all activities. You might give them a list like this one, or post it in the classroom.

> **I Am a Good Classroom Citizen**
> I disagree courteously.
> I show concern for others.
> I help others.
> I insist on equality for everyone.
> I help solve problems.
> I respect others.

➤ Discussion of affective qualities can become abstract, and gathering concrete examples of values, attitudes, and appreciations can make them easier to understand. Give students a questionnaire such as the following one, and have them fill it out individually. It can later serve as a basis for class discussion. The first section concerns values; the second, attitudes; the third, appreciations.

> Find examples of each of the following items.
>
> Standards of worth _____
> Standards of utility _____
> Standards of quality _____
>
> Disposition to act positively _____
> Disposition to act neutrally _____
> Disposition to act negatively _____
>
> Feelings of admiration _____
> Feelings of esteem _____
> Feelings of respect _____

➤ As they study people in a given unit, ask students to think about which virtues they demonstrate. You might include a checklist like this one.

Which Virtues Were Demonstrated by People in Our Unit?

_____ Self-discipline	_____ Honesty	_____ Empathy
_____ Self-control	_____ Integrity	_____ Patience
_____ Self-respect	_____ Perseverance	_____ Morality
_____ Respect for others	_____ Diligence	_____ Loyalty
_____ Concern for others	_____ Responsibility	_____ Rationality
_____ Open-mindedness	_____ Kindness	_____ Faith
_____ Cooperation	_____ Civility	_____ Hope
_____ Fairness	_____ Humility	_____ Modesty
_____ Other:_____	_____ _____	_____ _____

➤ In small groups, have students define and give examples of individual freedoms, individual responsibilities, and individual rights. You might give them a list to follow as they think of examples. You might scale down the list for a briefer activity.

Give examples of each of the following.

Individual Freedoms	Individual Responsibilities	Individual Rights
expression	respect for rights and freedoms of others	life, liberty, and the pursuit of happiness
worship		
conscience	honesty	dignity
thought and inquiry	tolerance	privacy
assembly	helpfulness	justice
political participation	self-control	equality
	compassion	due process
		private property

➤ To help students express their own emotions and develop empathy for those of other people, they could fill out a form like this one, which begins by tapping into the student's own feelings in order to think about those of others.

I feel best in discussion when _____.

Children in colonial times felt best when _____.

Teachers feel best when _____.

➤ In a discussion, ask students to think of examples of democratic behavior. You might focus on cooperation, responsibility, open-mindedness, concern for others, and creativity. Ask students to generate a variety of examples, such as what they have observed, what they themselves do, and what they have read about.

Concluding Activities

Highlight affective issues as students share reports, make summaries, complete booklets, present programs, and discuss main ideas. For example, new interests expressed by students, attitudes and values of civil rights leaders, helpful services provided by public and private agencies, progress in reducing discrimination, and ways to eliminate stereotypes and prejudice are key learnings in concluding activities.

Provide activities that focus attention on affective outcomes. For example, involve students in the making of summary charts with such titles as Contributions of Community Workers, Rights and Related Responsibilities, A Comparison of Values in Our Country and China, and Values Held by Notable Women and Men. Have students prepare entries for a dictionary of attitudes, appreciations, and values that include definitions and examples. Ask students to dramatize or role play selected incidents to demonstrate desirable attitudes, application of core values, and democratic behaviors.

Interrelate concluding and evaluating activities by asking students to complete sentences that express desirable attitudes and appreciations, as shown by these examples:

I can show self-control in class discussions by _____.

We are dependent on farmers for _____.

A responsibility I must assume to ensure others' property rights in school is

_____.

The customs of students who are refugees from other lands must be respected because _____.

I can promote gender equality in school by _____.

> ■ Education has for its object the formation of character. This is the aim of both parent and teacher.
> —**Herbert Spencer**

Evaluating Activities

Observe students' comments, questions, expression of feelings, and participation in learning activities, using Table 13.1 (p. 404) as a guide.

Conduct evaluative class and small-group discussions, posing questions such as these:

- What topics were most interesting? Why? least interesting? Why?
- Which topics should be given further study?
- What ideas did you find on ways to obtain gender equality in school and community activities? How will both girls and boys benefit?
- What attitudes are needed to ensure success?

■ **TABLE 13.1**

Checklist for Observation of Affective Outcomes

Interests

____ Expresses a desire to _____. (learn more about a topic, continue an activity, do an individual project, etc.)

____ Raises questions about _____. (where to find more on a topic, a project to undertake, a person to investigate, etc.)

____ Volunteers and participates actively in _____. (discussion, small-group activities, preparation of reports, etc.)

Attitudes

____ Demonstrates a disposition to act positively toward _____. (social studies activities, members of minority groups, etc.)

____ Frequently and consistently states _____. (preferences for learning activities, likes and dislikes, opinions, etc.)

Appreciations

____ Expresses high esteem, regard, or gratitude for _____. (contributions of civil rights leaders, Bill of Rights, etc.)

____ Shows appreciation by spontaneously making such statements as _____. ("That was really important!" "She worked hard to get voting rights for women." "I'm glad they didn't quit!" etc.)

____ Describes in detail the contributions of _____. (notable women and men, early civilizations to our culture, etc.)

Values

____ Defines in own words the meaning of such values as _____. (equality, justice, privacy, minority protection, etc.)

____ Uses values in decision making and gives reasons for _____. (choices, decisions, judgments, rating of alternatives, etc.)

____ Describes adherence or nonadherence to values in _____. (current and past events, topics of study, etc.)

Character Traits

____ Finds and shares examples of traits such as _____. (self-discipline, self-control, etc.)

____ Consistently demonstrates traits such as _____. (honesty, fairness, concern for others, etc.)

____ Urges others to act in accordance with traits such as _____. (kindness, diligence, humility, etc.)

Democratic Behavior

____ Defines and gives examples of behavior such as _____. (cooperation, responsibility, concern for others, etc.)

____ Demonstrates democratic behavior in _____. (class discussion, committee work, group projects, etc.)

____ Finds and describes examples of democratic behavior in _____. (school and community activities, instructional media, etc.)

As a capstone experience, provide students the opportunity to rate themselves on general affective outcomes or those explored in a unit of study (see Figure 13.1 and the rating devices in Chapter 14).

■ Strategies for Developing Values

To nurture the growth of key values, you can embed valuing strategies in regular instruction. This fits in naturally as students apply decision-making and critical thinking skills to issues. Teachers clarify value concepts and the significance of values in human behavior, but they avoid indoctrination, imposition of values, and one-sided interpretation. A reflective stance and an open atmosphere are maintained to stimulate students to think freely and critically about conflicting choices.

   Use multiple approaches to adapt instruction to fit issues and individual and group needs. For example, direct instruction may be used to teach core democratic values. Clarification strategies may be used to help students explore personal values and positions on issues in past and current events. Moral reasoning may be used to analyze what should be done by one facing conflicting choices. Rational analysis may be used when information can be gathered and used to make judgments, choices, or decisions. Action learning may be used to enable students to undertake projects designed to implement value decisions.

Direct Instruction

Direct approaches to values education include modeling, reasoned persuasion, behavior modification, and specific suggestions.

■ FIGURE 13.1

Self-Evaluation of Affective Learning

How Do You Rate Yourself?

Write A for very good, B for good, C for fair, D for poor, and F for very poor.

____ Respect for others	____ Sensitive to others' needs	____ Being honest
____ Interest in others	____ Fair judgment of others	____ Being frank
____ Listening to others	____ Cooperating with others	____ Helping others
____ Sticking to the job	____ Thinking before acting	____ Admitting errors

How can you improve on items marked C, D, and F?

_____

_____

Why are guided field trips to museums and cultural centers an integral part of a social studies program? What are some advantages of viewing original documents and exhibits and participating in cultural experiences?

Modeling

Present and discuss models as good examples of valued behavior such as fairness, responsibility, respect for others, and courage in the face of adversity. Members of the community, exemplary students, or the teacher may serve as models, as well as outstanding athletes, film and TV stars, characters in stories, notable women and men, and individuals from ethnic and minority groups. Ask students to find and share good examples and to criticize poor ones. Commend students who follow good examples and who set good examples for others.

Reasoned Persuasion

With students, analyze valid reasons for accepting and living by values such as human dignity, justice, and concern for others. Hold class discussions of issues to reveal how consideration of underlying value conflicts improves the making of sound decisions and judgments. Small groups can consider how values such as respect for others and fairness can be applied to specific problems in committee work or other activities. Individual conferences can benefit students who need specific help in behaving in accord with values such as respect for others and group welfare. Videos, stories, and other materials help students explore the importance of accepting and living by democratic ideals.

Behavior Modification

The following illustrate procedures for developing behavior that is consistent with desired values.

> ***State an objective:*** Sarah is to show respect for others in discussion by listening to others and not ridiculing their comments.
>
> ***State a criterion:*** Respect must be shown in all discussions.

Select a procedure: Use praise for reinforcement of positive behavior and removal from discussion to inhibit negative behavior.

Clarify and apply the procedure: Discuss these procedures with Sarah so that she fully understands her role in discussion. Give praise or remove Sarah as warranted by her behavior.

Evaluate and repeat procedure if necessary: Discuss improvement in behavior and ways to make further improvement, giving praise as it is earned and repeating the procedure as needed to achieve the objective.

Specific Suggestions

At times students may be told directly to adhere to standards, behave in accord with values, and consider the consequences of not doing so. Appeals to conscience and following the Golden Rule may get students to think more deeply about what is right or wrong in a given situation. Direct students to limit their choices to those consistent with stated values.

Questioning Strategies

Three strategies from the Taba Curriculum Project are closely directed by the teacher (Wallen et al., 1969). The first one (Table 13.2, p. 408) helps students clarify feelings of others and to identify with them. The second one helps students identify values in events and the reasons that underlie action in events. The third one is action-oriented and focuses on what should be done to deal with a problem. All three can be adapted for use in units at various grade levels. They can be applied to past and current events, incidents in stories, case studies, and problems faced by people under study.

Identifying Values in Educational Materials

The strategy presented in the set of guidelines on page 409 is adapted from one developed in the Taba Curriculum Project (Wallen et al., 1969). It may be used to identify desired values in stories, case studies, videos, or other learning materials. Students are guided to identify values through a series of questions.

Values Clarification Strategies

Strategies in this approach are designed to help students clarify personal values in an atmosphere that encourages students to respond freely. Students have the right to pass and are encouraged to respond honestly and to avoid comments that inhibit the expression of others. A *value* is defined as something chosen freely, prized and affirmed, and acted on repeatedly (Raths et al., 1978).

■ The American Civil Liberties Union website **http://aclu.org** provides teachers with programs aimed at protecting the First Amendment.

Many of the strategies can be adapted for use in social studies units to move beyond the clarification of personal values. The guiding principle is to apply them to value-laden topics in units and current affairs. In all strategies, taking the role of teacher-therapist, giving the impression that all values and views are of equal worth, and taking moral relativism to an extreme should be avoided. The following examples are adapted from Raths et al. (1978), Simon (1972), and Hendricks (1990).

Questioning Strategies for Affective Learning

■ **Clarifying Feelings**

Procedure	Focusing Questions	Application
Recall and clarify the event.	What is the problem? What happened? What did they do?	What promises did treaty signers make to the American Indians?
Infer possible feelings.	How do you think they (he, she) felt? Why might they feel that way?	How did the American Indians feel when the promises were broken? Why?
Infer the feelings of other persons.	How did others feel about it? The same? Differently? Why?	How did settlers feel? Why? How did others feel? Why?
Relate to experiences of students.	Has something like this ever happened to you? How did you feel? Why?	Have promises to you ever been broken? How would you have felt if you had been an American Indian? Why? a settler? Why?

■ **Identifying Values in Events**

Procedure	Focusing Questions	Application
Clarify the facts.	What is the situation? What happened?	What did the video show was happening to American Indian lands?
Identify main reasons.	Why did it happen? What reasons can you think of?	Why were settlers moving into American Indian territory?
Infer values from the reasons.	What do the reasons indicate is important to the people?	What was most important to the American Indians? to the settlers?
Identify possible student action and reasons.	What would you do in the same situation? Why?	What do you think should have been done? Why?
Identify student values from reasons.	How does this show what is important to you?	How does your view show what is important to you?

■ **Analyzing Problems**

Procedure	Focusing Questions	Application
Clarify the problem.	What is the problem? issue? difficulty?	How can American Indians protect the remaining lands they own as a tribe?
Identify alternative solutions and reasons for them.	What should be done? Why? What else might be done? Why?	What should be done? How can individuals be discouraged from selling their land?
Identify strengths, weaknesses, and possible reactions.	Which is the best solution? What might the reaction be to each one?	Which proposals are best? Which will be supported?
Relate to students' experiences.	Have you ever had a problem like this one? What did you do?	Which have been tried before? What did you do to help?
Evaluate past experience.	As you look back, was that a reasonable thing to do? Why?	What worked best? Would you do it again? Why or why not?
Consider alternatives and reasons for them.	Is there anything you would do differently? Why?	What might be done differently? What might work better? Why?

GUIDELINES FOR PLANNING A LESSON
Equal Rights for Women

Objectives   State the objectives to be achieved—for example, to identify equal rights that women should be accorded and to state action that can be taken to achieve equal rights.

Introduction   Present a reading, video, current event or other item and clarify the facts by asking such questions as: What is the problem? What information is presented? In what areas should women be given equal rights?

Development   Clarify dimensions of the problem and possible reasons for the situation by asking questions such as these: What are the main aspects of this problem? What reasons are given for the lack of equal rights for women in salaries? in entering certain professions? in other activities? Can you think of other reasons?

    Infer values that have been violated by asking questions such as these: What do the reasons indicate to be basic values that have been violated? How about equality of opportunity? How about freedom to choose?

    Identify steps that should be taken to remedy the situation by asking questions such as these: What suggestions are given for improving the situation? What reasons are given for them? What additional suggestions do you have? What are your reasons for them?

Conclusion   Clarify the values behind the suggestions for improving the situation by asking questions such as these: What do the suggestions and the reasons for them indicate to be important values that must be adhered to? Why should equality of opportunity and justice be extended to everyone?

Clarifying Questions

Pose nonjudgmental questions to stimulate students to think about values they hold and why they hold them:

Why do you feel (think, act) that way? How long have you felt that way? How do others feel about it? Why might some feel differently?

Can you use other words to tell what you mean? How might you explain your decision to others? Is this what you mean? (The teacher repeats or rephrases a student's comment.) Can you give an example?

What alternatives have you considered? What are possible consequences? What may happen if you do that? What might others do in your situation? Why?

Why is it so important? How does it compare in importance with other actions you might take? How much do you really value it?

What might you do if you were in their (her, his) situation? Why? What other actions might you take? Which would be most desirable? Why?

Values Sheets

■ The aim of education is
the knowledge not of
facts but of values.
—**William Ralph Inge**

Values sheets provoke thinking about value concepts, such as cooperation, friendship, concern for others, and fairness, or about value-laden topics that arise in units of study. They range in content from a single provocative statement to a paragraph or two on a problem, an issue, or an incident. Sometimes a picture, cartoon, part of a video, or some other resource is presented to stir thinking. The presentation is followed by directions or questions that call for choosing, prizing, or acting, as shown in this example.

A Word to the Wise Is Enough! (Benjamin Franklin)

What does this saying mean to you? What do you think it meant to patriots during the Revolutionary War? What do you think it meant to Tories? What do you think it meant to those who were not sure which side to choose? In what situations can it be used today? How can you use it in school and at home?

A values sheet is included in the facing lesson plan designed to develop democratic values and behavior. Values may be identified, surveyed, and compared on values sheets, as shown in Figure 13.2 (p. 408).

Here are other strategies and activities that you might use in values clarification.

ACTIVITY IDEAS ➤ *Values Clarification*

➤ Help students grasp values concepts by defining the concept and moving to an application of it. Here is a sample worksheet. You could extend it to include other values concepts as well.

> Cooperation means _____.
> I can cooperate in discussion by _____.
> I can cooperate better on committees by _____.

➤ Have students put themselves "in someone else's shoes" in order to understand that person's decisions, feelings, actions, words, and so on. You might supply a worksheet like this one to get them started.

> **If I Had Been . . .**
> If I had been one of the first settlers in our state, two wishes I would have made and reasons for them are:
>
> 1. _____
>   Reason: _____
> 2. _____
>   Reason: _____

LESSON PLAN   *Open-Mindedness*

Objective   To define open-mindedness and identify ways to be open-minded in social studies activities

Introduction   Ask students to read the following values sheet.

> **Open-Mindedness**
>
> Read these definitions, and be prepared to ask any questions you have about their meaning.
>
> Showing fairness and impartiality.
>
> Considering others' points of view.
>
> Being broad-minded and reasonable.
>
> Weighing the *pros* and *cons* of proposals.

Development   Respond to students' questions to clarify the meaning of each definition.

After discussing each definition, ask, What should we include in a definition that we can use in class activities?

Conclusion   Have groups of four to five students prepare definitions. Ask each group to report its definition. Discuss good ideas in each one, and guide the class to make a definition that includes the best elements.

Discuss how the definition can be applied to the following items:

committee work	preparing reports	analyzing issues
discussion	making decisions	planning a project

Evaluation   Ask students to note how they will be open-minded when

1. discussing current events.
2. choosing a committee.
3. giving a report.
4. discussing reports of others.

Sample Values Sheets

How Do You Rank English Settlements in These Places?

Write 1 for the settlement you think was best, 2 for the next best, and so on. Write a reason for your first and last choices.

_____ Boston _____ Charleston _____ Jamestown
_____ New York _____ Providence _____ Savannah

Reason for 1: _____
Reason for 6: _____

How Important Were These to Early Settlers in Our State?

Mark each item as follows: 3, most important; 2, important; 1, least important.

_____ Food _____ Shelter _____ Wealth _____ Family life _____ Law and order
_____ Clothing _____ Health _____ Happiness _____ Education

If I were a colonist, _____.

How Important Are These in Our State Today?

Mark each item as follows: 3, most important; 2, important; 1, least important.

_____ Food _____ Shelter _____ Wealth _____ Family life _____ Law and order
_____ Clothing _____ Health _____ Happiness _____ Education

Which ones did you rate the same in early times and now? Why? _____

Which did you rate differently in early times and now? Why? _____

How Do You Rate Yourself?

Mark each item as follows: 5, very good; 4, good; 3, fair; 2, poor; 1 very poor.

_____ 1. Showing respect for all students   _____ 4. Being a helpful committee member
_____ 2. Considering new ways to do things   _____ 5. Being the chairperson of a committee
_____ 3. Contributing ideas during discussion

How can you improve on those marked 3, 2, or 1? _____

If You Were a Colonist

Imagine you were living in New England during colonial times. How important do you think the items listed below would have been? Rate each one from 1 to 5, with 1 for the most important, 2 for the next, and so on.

_____ Health _____ Wealth _____ Hard work
_____ Patriotism _____ Peace _____ Strict laws
_____ Religious freedom _____ Education _____ Family life

Circle the one you think would be most important of all. Write a reason for choosing it: _____

_____

Underline the one you think would be least important. Write a reason for choosing it: _____

_____

How might K–8 students gain an understanding of such horrors as the Holocaust? How would you treat the Holocaust in your classroom?

➤ As another way to express values, have students list three wishes: one for their community, one for their state, and one for their country. Then discuss what values these wishes reveal.

Moral Reasoning Skills

You can foster moral development by guiding students to develop progressively higher levels of moral reasoning based on a growing conception of justice (Kohlberg, 1984). Conceptions of justice and types of reasoning vary across these levels and stages of moral development:

Preconventional level: Most 4- to 10-year-olds base reasoning on consequences of action. Stage 1 is characterized by a punishment and obedience orientation. Physical consequences determine goodness or badness, and justice may be viewed as "an eye for an eye." Stage 2 is characterized by an instrumental orientation, an exchange of favors, and the attitude expressed by "you scratch my back and I'll scratch yours."

Conventional level: Most 10- to 18-year-olds and many adults base reasoning on conformity and loyalty. Stage 3 is characterized by an interpersonal concordance orientation, conforming to get approval, and "being a good boy or a nice girl." Stage 4 is marked by a law-and-order orientation, respect for authority, loyalty to family and country, and "doing one's duty."

Postconventional level: Some adults base reasoning on ethical principles. Stage 5 is marked by a social contract and legalistic orientation. Right action is judged by adherence to contracts, general rights, and "a legal point of view."

Stage 6 is marked by a universal ethical principle orientation and is achieved by very few. Moral reasoning is based on self-chosen universal principles of justice that "respect the dignity of all human beings as individuals."

To give students practice in moral reasoning, you can present a moral dilemma to students orally or through a reading, a video, or another medium to highlight conflicting value choices. Here is an example.

What Should Jed Do with the Nuggets?

Jed's father has had poor luck prospecting for gold. They have no food and all their money is gone. Another prospector has "hit it rich." As he hurriedly loads a bag of nuggets on his horse, he does not notice that a few nuggets fall from the bag. Should Jed take the nuggets to his father or return them to the owner? Why or why not?

After brief discussion of the dilemma, ask students to take a position and give reasons for it. If there is little disagreement, more information may be given. For example, other miners will ask where the nuggets were obtained, or Jed's father will repay the rich prospector as soon as possible.

Next, provide small-group discussion (four to five students) so that students can analyze reasons and prepare questions about reasons, both for and against, for use in class discussion.

Finally, critically examine these reasons in class discussion, guided by questions such as these:

- What are reasons for keeping the nuggets? for returning them?
- What questions does each group have?
- Which is more important—helping one's family or not taking something that belongs to others?
- What if Jed's father had been the one who had "struck it rich" and then lost the nuggets?
- What might the consequences be if Jed keeps the nuggets? What if everyone kept things that someone lost?

Follow-up activities may be provided—for example, finding related examples, writing a solution that resolves the dilemma, or creating a dilemma story on the same issue or another one.

In discussions about moral reasoning, emphasize what the central character or group *should* do, not *would* do. A discussion of what a person *would* do shifts the focus from moral reasoning to an analysis of factors involved in predicting behavior.

Students' moral reasoning can be improved through probing questions such as the following:

Why is the use of children's literature an excellent strategy for exploring students' feelings and values? How might trade books help K–8 teachers connect affective, psychomotor, and cognitive elements of social studies learning?

Perception-checking questions to clarify the issue and identify points of agreement and disagreement: Are there questions about what is happening? What choice(s) does the person have?

Issue-related questions to clarify the issue: Should property rights be respected? Why or why not? What family obligation does Jed have? Why?

Interissue questions to focus on value conflicts: Which is more important—family welfare or property rights? Why?

Role-switch questions to consider various points of view: What if Jed's father had lost the nuggets? Should the finder return them? Why?

Universal consequences questions to consider broad implications: What if everyone did this? What might the consequences be? Why?

Teachers and students may prepare dilemmas after several have been analyzed. Identify issues that require an individual or a group to make conflicting value choices: telling the truth versus shielding a friend, sharing with others versus maintaining one's property rights, individual freedom versus obedience to authority, self-interest versus the good of the group, and keeping promises versus changing one's mind for personal gain.

Realistic issues may be identified in a unit, current event, or school activity. Here are some examples:

Should May tell on her friend who took an extra cup of water after the wagon train leader ordered everyone to a set limit until they reached the next water hole? Why or why not?

Should Susan join a demonstration to demand comparable pay for comparable worth at the factory where her mother works and may be laid off if the demand is met? Why or why not?

Should June, who is on probation because of being late to school, take time to help a person with disabilities cross a busy street? She has been told that she cannot serve as class president if she is late again. What should June do? Why?

You might prepare alterations or additions to the preceding list in order to spark a division of opinion that will stimulate group discussion. Finally, you can prepare probing questions to guide discussion and improve reasoning.

Rational Analysis

■ Visit the Renew America website **http://slostice. crest/environment/ renew_america/** to learn about America's environmental challenges.

A primary goal of rational analysis is to apply critical thinking and decision-making skills to value-laden issues. Many teachers use this approach because it employs skills related to many social studies topics. It is especially useful when information can be collected to support a value judgment or decision.

The following steps in rational analysis are adapted from the basic model presented by Metcalf (1971):

Clarify and define the problem or the issue: What is the problem? What is the main issue? What values are in conflict? What terms need to be defined? What is to be judged?

Gather information: What facts are available? What other facts are needed? Which items are facts, and which are opinions?

Assess the information: How can the facts be checked? Which are based on evidence? Which are unsupported? What do experts say?

Sift out relevant information: Which facts are related to the problem or the issue? Which are needed to make a value judgment or decision?

Make a tentative judgment or decision: What is a reasonable judgment or decision? Is it adequately supported by the facts? What are sound reasons for it?

Appraise the judgment or decision: Does it apply to other cases? Is it consistent with similar judgments or decisions? Does it apply to everyone, including ourselves? What are possible consequences if it is adopted universally?

Action Learning

A primary goal of this approach is to enable students to act on their values in the classroom, the school, and the community. It is most useful when students can be involved in projects such as making collections for the needy, helping the elderly, sharing scrapbooks with housebound children and adults, making holiday cards for absent students, and undertaking other activities that show concern for others or some other basic value. As with rational analysis, action learning puts basic thinking and decision-making skills to use.

The main difference between this and other strategies is the special emphasis on deciding whether or not to act; if the decision is to act, *action and evaluation follow,* as shown below.

> ***Clarify the need or the problem:*** What is the problem? What, if anything, should we do about it?
>
> ***Consider information and take a position:*** What are the facts? What additional facts are needed? What is our position on taking action?
>
> ***Decide whether or not to act:*** How can we help? Will our involvement be a contribution? What are possible consequences?
>
> ***Plan and carry out the action:*** What steps should we take individually and as a group? What materials are needed? Carry out the plan, making revisions as needed.
>
> ***Evaluate action and project future steps:*** Which procedures were most effective? Which were least effective? How can they be improved? What should we do in the future?

The action learning strategy is similar to the problem-solving and decision-making models discussed in Chapter 11. Action learning is not limited to school and community projects; it can take place in the classroom as students take action to secure gender equality, promote adherence to group rules, and demonstrate democratic behavior in group activities.

◼ Conclusion

The affective elements of learning are part of social studies. In most K–8 programs, cognitive, psychomotor, and affective elements are integrated and developed in a meaningful way for optimal student learning. The affective elements include opportunities for students to employ thinking skills as they examine controversial issues; explore their interests, appreciations, and attitudes toward social studies learning; acquire a rich understanding of our country's core civic values; gain an understanding of their own personal values; deal with the tension between societal and personal values; and acquaint themselves with strategies for developing strong values.

With its diversity of students, the social studies classroom is the ideal setting for affective learning. Children and young adults interacting with social studies content provides the ideal setting for exploration of personal values, learning core civic values, and internalizing those behaviors and actions consistent with living in a democratic society.

Questions, Activities, and Evaluation

1. Mark your position on the following items, and discuss it with colleagues.

	Yes	No	?
a. The schools should leave instruction on values to the family and the house of worship.	____	____	____
b. The schools must develop core democratic values, such as justice and equality.	____	____	____
c. The schools should teach students *how* to value, not *what* to value.	____	____	____
d. The social studies program should help students progress to higher levels of moral development.	____	____	____
e. If programs of character education are to succeed, basic values and virtues must be taught in school.	____	____	____
f. All of the above should be rejected.	____	____	____
g. A better point of view is _____			

2. The local school board is considering a policy that would significantly limit instruction in the affective elements of social studies learning. Your task is to develop a policy statement describing the importance of the cognitive, psychomotor, and affective domains and the integration of the three in social studies programs.

3. As you begin your professional career and speak with teachers, administrators, students, parents, and others about social studies instruction, are the affective elements of learning mentioned? Do the different groups view social studies differently? Which group(s), if any, emphasize the affective elements of learning?

4. Identify three episodes in U.S. history that illustrate local, state, or federal commitment to core civic values. Identify three individuals in U.S. history who are role models in exhibiting personal values that are consistent with democratic behavior. How might these episodes and individuals be integrated into units of study?

5. In your elementary and middle school observations, teachers indicate to you that children and young adults are more abusive toward each other and are more apt to resort to physical attacks against peers than they were a decade ago. If these observations are correct, do you believe that part of social studies is to address schoolwide problems? Who should address these problems?

6. State two affective objectives for a unit of your choice, and list activities you might use to achieve them. Refer to the activities noted in this chapter and in the activities in Chapter 2.

7. Examine a textbook and note examples of values, appreciations, and other affective elements. What questions might you use to guide study and discussion of them? What teaching strategy might you use? Make a plan to show how you would use it.

8. Prepare a list of ways to develop democratic behavior in a unit of your choice. Make a worksheet similar to the one presented in this chapter, including examples for each behavior of: (a) what students can do, (b) what students can observe, (c) what students can find in materials.

References

Bennett, W. (1993). *The book of virtues: A treasury of great moral stories.* New York: Simon & Shuster.

Braun, J. A. Jr. (1992). Caring, citizenship and conscience: The cornerstones of a values education curriculum for elementary schools. *International Journal of Social Education, 7,* 47–56.

Butts, R. F. (1988). *The morality of democratic citizenship.* Calabasas, CA: Center for Civic Education. (Chapter 4 on twelve core values)

Chance, J. M. (1993). On the development of democratic citizens. *Social Studies, 84,* 158–163.

Close, F. (1997). The fundamentals of character education. *Social Studies Review, 37,* 93–94. (Special edition on character education)

Coles, R. *The moral intelligence of children.* Cited in "The Bookshelf." (1997). *Education Week, 16* (34).

Fertig, G. (1995). Teaching collaborative skills to enhance the development of effective citizens. *Southern Social Studies Journal, 21,* 53–64.

Hannah, L. S., & Michaelis, J. U. (1997). *A comprehensive framework for instructional objectives.* Reading, MA: Addison-Wesley. (Chapter on attitudes and values)

Hendricks, W. (1990). *Building positive values: A handbook of classroom ideas and activities.* (Rev. Ed.). Mansfield, Ohio: Opportunities for Learning Inc.

Holder, B. H., et al. (1992). Each is home to all of us: Changing attitudes toward individual and shared responsibility. *Teacher Educator, 27,* 47–51.

Howe, H. II. (1997). Acting and understanding: What service learning adds to our academic future. *Education Week, 16,* 56.

Jarrett, J. L. (1991). *The teaching of values.* New York: Routledge.

Kohlberg, L. (1984). *Psychology of moral development.* New York: Harper & Row. (Detailed treatment)

Leming, J. S. (1993). In search of effective character education. *Educational Leadership, 51,* 63–71.

Lickona, T. (1997). *Educating for character: How our schools can teach respect and responsibility.* Cited in "The Bookshelf." (1997). *Education Week, 16* (34).

Mabe, A. R. (1993). Moral and practical foundations for civic education. *Social Studies, 84,* 153–157.

Metcalf, L. E. (Ed.). (1971). *Values education* (41st yearbook). Washington, DC: National Council for the Social Studies.

Mosher, R., Kenny, R. A. Jr., & Garrod, A. (1994). *Preparing for citizenship.* Westport, CT: Prager.

Raths, L. E., Harmin, M., & Simon, S. B. (1978). *Values and teaching.* (2nd ed.). Columbus, OH: Merrill.

Simon, S. B., Howe, L. W., & Kirschenbaum, H. (1972). *Values clarification.* New York: Hart. (Practical strategies)

Stevens, R. L., & Allen, M. G. (1996). Teaching public values: Three instructional approaches. *Social Education, 60,* 155–158.

Tibbitts, F. (1996). Education for citizenship. *Education Week, 15,* 29, 31.

Wagner, T. (1996). Creating community consensus on core values: An alternative to character education. *Education Week, 16,* 36, 38.

Wallen, N. E., et al. (1969). *Final report: The Taba Curriculum Project in the social studies.* Reading, MA: Addison-Wesley. (Valuing strategies)

Wright, I. (1993). Civic education is values education. *Social Studies, 84,* 149–152.

Chapter 14

Evaluating Students' Learning

Chapter Objective

To present guidelines and procedures for evaluating cognitive, psychomotor, and affective outcomes of instruction

Focusing Questions

- What guidelines are used to evaluate learning in social studies?

- How are authentic forms of assessment used to evaluate learning in social studies?

- How can portfolio building help improve student learning and enhance assessment and evaluation in social studies programs?

- What informal techniques and devices are useful in appraising cognitive and affective outcomes of instruction?

- How can student self-evaluation and peer evaluation improve learning?

- How can charts and checklists be prepared and used to appraise performance and products?

- What principles and procedures can be used to prepare test items and use published tests?

■ Making Use of Published Standards

Have you given much thought to assessment and evaluation in social studies? What do these two terms mean to you as you prepare to teach social studies in an elementary or middle school? The introduction of standards in the subject areas (i.e., social studies, mathematics, science, language arts, and reading) at the national level in the 1990s has helped to sharpen teachers', administrators', students', and parents' ideas on assessment and evaluation. (The use of standards is not the only method of looking at assessment and evaluation. However, because standards are so prevalent in education, they offer a helpful basis for assessment and evaluation in social studies.) National standards have been adopted and modified by states across the nation, further refined by individual school districts, and serve as a model of what teachers are asked to do—exactly which social studies cognitive, psychomotor, and affective elements must be taught at each grade level and the level of mastery students should master at each grade level. Turn to Chapters 1, 2, and 5 for an in-depth description of standards.

In Chapter 1 we highlighted standards in the social sciences (e.g., history, geography, economics, political science), and in Chapter 2 we described how each might be used in developing a unit of instruction, a course of study, or a K–8 or K–12 program. Because many states have adopted and refined the NCSS standards and view K–8 social studies as the integration of the social sciences, we will use the NCSS standards to guide our discussion of assessment and evaluation.

However, we do encourage you to look carefully at the social science standards and to incorporate information from these disciplines into your social studies program. And because social studies is sometimes part of interdisciplinary teaching, you may wish to look at standards in other disciplines. Ultimately, you should adopt elements of learning that reflect a general consensus reached among social studies educators, local educators, and the public on what K–8 social studies should consist of.

You may wish to use the NCSS standards as a guide as we describe assessment and evaluation in social studies instruction. The first few pages of the document provide a definition and purpose of social studies—the "anchors" needed to plan instruction. The standards represent the content (i.e., cognitive elements), are drawn from the definition and purpose of social studies, and illustrated as themes (e.g., culture; time, continuity, and change; people, places, and environment; global connections). Included as part of the standards are essential skills for social studies and democratic beliefs and values (i.e., psychomotor and affective elements). In short, the standards can be viewed as a model for teaching social studies and as a guide when selecting content, skills, and values to incorporate into a social studies program.

The next section of the NCSS document offers examples of meeting the standards in the elementary and middle grades. Here are two examples:

Culture—compare the ways in which people from different cultures think about and deal with their physical environment and social conditions; production, distribution, and consumption

Compare basic economic systems according to who determines what is produced, distributed, and consumed

These examples serve two purposes: (1) they suggest what teachers might do to address each standard, and (2) they identify how students might show a particular level of mastery of the standards.

The sections entitled "Standards into Practice: Examples in the Early Grades" and "Standards into Practice: Examples for the Middle Grades" provide classroom examples of how teachers address the standards and expectations of students with respect to each standard. Here are two examples:

People, places, and environment—locate and distinguish among varying landforms and geographic features, such as mountains, plateaus, islands, and ocean

Power, authority, and governance—identify and describe the basic features of the political system of the United States, and identify representative leaders from various levels and branches of government

These standards and examples offer teachers more than a "ballpark picture" of what U.S. social studies educators and classroom teachers believe should comprise K–8 social studies instruction for the new millennium. Whether you live in Oregon, Illinois, or Florida, state and districts have adopted the NCSS standards and modified them to reflect their particular needs. If you teach in one of these states, are you at liberty to modify these standards to fit your particular approach to social studies? Absolutely! The NCSS standards should be viewed as an ideal model of social studies instruction in K–8 schools; you will need to decide on how best to implement the NCSS standards. It is your responsibility to make decisions on the selection of content, modifications needed to address the strengths and weaknesses of students, and use of instructional approaches to keep students engaged in learning.

So, what will you find in this chapter to help you in the assessment and evaluation process? First, we include guidelines, techniques, and devices that help assess learning. Teachers in the primary grades devote part of their instruction to providing children with opportunities to learn how to stay on task, being courteous to others, not disturbing others, cooperating with the teacher, and the like. They provide activities that integrate these behaviors with core civic values as young children learn about themselves, others, neighborhoods, and our nation's history. Second, because classrooms are culturally diverse and students express learning in different ways (i.e., multiple intelligences, styles of learning, ways of thinking), we provide a wealth of resources to diagnose students' obstacles to learning and assess learning in social studies. Last, from a more expansive perspective, these same guidelines, techniques, and devices can help teachers assess their own performance and, by extension, offer input on ways of becoming more effective in the classroom. In short, effective assessment in the social studies is beneficial to both students and teachers.

■ Types of Evaluation

A primary function of evaluation is to inform decisions about instruction that will enhance the achievement of social studies objectives. The evaluation process includes stating objectives in measurable form, collecting related evidence, and using the evidence to make instructional decisions. *Diagnostic evaluation* is used to identify individual and group needs. *Formative evaluation* is done during instruction to appraise ongoing progress. *Summative evaluation* is done at the end of a unit or term to appraise the attainment of objectives.

Students' learning may be appraised at local, state, and national levels. Local assessment is most useful to teachers because it is directly related to the program of instruction. State assessment programs stress basic skills, although some include social studies or citizenship. The National Assessment of Educational Progress has included U.S. history, civics, and geography.[1] Information on state and national assessments, available in local school districts, will offer sample objectives, sample test items, and relative achievement of students.

Criterion-referenced measurement determines the extent to which defined objectives have been met. *Norm-referenced measurement* compares the achievement of students with that of a large sample in terms of percentile, grade equivalent, or other scores. Currently, *performance-based assessment* and *authentic assessment,* in which teachers create assessment materials that reflect students' learning styles, are favored methods of assessment.

---

1. National Assessment of Educational Progress, Educational Testing Service, P.O. Box 6666, Princeton, NJ 08541. Request NAEP Newsletter and the list of available reports.

The following example is drawn from the New York State list of principles for curriculum and assessment[2]:

High content and performance standards in the curriculum frameworks

Higher-order thinking and performance skills in realistic tasks and situations

Many ways and opportunities for students to show what they know and can do

Identification of students' strengths and needs, revealing ways to improve teaching and learning

Appraisal of learning over time and providing information on what students know and can do

Incorporation of state and local components

Use of different tasks, portfolios, records of achievement, and structured observation to get evidence on students' abilities and achievement

These principles have been addressed in a number of ways. Two examples—authentic assessment and portfolio building—illustrate the progress being made in the area of assessment. Authentic assessment refers to alternative methods that depart from traditional forms of assessment (e.g., true/false, multiple choice, essay, and matching questions). Over the past decade, as teachers have critically surveyed the cultural diversity in their classrooms, they have found traditional assessment wanting and have searched for alternatives. This trend has led to the modification of some diagnostic tools and new methods of assessing learning. Also, educational research has provided new insights into student learning (e.g., multiple intelligences, ways of thinking), and these have affected assessment. Today, more and more K–8 teachers possess tools that can be characterized as traditional and authentic.

Portfolios, samples of students' work gathered over a period of time, have become a widely used tool for assessment. Portfolios include student work selected by the teacher, teacher and student, and the student. Teachers have differing philosophies about and approaches to portfolios, but many agree that portfolios have these benefits: (1) they offer teachers the opportunity to observe students in a broader context, (2) they give students the opportunity to influence the assessment and evaluation processes, and (3) they encourage students to become independent and self-directed learners. Because portfolios are intended to show growth in learning over time, they are constantly evolving.

The process of using portfolios is quite simple. If the student is to be solely responsible for the portfolio, the following steps might be followed:

1. Students collect work in folders.
2. They periodically select work from their folders to be revised, adapted, or polished for inclusion in their portfolios

---

2. New York Teacher, May 30, 1994. For a detailed review see Learning Centered Curriculum and Assessment for New York State. Report of the State Curriculum and Assessment Council to the Commissioner of Education and the Board of Regents, Nov. 1993, 15–16.

3. Students regularly reflect on competed work or work in progress
4. Ultimately, students reflect on the whole body of work in the portfolio in order to assess their own learning, accomplishments, and strengths, and to set future goals.

The guidelines, techniques, and devices presented in this chapter can be characterized as both traditional and authentic. In addition, they should be viewed as "generic" because they were developed based on the general characteristics of children and young adults. As you look at these examples, reflect on the cultural diversity you will encounter in your classroom as well as the students with exceptionalities. How might some of these guidelines, techniques, and devices be modified to accommodate the student who has hearing impairments, the student who is a recent immigrant from Yugoslavia, or the student who does not value social studies? And, once you begin your professional career, continue to look for assessment tools that are flexible and can be modified to address the diversity and exceptionalities found among students. Last, the following tools for social studies assessment might be recorded in students' folders and ultimately included in students' portfolios.

Guidelines for Evaluation

The following guidelines will help you plan a thoroughgoing process of evaluation that will help guide instruction and support learning for all students.

Plan and Conduct Evaluation Systematically   Evaluation should not be done randomly or casually. To truly grasp students' achievement and needs, you must plan and implement a system of evaluation. First, determine the purpose. Second, select the technique(s) to be used. Third, collect assessment data and judge the results. Fourth, use the results to make a decision on what to do to improve teaching and learning. Fifth, implement the decision and continue the evaluation process.

Consider All Objectives   Knowledge, skills, attitudes and values, and participation may vary in emphasis, but none of them should be neglected as you plan instruction and evaluate outcomes. For example, assessment of unit outcomes might include test items on knowledge and skills, a brief questionnaire on attitudes, and a checklist on participation—all related to unit objectives. Don't evaluate attainment of just one or two objectives.

Evaluate Continuously   Use diagnostic or preassessment to identify individual and class needs. Make a needs assessment by determining the gap between current performance of students and the desired performance. Use formative assessment during instruction and make adjustments. Use summative assessment to determine whether objectives have been achieved. Use of the full rage of assessment techniques ensures complete information about students' learning.

> ■ Not everything that counts can be counted and not everything that can be counted counts.
>
> **—Albert Einstein**

Integrate Evaluation and Instruction   This is vital in social studies because learning activities provide useful evidence of achievement. For example, discussion, reporting, and committee activities can be observed to assess understanding of concepts and expression of attitudes. Also, be sure there is a match between what you teach and what you evaluate.

Select Appropriate Techniques and Devices   Observation, discussion, charts, portfolios of students' work, and checklists are helpful evaluation tools. Computer testing, teacher-made tests, and test items in textbooks and workbooks are related to instruction and can be modified to fit unit objectives. You may also base evaluation on self-reports such as attitude questionnaires and value scales, logs or diaries or videos of activities, completed task cards, learning progress charts or maps, quality circles, and anecdotal records or behavior journals.

Provide for Student Self-Evaluation and Constructive Peer Evaluation   Skill in self-evaluation is essential to the development of self-direction that is an attribute of effective citizenship and lifelong learning. Constructive peer evaluation adds a valuable dimension to the appraisal of students' learning. Checklists, rating forms, and other devices may be used to develop students' evaluation skills. Differences among self-evaluations, peer evaluations, and teacher evaluations should be discussed to find ways to improve evaluation procedures.

Use Assessment Data Constructively   Observation, discussion, charts, and checklists yield data that can be used immediately to modify instruction, provide feedback, and enhance learning. Summaries of data from tests, portfolios of work samples, observation, and other appraisals should be used to determine grades, report to parents, and implement the accountability program in accord with school district policies.

Why is teacher observation an effective method of evaluating students' learning in social studies? Are you familiar with student self-evaluation and peer evaluation?

■ Assessment Techniques and Devices

Observation by the Teacher

A most useful technique is daily observation of students as they participate in discussion, committees, and other social studies activities. You might assess interests, attitudes, work habits, acceptance of responsibility, and other behavior. For example, information on students' attitudes can be obtained by looking for the following:

1. Positive or negative statements about a person, a group, an activity, an object, or an organization
2. Number of times reference is made to the above in positive or negative terms
3. Willingness or unwillingness to work or interact with an individual or a group or to defend or help others in time of need
4. Expressions of likes, dislikes, preferences, and opinions regarding individuals, groups, and activities

Checklists are used to focus observation (and student self-evaluation). For example, Figure 14.1 contains specific behavior to observe and is easy to use in a variety of situations. Columns containing students' names may be added to the right to keep a record of the behavior of members of a committee, other groups, or the class. Other examples are presented later in this chapter.

Items to include in checklists and charts may be identified through teacher observation. For example, after observing the use of sexist language in discussion, one teacher guided the class to develop a chart for future evaluation that included these items: (1) use terms such as *active* and *strong* to describe both women and men; (2) give examples of both men and women when discussing notable people; (3) describe roles and contributions of both women and men in discussions of historic events; (4) use terms such as *firefighter, chairperson,* and *homemaker* instead of

■ FIGURE 14.1

Observation Checklist

Appraisal of Open-Mindedness

Rate as follows: 1, good; 2, fair; 3, poor.

_____ 1. Considers differing ideas

_____ 2. Tries new ways to do things

_____ 3. Puts facts before feelings

_____ 4. Seeks all sides of an issue

_____ 5. Willing to change views

_____ 6. Judges others fairly

Appraisal of Work in Small Groups

Rate as follows: 1, good; 2, fair; 3, poor.

_____ 1. Keeps the task in mind

_____ 2. Cooperates with the leader

_____ 3. Does not disturb others

_____ 4. Is courteous to others

_____ 5. Does a fair share of the work

_____ 6. Helps find ways to improve

fireman, chairman, and *housewife;* and (5) include examples of women in leadership positions along with those of men.

As suggested earlier, you may wish to modify the checklists and charts provided in this chapter to improve the quality of observation. First, focus on a few students, looking for specific behaviors. Second, do not be influenced by your overall impression of a student (the halo effect). Third, look for both positive and negative instances of behavior, being sure not to be caught in the trap of fault finding. Fourth, note reactions later so that observation will not be obscured by personal feelings and data may be interpreted as objectively as possible.

When interpreting observations, keep in mind that similar types of behavior may not indicate similar learning. For example, some students may help others because of concern for others; other students may help because they want to move in on the activity. Some students may carry out a responsibility because it is in line with group plans, while others may do it merely to obtain approval of the teacher. By and large, however, most observed behavior can be interpreted at face value when students are engaged in meaningful activities.

Group Discussion

Discussion is widely used to assess progress in daily activities, use of concepts, attitudes toward specific social studies learnings, use of thinking skills, and so on. Typically, the teacher develops standards in each area of instruction (though students may also develop them), and assessment is completed in a systematic and timely fashion. Outcomes for both the students and teacher include the following: knowledge of progress in skill attainment, strengths and weaknesses of group projects, and next steps to take.

Guide discussion with questions that focus attention on unit objectives. For example, questions for community studies might include these: What special features make our community different from others we have studied? Why do you think so many early communities were located near waterways? Who can describe the different zones in a city? In which of the cities we have studied would you most like to live? Why? Questions for a unit on regions might include these: How are regions defined? What characteristics might be used to define regions of our country? Which regions are best for agriculture? Why? Which ones are most densely populated? Why? Other examples may be found in the focusing questions presented in Chapters 2 and 4.

Figure 14.2 shows a checklist that students might use to evaluate their participation in a discussion.

Quality Circles

Quality circles include four or five students whose task is to evaluate and suggest improvements in learning activities. They note difficulties, needed changes, ways to improve, and progress in making improvements. Students might use questions like these to appraise an activity: What strengths should be continued? What weaknesses should be eliminated? What difficulties arose? How can they be overcome? What specific recommendations should be made to improve the quality of our work?

■ **FIGURE 14.2**

Discussion of Self-Evaluation

Which Do You Do?	**Discussion Standards**
_____ Use questions to guide study.	_____ I wait to be recognized.
_____ Get ideas from reading materials.	_____ I give others their turn.
_____ Get ideas from audiovisual materials.	_____ I make a contribution.
_____ Take and organize notes.	_____ I stick to the topic.
_____ Share ideas during discussion.	_____ I listen to others.
_____ Help to plan next activities.	_____ I help find ways to improve.

Some activities or units of study require more specific questions related to content or skills. For example, one group used the following to find ways to improve the quality of map work: What changes are needed in (1) use of symbols, (2) use of color, (3) printing of place names, (4) accuracy of location of items, and (5) clarity of the legend? Another group was guided by these questions as they appraised the quality of committee work: What can the chairperson do to get each member to contribute? How can each member do a fair share of the work? What changes are needed in work standards? What should be done to get all members to follow work standards? Which standards are most difficult to follow? Why? What should be done to meet them?

Committee procedures may be used, with a chairperson as leader and a recorder to report recommendations for improvement. Student involvement in devising questions, identifying needed changes, and making recommendations keeps responsibility on students for the continuing improvement of learning activities. A desirable spinoff is growth in self-direction, a key element in lifelong learning.

More Assessment Tools

Table 14.1 (p. 430) gives criteria that you may use in developing your own evaluative charts and checklists, both for your own use and for student use in peer evaluation and self-evaluation. Various types of scales can be designed. The following guidelines are helpful in preparing evaluative charts and checklists:

■ For a look at the many assessment tools employed by schools across the nation turn to **http://www.sdcoe. k12.ca.us/welcome. html**, San Diego County Office of Education's website.

1. Identify specific items to include by checking teaching guides, standards documents, and other appropriate materials.
2. Observe students, and analyze their work to note specific needs and to modify instruction.
3. Vary the number of items for students to use in self-evaluation to achieve adequate evaluation of a defined knowledge, skill, or attitude domain.
4. Involve students in discussion of the evaluation tools so that students will understand how to use them and why.

Figure 14.3 (p. 431) shows formats that may be used to design these instruments.

■ **TABLE 14.1**

Evaluating Different Types of Student Work

Outline Maps

Title descriptive of content?

Compass rose drawn accurately?

Data double-checked?

Symbols defined in legend?

Neat and legible printing?

Places located accurately?

Source(s) of data given?

Social Studies Reports

Significant topic selected?

Social studies concepts used?

Main ideas supported by details?

Main ideas in proper order?

Effective use of maps and illustrations?

Clear title, introduction, and summary?

Sources of information noted?

Defining Terms and Issues

Clear definitions?

Similarities to and differences from other issues or problems noted?

Appropriate questions raised?

Relevant ideas expressed?

Individual and group values embraced?

Issue, problem, or terms clearly expressed in own words?

Judging and Using Information

Evidence related to problem is presented?

Inconsistencies and contradictions are identified?

Facts, opinions, and reasoned judgments are differentiated and stated clearly?

Assumptions, bias, stereotypes, and propaganda identified?

Drawing Conclusions

Conclusions based on evidence?

Inferences drawn correctly?

Implications identified?

Inferences distinguished from generalizations?

Conclusions used to formulate hypotheses and make predictions?

Faulty generalizations and conclusions identified?

Questionnaires and inventories are self-report devices used to assess feelings, interests, attitudes—affective outcomes of instruction. Formats vary from those that require marking a smiling or nonsmiling face on a worksheet and yes/no to five- and seven-place scales. Attitude scales often have five places, ranging from *strongly agree* to *strongly disagree, strongly favor* to *strongly disfavor,* or other appropriate terms. Figure 14.4 (p. 432) shows examples of these formats.

The semantic differential is used to assess attitudes toward a group, a person, an activity, a place, an object, or an event. Students mark their position on a scale between bipolar adjectives, as shown in Figure 14.5 (p. 433). Examples of other adjectives are brave–cowardly, calm–agitated, clear–hazy, fair–unfair, high–low, honest–dishonest, relaxed–tense, sweet–sour, and valuable–worthless.

Titles of scales used in the social studies might be called: Living in Our Community, Using Computers, Veterans Day, Living in a Desert Region, Our Country's Future, Moving West in a Covered Wagon, Life in China, Contributions of the Romans, and Life in the Middle Ages. Feelings about social studies activities may be assessed by scales with titles such as Working on Committees, Preparing Individual Reports, and Group Discussion.

■ **FIGURE 14.3**

Formats for Assessment Instruments

■ **Horizontal Scale for Teacher Use**

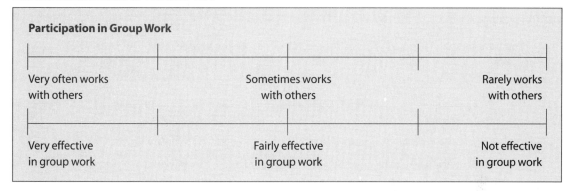

Participation in Group Work

| Very often works with others | Sometimes works with others | Rarely works with others |

| Very effective in group work | Fairly effective in group work | Not effective in group work |

■ **Checklists for Student Use**

How Good Is Your Work on Committees?

Mark each item as follows: 5, very good; 4, good; 3, fair; 2, poor; 1, very poor.

_____ Making plans for work   _____ Sticking to the job

_____ Being a helpful member   _____ Following work rules

_____ Chairing a committee   _____ Doing a fair share of work

_____ Respecting all members   _____ Finding ways to improve

How can you improve on those marked 3, 2, and 1?

Rate Yourself on Media Literacy!

Grade yourself as follows: A, always; B, frequently; C, sometimes; D, rarely; E, never.

Which of these do you analyze and evaluate to detect good and bad features?

_____ Newspapers	_____ Magazines	_____ Radio	_____ TV
_____ Video	_____ Film	_____ Trade books	_____ Textbooks
_____ Computer programs	_____ References	_____ Other _____	

Which of these do you use to analyze and evaluate media?

_____ Purpose	_____ Motive	_____ Point of view	_____ Assumptions
_____ Values	_____ Facts	_____ Opinions	_____ Emotional appeals
_____ Persuasion techniques	_____ Other _____		

How can you improve on those marked C, D, and E?

Formats for Questionnaires and Inventories

Mark the Face that Shows How You Feel

1. Studying our community 😊

2. Reading about regions ☹️

Are You Interested in These Hispanic Unit Activities?

1. Reading about leaders   Yes   No
2. Interviewing leaders   Yes   No
3. Giving a report   Yes   No
4. Making a booklet   Yes   No

Social Studies Attitudes

Mark as follows: SA, strongly agree; A, agree; U, uncertain; D, disagree; SD, strongly disagree.

_____ 1. Students learn how to be good citizens in social studies.

_____ 2. More time should be given to history of our country.

_____ 3. More time should be given to global studies.

Preference for Group Work

Rank in order your preference for working on the following committees, beginning with 1 for your first choice.

_____ Crafts   _____ Dioramas   _____ Interviewing

_____ Mapping   _____ Murals   _____ Quality circle

How Do You Rate Social Studies Instruction?

1. Rank these in order of importance. Use 1 for the most important, 2 for the next most important, to 5 for the least important.

   _____ Art   _____ Arithmetic   _____ Reading   _____ Science   _____ Social Studies

2. Should we have *more* or *less* of the following in social studies?

Library books	More	Less	Individual reports	More	Less
Field trips	More	Less	Arts and crafts	More	Less
Role playing	More	Less	Class discussion	More	Less
Committee work	More	Less	Computer projects	More	Less
Simulations	More	Less	Gender equality rules	More	Less
Geography	More	Less	History	More	Less
Civics	More	Less	Economics	More	Less

3. What is the best part of social studies instruction? _____

4. What is the worst part of social studies instruction? _____

■ **FIGURE 14.5**

Semantic Differential Scale

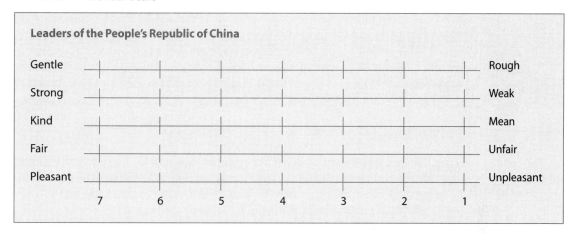

Students may participate in the preparation of useful scales by suggesting topics and proposing or adding adjectives. For example, one group proposed the following bipolar terms for a scale on Our Public Transit System: bright–dull, cheap–costly, easy–hard, fast–slow, and good–bad. Another group planned a scale entitled The Gold Rush and Miners, and they used the dictionary and the thesaurus to double-check these antonyms: bold–timid, excited–calm, gritty–smooth, lucky–unlucky, and wealthy–poor.

Both individual and group logs or diaries contain information for use in evaluation. The group-made log contains material dictated by the class, may be entered on an experience chart, and is related to daily activities. Individual logs or diaries are kept by each student. A helpful recording form is shown in Figure 14.6.

■ **FIGURE 14.6**

Individual Learning Log

Daily Learning Log

Name _____ Unit _____ Date _____

New concepts learned _____

Other learning _____

Difficulties _____

Most interesting activity _____

Least interesting activity _____

Most valuable activity _____

Other comments _____

Anecdotal Records

Teachers may make brief notes on a student's behavior in order to gather data on interests, learning difficulties, misbehavior, and special needs. Teacher comments are added later to indicate steps to take to improve learning. The excerpts in Figure 14.7, from a behavior journal on a student who had been doing poorly in social studies, illustrate how anecdotal records may be used. Because of the extra time and work involved, such records should be limited to situations of special importance for which evaluation data are not otherwise available.

Portfolios

A portfolio put together by a teacher, for example, may provide for summative as well as formative evaluation. Students' reports, map work, social studies artwork, semantic maps, and other materials may be examined to appraise learning and identify points to clarify in instruction. Samples gathered at the beginning and the end of a term or a unit may be compared to appraise students' progress and to report to parents. Tape recordings of discussions and oral reports may be used by students as well as by the teacher to appraise verbal skills and use of concepts. Positive ways to improve should be emphasized so that students benefit without feeling embarrassment for their mistakes or weaknesses.

Individual Conferences

In serious cases a conference with a student can help identify needs, difficulties, interests, and reasons for behavior. Special care should be taken to be a good listener, focus on specific examples of behavior, elicit suggestions from the student, and maintain rapport throughout the conference. Specific appraisals may be made by having a student think aloud while interpreting a map or table, using an index or table of contents, or engaging in another activity in need of evaluation.

■ FIGURE 14.7

Example of an Anecdotal Record

Excerpts from Behavior Journal on Mae R.

Date	Incidents	Comments
10/4	Did not volunteer for an individual project.	May be interested in making a study of a notable woman.
10/6	Asked if materials were available on black women.	Must check with librarian.
10/7	Asked if anyone was reporting on Sojourner Truth.	Great! Materials available.
10/11	Volunteered to make a booklet.	Must give help as needed to ensure success.

Evaluation of student learning is not the sole responsibility of the classroom teacher. K–8 teachers interact with a number of professionals when assessing and evaluating students' experiences in social studies.

Peer Evaluation

Students' evaluation of each other goes on constantly and should be put to constructive use. Benefits to students include development of skill in making positive comments and constructive suggestions, in self-appraisal by comparing one's own work with that of others, and in applying standards objectively and fairly. Peer evaluation also gives students immediate feedback expressed in terms they understand and grounded in learning activities that they've participated in. Perceptions of fellow students can be insightful and helpful.

To ensure that peer evaluation is truly constructive, give students guiding principles and rating forms to support the evaluation process. Sample guidelines and a form are given in Figure 14.8 (p. 436).

■ Constructing and Using Tests

Criterion-referenced and norm-referenced tests, many of which reflect the knowledge, skills, and affective elements found in social studies national and state standards, are used to assess and evaluate learning in social studies. Criterion-referenced tests are designed to assess achievement in defined domains such as knowledge of state historical events and development of map skills. Norm-referenced tests provide percentile, grade-equivalent, or other scores to compare the achievement of local students and classes with the achievement of a large sample of other students in the same grade or age group.

Criterion-referenced tests are being used with increasing frequency because they fit local instruction, reveal what each student has mastered, and provide data needed to individualize instruction. For example, mastery of map skills may be assessed by items that require students to interpret the legend, use the scale, identify

■ American students are the most tested and the least examined in the world.

—**Daniel Resnick and Lauren Resnick**

■ **FIGURE 14.8**

Peer Evaluation Forms

■ **Principles**

> **Good Evaluators**
>
> _____ Have clear standards in mind, and use them to make an appraisal.
>
> _____ Apply the standards fairly and honestly to everyone.
>
> _____ Find good points that should be developed further.
>
> _____ Find needs for improvement, and make constructive suggestions.
>
> _____ Double-check to ensure accuracy and fairness of the evaluation.
>
> _____ Reserve judgment when there is lack of evidence or uncertainty.

■ **Rating Form**

> **Rating Each Other in Cooperative Work**
>
> Name of member _____   Name of evaluator _____
>
> | | | | |
> |---|---|---|---|
> | 1. Listens to the chairperson | Always | Usually | Rarely |
> | 2. Listens to other members | Always | Usually | Rarely |
> | 3. Sticks to the job | Always | Usually | Rarely |
> | 4. Follows committee rules | Always | Usually | Rarely |
>
> Strongest point: _____
>
> Needed improvement: _____

directions, and locate places. The ability to use thinking skills may be assessed by items that call for generalizing, analyzing, and evaluating, as shown in the next section. The guiding principle is to note the desired outcomes or competencies in a given domain of instruction and then to prepare related test items.

Computerized testing may be done in an interactive format. Students' responses will prompt the computer to present a related item next (Bracey, 1990).

Testing Students' Thinking Skills

You will test students' thinking skills and mastery of selected concepts on six levels of cognition: knowledge, comprehension, application, analysis, synthesis, and evaluation (Bloom, 1956). Thinking skills are discussed in Chapter 11. Figure 14.9 shows how these skills were tested in a unit about the students' home state.

Testing the Six Levels of Thinking Skills

■ Knowledge Level

Recalling	Which ocean is on the western edge of North and South America?
	A. Arctic B. Atlantic C. Indian D. Pacific
Observing	Write the names of three resources shown on the map on page 72 in our textbook.
	_____ _____ _____

■ Comprehension Level

Interpreting	The graph on page 76 shows that population growth was greatest from
	A. 1881–1910 B. 1910–1940 C. 1940–1970 D. 1970–2000
Generalizing	Which statement best expresses the main idea in the section "Location of Cities"?
	A. The largest cities are near productive resources.
	B. The largest cities are near natural waterways.

■ Application Level

Inferring	What seems to be the purpose of the author of the report "The Coming Water Shortage"?
	A. To urge dam construction C. To cut industrial use
	B. To urge use of rivers D. To promote recycling
Hypothesizing	Complete the following to state a hypothesis that can be tested by gathering evidence:
	The area of our state that would be hurt most by a water shortage is _____.
	A good source of evidence to test the hypothesis is _____.
Predicting	Based on trends shown in the graph on page 78, what do you forecast the population of our state to be in 2010? _____

■ Analysis, Synthesis, and Evaluation Levels

Analysis	Use an outline map to divide our state into major landform regions.
Synthesis	Make and illustrate a tourist map that shows at least four scenic attractions in our state.
Evaluation	If you could choose, where would you most like to live in our state? _____
	Write two reasons for your choice: _____ _____

Testing Affective Outcomes

Most units include objectives related to desirable attitudes, appreciations, interests, or values that involve students' feelings. They may be assessed by requiring students to give ratings, make rankings, or respond on a continuum such as *strongly agree* to *strongly disagree.* Various levels may be assessed, ranging from receiving and responding to valuing and holding a system of values (Krathwohl et al., 1964; Hannah & Michaelis, 1977). The examples presented in Figure 14.4 illustrate useful self-reports. Figure 14.10 shows examples designed to assess seriousness of problems, preferences, degree of importance and interest, and willingness to act on values.

Tests Based on Instructional Materials

Useful criterion-referenced items can be based on material presented in textbooks and other media. Such tests can increase the level of complexity with each test item, beginning with remembering in the first item and moving to interpreting in the second, analyzing in the third, and evaluating in the last. Figure 14.11 (p. 440) shows this progression.

Situation and Problem Test Items

You can test students' ability to apply concepts and main ideas by presenting a situation or a problem, as shown in Figure 14.12 (p. 441).

The model depicted in Figure 14.13 (p. 441) can address realistic and challenging situations that surface in units of study. The model goes beyond identifying a problem to include important aspects of problem solving and decision making.

■ Guidelines for Constructing Test Items

> ■ Authentic assessment means the assessment tasks are real instances of learning rather than indirect estimates of actual learning goals.
>
> —**June R. Chapin and Rosemary G. Messick**

Two main types of test items need to be prepared to fit units of study. Selection-type items, such as multiple choice, binary choice (true–false, yes–no), and matching, are objective and relatively easy to score. Supply-type items, such as short-answer (completion) and essay, are useful when students should respond by expressing the answer rather than choosing one.

A sound procedure is to begin by preparing multiple-choice items, followed by preparing others as needed to assess desired outcomes. For example, true–false items may be used when there are only two alternative responses. Matching items may be used to assess the ability to associate or relate two sets of information. Completion and essay items may be used when students should be able to construct the answer.

All well-prepared test items have clear directions, an appropriate reading level, and correct sentence structure. No items should be trick questions, contain double negatives or unintended clues to answers. Textbook wording should be avoided because it tends to foster rote memorization. Items of the same type (multiple-choice, matching, and so on) should be grouped in separate sections in a test.

Testing Attitudes, Appreciations, Interests, and Values

How Serious Are These Problems in Our State?

Mark each item as follows: A, very serious; B, serious; C, fairly serious; D, not serious; E, not sure.

_____ 1. Acid rain   _____ 3. Air pollution   _____ 5. Mass transit

_____ 2. Toxic waste   _____ 4. Urban blight   _____ 6. Water pollution

---

Which State Do You Prefer?

Rank the following in order of your preference as a state in which to live, beginning with 1 for your first choice.

_____ Alaska   _____ California   _____ Florida   _____ Hawaii

_____ Illinois   _____ New York   _____ Oregon   _____ Texas

Reason for first choice: _____

Reason for last choice: _____

Rate the Following Topics

Mark an X on the lines below each topic to show how important and how interesting it is to you.

1. History of Our State

Very important   Not important

Very interesting   Not interesting

2. Contributions of recent Immigrant Groups

Very important   Not important

Very interesting   Not interesting

What Should All Students Do? What Do You Do?

1. Everyone should show respect for minority group members.

    Strongly agree   Agree   Undecided   Disagree   Strongly disagree

2. I show respect for minority group members.

    Always   Most of the time   Sometimes   Seldom   Never

3. Everyone should find and correct unfairness to minority groups.

    Strongly agree   Agree   Undecided   Disagree   Strongly disagree

4. I find and correct unfairness to minority groups.

    Always   Most of the time   Sometimes   Seldom   Never

■ **FIGURE 14.11**

A Test That Incorporates Instructional Materials

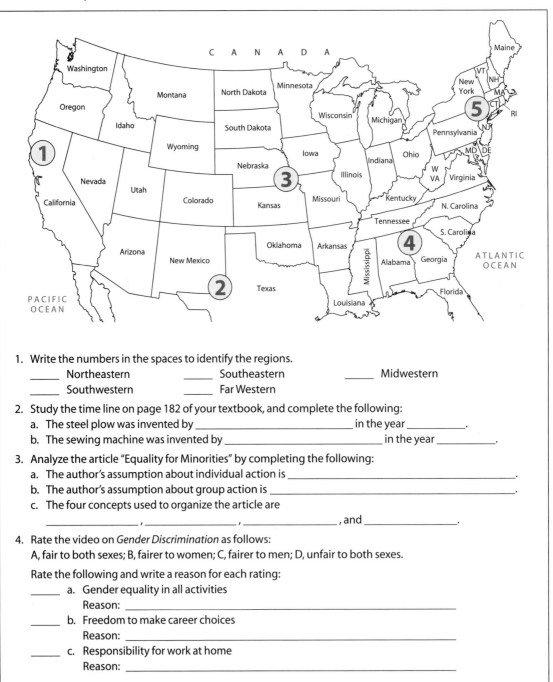

1. Write the numbers in the spaces to identify the regions.
    _____ Northeastern   _____ Southeastern   _____ Midwestern
    _____ Southwestern   _____ Far Western

2. Study the time line on page 182 of your textbook, and complete the following:
    a. The steel plow was invented by _____ in the year _____.
    b. The sewing machine was invented by _____ in the year _____.

3. Analyze the article "Equality for Minorities" by completing the following:
    a. The author's assumption about individual action is _____.
    b. The author's assumption about group action is _____.
    c. The four concepts used to organize the article are
        _____ , _____ , _____ , and _____ .

4. Rate the video on *Gender Discrimination* as follows:
    A, fair to both sexes; B, fairer to women; C, fairer to men; D, unfair to both sexes.

    Rate the following and write a reason for each rating:
    _____ a. Gender equality in all activities
              Reason: _____
    _____ b. Freedom to make career choices
              Reason: _____
    _____ c. Responsibility for work at home
              Reason: _____

Using Problems for Assessment

Pioneer Problems

Pioneers moving westward had to select food to take in their covered wagons.
Mark a + by each item that they would take.

_____ Apples	_____ Carrots	_____ Flour
_____ Bacon	_____ Cheese	_____ Milk
_____ Bread	_____ Dried beans	_____ Rice
_____ Cake	_____ Eggs	_____ Salt

Committee Problems

Members of a committee have had trouble working together. Suggestions for
improvement are listed below. Mark each item as follows: A, agree; D, disagree.

_____ Ask the teacher to step in when a problem arises.

_____ Ask the chairperson to straighten out problems.

_____ Each member should ignore troublemakers.

_____ Any troublemaker should be removed by the chairperson.

_____ Members should go to their seats if trouble arises.

_____ Ask the troublemaker to stick to the job.

■ FIGURE 14.13

Assessing Problem-Solving Skills

Problem, Solutions, Consequences, Decision, Reasons

Complete the following by stating a problem, listing possible solutions and
consequences, making a decision, and noting the reason(s) for it.

The problem: _____

Solution 1: _____

Consequences: _____

Solution 2: _____

Consequences: _____

Decision: _____

_____

Reason(s): _____

_____

Examples of all these test items are given at the end of the chapter (Figures 14.15–20). Together, these guidelines and examples should help you design meaningful, useful test items.

Multiple-Choice Items

These items consist of a question or an incomplete statement (called a *stem*) followed by three or more plausible responses. The correct one or the best one is the answer; the others are distractors that are useful in diagnosing errors and identifying areas in need of review or reteaching. Sometimes variations on selecting the correct response are used, such as selecting the incorrect answer and selecting two or more correct answers. Such optional responses as *all of the above* and *none of the above* should be used rarely if at all, because they confuse many children.

Guidelines

1. The stem should present one question or one problem and should contain most of the item's content.

2. Avoid negatively stated items if possible, and be sure that one alternative is the correct or the best answer.

3. Select plausible alternatives, make them about the same length, distribute them evenly among answer positions, and keep all choices in the same category— that is, do not mix persons, places, and things.

4. Be sure that each alternative is grammatically consistent with the stem.

5. Avoid alternatives that overlap each other as in this example:

   Over the past decade the employment of women in executive positions has increased by
   A. less than 10 percent.
   B. more than 30 percent.
   C. less than 20 percent.
   D. more than 40 percent.

6. Avoid clues, such as words in the stem that are also in the answer, or the use of *a* or *an* at the end of the stem when the alternatives do not all begin with a vowel or a consonant. For example, note how the use of *an* gives a clue in this item:

   A strait is an
   A. hilly area.
   B. inlet of water.
   C. small bay.
   D. strip of land.

Matching Items

These items are a space-saving modification of multiple-choice items. They are used to assess students' ability to associate terms and meanings, persons and events, causes and effects, and other related items. Matching pictures with descriptions or names and matching word pairs or parts of sentences are widely used in early grades. A variety of items may be used in later grades.

Guidelines

1. Place related material, such as people and events or causes and effects, in each column; do not include unrelated content.
2. Keep the number of items small (three to seven), provide extra responses in one column, or permit some responses to be used more than once to minimize guessing by middle- and upper-grade students.
3. Arrange the items in one column in alphabetical, chronological, or some other logical order and those in the other column in random order.
4. Keep the columns on the same page so that students will not have to turn the page to match items.

Binary-Choice Items

True–false, yes–no, right–wrong, and other two-choice items should be used only when two plausible answers are possible. A variety of formats may be used, ranging from the typical true-false item to the cluster format.

Guidelines

1. Include an equal number of true and false items of equal length, and arrange them in random order.
2. Avoid use of *all, none, always, never,* and other specific determiners that are usually false, and *generally, should,* and *may,* which are usually true.
3. Make each item definitely true or false; avoid use of *few, many, important,* and other ambiguous terms.
4. Place the key element in the main part of the statement or the question, not in a phrase or a subordinate clause. Do not use double negatives.
5. You might use these extensions with students in upper grades: if an item is false, rewrite it to make it true; if an item is true, explain why; find proof for each answer by checking the textbook or other source; add a third column *O* to be marked if the item is based on opinion or *E* to be marked if more evidence is needed.

Many teachers use paper and pencil tests to evaluate students' learning in social studies. What are the strengths of this form of evaluation? weaknesses?

Short-Answer Items

These items require students to complete sentences, give examples, define terms, state analogies, write main ideas, and supply other answers to unit-related questions. A broad range of cognitive and affective outcomes can be assessed with these test items.

Guidelines

1. Omit only key words, phrases, or dates, not minor details. Do not write a statement such as "The role of mayors is _____ ." Many different responses are acceptable.

2. Use blanks of uniform size, and do not use *a* or *an* before a blank so that no clues are given.

3. Use definite statements with omissions that call for one correct response. Give students credit for other acceptable responses.

4. Do not omit so many words that meaning is obscured, as in "The Puritans left _____ to settle in _____ because _____."

5. Provide blanks as shown in the preceding examples to facilitate writing by students and scoring answers.

Essay Items

Two types of essay items may be used with students who have adequate writing skills to assess complex learning at the application, analysis, synthesis, and evaluation levels. Restricted-response items set clear limits for the response. Extended-response items provide for greater freedom of response. Both types provide evidence of complex learning not obtained from objective tests. However, scoring is more difficult and time-consuming.

Another form of essay text is a writing assignment that is similar to a learning exercise or an independent study project. Students are required to write and edit a report and to double-check it for accuracy of content, spelling, and grammar.

Guidelines

1. Prepare questions or statements that clearly define the task, require the use of high-level skills, and do not call for long answers beyond the writing competence of students.

2. Write model answers, and use them to check the intent and the clarity of each item; make any needed revisions.

3. Use model answers to score essay items that do not call for divergent responses. For items with divergent answers, use criteria such as completeness, organization, originality, use of examples, and use of key concepts.

4. Score papers anonymously to avoid the halo effect. (Have students write their names on the back of the test paper.) Score all students' answers to one question before going to the next one so that scoring standards will be applied consistently.

5. Inform students when spelling and grammar are to be scored. Give separate scores for them, and do not let their scoring influence the scoring of content.

Test Banks and Published Tests

Teachers can create a bank of test items on file on their computers. Items may be swapped with fellow teachers and thus increase the size of the test bank. A variety of test-bank computer programs is available in most school systems and college libraries. Examples are *Examwriter, QuickTests, Test Quest, Testmaster, Test It!, Quiz Program, Test Factory, Test Generator,* and *All of the Above.*

Some school systems maintain test item banks from which teachers select items. If the item bank is computerized, teachers can locate useful items, run a printout, and use the items in their own tests.

Tests available from organizations and commercial publishers contain a variety of items that are useful in the social studies. Standardized tests with sections on the social studies contain items on skills and concepts that are useful and suggestive of items that teachers can construct. See the following in the college or school district library: *California Achievement Tests, Iowa Tests of Basic Skills, Metropolitan Achievement Test, Sequential Tests of Educational Progress, SRA Achievement Series, Stanford Achievement Test.* Test makers use items such as those shown in Figure 14.14 (p. 446) to assess commonly taught concepts and skills.

Pitfalls to avoid when using published tests are (1) expecting all students to be "at or above the norm," (2) failing to interpret students' achievements in light of capabilities, (3) not taking time to diagnose individual needs, and (4) making a self-fulfilling prophecy by setting low expectations for low achievers.

■ **FIGURE 14.14**

Sample of a Published Test

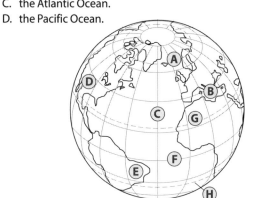

Money to pay for the cost of roads comes from

A. contributions.
B. dividends.
C. dues.
D. taxes.

Which map is best for locating state capitals?

A. highway map
B. political map
C. population map
D. relief map

Which one of these workers provides a service?

A. farmer
B. home builder
C. manufacturer
D. store clerk

The area with letter C on it is

A. part of Europe.
B. North America.
C. the Atlantic Ocean.
D. the Pacific Ocean.

Guiding principles for effective use of standardized tests are: (1) select a test that fits what has been taught, (2) interpret achievement levels in terms of each student's background and capabilities, and (3) follow-up by providing instruction to meet individual needs.

■ Test-Taking Tips

■ FairTest: The National Center for Fair and Open Testing **http:// www.firtest.org** focuses on efforts to ensure that evaluation of students is fair, open, and educationally sound.

Knowing how to approach different testing situations definitely prepares students to succeed. Tips such as these should be discussed with students to help them develop effective test-taking procedures:

- Ask questions if directions are not clear. Do the sample items, and raise your hand if you have any questions.
- Concentrate as you read each item, then choose the best answer. Work rapidly, but carefully. Skip an item if you do not know the answer. Return to it later.
- Do try to answer all items. Choose the answer you think is best. Be sure the number of each item matches the number on the answer sheet.
- Clearly mark the space on the answer sheet. Erase all of it if you make a change.
- Start immediately when told to begin. Do not let anything or anyone distract you!

■ A Gallery of Test Items

The following tests exemplify the test items described earlier in this chapter. Use them as models as you design your own tests. The items progress from those appropriate for primary grades to more challenging items for the middle school levels.

■ FIGURE 14.15

Multiple-Choice Test Items

Draw a line under the best word to end the sentence.

1. A person who buys goods and services is a

   consumer.   producer.   worker.

Draw a circle around the best answer.

1. What are food, shelter, and clothing?

   A. basic needs   B. human wants   C. three wishes

Directions. Write the letter of the correct answer in the blank space by each item.

   _____ 1. Who helped to survey and plan Washington, D.C.?

   A. Banneker   B. Franklin   C. Jefferson   D. Washington

Directions. Circle the letter by the best answer.

1. Which nation has the largest population?

   A. Russia   B. India   C. U.S.A.   D. Japan

Directions. Mark the space on the answer sheet to show the answer you select.

1. What is the Ring of Fire?
   A. volcanoes around the Pacific Rim
   B. volcanoes that created Hawaii
   C. volcanoes around Mexico City
   D volcanoes in the Andes

Directions. Write a + in one of the blank spaces below each item to show how you feel.

1. What is your position on the plan to involve students in the anti-litter project?

   _____ Strongly   _____ Agree   _____ Not sure   _____ Disagree   _____ Strongly
   agree   disagree

■ **FIGURE 14.16**

Matching Test Items

Draw a line to show the provider of each service.

Provider	*Service*
Clerk	Education
Nurse	Protection
Police	Business
Teacher	Health

Draw a line between the following to make correct sentences.

Carpenters work to produce	clothing.
Farmers work to produce	shelter.
Tailors work to produce	food.

Matching People and Contributions

Write the letter by the contribution in the space by the person who made it.

_____ 1. Jane Addams	A. founded Tuskegee Institute, a school for blacks
_____ 2. Susan B. Anthony	B. helped to found the NAACP
_____ 3. W. E. B. DuBois	C. founded Hull House to help the poor
_____ 4. Booker T. Washington	D. worked for women's right to vote
	E. worked for reform in politics
	F. worked to end monopolies

■ **FIGURE 14.17**

Binary-Choice Test Items

True	False	1. Cooking and sewing are examples of goods.
T	F	1. Opportunity cost is the best thing one gives up to get something else.
Yes	No	1. Are tools, materials, and equipment productive resources?
Y	N	1. Division of labor occurs when Joe dries dishes washed by May.

Mark N by items that are part of the national environment. Mark C by items that are part of the cultural environment.

_____ 1. Lumber	_____ 4. Steel	_____ 7. Minerals	_____ 10. Animals
_____ 2. Gardens	_____ 5. Plants	_____ 8. Pollution	_____ 11. Zoos
_____ 3. Dams	_____ 6. Rivers	_____ 9. Forests	_____ 12. Air

■ **FIGURE 14.18**

Short-Answer Test Items

An example of a *service* is *health care*. Other examples are _____ , _____ , and _____ .

A mayor is _____ .

Read pages 78–81 and list *three of our state's natural resources.*

_____   _____   _____

Farm is to *rural* as *city* is to _____ .

Classify the cities *included in today's reading* by writing their names in the correct column.

Banking Centers	*Trade Centers*	*Resort Centers*
_____	_____	_____
_____	_____	_____

To *consume* means _____ .

Complete the following outline of *main ideas* and *supporting detail*s as you read pages 40–43.

A. _____

   1. _____

   2. _____

B. _____

   1. _____

   2. _____

Study the *table* on page 54, and *rank the countries in order,* beginning with 1 for the country largest in land area. Next, rank them in order by population.

Country	*Land Area*	*Population*
Brazil	_____	_____
Canada	_____	_____
Japan	_____	_____
Russia	_____	_____
U.S.A.	_____	_____

We should *support equal rights* for others because _____ .

Activities in *school* in which I like to participate are _____ .

Essay Test Questions

Describe the land, climate, and resources of Mexico. Next, describe the resources that are used to make products for foreign trade.

Summarize the key ideas in today's reading selection. Be sure to place them in the order in which they were presented.

Describe three different map projections. Write a critique of each one that includes attention to recommended use, distortion of land areas, distortion of water areas, and distortion in polar areas.

Writing Assignments as Tests

The Middle Colonies

1. Write the names of the colonies that were between the New England and the southern colonies.

2. Write a paragraph about each middle colony that includes the following:
   a. Name of the colony
   b. Founder of the colony
   c. Why it was founded
   d. Name and date of the first settlement
   e. Country of origin of settlers
   f. A distinctive feature of the colony

3. Proofread your report and make needed changes to ensure accuracy of content, spelling, and grammar, which will be used to grade your report.

Accomplishments of Ancient Greeks

1. Write a paragraph about each individual listed below. Describe the accomplishment for which each one is recognized.
   a. Homer   c. Sappho   e. Aesop   g. Herodotus
   b. Anaxagoras   d. Socrates   f. Plato   h. Aristotle

2. Proofread and revise each paragraph to be sure that content, spelling, and grammar are accurate. Grading will be based on clarity of expression and accuracy of content, spelling, and grammar.

Individual Reports

1. Choose a person, an event, or another topic related to our unit of study.

2. Write a two-page report that includes the following:
   a. Title, introduction, development, conclusion
   b. Sources of information

3. Your report will be graded in terms of originality, clarity of expression, and accuracy of content, spelling, and grammar.

▉ Conclusion

Evaluation and assessment are integral parts of social studies. Guidelines for evaluation include addressing all objectives; evaluating continuously; selecting appropriate techniques and devices, including providing for student self-evaluation and constructive peer evaluation and teacher evaluation; and using assessment data constructively. Teachers are sensitive to and knowledgeable about issues relating to diversity (e.g., culture, exceptionalities, gender) and integrate traditional (e.g., essay, multiple-choice test items) and alternative forms of assessment (e.g., student self-evaluation, portfolios) into their social studies programs. These tools for assessment also are used by teachers as they assess and improve on their own classroom performance.

Last, teachers are aware that social studies programs are shaped by the wishes of the local community, state guidelines and regulations, and national trends, such as the standards movement. At state and local levels, the definition and purpose of social studies is translated into student expectations, and cognitive, psychomotor, and affective objectives for learning become the focus of testing. Results of assessment and evaluation will communicate to interested parties how well students are meeting expectations for learning.

 Questions, Activities, and Evaluation

1. What is your position on the use of standards to assess and evaluate learning in social studies? What role, if any, should standards play in determining what constitutes social studies in the K–8 curriculum? What role, if any, should local interests play in influencing the K–8 curriculum?

2. Do you view portfolios as a viable approach to assess social studies learning? What are some advantages to using this approach? disadvantages?

3. Consider practical ways to use each of the basic guidelines to effective evaluation presented in the first section of this chapter. Which do you believe to be the most difficult to apply? Which do you believe now need greater emphasis?

4. In what ways can you provide for student self-evaluation in a unit you are planning?

5. Note ways in which you might use each of the following in a unit of your choice: observation, examination of samples of work, interviews, discussion, charts, checklists, rating scales, and questionnaires.

6. Survey the examples provided in this chapter, and describe how they might be modified to assess social studies learning among each of the following:

    a. a student who speaks very little English

    b. someone with hearing impairment

    c. a student with an emotional disorder

    d. a gifted student

7. Prepare several test items in each form discussed in this chapter. Plan items for assessing both affective and cognitive objectives.

8. Examine the teacher's edition of a social studies textbook and note the suggested evaluation activities. What additions and changes can you make to improve them?

9. What is your position on the following? Check your position and discuss it with others, and then change each statement so that it reflects your views.

	Yes	No	?
a. Priority should be given in the social studies to evaluation of such lasting outcomes as concepts and skills.	____	____	____
b. Teachers at all levels should emphasize self-evaluation by students.	____	____	____
c. Observation of students is one of the most useful and practical ways to evaluate learning in the social studies.	____	____	____
d. Charts and checklists are among the best devices for teacher appraisal of students and for self-evaluation by students.	____	____	____
e. Teachers should make their own test items for each unit.	____	____	____
f. Teachers should be held accountable for achievement in social studies as well as in reading and arithmetic.	____	____	____
g. The best way to appraise teacher effectiveness is by the amount of pupil gain as shown by tests.	____	____	____

References

Baugh, I. W. (1994). Hypermedia as a performance-based assessment tool. *Computing Teacher, 21,* 14–17.

Bloom, B. S. (Ed.). (1956). *Taxonomy of educational objectives. Handbook I: The cognitive domain.* New York: D. McKay.

Bracey, G. (1990). Computerized testing: A possible alternative to paper and pencil? *Electronic Learning, 9,* 16–17.

Brophy, J., et al. (1991). Social education professors and elementary teachers: Two purviews on elementary social studies. *Theory and Research in Social Education, 19,* 173–188.

Campbell, J. (1992). Laserdisk portfolios: Total child assessment. *Educational Leadership, 49,* 69–70.

Darling–Hammond, L., et al. (1995). *Authentic assessment in action: Studies of schools and students at work.* New York: Teachers College.

DeFina, A. A. *Portfolio assessment: Getting started.* Cited in "The Bookshelf." (1996). *Education Week, 15* (38).

Doolittle, P., Halpern, M., & Rudman, L. M. (1994). The ERIC/AE Test Locator Service. *Educational Research, 23,* 34–35.

ERIC Clearinghouse on Tests, Measurement, and Evaluation. American Institutes for Research, 1055 Thomas Jefferson Street N.W., Washington, DC 20007–3893. Write for list of materials.

Fischer, C. F., & King, Rita M. (1995). *Authentic assessment: A guide to implementation.* Thousand Oaks, California: Corwin.

Frisbe, D. A., et al. (1993). An evaluation of elementary textbook tests as classroom assessment tools. *Applied Measurement in Education, 6,* 21–36.

Gronlund, N. E. (1993). *How to make achievement tests and assessments.* (5th ed.). Boston: Allyn & Bacon.

Grosvenor, L., et al. (1994). *Student portfolios.* Washington, DC: National Education Association.

Hannah, L. S., & Michaelis, J. U. (1977). *A comprehensive framework for instructional objectives.* Reading, MA: Addison–Wesley. Sample items, charts, and checklists on various levels for cognitive and affective assessment.

Herbert, E. A. (1992). Portfolios invite reflection—from students and staff. *Educational Leadership, 49,* 58–61.

Herman, J. L. (1992). What research tells us about good assessment. *Educational Leadership, 49,* 74–78.

Krathwohl, D. H., Bloom, B. S., & Masia, B. B. (1964). *Taxonomy of educational objectives. Handbook II: The affective domain.* New York: D. McKay.

Lescher, M. L. (1995). *Portfolios: Assessing learning in the primary grades.* Washington, DC: National Education Association.

Lockledge, A. (1997). Portfolio assessment in middle school and high school social studies classrooms. *The Social Studies, 88,* 65–69.

Martin, C. L. *Geography textbook assessment for middle and high school educators.* (1996). Washington, DC: Geographic Education National Implementation Project.

Meisels, S. J. (1996). Using work sampling in authentic assessments. *Educational Leadership, 54,* 60–65.

National Center for Innovation. (1995). *Assessing learning in the classroom.* Washington, DC: National Education Association.

National Council for the Social Studies. (1991). *Social studies in the middle school: A report of the task force on social studies in the middle school* and *Testing and evaluation of social studies students.* (Position Statement and Guidelines.) Washington, DC: Author.

Nickell, P. (Ed.).(1992). Special section: Student assessment in the social studies. *Social Education, 56.*

North Carolina State Department of Education. (1994). *A guide to quality early childhood and elementary school programs.* Raleigh, North Carolina: Author.

O'Brien, J. (1997). Statewide social studies assessment: Threat or treat? *The Social Studies, 88,* 53–59.

Office of Educational Research and Development. (1993). *Blue Ribbon Schools: Outstanding Practices in Geography Education, 1989–90, and History Education, 1990–92.* Washington, DC: Author.

Pomplun, M. (1996). Cooperative groups: Alternative assessment for students with disabilities? *Journal of Special Education, 30,* 1–17.

Ravitch, D. (1995). Standards in U.S. history: An assessment. *Education Week, 14,* 48.

Rosaen, C. L. (1992). *The potential of written instructional materials to improve instructional practice.* East Lansing, Michigan: Center for the Learning and Teaching of Elementary Subjects.

Rothman, R. *Measuring up: Standards, assessment, and school reform.* Cited in "The Bookshelf" (1996). *Education Week, 15* (38).

Wiggins G. (1996). Practicing what we preach in developing authentic assessments. *Educational Leadership, 54,* 18–25.

Wiggins, G. (1992). Creating tests worth taking. *Educational Leadership, 49,* 26–34.

Chapter 15

Teaching Social Studies in Today's Classrooms: Am I Prepared?

Chapter Objective

To present preservice teachers with a list of suggestions that can lead to becoming an effective social studies teacher

Focusing Questions

- What did you learn from this course and textbook that helped you grow professionally?

- What is the meaning of the phrase "becoming a social studies teacher"?

- How can personal and professional introspection help you in becoming an effective teacher?

- Why is becoming a good planner an effective method of growing professionally?

- How can developing a personal definition and purpose for social studies enhance your success in social studies instruction?

■ Am I Really Prepared?

If you are reading this chapter, you are about to finish this methods course and begin student teaching. Are you uncertain about your selection of teaching as a profession? Are you feeling unprepared for the task that lies ahead because you believe you lack a firm grasp of the social sciences and knowledge of how to implement social studies instruction? Are you feeling a bit of insecurity over the level of diversity you may encounter in the classroom? Rest assured you are no different from the many preservice teachers—both elementary and secondary—who, each fall and spring, begin their student teaching experiences. It is quite normal to be apprehensive. Who wouldn't be, knowing that in a few short weeks, they will be responsible for the education of a group of children or young adults! How you address this apprehensiveness and how you begin your student teaching experience and explore a career in elementary or middle school education are important points.

Let's begin by sharing with you paths some student teachers have taken which we believe you should avoid. Sometimes student teachers are overheard saying, "Give me the social studies textbook, tell me what to do, and let me teach." These are the textbook-bound teachers. They have forgotten what they learned in foundations, educational psychology, field experiences, and methods, and they will place their faith in the textbook. Regardless of the students, what is occurring in the world, and contemporary developments in education, the textbook and its ancillary materials will rule supreme among these teachers. These student teachers are willing to relinquish their role in the classroom (even before assuming it) and pass it on to the textbook. Other student teachers are overheard saying, "I want students to enjoy themselves in my classroom. I will do what the students will find fun." In this case, entertainment will dictate what goes on in these teachers' classrooms. The last group is often heard saying, "I'll develop social studies instruction that I experienced when I was in elementary and middle school and that I found enjoyable." Although these preservice teachers may have experienced valuable learning and fun, they are trying to clone their own experiences in school—becoming a teacher of the 1980s. In this scenario, the contemporary world and the needs of students succumb to a re-creation of a bygone era.

What do the preceding scenarios share in common? Why should you avoid these paths? First, these student teachers have distanced themselves from what they learned in their teacher preparation programs. Their plans are based more on past experiences than an integration of theory and practice. Second, they have abandoned a major part of their responsibility in the classroom by not assuming the role of teachers of social studies. The first group of student teachers has relinquished its role to the textbook; the other to fun activities; and the third to past experiences that may or may not have any value in today's classroom. Moreover, by relinquishing their role as instructional leaders, they have identified themselves as "controllers" of the classroom, using textbooks to keep students busy and activities to keep students entertained; such behavior and actions do not guarantee that social studies learning will take place. Third, by giving up the role of instructional leaders, these student teachers have lessened their chances of experiencing a sense of self-efficacy—the feeling that they are helping students learn social studies—and self-fulfillment—that they make a difference in the classroom. Experiencing these feelings is vital in student teaching and essential in the professional development of beginning teachers.

Have you been tempted to follow one of these paths? Many preservice teachers do, to some degree. Reflect for a moment on why you decided to become a teacher. Did you embark on a teaching career because of your admiration for a teacher? Is it because you like being around children and young adults? Do you want children to like you? Do you feel that having fun with students is a prerequisite to learning? Did you choose teaching because you want to help children and young adults grow intellectually, socially, emotionally, and physically? There is nothing wrong with beginning the process of becoming a teacher by following one of these paths. However, one purpose of a teacher preparation program is to help you incorporate and perhaps modify your reasons for choosing teaching as a profession into a sound educational philosophy.

In the next few pages we suggest ways to avoid unproductive teaching paths while remaining committed to your reasons for selecting teaching as your profession. The suggestions are based on the principle that becoming a K–8 social studies teacher is a lifelong process.

■ Becoming an Effective Teacher

In this chapter, we reintroduce you to basic principles that a cross section of social studies educators agree are essential to success in the classroom. Adhering to these suggestions will increase your chances of having a successful student teaching experience and being prepared to become a member of the teaching profession.

1. Reflect upon and Use Knowledge and Experiences

Value what you learn and experience in teacher education. Whether the experience is good or bad, take something from it. Let's begin by reviewing what you have learned in this social studies methods course. Has this textbook helped you become an effective teacher?

Have you gained a greater appreciation for social studies as a subject area in the elementary and middle school curriculums? Do you appreciate the national and global perspectives social studies offers students, and have you acquired an understanding of the knowledge, skills, and dispositions you can bring together to provide students with creative instruction? Do you have a stronger understanding of America's diverse population and are you more aware of the strengths and challenges students bring to the classroom? Have you gained a stronger sense of the many ways you can help students make connections with social studies? Are you more aware of the complex nature of planning and implementing instruction, and assessment? Are you excited to learn more about these questions as you get ready to student teach?

If you have addressed some of these questions proactively, we have succeeded in helping you become an effective social studies teacher. By "proactively," we mean reflecting on the questions posed, offering honest responses, listening to alternative responses, and using these reflections as a method of growing professionally. We anticipate, as you begin teaching, that you will turn to chapters in this textbook to address a number of issues including the following: making sense of the social studies program you are asked to implement, reviewing the social sciences to identify concepts to include in your program, and adding a global perspective to units such as "We Are All Americans," "Americans Form a Nation," and "Living in the Twenty-First Century."

This textbook and other professional books on the social sciences and social studies can help you learn more about the social sciences, social studies, definition(s) and purpose(s) of social studies, and the content identified as social studies. Once on this path you will also pursue your own interests and the interests of children and young adults to personalize instruction in your classroom.

2. Accept the Notion of Becoming an Effective Social Studies Teacher

Becoming is a good term for describing the student teaching experience (Goodman & Fish, 1997). There is a popular but erroneous belief that teacher education programs prepare teachers to *be*. That is, once you have matriculated through your program, you will be prepared, and on the day you graduate and receive state certification, you will possess the knowledge, skills, and dispositions necessary to be a successful teacher. According to this view, there is little else to learn and, since you are prepared, what difficulties you experience in the classroom do not reside in your teacher education program or within you but elsewhere.

We do not accept this belief. We subscribe to the view that teacher education programs prepare teacher candidates for *becoming* (Bullough, Crow, & Knowles, 1992). We believe good programs provide you with the "bare essentials" for becoming a teacher. They introduce you to a generalization such as the following: "One is always becoming a teacher, and to remain effective, one is continually working at improving his or her performance in the classroom." Over your many years of teaching, you will grow professionally by building on the bare essentials and adopting a proactive disposition toward teaching.

Becoming also means accepting the proposition that teaching is a lifelong process; you can never be completely satisfied with your teaching (Cochran-Smith & Lytle, 1992). You will always look for ways of improving your performance in the

■ If we think about our own lives, we'll remember how much we learned from those who encouraged us.
—**Joe Nathan**

classroom: if an activity was successful, you will want to make it more successful the next time you use it; if only a few students were daydreaming when you reviewed the causes of the Civil War, the next time you teach the unit you will make modifications to minimize daydreaming in the classroom; as you make progress meeting the needs of students with disabilities, you are also learning Spanish to address the needs of the growing Hispanic student population in your school. Accepting the notion that teaching is *becoming* and a lifelong process is no easy task; but when you do accept it, you will find yourself being more and more successful in the classroom. That is, you will experience feelings of self-efficacy and self-fulfillment.

3. *Practice Personal and Professional Introspection*

A fundamental element is missing in each scenario of student teachers presented at the beginning of the chapter—the personal and professional qualities of the individual. Because becoming a teacher includes coming to terms with our personal and professional selves, we think prospective teachers should explore these two areas as they embark on a teaching career (Bullough, Crow, & Knowles, 1992). In fact, many leading experts in teacher education suggest that a prerequisite to becoming grounded in the mechanics of teaching is learning more about self in a reflective manner (Bennett & Spalding, 1992). It means coming to terms with why we selected teaching as a profession, learning to integrate theory and practice from the rich understandings provided in a teacher preparation program, and making sound decisions in the classroom (Schon, 1987; Zeichner & Liston, 1996).

Probably reflection is a major part of your teacher education program. What does it mean to be reflective? As you have matriculated through the program, you have explored the meaning of reflection, targeted some basic questions, and moved to questions related to your professional self. The personal questions may have included these:

- Why do I want to be a teacher?
- What in my personal background has influenced my decision to choose teaching as a profession?
- What are my feelings about children and young adults?
- What is happening to me personally as I prepare to become an elementary or middle school teacher?
- How open am I to change?
- Am I comfortable with the changes I am experiencing?

■ Phi Delta Kappa **http://www.pdkintl.org** is an international organization aimed at promoting quality education, particularly in publicly supported education, as essential to the development and maintenance of a democratic way of life.

Questions relating to the professional self are similar. Typically, teacher education programs take the position that becoming a teacher is a lifelong process. These programs encourage reflection about assuming the role of a professional. This includes adopting the disposition that there are multiple ways of improving performance and good teachers explore all possibilities. Teachers attempting to address classroom problems are continually gaining new knowledge and experiences that will provide them with greater and greater insight into problems. These teachers are committed to the belief that self-examination, reflecting on experience, and pursuing professional development are the keys to success in the classroom (Clandinin & Connelly, 1995). As part of their professional development, they ask themselves questions like these:

- How do my views on teaching and learning fit with professional and community expectations of teachers?
- How can I improve my perspective on teaching and learning?
- Am I willing to accept prevailing definitions and purposes for social studies?
- Do I accept constructive criticism?
- How will I grow professionally—join teacher organizations or learn on my own, from other teachers, or from a mentor?
- How will I go about gaining a knowledge base in social studies?
- Do I have a realistic view of schools and communities?
- How will I keep abreast with current trends in elementary and middle school education?
- What does it mean to teach in the twenty-first century?

There is no end to the questions that teachers can ask themselves as they improve their performance in the classroom (Brubacher, Case, & Reagan, 1994; Gipe & Richards, 1992).

4. *Adopt a Definition and Purpose of Social Studies*

In the third part of this book you learned about planning for social studies. In this chapter, we suggest that adopting a definition and purpose of social studies is a prerequisite to planning an instructional program. These two elements are instrumental in providing direction and focus to the planning process. And, when teachers reflect and refine their thoughts on definition and purpose they (1) bring to the surface their views on social studies, (2) lend a sharper focus to planning, and (3) align their views of social studies with those of leading educators and state and local education officials.

What is social studies, and what is its purpose in the elementary and middle school curriculums? Simple questions? Hardly. Ever since the social sciences and social studies became part of the K–12 curriculum, educators have reflected on definition and purpose. And in the twenty-first century, the debate continues. (Review Chapter 1 to examine some of those arguments.) Prior to entering this program, you probably held some ideas about social studies. Have those views changed? As you move closer to student teaching, have your views been influenced by your university experiences—a reading, class discussions, a planned activity? Have field experiences played a greater role—observing teachers, listening to students, reading a school document describing social studies (Bennett & Spalding, 1992; Goodman & Fish, 1997)?

As you prepare to student teach, and before taking sole responsibility of a classroom, we encourage you to do more than reflect on questions relating to definition and purpose. We encourage you to adopt a definition and purpose of social studies. When you meet your cooperating teacher, inquire about the district's position on social studies. Ask your cooperating teacher about units of instruction and the definition and purpose of social studies. Review social studies documents produced by the state and school district. Inquire about the role of textbooks and ancillary materials in instruction. Interview a cross section of students, and ask them what they believe is the definition and purpose of social studies. Your definition and purpose should approximate what is expected of you in your student teaching experience. It should be a tentative definition. Let your student teaching experience and your first few years in the profession help shape a firmer definition and purpose of social studies.

A definition and purpose allows you to plan for instruction with purpose. When you meet with your cooperating teacher and as you plan for instruction, keep these questions in mind:

- Does your planning reflect a definition and purpose for social studies?
- Are you and your cooperating teachers in general agreement on definition and purpose?
- How do you feel about standards?
- Do you feel comfortable teaching social studies?
- What units of instruction do you enjoy putting together?
- If you have had to modify your views on definition and purpose for social studies, will you be comfortable with those changes?
- How did you go about making the changes? Is there tension between your personal and professional selves? What can you do to reduce the tension? Do you think that most effective teachers live with this tension? Can you live with it?

5. *Develop a Plan for Implementing Social Studies Instruction*

Grasping how to implement instruction puts the definition and purpose for social studies into action. We define *implementation* as the process of developing lessons and units of instruction, selecting teaching strategies, identifying the appropriate content for instruction, and carrying out instruction. We focus on the importance of selection of content (i.e., knowledge, skills, dispositions) when developing social studies instruction.

As you have read in this textbook and elsewhere, there are a number of guidelines to consider when selecting content for instruction. In this chapter we focus on one criterion—the purpose of social studies. The NCSS definition we have been using in this textbook states that the purpose of social studies is "to help young people develop the ability to make informed and reasoned decisions for the public good as citizens of a culturally diverse, democratic society in an interdependent world." What does this phrase mean to you? Are there differences between your views and those of your school district? Do you need to align your views with those of your school district?

> ■ The art of teaching is the art of awakening the curiosity of young minds.
>
> **—Anatole France**

Once you have a settled on a purpose of social studies, the next step is to sharpen its focus by gaining a greater understanding of the social sciences, social studies, and community. A greater sensitivity to community (local, national, global perspectives), for example, will help you identify concepts, concept clusters, and generalizations you may wish to include in social studies. Many preservice teachers begin by examining and selecting content from social studies textbooks, gathering materials, and listening to the advice of cooperating teachers. Once they gain confidence using these resources, they may look to the social sciences for additional information. This process leads to a greater pool of content to select from, and it helps student teachers (1) focus on the definition and purpose of social studies; (2) make connections, where possible, among local, national, and global perspectives; (3) reflect a variety of the social science disciplines; (4) target the interests of students; and

Teachers are professionals who continually strive to reach out to all students. How are you preparing to know students and engage them in social studies learning?

(5) provide for sound social studies learning. In short, one way teachers provide students with instruction that is valuable and fun is by increasing their knowledge base of the social sciences and choosing content that aligns with the purpose of social studies (National Board for Professional Teaching Standards, 1996).

6. *Incorporate Knowledge of Community and Students in Social Studies Instruction*

Why are some student teachers intent on controlling students with textbooks and entertaining activities? One explanation could be that in their field experiences, they experienced little success in connecting students to social studies learnings. This may have happened because they did not take into account the community in which they were teaching social studies or the students in their classrooms as these student teachers planned instruction.

In this context, community refers to the location of your field experience and student teaching placements and the communities where your students live. What community characteristics might influence social studies planning? Reflect, for the moment, on your field experiences. Where was the school located? What are the socioeconomic characteristics of the community? What are some of its historical experiences? What contemporary issues and problems might be identified as social studies material? When student teachers can identify community social studies information, they can develop a social studies program that relates to the experiences of students and captures their interest. In what ways, if any, would a primary grade social studies program for a rural community in Iowa differ from one in a suburban community in Virginia? Examining a community also allows teachers to gain an understanding, in general terms, of what areas in social studies might need greater coverage.

Knowledge of students is an equally important element. In Chapter 3 we provide you with general characteristics of students. For example, students share basic wants and needs, but their home environments and previous school experiences may suggest different approaches to meeting those needs. Issues of cultural background, gender, and exceptionalities can make this even more complex. The information in Chapter 3 can help you gain a detailed understanding of the students in your classroom. It is *your* responsibility to learn specific information about them.

Teachers who understand their communities and students can make better use of the resources (Colsant, 1995; Ladson-Billings, 1994). For example, review the ideas included in Chapter 4, think of the students in your classroom, and identify how these ideas might be modified to fit the interests of your students.

7. Adopt a Creative Approach to Assessment in Social Studies

In Chapter 14 and in other parts of this textbook, you learned of a number of ways of assessing social studies learning. But these suggestions become powerful tools only when they have been modified to meet the specific needs of students. To do this, you must get to know your students.

When you explore students' backgrounds, a deep and enriching pool of information emerges. Think of how you might use student information in the area of assessment and evaluation in the following examples: John (his American name), a recent immigrant from Kosovo who speaks no English joins your kindergarten class; Samantha, who does not respond to paper and pencil techniques and, because of behavioral difficulties, does not work well in group settings; Jenny McDonald, who while constructing a family tree in third grade, has become interested in her Irish heritage; Peter, a middle school student who seems unchallenged by your whole instructional program; and Jackie, who is in the fifth grade but reading at the second-grade level (Wiggins, 1993). Can you recall any examples from your field experiences similar to these? How might you modify the guidelines, checklists, and techniques provided in Chapter 14 and elsewhere in this textbook to assess learning for these students and others in your classroom?

8. Meet the Challenges of Social Studies Instruction Proactively

Challenges are part of teaching; no classroom is free of them. They appear when you are student teaching and continue until you retire from the profession. In the following paragraphs we offer one approach to addressing the challenges you will encounter teaching in a K–8 classroom.

■ Kappa Delta Pi, **http://kdp.org**, an international honor society in education, is dedicated to scholarship and excellence in education.

First, take a proactive approach to classroom situations by viewing them as challenges and not problems. By approaching situations as challenges, you assume a positive approach to what is occurring in the classroom. Challenges can be overcome, but problems seem to fester and linger indefinitely. What sorts of challenges will you encounter in the classroom? Some will relate to implementing units of study; others to learning about the social sciences and social studies; others to your attempts to reach out to your students and their attempts to reach out to you.

Second, learn how to deal with challenges. Yes, the first step is to take a positive stance, but equally important are your actions. We suggest you become an analytical teacher. For example, what would you do if more than a few students said to you that social studies learning in your classroom is boring? How would you address this challenge? If you are an analytical teacher, you might take the following steps: (1) collect information by asking the students what they mean by "boring" and by reflecting on your teaching; (2) identify a possible explanation for the so-called boredom (e.g., social studies instruction occurs early in the morning and the students show little interest in academic activities at this time of day); (3) collect additional information (common teaching strategies and student activities you employ); (4) identify other explanations for the boredom (instruction is too textbook-driven); (5) from the evidence collected select a possible explanation for the boredom and make changes (develop lessons that include more student activities); (6) return to the students and ask them to comment on the changes to their social studies program; (7) if the changes you have made do not address the challenge, return to the first item and begin the process again (Cochran-Smith & Lytle, 1992; Hubbard & Power, 1993; Powell, Zehm, & Garcia, 1996).

Teachers who are proactive in the classroom are problem solvers. They successfully address challenges, learn from them, and move on to others. They enjoy the role of the proactive teacher because it increases their opportunities for success in the classroom.

9. *Take Advantage of Mentoring Opportunities*

When you begin student teaching, ask your cooperating teacher to serve as your mentor. What is a mentor, and what is a mentoring relationship? Mentors provide guidance and support as they bring out the best in an individual. Because mentoring is about bringing out the best in an individual, it is a learning relationship. It is not about a mentor rubber-stamping the actions and behaviors of a preservice teacher; nor is it about becoming a mentor's clone. Mentors allow student teachers to meld their special talents with the responsibilities of a teacher. They model professional behavior in the classroom, observe student teachers, and offer them constructive criticism. They meet with their student teachers, highlight their growth, and identify areas needing improvement. Mentors see themselves as accomplished teachers and wish their student teachers to become equally competent.

We target cooperating teachers to serve as mentors because they are excellent teachers, respected by their peers, and wish to see you grow professionally. (They too wish to grow, and they see the opportunity of interacting with potential teachers as a way of learning more about social studies.) Cooperating teachers know you, respect you, and are willing to nurture a relationship with you. What should student teachers bring to this relationship? Respect for the cooperating teacher, honesty, acceptance of student teaching as a learning situation, and the willingness to accept constructive criticism as a method of growing professionally (Brennan, Thames, & Roberts, 1999; Tatum & McWhorter, 1999).

How would you go about establishing a mentoring relationship with your cooperating teacher? We suggest you sit down together, and discuss expectations. If it seems that the relationship would work, ask the person to enter a mentoring relationship with you. Mentoring works when both parties act in a professional manner.

10. *Become Aware of Opportunities for Lifelong Learning*

There are many opportunities for lifelong learning in social studies. For example, some student teachers join networks and support groups (chat on the Net) where they can talk with other student teachers or with established teachers about their triumphs and challenges. Student teachers find these networks helpful because they provide (1) ideas about lessons, activities, and the like to improve social studies instruction; (2) a forum where they learn that they are not the only ones experiencing

There is no greater satisfaction to teachers than knowing their students are learning.

challenges in the classroom; (3) suggestions on how to experience greater efficacy and fulfillment in the classroom; (4) colleagues to speak with about general and specific issues relating to K–8 teaching; and (5) a place to vent (Olebe, Jackson, & Danielson, 1999; Rogers & Babinski, 1999).

Professional organizations offer excellent opportunities for lifelong learning. There are teacher organizations (e.g., National Education Association, American Federation of Teachers, Kappa Delta Pi), sponsored by university faculty, offering student teachers information about state certification, job opportunities, salary trends, and fresh perspectives on issues and problems affecting K–8 teaching. Content-oriented organizations are sponsored at the local level by teachers (e.g., NCSS, National Council for Geographic Education, National Council for Economic Education) and focus on issues relating to the teaching of the social sciences in the K–8 curriculum.

Many student teachers are attracted to these organizations because they offer opportunities to interact with new and established teachers and listen to and participate in discussions of common interest. These organizations also offer student teachers the opportunity to attend annual meetings sponsored at the local, regional, and national levels. At these meetings, student teachers hear of new ideas in the teaching of social studies and visit exhibit areas where publishing companies display the latest materials available. It is a great opportunity to learn more about teaching social studies, and teachers grow professionally by speaking at these conferences and presenting to colleagues the many wonderful things they are doing in the classroom.

■ Am I Prepared to Teach Social Studies?

You bet! You learned a lot in this course, and in this book you found information on social studies, principles of good social studies teaching, and countless examples of how to promote social studies learning in the K–8 classroom. Last, we provided you with a list of suggestions that should place you on the proper path as you begin your student teaching experience. It is now up to you. We are betting that you will be successful, have an impact on social studies education, and enjoy teaching. Are you still a bit apprehensive? Don't worry—that feeling will begin disappearing with the many successes you will experience on your first day of student teaching.

References

Bennett, C., & Spalding, E. (1992). Teaching the social studies: Multiple approaches for multiple perspectives. *Theory and Research in Social Education, 20,* 263–292.

Brennan, S., Thames, W., & Roberts, R. (1999). Mentoring with a mission. *Educational Leadership, 56,* 49–52.

Brubacher, J. W., Case, C. W., & Reagan, T. G. (1994). *Becoming a reflective educator: How to build a culture of inquiry in schools.* Thousand Oaks, CA: Corwin Press.

Bullough, R. V. Jr., Crow, N. A., & Knowles, J. G. (1992). *Emerging as a teacher.* New York: Routledge.

Clandinin, J. D., & Connelly, F. M. (1995). *Teachers' professional knowledge landscapes.* New York: Teachers College Press.

Cochran-Smith, M., & Lytle, S. L. (1992). *Inside outside: Teacher research and knowledge.* New York: Teachers College Press.

Colsant, L. C. (1995). Hey, man, why do we gotta take this? Learning to listen to students. In J. G. Nicholls & T. A. Thorkildsen (Eds.), *Reasons for learning: Expanding the conversation on student–teacher collaboration.* New York: Teachers College Press.

Goodman, J., & Fish, D. R. (1997). Against the grain teacher education: A study of coursework, field experience, and perspective. *Journal of Teacher Education, 48,* 96–107.

Hubbard, R. S., & Power, B. M. (1993). *The art of classroom inquiry: A handbook for teacher-researchers.* Portsmouth, NH: Heinemann.

Ladson-Billings, G. (1994). *The dreamkeepers: Successful teachers of African American children.* San Francisco: Jossey-Bass.

National Board for Professional Teaching Standards. (1996). *Social studies–history standards for national board certification.* Washington, DC: Author.

Olebe, M., Jackson, A., & Danielson, C. (1999). Investing in beginning teachers—the California model. *Educational Leadership 56,* 41–44.

Powell, R., Zehm, S., & Garcia, J. (1996). *Field experience: Strategies for exploring diversity in schools.* Englewood Cliffs, NJ: Prentice-Hall.

Schon, D. A. (1987). *Educating the reflective practitioner: Toward a new design for teaching and learning in the professions.* San Francisco, CA: Jossey-Bass.

Tatum, B., & McWhorter, P. (1999). Maybe not everything, but a whole lot you always wanted to know about mentoring. In P. Graham, S. Hudson-Ross, C. Adkins, P. McWhorter, and J. M. Stewart (Eds.), *Teacher/mentor: A dialogue for collaborative learning.* New York: Teacher College Press.

Wiggins, G. P. (1993). *Assessing student performance: Exploring the purpose and limits of testing.* San Francisco: Jossey-Bass.

Zeichner, K. M., & Liston, D. P. (1996). *Reflective teaching: An introduction.* Mahwah, NJ: Erlbaum.

Index

468

Short-answer test items, 444, 449
Sight vocabulary, 242–243
Silent letter list, 244
Silvern, S. B., 366
Simon, S. B., 407
Simulations, 378–379
Situational tests, 438
Skills inventory, 189
Skimming books, 254
Skits, 371
Slavin, R. E., 224
Slide presentations, 279
Small-group activities, 212–214
    guidelines for, 220–222
Social competence, 10
Social Education magazine, 3, 167, 271, 278, 292
Social Science Education Consortium, 292
Social studies, 3, 9–14
Social Studies and the Young Learner, 3, 130, 292–293
Social Studies School Services, 17, 278, 293
Socioeconomic status (SES)
    differences, understanding, 85–86
    IQ tests and, 185
    needs assessment and, 186
Sociology, 26, 54–56, 66
Sociopolitical literacy, 27
Software. *See* Computers
Source materials. *See also* Instructional materials
    for background building, 156
    for current affairs studies, 129
    for environmental/energy studies, 122
    gender equality education, 110–111
    for global studies, 117–118
    information gathering and, 65, 67
    for law-related education, 114–115
    in multicultural education, 106
    people as, 254–255
    for process knowledge, 64
    in sample unit plan, 164–165
    for special events studies, 135
    for unit plan, 161
Space arrangements, 219–220, 221
Spalding, E., 458, 460
Spanish-speaking students, 86–87
Spatial intelligence, 90
Speaking skills, 257–258
Special events, 129–135
Special students, 86, 178–184
Speech disorders, students with, 184
SQ3R reading strategy, 201–202
SQUIRT (Super Quiet Undisturbed Reading Time), 203
SRA Achievement Series, 445
SSR (Sustained Silent Reading), 203
Standards, 7, 8
    for committee work, 222
    emotional disorders, students with, 181
    in geography, 40
    for group learning activities, 226
    history standards, 31–33
    NCSS standards, 422–423
    published standards, using, 421–423
Stanford Achievement Test, 445
Stereotyping. *See also* Affective learning
    in materials, 291
Stone, M. E., 184
Storyboards, 281
Structural analysis for words, 244–245
Student Letter Exchange, 105
Student self-evaluations. *See* Self-evaluations

Students Team-Achievement Divisions (STAD), 224
Study guides
    for cooperative learning, 227–231
    lesson planning and, 140
    planning study guides, 230
    student-prepared guides, 230
Study skills, 13, 205–206
    lesson plan objectives and, 145
    reading skills and, 251–253
Study trips, 288, 289
Summative evaluation, 423
Supply-type test items, 438
Surveys. *See* Polls and surveys
Symbolic materials, 281–282
Symposium presentations, 223
Synonyms, 344
Synthesizing information, 352–355
    history concepts, 30
    testing on, 437

Taba, H., 345
Taba Curriculum Project, 407
Tables, 282
    comprehension skills and, 250
Taking Turns groups, 224
Tape recordings, 67, 278
    listening skills and, 255
    logs, 172
Tatum, B., 464
Taxonomies, planning with, 167–168
Teacher-observations, 427–428
Technology in the classroom, 8
Television, 275–276
    critiquing, 290–291
    The History Channel, 292
    music on, 380
Tests
    of affective outcomes, 438
    attitudes, testing, 439
    bank of test items, creating, 445–446
    binary-choice items, 443, 448
    clarity in, 438
    criterion-referenced tests, 435–436
    essay items, 444–445, 450
    guidelines for constructing, 438–445
    on instructional materials, 438, 440
    interests, testing, 439
    matching items, 443, 448
    on modules, 151
    multiple-choice items, 442, 447
    norm-referenced tests, 435–436
    problem items tests, 438
    on problem solving skills, 441
    published tests, 445–446
    short-answer items, 444, 449
    situation tests, 438
    thinking skills, testing, 436–437
    tips for taking, 446
    values, testing, 439
    writing assignments as, 450
Textbooks
    lesson plans based on, 140
    maps in, 309
    as reading materials, 267–268
    unit plans relying on, 165
Thames, W., 464
Thesauruses, 253, 260
Thinking skills. *See also* Creative thinking;
    Decision making; Problem solving
    acquisition of knowledge, 340–347

analyzing information, 352–355
clarifying procedure and, 359–360
classroom examples of, 331–332
forms of thinking, 332–337
lesson plan objectives and, 145
model of teaching, 357–361
questions to ask, 331–332
synthesizing information, 352–355
testing, 436
Thorndike, Edward, 4
Time charts/time lines, 282–284, 283
Time concepts, 29, 347–348
Time zones, 306, 307, 313–314, 322
Tompkins, J. R., 86
Topical approach, 17–18
Topics
    for community surveys, 287
    concepts, development of, 351
    for creative thinking, 335
    for discussions, 215
    generalizations, development of, 351
    lesson plans by, 140
Tsujimoto, J. I., 367

Underlining activities, 198
Unfinished stories, 372
Units of instruction, 154–156
    preplanned units, 166–167
    taxonomies, using, 167–168
Unit words, 237–238
Universal consequences, 415

Value-laden concepts, 344
Value-neutral concepts, 344
Value-neutral generalizations, 349
Values
    affective elements of learning and, 393–394
    process knowledge teaching, 64
    testing, 439
Values clarification. *See* Affective learning
Videos, 67, 278
    resources, 276
    unit plans and, 165–166
Visual learners, 187
Visually impaired students, 86, 182–183
Vocabulary, 15
    background building for, 240–242
    challenging vocabulary, 238–239
    charts, 269
    sight vocabulary, 242–243
    understanding use, 236

Wallen, N. E., 407
Wesley, Edgar B., 4
Whole-group activities, 212, 213
Whole-language learning, 270
WIERD (We're Involved in Enthused Reading Daily), 203
Wiggins, G. P., 463
Wiseman, D. L., 203
Writing skills, 168, 258–261
    activities, 198
    creative writing, 366–369
    reports and, 259–260
    test, writing assignment as, 450

Yearbooks, 253

Zehm, S., 463
Zeichner, K. M., 458

470